O9-BTN-036

KLANSVILLE, U.S.A.

KLANSVILLE, U.S.A.

The Rise and Fall of the Civil Rights-Era Ku Klux Klan

David Cunningham

OXFORD UNIVERSITY PRESS

Oxford University Press is a department of the
University of Oxford. It furthers the University's objective
of excellence in research, scholarship, and education
by publishing worldwide

Oxford New York
Auckland Cape Town Dar es Salaam Hong Kong Karachi
Kuala Lumpur Madrid Melbourne Mexico City Nairobi
New Delhi Shanghai Taipei Toronto

With offices in
Argentina Austria Brazil Chile Czech Republic France Greece
Guatemala Hungary Italy Japan Poland Portugal Singapore
South Korea Switzerland Thailand Turkey Ukraine Vietnam

Published in the United States of America by
Oxford University Press
198 Madison Avenue, New York, New York 10016

Library of Congress Cataloging-in-Publication Data
Cunningham, David, 1970–
Klansville, U.S.A. : the rise and fall of the civil rights-era Ku Klux Klan / David Cunningham.
p. cm.
ISBN 978-0-19-975202-7 (hardcover : alk. paper)
1. Ku Klux Klan (1915–)—North Carolina. I. Title.
HS2330.K63C75 2013
322.4'209756—dc22
2012006207

3 5 7 9 8 6 4 2

Printed in the United States of America
on acid-free paper

For Sarah

CONTENTS

ACKNOWLEDGMENTS

My interest in this book's topic emerged somewhat unconventionally, through a previous project on Federal Bureau of Investigation (FBI) counterintelligence programs that exposed me to thousands of pages of Bureau intelligence memos targeting the civil rights-era KKK. There, amid the expected documentation of cross-burnings, beatings, shootings, and other acts of racist terror, much of what I read seemed surprising. While the memos reflected FBI agents' conflicted orientation to the klan during that period, they also offered strong evidence countering conventional accounts of the 1960s KKK as thriving predominantly within isolated communities in the Deep South, lacking organizational sophistication, and benefiting from the active support of segregationist officials. Instead, I learned that the era's largest and most powerful KKK resided in North Carolina, where officials chose not to "massively" resist desegregation mandates and instead consistently opposed the klan's presence. The Bureau's accounts also provided me with cause to ponder, for the first time, the organizational acumen behind the klan's elaborate public rallies and street walks, church services and barbecue suppers, promotional billboards and bumper stickers, networks of "klaverns" and parallel family oriented "Ladies Auxiliary Units," monthly newspaper and group life insurance plan.

This book documents and explains this textured reality, an effort made possible only by the benevolent assistance and encouragement of many others. An unexpected, and somewhat bewildering, spark came even before I began formal work on this project, when I crossed paths in 2002 with Robert Shelton, the most influential KKK leader of the civil rights era. Agreeing to meet me at his local haunt, a Burger King near his Alabama home that he claimed his cohorts offered to "keep in business" in return for endless cups of steeply discounted coffee (to make his point, he had me follow him to the registers, where he slapped a dime, nickel, and four pennies on the counter and promptly received a freshly brewed cup), he brought me a pile of materials intended to demonstrate the vitality of his KKK outfit, the United Klans of America (UKA), in the face of the FBI surveillance and harassment the group had weathered.

Soon after, in response to a loosely related email query, Rory McVeigh offhandedly suggested that "somebody really needs to write a good book about the civil rights-era Klan," a proposition that I appropriated as a mandate to embark on this project. In North Carolina, the hospitality of Bob Edwards and his family in Greenville eased tremendously my initial tentative efforts to spend time in and learn about former KKK hotbeds. At different points, Charlie Kurzman, Andy Andrews, and Larry Griffin offered sage advice and shared good food in Chapel Hill, as did Christian Davenport in Washington, DC, Will Campbell in Nashville, and Peter Young in Massachusetts. In Jackson, Buddy and Frenchie Graham, Adam and Jessica White, and Lara and Chris Kees raised the bar so high as to redefine my conception of hospitality. Jill Williams helped track down newspaper articles and more importantly provided indispensable guidance and advice in Greensboro. She also introduced me to Lewis Brandon, who in a brief conversation provided a kernel of wisdom about the role of North Carolina A&T in the city's civil rights struggle; this chance encounter ultimately informed much of the argument in Chapter 6.

Invitations to present different parts of this project in North Carolina at UNC–Chapel Hill, East Carolina University, Barton College, and Greensboro's International Civil Rights Center and Museum provided the dual benefit of thoughtful feedback from those audiences as well as introductions to local people with vital firsthand perspectives on the Carolina Klan. Roy Hardee generously shared materials from his personal KKK archive, gleaned from his years as a journalist in eastern North Carolina (and collected at considerable risk—while covering a UKA rally in Pitt County, he was injured after being hit in the head by a ball-bearing fired by a klansman). Michael Frierson allowed me to listen to interviews with his father, a retired FBI agent charged with developing KKK informants, and klan leader George Dorsett, a major figure in the UKA's rise and fall. His documentary about their relationship, "FBI-KKK," is a crucial and compelling story about family and southern racial politics. John Drabble demonstrated unsurpassed collegiality when he volunteered to copy, bind, and send (from Turkey no less!) an exhaustive report compiled by the FBI's Charlotte office and obtained through his Freedom of Information Act request. E. M. Beck kindly shared the historical lynching data that he and Stuart Tolnay had gathered for their important book *A Festival of Violence*. Patsy Sims provided helpful contact information. Ryan Arp offered technical assistance at a decisive point in the project. Peter Owens, Crystal Null, Josephine Hsai, and Gilberto Bardales from George Tita's Geographic Information Systems seminar at UC-Irvine created the rally attendance maps that appear in Chapter 2. Kirsten Moe contributed to the research in many ways; it will be hard for future research assistants to top her heroic effort to operationalize the often indecipherable network of North Carolina state roads. One day in the midst of that effort, she arrived at my office with a set of enormous North Carolina state road maps inherited from her grandfather. Two of them have adorned my office wall ever since.

With related endeavors that regularly overlapped with this one, Dan Kryder, Geoff Ward, Margaret Burnham, Susan Glisson, Charles Tucker, and Robby Luckett provided insight, support, and good company in equal measure. Dan's zeal for barbecue and advice about the research process aided my navigation of the project at several challenging points. A number of friends, colleagues, and students read part or all of the manuscript, offering trenchant comments and saving me from embarrassing missteps; that group includes Andy Andrews, Chip Berlet, Wendy Cadge, Charles Eagles, Nicky Fox, Larry Griffin, Clare Hammonds, Randy Hart, Jenny Irons, Joseph Luders, Gary T. Marx, Rory McVeigh, Sara Shostak, Sarah Soule, Stefan Timmermans, Jocelyn Viterna, Steve Whitfield, students in the 2009 "Approaches to Sociological Research" proseminar, and a number of anonymous reviewers (Wendy and Sara get extra credit for patiently talking me through a forty-five-page, single-spaced chapter outline at a particularly muddled juncture). My dissertation advisor, Peter Bearman, offered helpful advice and, as ever, contributed indirectly by example. I also am grateful to audience members and fellow panelists at meetings of the American Sociological Association and the Southern Political Science Association, the Porter L. Fortune, Jr. Symposium at the University of Mississippi, the Hixon-Riggs Forum at Harvey Mudd College, and colloquia and workshop sessions at the University of Connecticut, East Carolina University, the University of North Carolina at Chapel Hill, Princeton University, and Columbia University. Teaching alongside Mark Auslander in Waltham and the Mississippi Delta broadened my perspective in helpful ways. My friend and colleague John Plotz allowed me to connect some of this work to *Birth of a Nation* in his narrative film course, and guest lectures in several other Brandeis classes and in Marc Dixon's Political Sociology seminar at Dartmouth College helped to clarify my thinking as well.

I'm not sure what I've done to deserve the good fortune of carrying this project through in the supportive and invigorating atmosphere at Brandeis

University. My colleagues in the Sociology Department provided unflagging models of engaged scholarship. Judy Hanley, Cheryl Hansen, and Elaine Brooks served up administrative aid, crisis management, laughter, and chocolate at every turn. My students keep outdoing each other, even as I continue to fret annually that no incoming group could surpass previous cohorts' energy, curiosity, and enthusiasm. While unfortunately I lack sufficient space to name the dozens of students who have, mostly unknowingly, inspired and shaped the pages that follow, I would like to single out two particular groups. During the summer of 2001, as this project incubated in my head, I spent thirty-two days living in a sleeper bus with fourteen Brandeis students examining social change efforts across America as part of a traveling program we formally dubbed "Possibilities for Change in American Communities" (but then proceeded to refer to simply as "the bus"). For abetting my reintroduction to the South during that trip, and more generally for the inspiring example they set that summer and have only surpassed since, I thank April Alario, Adam Brooks, Barb Browning, Aaron Kagan, Nicole Karlebach, Cheryl Kingma-Kiekhofer, Dan Lustig, George Okrah, Tameka Pettigrew, Allison Schecter, Andrew Slack, Suzy Stone, Lee Tusman, and Jasmine Vallejo. Exactly a decade later, eleven Brandeis students traveled south with me as part of a special summer Justice Brandeis Semester program titled "Civil Rights and Racial Justice in Mississippi." For their invigorating and unswerving belief in the synergies between research and social justice (and for their willingness to become roadfood enthusiasts), I thank my co-instructors Ashley Rondini, Elena Wilson, and Robby Luckett, along with Anwar Abdul-Wahab, Yosep Bae, Jesse Begelfer, Micha Broadnax, Edwin Gonzalez, Jermaine Hamilton, Talya Kahan, Elly Kalfus, Molly Schneider, Gabi Sanchez-Stern, and Jake Weiner.

Few aspects of the research process are as affirming as one's interactions with archivists who share their immense knowledge of their collections while often simultaneously immersing themselves in your topic despite having dozens of other tasks to juggle. Two truly fortuitous events occurred through their herculean efforts. First, archivists' follow-up to my repeated, seemingly futile requests to view the sealed investigatory files from the 1965–1966 House Un-American Activities Committee–KKK hearings helped to procure a special authorization to open the records several years ahead of schedule. Those files proved a vital resource. Second, at the LBJ Archives an intern named Laura (I regret that I don't know her last name) tenaciously tracked down the present whereabouts of Peter B. Young, who became my most valuable and colorful source (amazingly, though the effort was spurred by the work he did in North Carolina and the archives he deposited in Texas, it turned out that Mr. Young resided literally down the road from me in Massachusetts).

For their aid, advice, and abiding responsiveness, I thank Kate Mollan and the staff at the National Archives; Maury York, Dale Sauter, and the staff at the Special Collections Department in East Carolina University's Joyner Library; Marilyn Schuster, Bob McIness and the Special Collections staff in the Atkins Library at UNC-Charlotte; Allen Fisher and the Research and Archives staff at the Lyndon Baines Johnson Library and Museum; Randall Burkett, Kathy Shoemaker, and the staff of the Manuscript, Archives, and Rare Book Library at Emory University; Donald Davis at the American Friends Service Committee Archives in Philadelphia; Earl James and the North Carolina State Archives staff; Aimee Boese and Mike Taylor at the Pender County Public Library in Burgaw; Timothy J. Cole and the staff of the Greensboro Public Library; Keith Longiotti and the staff of the Wilson Library at UNC–Chapel Hill; and the helpful staffs of the Perkins Library at Duke University, the Moorland-Springarn Research Center at Howard University, the McCain Library at the University of Southern Mississippi, the Sheppard Memorial Library in Greenville, the Kinston-Lenoir County Public Library, the Caldwell County Public Library, the Charlotte Mecklenburg Library, the Montgomery County Library, and the Boston Public Library.

None of this work would have been possible without crucial funding and other research support. I thank Brandeis University for awarding me a Bernstein Fellowship, which provided a semester of research leave at the outset of the project, as well as three separate grants from the Theodore and Jane Norman Fund that enabled everything from research travel to the use of many of the photos that appear in this book. I also acknowledge, with great appreciation, a grant from the Harry Frank Guggenheim Foundation, which furnished an additional semester leave to complete preliminary analyses, as well as research travel awards from the Lyndon Baines Johnson Foundation and the East Carolina University Special Collections Department. Sudbury's Goodnow Library offered an ideal and much-needed work refuge during cold winter months.

Earlier versions of Chapters 4–8 benefited from development as articles in other venues. I thank the publishers of the *American Journal of Sociology*; *Qualitative Sociology*; *Research in Social Movements, Conflict and Change*; *Social Forces*; *Southern Cultures*; *and Theory and Society* for permission to draw upon that work,[1] as well as several of their anonymous reviewers for suggesting improvements. At Oxford University Press, James Cook has offered a sharp eye and unfailing judgment, and otherwise has been everything one can ask for as an editor—supportive, responsive, and, most important, patient.

Patterson Lamb provided helpful and judicious editing suggestions, and Rebecca Clark, Alana Podolsky, and Rick Stinson have deftly managed a variety of matters great and small.

My deepest debt and appreciation goes to my family. As ever, my parents Bill and Ninette Cunningham have been a fount of unwavering love and support. For them, there is no concern or even question that my work will turn out well; they just want to know that I'm happy doing it. David and Ridley Boocock, Lizzie and Adam Dobkowski, and Ann Carroll always offer ardent backing and frequent occasions for celebration. I embarked on this project alongside Sarah, now my wife, who at the outset had no legal bond to indulge the undue attention that it occupied. Back in 2003, she agreed to drive the getaway car during a particularly precarious effort to secure an interview, and to my endlessly great fortune she remains with me, joined more recently by our children, Andrew and Charlotte. I am pleased beyond words about their apparent conspiracy to demonstrate enthusiasm for this and related topics, even weathering the heat of an entire Mississippi summer with me. (Last year, four-year-old Andrew told his pre-school class during a Thanksgiving exercise that he was thankful for "civil rights," apparently even more than for his beloved superheroes, though I think he sagely senses the connections.) I am even more pleased that they insist I remain enthusiastic about a host of other things, superheroes included. For making all this possible, and for allowing me to see with certainty even brighter days ahead, this book is for Sarah.

KLANSVILLE, U.S.A.

INTRODUCTION

"Quit playing with them niggers," commanded J. Robert "Bob" Jones. "I didn't invite them, but I've got a few choice words for them." It was a sultry Sunday afternoon in August 1966, and Jones was addressing a packed house at the Memorial Auditorium in Raleigh, North Carolina. More than 2,000 additional supporters milled around the parking lot outside, having arrived after the auditorium's 3,067 seats had filled; Jones and other featured guests would later climb out onto the auditorium's ledge above the parking lot, greeting those supporters to reward their patience. This event, the largest political gathering in the state that year, was hosted by the North Carolina Realm of United Klans of America (UKA), Knights of the Ku Klux Klan (KKK), Inc.

Squat and square-faced, with a prominent scar across his cheek, Jones was dressed in a shirt and tie, covered by the ornate, knee-length green silk robes reserved for the United Klans' state leaders, or "Grand Dragons." His three-year run in North Carolina marked him as by far the most successful Grand Dragon in the UKA's five-year history. Perched behind a podium on the auditorium's stage, he was charged with introducing a long list of speakers, including several fellow Dragons and the UKA's national leader, "Imperial Wizard" Robert M. Shelton. Jones directed his crude invective to a small group of African Americans who had defiantly filled a handful of the hall's seats, following a city council ruling that ordered the rally open to any member of the public. State police interspersed around the hall, reinforced by 220 National Guard troops stationed nearby on orders from the governor, kept the general peace, while verbal abuse from klan members and sympathizers rained down on the black rally crashers.

Jones, gauging the significance of the occasion, wanted his followers to remain on their best behavior. Imperial Wizard Shelton, the UKA's most prominent figure, reinforced that message. Never known for his dynamism—one reporter compared him to Art Carney—Shelton delivered a typically measured speech, downplaying race issues in favor of a focus on their supposed root cause. "Black power and civil rights are not true issues in America today,"

Shelton argued. "They are taken-for-granted means of the international communist conspiracy spreading frustration, animosity, and ill will." Later, "Imperial Kludd" George Dorsett—the UKA's national chaplain, the biggest draw at the group's nightly rallies, and, secretly, an informant on the payroll of the Federal Bureau of Investigation (FBI)—would offer the day's most "choice" words. "I'm fighting not for myself, but for the children of America, to keep them from being raped, mugged, and knifed," Dorsett warned, prompting the largest cheer of the day. "We don't believe in violence, and we're not going to have violence, *if we have to kill every nigger in America*!"[1]

The UKA organized this Memorial Auditorium rally to defend Jones, Shelton, and its other leaders against pending federal prison sentences. Throughout the preceding year, the US House of Representatives had conducted massive hearings on the civil rights-era KKK revival. Dozens of klan leaders refused to turn over subpoenaed records, and now seven of them faced contempt of Congress charges. Though the hearings targeted a wide range of organizations, the UKA was by far the most prominent of the seventeen Ku Klux Klan groups identified by House investigators. Longtime FBI director J. Edgar Hoover noted that the UKA was so dominant as to be synonymous with the broader KKK among the general public. By 1966, more than 500 chapters—referred to, in klan parlance, as "klaverns"—scattered across nineteen states retained an estimated 25,000 UKA members.[2]

The location of those klaverns was perhaps the investigation's most unexpected finding. Deadly KKK violence in Mississippi, Alabama, and Georgia had garnered the lion's share of klan publicity, but the United Klans' real stronghold was in fact North Carolina, long considered the region's most progressive state. While governors elsewhere in the South sometimes stood—literally or figuratively—in schoolhouse doorways to demonstrate their militant support of segregation, in North Carolina no viable candidate could even consider defying looming federal civil rights legislation. But alongside this pronounced moderation, North Carolina's UKA boasted between 10,000 and 12,000 dues-paying members spread among approximately 200 klaverns. Across the state, newspaper editors, religious leaders, and other officials denounced this UKA presence, regularly referring to the group as "basically un-American," "anti-Christian," and "poisonous" to the state's interests, and characterizing its rallies as "revolting," "deplorable," and "sickening" spectacles.[3] In the face of this opposition, however, the UKA regularly attracted the largest crowds of any political organization in the state. At public rallies, adherents welcomed the sort of heated racist rhetoric that

George Dorsett delivered during the Memorial Auditorium event. Members proudly referred to their state as "Klansville, U.S.A.," and such claims were not mere hyperbole. As Figure I.1 shows, at its mid-1960s peak the UKA's presence in North Carolina eclipsed klan membership in all other southern states combined.

The UKA enjoyed a spectacularly rapid rise in the state. United Klans had initially formed in 1961, with members confined mostly to Alabama and Georgia. Over the next two years, only a handful of North Carolinians joined the organization. Jones took over as the Tar Heel State's Grand Dragon in 1963, and his pioneering organizing approach emphasized the UKA's public face. By the summer of 1964, the Carolina Klan established a demanding schedule of nightly rallies across the state, where they enlisted thousands of dues-paying members. Held generally in cow pastures or local air strips, these klan rallies resembled skewed county fairs, complete with live music, concessions, souvenirs, and raffles and other games for adults and children. Several self-styled preachers and political theorists spoke in support of states' rights and the South's segregationist traditions. Most of their rhetoric militantly opposed the looming changes in the political and racial landscape, which the klan rooted in hypocritical liberal Washington politics, the encroaching civil rights movement, and a sweeping "Communist-Jew" conspiracy. Each rally climaxed with a ritualized burning of a cross that reached as far as seventy feet into the sky.

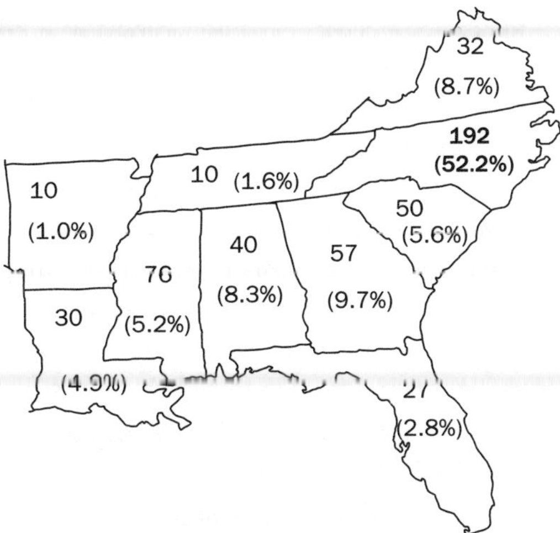

FIGURE I.1. Number of UKA klaverns, and percentage of total membership, by state (1966)

By 1965, hundreds of thousands of North Carolinians had attended these UKA gatherings—crowd estimates by the State Highway Patrol ranged between 200 and 6,000 each night, depending upon the location and time of year. Smaller numbers participated in periodic "street walks" (daytime marches by robed klan members and helmeted members of the UKA "Security Guard") and members-only barbecues, fish frys, and turkey shoots. While such events defined many adherents' klan involvement, a militant core within the UKA also pursued more nefarious efforts to intimidate black residents or white liberals through cross burnings, beatings, and shotgun fire.

The hearings of the congressional House Un-American Activities Committee (HUAC) marked a turning point in the UKA's fortunes. In the face of the committee's findings, North Carolina officials shifted their policing approach. Wide-ranging suppressive tactics increased the costs and risks of membership, sapped the group's resources, and hindered its ability to organize. While the massive Memorial Auditorium rally seemed to flaunt the UKA's strength in the face of state opposition, in fact it signaled a last gasp by a crumbling organization. The UKA's state office began to shed dollars and members far more quickly than it could replace them. Resulting infighting and schisms produced several competing KKK organizations in the state, which, alongside significant overall attrition among the rank-and-file, meant that more groups were battling over the klan's dwindling membership and financial resources. Shelton and Jones began year-long prison sentences for their contempt convictions in 1969, and the resulting leadership vacuum proved a fatal blow to the UKA.

But for much of the decade, the Carolina Klan was a force. After more than a thousand UKA supporters protested his 1966 speech, Martin Luther King Jr. pondered how "the state that prides itself on being the most liberal in the South can have the largest marches of the Ku Klux Klan." Charlotte-based writer Harry Golden expressed similar frustration. Everywhere he traveled, incredulous audiences wanted to know: "North Carolina, the largest Ku Klux Klan state? Is this possible in 'liberal' North Carolina?"[4] This book focuses on that puzzle, to explain why and how the dominant KKK outfit of the past half-century emerged not in the militantly segregationist Deep South, but rather in a state lauded for its southern-style progressivism.

The following chapters use the case of the UKA's North Carolina Realm to understand how the civil rights-era Ku Klux Klan in general reflected, and often stood apart from, the politics of resistance, moderation, and capitulation that represented prevailing southern responses to civil rights reform. Focusing on a single state provides an ideal standpoint for understanding the

UKA's appeal, actions, and trajectory. Organizationally, the group was a confederation of state realms led by their own cadres of officers, each of whom developed distinct participation styles and recruitment strategies. Each state's financial and organizational infrastructure was in large part independent as well. When, for instance, North Carolina State Officer Bob Kornegay was sent to Virginia to serve as that state's Grand Dragon, Bob Jones sent a letter to his Tar Heel membership, announcing that Kornegay was "no longer with us," and instructing them to "refrain from bothering him with North Carolina problems." The autonomy of the UKA's state realms was compounded by the presence of more than a dozen other self-proclaimed authentic Ku Klux Klan organizations across the South.[5]

The account here takes seriously the differences among these varied klan manifestations, and adopts the unconventional lower-case "klan" label to challenge prevailing treatments of "The Klan" as implicitly uniform across organizations, eras, and locales. Civil rights histories have further obscured such distinctions by focusing disproportionately on KKK action in protest "hot spots" such as Birmingham, Alabama; St. Augustine, Florida; and various Mississippi locales.[6] Widespread reportage of the klan's visible—and often brutal—opposition to civil rights activists in those areas reinforces the tendency to view such cases as typical of KKK organization everywhere in the South. However, even a cursory examination of existing evidence reveals that klan groups varied considerably in their recruitment strategies, ideology, militancy, level of activity, and connections to mainstream political and civic leaders. Focusing on the North Carolina story unearths this variation and considers it in light of the interplay between the KKK and the local, state, and national settings within which its membership thrived or withered.

Theoretical Framework

The chapters that follow introduce and draw on a *mediated competition model* to explain the rise of the Ku Klux Klan in North Carolina. The model demonstrates that the UKA organized most successfully where (1) white residents perceived civil rights reforms to be a significant threat to their status; (2) mainstream outlets for segregationist resistance were lacking; and (3) the policing of the KKK's activities was laissez-faire, limited to attempts to prevent acts of organized violence. While federal pressures to desegregate schools, workplaces, and public spaces transformed race relations in every southern community, they hit hardest where white residents' privileged standing most relied on maintaining segregation. When the political environment in those settings also limited mainstream defenses of the racial status quo and rejected hard-line policing of the klan's presence, the UKA was most likely to thrive.

This model follows previous research that views the KKK as perhaps the archetypal example of a reactive movement—one that mobilizes in response to threats to the political, economic, or social status quo. It builds on the most powerful framework for understanding reactive political action: ethnic competition theory, which suggests that individuals are motivated to join groups like the klan when they see themselves as competing for scarce resources with members of other racial or ethnic groups.[7] As an explanation for many forms of political contention—from riots and church burnings, to hate group membership and electoral support for divisive candidates—ethnic competition theory suggests that when multiple groups vie for a limited pool of resources, the boundaries that define and separate those groups harden. As a result, individual members of any particular group more easily attribute their tenuous status to other factions, increasing the likelihood of conflict between the groups in question. Organizations like the UKA exploited these kinds of insecurities, attracting followers convinced by claims that civil rights reforms unjustly threatened whites' entrenched advantage in political, economic, and social arenas.[8]

The mediated competition model developed here extends previous competition-based analyses in two ways. First, by examining how perceived competition relates to factors associated with statewide political cultures, county demographics, local community associations, and individual social locations, this account outlines and assesses processes occurring at multiple levels. This approach adds precision to conventional competition explanations that focus on how general, or "macro-level," environments shape possibilities for political action.[9] Consistent with past research, this analysis of the UKA shows that the general composition of states, counties, and communities defines the degree to which racial groups overlap and thus compete for economic, political, and social resources. But the argument here additionally emphasizes how potential klan adherents experience that general overlap within their local social worlds, through the structure and orientation of neighborhoods, community associations and institutions, and interpersonal ties. Those mediating contexts shape the extent to which individuals perceive racial overlap as a potential threat, construct grievances in racialized ways, and in some cases view the UKA as a vehicle to combat threats to the racial status quo.

Second, this account explains *how* the UKA mobilized racial threat, by drawing on concepts typically associated with social movement theory to identify and analyze the processes through which racial threat translates into racist action. While competition-based explanations typically focus on when and where threats emerge and view subsequent political action as a straightforward product of those threats, social movement scholars often seek to understand how such threats translate into collective action. In that vein, rather than assuming that shared grievances coalesce into coordinated action, the following chapters emphasize the ways in which political contexts and organizational resources mediate such baseline conditions—that is, how the UKA drew upon, and often aggravated, racially charged environments to mobilize thousands of white North Carolinians to act together to preserve the segregationist status quo.

To uncover the processes that link the presence of racial competition to klan action, the analysis here shows how the broad political environment shaped klan recruits' shared sense of racial threat. In moderate North Carolina, where officials would abide by the Civil Rights Act, klansmen could more effectively argue that only the KKK would offer an organized defense of "authentic" white interests. The UKA in Mississippi and Alabama, in contrast, competed with a variety of mainstream institutions—from elected political leaders and school board officials, to local employers and Citizens' Council chapters—dedicated to defying federal civil rights statutes to maintain the segregationist status quo.[10] In the Deep South's more expansive segregationist field, the klan filled a narrower niche. Also crucial was the orientation of local and state police. By adopting laissez-faire policies that sent a tacit message of support for the UKA or instead by unambivalently and aggressively suppressing klan organization, police could shift the stakes of klan affiliation, helping or hindering the UKA's efforts to build active mass support.[11]

This account also emphasizes how competition dynamics were mediated by aspects of UKA organization, including the group's ability to marshal and deploy resources to build and nourish its membership. By organizing rallies and other events to secure funds, drawing on social networks to connect and align with sympathetic constituencies, and adopting strategies intended to enhance the visibility and resonance of their appeals, UKA officials worked to extend the group's reach and impact. Efforts to build a sense of racial solidarity and collective identity around the ideal of "authentic whiteness" were especially important. Crafting compelling ideological arguments that aligned with their constituencies' bedrock religious and nationalistic sentiments and then using klan-centered rituals and events to reinforce such frames, UKA recruiters sought to solidify a shared sense of racial threat among sympathetic white North Carolinians.[12]

In sum, the mediated competition approach here strengthens existing formulations of ethnic competition theory by integrating key elements from research on social movements to explain how UKA organizers mobilized racial grievances, often in uneven and unpredictable ways. The analysis moves beyond conventional conceptualizations of ethnic competition, comparing how competition dynamics emerged and played out at the state, county, community, institutional, and interpersonal levels. Rather than suggesting simply that KKK organization was produced by the broad makeup of surrounding communities, this framework emphasizes how associated social arrangements shaped individuals' perceptions of competition, and then how such perceptions translated into KKK organization.

What's to Come?

The pages that follow draw on this framework to tell the story of the UKA's rise and fall. The opening chapter traces the long history of the KKK to situate the UKA's seemingly phoenix-like rise in 1960s North Carolina. Though historical accounts of the KKK have generally emphasized its waves of growth and decline, the trajectory of the klan owes much to continuities in personnel and ritualized organization that supported successive iterations of the klan. A long view of the KKK's history also underscores the central role played by police officials in shaping the klan's fortunes and impact.

Chapter 2 extends this historical portrait to develop a close account of the UKA's move into North Carolina. Mapping the civil rights–era klan's key players, organizational routines, and major events reveals much about the klan experience in North Carolina and across the South generally. To build solidarity and grow its resource base, UKA leaders organized frequent rallies, emphasized membership rites, reinforced strict boundaries between the "white public" and outsiders, and developed a tactical repertoire that—for a brief period—deftly balanced public civic action and clandestine violence. These organizational elements provide a key backdrop to the group's rapid rise in 1964 and 1965.

The UKA's most spectacular success poses a complex puzzle because it occurred within a state widely perceived as a bastion of southern liberalism. To explain this seeming paradox, Chapter 3 focuses on the history of race relations and economic progressivism in North Carolina. The state's shifting economy and postwar political campaigns, alongside its officials' ambivalent efforts to police the KKK and other white supremacist vehicles, created a distinctive political setting, where segregationist interests consolidated around constituencies largely detached from political elites who charted a moderate course with race relations. In 1964, the UKA emerged as the central outlet willing to resist the fall of Jim Crow segregation and thus had broad appeal in communities where white residents were most threatened by direct competition with African Americans. For a time, this appeal remained largely unchecked by police action. North Carolina's state policing agencies, unlike other moderate states like Florida, adopted a lax approach to the klan's presence, which allowed the UKA to organize freely in communities across the state.

The three chapters that follow focus on the ways in which the racial competition that drove the klan's growth emerged and evolved. Each tackles the issue from a different vantage. In Chapter 4, the broad analysis of change in North Carolina places the roots of threats posed by racial reform in the makeup of the state's counties. White resistance to civil rights claims stemmed from a sense that integration would affect the economic, political, and social status quo—altering existing arrangements in local communities in different ways and impacting the breadth and depth of associated racial anxieties. Much of the difference in UKA strength across the state was due to county-by-county shifts in factors associated with this perceived racial threat, including the degree of overlap between black and white workers, black electoral strength, the vibrancy of civil rights activism, and the level of interracial contact in schools, shops, and other public venues.

Chapter 5 focuses on the same issue from the opposite perspective, by considering how individuals came to the UKA. Focusing on the ways in which family, workplace, and friendship ties helped and hindered prospective members' connections to the klan, the chapter demonstrates that although UKA appeals resonated in areas characterized by high levels of racial competition, klan members were not necessarily drawn from those who themselves competed with African Americans for jobs and other resources. Instead, in competitive environments, klan recruiters exploited the diffuse character of racial threat—the ways in which shared anti–civil rights sentiments could spread across family, friendship, and civic networks—and worked to build a sense of collective identity around the UKA's brand of authentic whiteness. Combined with the county analysis in Chapter 4, this account of individual paths to participation in the UKA underscores the ways in which local community environments shaped ideas about race and the "threat" of desegregation.

Local networks and institutions also shaped community officials and other elites' complex, frequently ambivalent and contradictory orientations to the klan. For sometimes idiosyncratic reasons, sheriffs and local police officers might vociferously oppose the klan's presence. Or instead they might enable KKK activities, by taking a hands-off approach to klan violence or even covertly aligning with a local klavern. Similarly, business owners could post subtle klan-supporting stickers on their windows (the best known were "Keep Kool Kid" and "TWAK," which implored supporters to "trade with a klansman"), or else defy klan pressure and desegregate their premises. Religious leaders frequently offered anti-klan proclamations, though the UKA also included dozens of preachers in its ranks. Local editors sometimes risked significant losses in advertising dollars to criticize the klan in print. Other newspapers willingly published UKA rally flyers and other propagandizing material.[13]

Chapter 6 focuses on these complexities, to show how the makeup of three North Carolina communities helped or hindered klan organizing. Two of those communities—Charlotte and Greensboro—are located in the central Piedmont region, with seemingly similar profiles but drastically different klan histories. Charlotte, the home of the state's NAACP headquarters, remained relatively insulated from klan activity and managed to retain an overall reputation for racial progressivism, despite the smudge of a series of high-profile bombings targeting civil rights leaders in 1965. Greensboro, ground zero for the 1960 sit-in movement and an early adopter (along with Charlotte and Winston-Salem) of a school desegregation plan, was the Piedmont's most highly organized klan city. A third community, Greenville, typified the state's largely rural coastal plain and demonstrates how economic and social arrangements in the eastern part of the state created a climate where the UKA could thrive.

Ultimately, the Klan's rapid rise in North Carolina was matched by an equally spectacular fall, with membership dropping off severely and the UKA breaking into several competing factions by 1969. The roots of this decline relate in part to the successes of the civil rights movement and consequent shifts in the political climate. The primary driver of the Carolina Klan's decline, however, was the increasingly aggressive efforts of state and federal officials to suppress the UKA's actions. Chapter 7 demonstrates these shifts and shows how, as with the KKK in previous eras, the UKA's fall was predominantly a policing story.

The epilogue considers the lessons derived from the rise and fall of the civil rights–era Ku Klux Klan. While the UKA disintegrated into small, mostly ineffectual factions in the 1970s, its legacy endures in surprising ways. Patterns of 1960s klan activity help to explain two distinct but hugely significant trends in subsequent decades—the South's move away from its longtime solid support of the Democratic Party, and its disproportionately high homicide rates. In former UKA strongholds, both Republican voting and violent crime occur much more frequently than in other similar communities across the region. While obviously quite different in type and character, both of these trends lend insight into how organized vigilantism powerfully and enduringly shapes community landscapes. Considering the complex role played by the UKA in "Klansville, U.S.A." provides an opportunity to rethink conventional understandings of the political evolution of the South and nation over the last half-century, as well as how to productively address the klan's more deleterious effects.

The KKK: Explanations and Orientations

Few groups evoke more intense emotional reactions than the Ku Klux Klan. A half-century after the UKA's heyday, striking an appropriate tone when writing about the Carolina Klan remains difficult. The group's open and intense racism grow no less abhorrent with repeated study. The fact that many of its members engaged in what *Saturday Evening Post* reporter Stewart Alsop described as "a kind of brutal monologue"—reflecting endlessly on white supremacy, "nigger" deficiencies and conspiracies, and their own facility with firearms—makes it difficult to dig beneath the rhetoric to comprehend deeper anxieties and motivations.[14]

But explanation requires just that, to understand how and why particular settings enabled the klan's brand of racism and lawlessness. To understand the UKA on its own terms, much of what follows takes seriously the views of members and sympathizers and how they interacted with their historical milieu. While I do not pretend to be an unbiased observer, the account here reflects a sense that respectful engagement with klan personas and worldviews is crucial to comprehend organized racism and to acknowledge sometimes uncomfortable truths about how political extremism intersects with mainstream institutions and ideals. To argue, as this book does, that the KKK is never entirely separable from its surroundings requires rigorous scrutiny of the degree to which klan adherents were, as many local officials and civic leaders claimed, "alien" to the community. Doing so also humanizes those connected to the klan, to seek comprehensibility in the "awful disaster" of a mass movement motivated by vehement racism. As segregationist fervor took many forms, examining why the KKK's brand of white supremacy resonated with certain individuals in particular places and times provides a more nuanced window into a process often subsumed under faceless monikers like "massive resistance" and "white backlash."[15]

Perhaps most important, taking the klan seriously helps to uncover and elevate the experiences of those victimized by its actions and ideas. While researching the UKA, I was challenged periodically by the argument that focusing on the Carolina Klan's distinctive size and organizing capacity neglected the fact that the group largely avoided deadly violence. The "real" klan story, according to this critique, resided with more militaristic KKK factions in Alabama and Mississippi. Such claims echoed those regularly advanced by reporters, police, and other North Carolina officials throughout the 1960s. Now, as then, such a narrow view of the klan's impact ignores the lived reality of the untold thousands of residents harmed, directly or not, by its presence. Though few klan members were arrested prior to 1966, police files document hundreds of acts of klan violence in North Carolina, including shootings, cross burnings, physical beatings, and written and verbal intimidation. These crimes were only the tip of the iceberg. As historian David Cecelski notes:

> This litany of crimes in the public record includes only a fraction of Klan outrages.... Several oral history projects... have recently interviewed large numbers of local black citizens who lived through the KKK revival. Undocumented Klan atrocities emerge in nearly every interview. Newspapers almost never mentioned these racial attacks, nor did law enforcement agencies investigate them. They represented the real Klan that tens of thousands of... North Carolinians crowded to see and hear.[16]

Indeed, though often invisible in a legal and historical sense, the impact of klan violence was all too real to its targets and to bystanders who feared similar retribution. I sometimes learned those lessons at unexpected times. Between sessions of a conference in Boston, a woman who knew I was researching the Carolina Klan shared her story with me. She had been raised in a mixed-race household in the North Carolina Piedmont. One night in the late 1960s, as retribution for her family's apparent racial transgression, klansmen burned a cross on her front lawn. Terrified, they moved away soon after, and she herself never returned. Nearly forty years later, the experience clearly remained a painful one.

Two years later, I heard Natasha Trethewey, also from a mixed-race family in the South, deliver a powerful reading of her poem "Incident." The poem recounts an act of klan terror, where "a few men gathered, white as angels in their gowns" to light a "cross trussed like a Christmas tree" on a front lawn, while the house's occupants "peered from the windows, shades drawn." It concludes:

> *When they were done, the men left quietly. No one came.*
> *Nothing really happened.*
> *By morning all the flames had dimmed.*
> *We tell the story every year.*[17]

Even as the UKA attracted thousands to its nightly rallies, many of North Carolina's most influential officials believed that klan action usually amounted to "nothing." Several high-ranking police agents during that period confided to me that although they considered the prevention of klan violence a top priority, they often wouldn't take cross burnings and the like seriously because in the end such acts "didn't really hurt anyone." But as Trethewey conveys, such narrow conceptions of meaningful racial violence clearly belie the experiences of hundreds of the klan's targets.

The legacy of the civil rights-era KKK is, in an important sense, cemented by the telling of these sorts of stories, including those in which "nothing really happened." Ultimately, a complete reckoning will bring such accounts into the open, in conversation with those on other sides of the civil rights struggle, including the UKA's side. Airing all of these perspectives is an important step, though engaging with contending accounts in a manner that demands truth and accountability requires that we interpret them in their historical and social context. This is especially true of the versions recounted by representatives of less palatable factions such as the KKK. In a spirit of hope that this dialogue someday will occur, this book is an attempt, above all else, to provide a foundation for understanding that side of the story.

1 BEGINNINGS

THE KU KLUX KLAN IN NORTH CAROLINA AND THE NATION

The people of North Carolina are ready for the Klan, and nothing can keep it down when the people are ready!

—THOMAS HAMILTON, founder and leader of the Associated Carolina Klans, during a Charlotte organizing meeting in 1949.[1]

I think about as much of the Ku Klux Klan idea as I do of infantile paralysis.

—CHAPEL HILL MAYOR EDWIN LANIER, in response to Hamilton's proposed organizing drive.[2]

On Veterans' Day 1963, Capus Waynick enjoyed a barbecue dinner at an event in Salisbury, a small city forty miles north of Charlotte, North Carolina. A distinguished former US ambassador to Nicaragua and Colombia, Waynick had recently signed on as Governor Terry Sanford's unofficial "racial troubleshooter." That high-profile role earned him an invitation to address community leaders at Rowan County's Veterans Administration Hospital. The pre-dinner speech went well, in part because Waynick decided to avoid his usual controversial rhetoric of racial moderation. "The only reference I made to the race problem," he recalled, "was to suggest that unless we could deal in brotherly cooperation with our own people, regardless of our race, we would be weak in the projection of our images."

Even that sentiment did not sit well with Bob Jones, a Navy veteran and local awning salesman. As a mid-level leader in the US Klans throughout the latter half of the 1950s, Jones had earned a reputation as an aggressive and hard-drinking defender of the Jim Crow status quo. Earlier in 1963, another KKK organization, the Alabama-based United Klans of America (UKA), had enlisted Jones to reorganize North Carolina for the klan. Brashly approaching Waynick at the barbecue, Jones announced that he was the Grand Dragon of the KKK in North Carolina and, as such, would vote for no politician who sought "nigger support." Waynick was taken aback. "His conception of what he is against was no less depressing than that of what he was for," he thought as he took the brunt of Jones's tirade. "What an anachronism!"[3]

In fact, Jones was an emerging force in North Carolina politics. Waynick's "anachronistic" take reflected the KKK's marginalization and organizational disarray in the decades following its 1920s heyday, when klan membership nationally numbered in the millions. That fractured history changed, however, in the months that followed Waynick's VA speech. While Governor Sanford's calls for racial moderation struggled to take hold in many North Carolina communities, Jones was in the headlines daily, delivering missives against desegregation and its underlying communist-Jew conspiracy with a savvy balance of fiery and folksy rhetoric. By 1965, the klan's nightly rallies were the largest political gatherings of any kind in the state. Upwards of 10,000 dues-paying members spread across more than 200 klaverns organized within the state's borders. During its mid-1960s heyday, the "Carolina Klan" became the largest and most successful manifestation of the postwar Ku Klux Klan.

This paradoxical phenomenon—in which the largest klan of the past seventy years rose up seemingly in a matter of months in ostensibly the most progressive state in the South—did not of course occur in a vacuum. Far from being cut from whole cloth, the Carolina Klan drew upon a century of KKK history and derived its core membership, rituals, and organizational style from earlier klan incarnations. As the UKA's 1964 constitution declared, "the principle and spirit of Klankraft will at all times be dedicated in thought, spirit and affection to our Founding Fathers of the Original Ku Klux Klan organization in the year 1866, and active during the period of Reconstruction History; and to their predecessors in the years 1915 & 16."[4] Examining the Ku Klux Klan's long history lends insight into how the actions of core leaders during the KKK's fallow abeyance periods enabled continuity across seemingly discrete waves of klan mobilization; how earlier klan waves provided those leaders with crucial organizational and cultural resources in their subsequent mobilizing campaigns; and the central role played by often-obscured modes of policing in the KKK's emergence, decline, and continued rebirths.

The Origins of the KKK

The "Founding Fathers" referenced in the KKK constitution were in fact six young Confederate veterans in Pulaski, Tennessee. In 1866, they gathered with the intention of forming a sort of fraternal organization. Their motivation, by most accounts, was boredom, a "hunger and thirst" for excitement.

The group's initial meeting took place at the law office of a local judge, the father of one of the six original members. They selected the group's name by following a practice standard in fraternities on American college campuses, drawing upon a Greek word, *kuklos*, supplemented, for alliterative purposes, by the word "klan." These founders also established much of the klan's enduring iconography, including elaborate initiation rituals, complex slates of offices, and regalia employing long robes and conical hoods.[5]

At first, the KKK's aims bent toward amusement, especially the playing of "pranks" on local black residents. Members designed costumes that featured long white sheets covering the head and body, to create the impression that members on horseback were in fact ghosts. Groups of klansmen would embark on nighttime rides, paying unwelcome visits to black families. They would often construct elaborate ruses, requesting and pretending to drink enormous quantities of water as "thirsty dead returning from hell," or removing false heads and limbs to demonstrate their extraordinary powers.[6]

These tricks were not merely for the harmless pleasure of bored klan members. From the beginning, the klan's actions drew upon themes and tactics employed in the antebellum patrol system, which had enforced strict curfews to control the movement of slaves. Like those slave patrols, early klan activity maintained racial subjugation by terrorizing the black population. In much of the Reconstruction-era South, black freedpersons remained subject to curfews limiting free assembly and especially the formation of schools. Klan members would beat and whip violators of such racial codes.[7]

New members' desire to use these means to maintain the racial and legal order quickly superseded the KKK's fraternal bent. Such aims resonated widely in the years following the Civil War, when lawlessness, motivated in part by federal Unionist efforts to "reconstruct" the southern economic and political system, pervaded Pulaski and many other communities across the South.[8] The editor of the local newspaper, the *Pulaski Citizen*, noted the "chronic drunkenness and debauchery" that plagued the town, which often was exacerbated by mixed-race conflicts. Such racially motivated fracases frequently targeted Republican "carpetbaggers" (northerners who settled in the South during this period) and "scalawags" (white southern Republicans) who worked to enforce Reconstruction reforms, enfranchising newly freed slaves and in the process subverting the power of antebellum white elites.

In this context, the klan spread slowly at first, as its founders granted residents of rural areas surrounding Pulaski permission to form their own "dens" during the summer of 1866. A meeting the following year in Nashville spurred its broader growth. Several prominent Confederate officers attended, and their influence extended well beyond central Tennessee. The meeting yielded an official Prescript, which carefully specified the organization's strict membership criteria, elaborate secret rituals, and slate of nested local, state, and national officers. Confederate General Nathan Bedford Forrest was named "Grand Wizard," the group's first national leader.

Forrest and his associates proceeded to recruit extensively, mobilizing Civil War veterans throughout the South as local leaders. With the added assistance of various newspapers supportive of anti-Reconstruction southern Democrats, the KKK grew significantly throughout 1868. While the group's many apologists would regularly claim that the klan was a defensive organization, a response to the upheaval engineered by newly freed blacks and their Republican allies, its members in fact aggressively advanced the southern Democratic agenda in the face of Republican control. Indeed, the klan thrived where Democrats posed an effective challenge to the policies of racial equity promoted by Radical Republican political institutions. In such places, KKK adherents drew upon the resources of strong Democratic infrastructures, and used them to spread the perception that white supremacy, the purity of white womanhood, and law and order itself were under siege.[9]

Along with similar vigilante groups such as the Order of Pale Faces and the Knights of the White Camellia, the KKK violently intimidated black community leaders and the carpetbaggers and scalawags who supported them. While this violence had a pervasive logic—to consolidate support for white supremacy—it also occurred in the absence of significant regional or national klan coordination. Members rarely followed the Nashville Prescript; in retrospect, the document's importance lay mostly in its role as a blueprint for *future* waves of klan activity, including the 1960s UKA. By the end of 1868, despite their nominal ties to the overall KKK organization, local dens became largely autonomous and increasingly engaged in unregulated terrorist activity.

This pattern generally held in North Carolina, where in a crowded field of vigilante groups the klan's origins were somewhat murky. In the Tar Heel State, the White Brotherhood (WB) and the Constitutional Union Guard (CUG) emerged in parallel with the KKK's rise in Tennessee. By 1868, they were joined by the Invisible Empire, an organization commonly assumed to be a KKK alias. In many communities, membership across all three organizations overlapped. William L. Saunders, a Wilmington newspaper editor, ostensibly headed the statewide Invisible Empire, though in practice he held little influence over county-level klan officials and most of the state's 40,000 members. Similarly, Grand Wizard Forrest and other national officers had no practical connection to klan activities in the state.[10]

KKK action intensified following the 1868 elections. Republican William W. Holden, the president of the state's anti-racist Union League, had been elected North Carolina's governor. Faced with Holden and a Republican-dominated legislature, the KKK became an increasingly violent tool of displaced white Democratic interests. White vigilantes frequently targeted black residents for various, often fabricated indiscretions. But victims also included prominent Republican officials. Jones County Sheriff O. R. Colgrove, a white northerner who benefited from black electoral support and had the audacity to arrest several CUG members, was ambushed and killed in May 1869. State Senator John W. Stephens, a Unionist and Republican who had worked actively with his black constituency, was murdered the following year, after being lured to a storage room in the county courthouse and stabbed to death by a klan contingent that included several local elites.[11]

As organized vigilante acts occurred more frequently in 1869 and 1870, Democratic elites had an especially complex relationship to the group. Prominent Democrats often joined the klan when it seemed politically expedient to do so. In more than one case, self-described political moderates helped form local dens as a means to ensure "order," only to withdraw when members engaged in outrages against black and Republican citizens. But even after breaking with the KKK, self-interest dictated that these men not openly criticize the group. "Democrats sympathized with the Klan, benefited by it, were intimidated by it, and were ashamed of it, often simultaneously," historian Allen Trelease explains. "This was part of the psychological burden of white supremacy."[12]

In the face of a growing and increasingly militant KKK, Grand Wizard Forrest issued an order in 1869 to severely curtail members' actions. Largely unsuccessful across the region, the order had no discernible impact in North Carolina. Governor Holden frequently spoke out against the klan's increasing boldness, but his efforts were only marginally more effective. On two occasions, Holden summoned the militia to suppress racial disorders, but more often he responded to KKK outrages with softer measures, attempting to appease rather than eliminate klan dens.

The forces of order became increasingly desperate. Following Senator Stephens's murder and a series of outrages in Alamance County, the *Raleigh Daily Standard*—Holden's staunchly anti-klan newspaper—began calling for armed self-defense. "Load your guns and fire on these midnight assassins whenever they attack you," the paper counseled. "A shot or two in every county in this State will break up these bands of outlaws and murderers." Governor Holden declared a "state of insurrection" and enlisted former Union Army colonel George W. Kirk to regain control in Alamance and several western counties. When Kirk's militia arrested klan adherents, the governor suspended the local courts in favor of military trials, in violation of the state's constitution.

This unstable climate, combined with widespread klan intimidation of Republican supporters, allowed the state's Democrats to regain congressional control following the 1870 elections. The new legislature promptly voted to impeach Holden for his actions in what had become known as the "Kirk-Holden War." Holden was ultimately found guilty of charges related to the deployment of militia troops during the conflict and, on March 22, 1871, he became the first governor in US history removed from office by impeachment.[13]

Though this political realignment suppressed Republican-led Reconstruction efforts, KKK action continued, especially in the mideast and western regions of the state. Only federal government intervention shifted the tide. In 1870, Congress passed the first of two Enforcement Acts, which made interference in voting efforts a federal offense and also forbade conspiracies that infringed upon the exercise of constitutional rights. The following year's Ku Klux Klan Act went even further, allowing federal district attorneys to prosecute a range of conspiratorial efforts to limit constitutional expression. This latter act also included provisions authorizing federal military intervention and, for a time, the suspension of the writ of habeas corpus. The first trials under these acts took place in North Carolina in 1871, the result of arrests stemming from a series of outrages in Rutherford County in the western mountains. These trials resulted in forty-nine convictions for a range of offenses, including simple membership in the klan, which the prosecution argued made individuals a party to unlawful conspiracy.

That same year, the US Senate embarked on an investigation of vigilante violence in the South, including the outrages in Alamance and Caswell counties. A broader Joint Select Committee focused on the "Condition of Affairs in the Late Insurrectionary States" began a second investigation soon after. This momentum led to mass arrests of klan members across the South. Results were mixed, as subsequent prosecutions and convictions lagged behind the large number of pardons awarded to early arrestees. But despite this lack of follow-through, these efforts, along with the lessening threat of Republican political influence as Reconstruction waned, hastened the klan's decline. While sporadic klan-perpetrated violence occurred through the end of 1872, that year's elections were relatively peaceful, and the KKK no longer had a grip on southern communities.[14]

Which of course is not to say that the subjugation of African Americans came to an end. To the contrary, racial oppression, frequently by violent means and committed with virtual impunity, remained a defining feature of postbellum southern life. Even prior to the klan's rise in 1866, North Carolina and the other former Confederate states each established Black Codes limiting newly freed slaves' economic, political, and legal freedoms. The 1876 elections, which resulted in the ceding of local political control to southern Democrats, ended Reconstruction and destroyed any hope of a radical overthrow of white supremacy.

Emboldened by their consolidation of power, political leaders institutionalized a system of strict racial separation, commonly referred to as Jim Crow, and employed a variety of means to disenfranchise black citizens. In North Carolina during the 1890s, a "Fusionist" coalition of Populists and Republicans supported by African Americans as well as white farmers opposed such efforts. In 1894, Fusionists had undermined Democratic control, winning a majority of seats in that year's state General Assembly election. These victories fueled a Democratic backlash, in which party elites curried favor with poor and working-class whites by advancing spurious claims of black economic domination and black-on-white rape.

This racist campaign was astonishingly successful. In scenes reminiscent of the Reconstruction KKK's heyday twenty years earlier, Democratic supporters joined "Red Shirt" clubs, designed to intimidate voters and engineer widespread electoral fraud. In Wilmington, a major port city in North Carolina's southeastern corner, a mob of white vigilantes engaged in a systematic effort to consolidate white political and economic control, abandoning any pretense of law and order. The insurgents took the city by force, exiling black elites and city officeholders, burning the printing press of the city's black-owned newspaper, and installing their own members as city political leaders. During the takeover, a number of African Americans were killed (estimates ranged between nine and ninety) and 1,400 others fled the city. The following year, state lawmakers imposed a series of voting restrictions designed to decimate the black electorate. A series of statutes restricting race mixing in public and private venues followed. "By the eve of World War I," writes historian Raymond Gavins, "almost every visible space had been separated."[15]

Such measures, of course, were consistent with those that the KKK had championed in the face of postbellum Republican control. The klan's continued resonance among white southerners was evident in the occasional rise of klan-like groups, such as North Carolina's Red Shirts and, in Mississippi, the Whitecaps, who drove black tenants off farmland during the 1890s. Among white Democrats, memories of the Ku Klux Klan were often tinged with a gauzy romanticism. Apologist accounts featuring heroic klan forces defending the honor of the white South provided a foundation for such increasingly sentimental depictions. The 1871 Joint Select Committee's Democratic minority report provided a clear and influential example of such accounts. According to the report, the klan was wholly a product of "wanton oppression in the South [due to] the rule of the tyrannical, corrupt, carpet-bagger or scalawag." As a valorous reaction to this unjust repression, the KKK sought to restore stability and justice across the region, a heroic effort divorced from any political agenda centered on white supremacy.[16]

Following this general script, in the early years of the twentieth century southern newspapers would periodically publish nostalgic KKK stories, usually based on firsthand accounts of surviving klan members. One such tale drew upon the diaries of North Carolinian Randolph Shotwell, a Rutherford County klan leader who later served two years in a federal penitentiary for his role in a 1871 raid on Rutherfordton, the county seat. Shotwell characterized the klan as a reaction to "the humiliations, the exactions, the persecutions and personal annoyances" placed on white southerners by the "unjust" Freedmen's Bureau and other federally controlled agencies. These sorts of interventions stirred up racial antagonisms, he argued. "Uninfluenced by outsiders," Shotwell explained, the freedmen "would for the most part have continued to work and sing and dance on the old plantation." Instead, faced with the "oppression" that resulted from Reconstruction's various corruptions, the klan corrected abuses and "shielded women and children from the insolence, rapacity and brutal passions of vile desperadoes, white or black." Echoed in various early twentieth-century historical volumes, including J. G. de Roulhac Hamilton's influential *History of North Carolina*, this basic account was viewed as authoritative in much of the South.[17]

"Rebirth" in the 1920s

Such romanticized klan stories also reached the masses through Thomas Dixon's well-received turn-of-the-century novels *The Leopard's Spots* and *The Clansman*, which served as the basis for the epic D.W. Griffith film *Birth of a Nation*. The film's 1915 release coincided with the fiftieth anniversary of the Civil War's end, and in Atlanta a failed minister and salesman named William

J. Simmons capitalized on that year's cresting Confederate nostalgia. Simmons claimed to have long dreamed of reviving the KKK, and shortly before the Atlanta opening of Griffith's film, he gathered a handful of sympathetic fraternal types and led them up nearby Stone Mountain for the klan's official re-founding. Despite nasty weather, the ceremony featured the first klan cross burning; while Dixon had included the ritual in his novel, no evidence exists that it was ever performed by adherents of the original klan.

At first, Simmons's revived KKK grew rather slowly, claiming a membership of several thousand in Georgia and Alabama by 1920. That year, in an effort to bolster the group's appeal, Simmons hired professional marketers Edward Clarke and Elizabeth Tyler to build the organization. Clark and Tyler hired on commission hundreds of klan recruiting agents, or "kleagles." In a nation beset by post–World War I nativist tendencies, along with racial and labor strife, an agricultural crisis, and the start of Prohibition, the klan's message of racial purity, Protestantism, and patriotic "100 percent Americanism" resonated with many white Americans who felt their status devalued by looming changes. Kleagles targeted leaders of Protestant congregations and existing fraternal organizations, in hopes of recruiting followers in blocs. They often also successfully tailored the klan's message to the concerns of local communities, and soon the group was seen as the solution to a variety of political, economic, and moral ailments.[18]

Nationwide attention from the *New York World*'s three-week KKK exposé series bolstered these organizing efforts. Though critical of the group and its violent tendencies, the series proved an effective recruiting tool. Eighteen newspapers across the nation ran the story, providing the klan with the widespread visibility it had lacked, along with the backhanded cachet of being important enough to be smeared by the elite eastern press. This media attention also led to an investigation by a congressional committee, further raising the klan's public profile. When called to testify, Imperial Wizard Simmons emphatically defended the klan's good name, lamenting its "persecution" by criminals and troublemakers and swearing "in the presence of God... [to] forever disband the Klan in every section of the United States" if it was in fact guilty of any of the charges brought against it.[19]

In part because of Simmons's successful performance, the committee decided not to pursue action against the KKK. Within the year, klan membership skyrocketed, numbering 85,000 in 1921 and somewhere between 3 and 5 *million* by 1925. Unlike the KKK's Reconstruction-era "first-wave," klaverns were not confined to rural communities or to the South. The group claimed tens of thousands of members in cities across the nation—including

50,000 in Chicago, 35,000 in Detroit, and 17,000 in Denver. Membership in many states exceeded 100,000, and the group's strongholds included Indiana, Ohio, Oregon, Texas, and Alabama. Far from marginal, klan members came from both blue- and white-collar sectors, and frequently included prominent community leaders. Thousands of women also joined the parallel Women of the Ku Klux Klan, and similar numbers of boys claimed membership in the Junior Klan.

In North Carolina, eighty-six klaverns held a membership that approached 50,000, close to the average among states during that period.[20] From 1922 to 1927, Henry A. Grady, a judge on the state Superior Court, served as North Carolina's Grand Dragon. Across the state, many prominent individuals joined, and the group cultivated a public image centered on Protestant morality and fraternal solidarity. Judge Grady strongly opposed nightriding, though his leanings did not prevent his membership from engaging in scattered floggings and various other vigilante activities, including at least one bombing.[21]

In 1923, a bill introduced in the state legislature to prohibit organizations from keeping their memberships secret or wearing masks in public posed a major challenge to the klan's North Carolina support base. Throughout those proceedings, many voiced public support for the KKK on the House and Senate floors. Even the klan's opponents generally avoided discussion of the group's violent actions, instead framing their concerns around the importance of preventing hypothetical future abuses. In the end, the bill failed, a testament to the klan's political influence and broad support base.

Across the nation, similar widespread appeal allowed the KKK to become a player in local and statewide elections. Klan-backed candidates were elected as governors or US senators in a number of states, including Indiana, Texas, Alabama, Colorado, and California. By the 1924 elections, the KKK's national influence was peaking. Its positions influenced both the Democratic and Republican party platforms, and its political machine also strongly and effectively attacked Progressive Party presidential candidate Robert LaFollette.[22]

Though the group retained its violent reputation, the KKK's militance co-existed with its strong emphasis on civic populism. In North Carolina and elsewhere, the klan had ties to a range of fraternal and church groups, and sometimes organized around issues such as law enforcement and good schools. While such emphases have caused some historians to suggest that racism was not primary to this second-wave klan, the intersection of class and race issues in many communities allowed the KKK's civic efforts to link a white supremacist agenda to its campaigns against the immigrants, communists, Catholics, and Jews who ostensibly threatened the prevailing social order.

After 1925, a shifting political and economic landscape, along with moral and financial scandal within the organization, caused the KKK to rapidly lose momentum. Unlike the first-wave KKK, Simmons's klan was a highly centralized outfit, profiting tremendously from initiation fees and the sale of regalia and other klan-related products. This lucrative, top-heavy structure made the klan vulnerable to conflicts over financial control. Such rifts had, in 1923, led to Simmons's ouster from the group's top leadership, with Hiram W. Evans and klan recruiter extraordinaire D. C. Stephenson taking command of the organization. Judge Grady was not immune from these organizational battles. In 1926 and 1927, he clashed with his own membership and with Evans, leading to his split from the klan and a precipitous drop in North Carolina's KKK membership. By late 1927, klan supporters were still able to defeat a reprise of the 1923 unmasking bill, but its mass support had dwindled drastically.[23]

Among national officers, a series of even more spectacular scandals followed. Accusations of staggering financial corruption dogged Evans and other leaders. D. C. Stephenson was charged with second-degree murder stemming from a tragically bizarre incident with a state office worker, who died from the effects of poison she ingested after being kidnapped, assaulted, and raped. Amid this fallout, larger political forces no longer aligned in the KKK's favor. The widespread discontent that the klan had exploited to drive its wide appeal was eroding, klan politicians often failed to fulfill their varied campaign promises, and mainstream political parties increasingly addressed grievances shared by much of the klan's base. By the end of the 1920s, the KKK had almost entirely lost its mass support and political influence. The formal organization limped along for more than a decade, and officially disbanded in 1944 after the Internal Revenue Service filed a lien for back taxes totaling nearly three-quarters of a million dollars.

Disarray (and Continuity) in the Postwar Doldrums

By the close of the 1940s, political scientist V. O. Key pronounced the klan a "dying movement in which southerners take no pride." Hard-line white supremacy, however, had not entirely lost its appeal, and the klan's hoods and burning crosses were perhaps its most evocative manifestation. In this sense, the fall of the second-wave KKK presented an entrepreneurial opportunity, and the first of many new klan organizations emerged during the fall of 1945, when Atlanta obstetrician Samuel Green organized a Stone Mountain cross burning to introduce his Association of Georgia Klans.[24]

Green's organization wasn't entirely "new," as he himself was a bridge back to Simmons's early 1920s KKK. He had remained with the klan during its sharp fall and in the 1930s became the group's Georgia Grand Dragon. When the IRS effectively shut down the second-wave klan in 1944, Green retained a network of klan associates in several southern states. Shortly before his 1945 Stone Mountain ceremony, he reactivated the klan's Georgia corporate charter.

Green's klan grew steadily enough, though its presence polarized the public. The group could count friends in high places; its admitted members in 1946 included Mississippi Senator Theodore G. Bilbo, future West Virginia Senator Robert Byrd, and scores of local political and law enforcement officials. But at the same time, even in the klan's Georgia strongholds, many local and state officials attempted to outlaw the order. Elsewhere in the South, the group received even sharper criticism from public figures. Florida Governor Fuller Warren referred to them as "hooded hoodlums and sheeted jerks," and his Alabama counterpart, "Big Jim" Folsom, pushed hard for a state antimasking law. Nationally, the writer Stetson Kennedy leaked information about the KKK to influential reporter Drew Pearson and the writers of the popular *Superman* radio show, transforming many of the klan's ritualistic secrets into objects of public ridicule.[25]

Green needed to manage various internal divisions as well. In 1948, two Georgia klaverns split from the Association of Georgia Klans and formed a competing organization, and the following year Green ordered three Tennessee units to disband. But the biggest blow to the klan's prospects came in August 1949, when Green himself died suddenly from a heart attack while working in his yard. His replacement, Sam Roper, was a longtime Atlanta police officer and former head of the Georgia Bureau of Investigation. When Roper struggled, not very successfully, to hold various klan factions together, a number of independent organizations soon emerged to compete for members.[26]

While most of these new groups were in the Deep South, perhaps the most volatile organization was headed by Thomas L. Hamilton, a forty-six-year-old South Carolina grocer. Hamilton had first joined the KKK in 1926 and by the mid-1940s had become Green's trusted assistant, charged with building the organization's strength in South Carolina. He also built an active life for himself there, as a Baptist church deacon, 32nd degree Mason, and owner of a wholesale grocery business. His efforts for the Association of

Georgia Klans were confined primarily to South Carolina, though under Green's direction he made an early foray across the state's northern border into Gastonia, North Carolina, west of Charlotte. An initial organizing meeting there attracted a handful of men in March 1949, and the following month members of the group responded to a series of scalding editorials in the local *Gastonia Daily Gazette* by burning a cross outside the newspaper editor's home.[27]

But Hamilton's real move into the Tar Heel State occurred after Green's death, when he acrimoniously split from the Association of Georgia Klans. Demonstrating a newfound ambition, Hamilton shook off Roper's claims that he was a "traitor to the cause of Klancraft" and began taking steps to expand his South Carolina stronghold. Public reaction to Hamilton's initial organizing meeting in Charlotte in December 1949 was decidedly critical. The *Durham Morning Herald* dismissed the KKK as "foreign to the people of North Carolina," and Chapel Hill mayor Edwin Lanier hyperbolically compared the klan's appeal to that of infantile paralysis. The Raleigh Ministerial Association passed a resolution to express "complete condemnation of this movement and unalterably oppose... the extension of its nefarious activities in our city." Both the Raleigh and Charlotte city councils adopted ordinances barring the klan from appearing in public wearing masks or hoods.[28] All of this heated rhetoric and action, in response to boasts made by a klan leader who at that point had held only a handful of meetings in a single area of the state, betrayed the significant unease of community leaders. Newspaper editors and politicians knew that the klan wasn't in fact "foreign" to the state and were wary of the emergence of a political force not easily controlled.

Such concerns proved to be well founded. At first, Hamilton focused primarily on extending the reach of his organization. He employed Tommy H. Panther as his North Carolina "klokard," charging him with starting klaverns in Greensboro, Wilmington, Chapel Hill, Raleigh, and other communities. But while the breadth of the klan's membership failed to coalesce into a significant threat, a sustained terror campaign in a single concentrated region of the state ultimately brought national infamy to Hamilton's klan.

On July 22, 1950, thirty carloads of Hamilton's klansmen caravanned across the state line to Tabor City, a small town just north of the border in North Carolina's rural southeast corner. The lead car held four hooded klansmen, announced by a two-foot-high illuminated cross mounted on its hood and "KKK" written in red across its windshield. Members in other cars threw handbills out to curious onlookers, announcing a "chance to do your part toward saving America from the Jews, nigger, and integrationist quacks who are communists and nigger lovers," and inviting all white men to join them "when the opportunity knocks on your door." The motorcade sparked a harsh editorial from Horace Carter, the publisher of the local *Tabor City Tribune*, who advised readers to "turn your back on the KKK." His assessment of the klan was unambiguous: "the long history of this infamous band of vigilantes guarantees that their very presence in this community will bring violence, despair, lawlessness and tragedy if they succeed in organizing and survive."[29]

Hamilton swiftly retaliated. Carter found a note from the klan on his car windshield the following morning, calling him a "nigger-loving son of a bitch" and warning that the KKK "knows how to deal with trouble-makers like you." A week later, another klan motorcade provoked a shootout outside a black-owned establishment in Myrtle Beach, South Carolina. Membership grew quickly, helped by a November rally that attracted thousands and by Hamilton's appointment of Early Brooks, a well-known former local police officer and lightning rod salesman, as recruiter and head of the local klavern. The following January, a set of klansmen broke down the front door of a house in rural Columbus County, under instructions from Hamilton to whip the husband and wife living there. One of the victims, Evergreen Flowers, later testified that she was struck on the head and bound and gagged, before escaping from the mob and hiding under her house. That same night, across the South Carolina border, two white farmers were beaten by ten hooded klan members.[30]

A series of floggings against various local residents followed. Often, the stated reasons for the punishments were moral ones—abusing one's mother, for instance, or disrespecting the church, committing marital infidelities or drinking excessively. But as in earlier eras, much of this regulative action responded to violations of racial codes and anxiety over the looming possibility of government-mandated desegregation. Klansmen disproportionately targeted black residents, in particular those they suspected were involved in interracial relationships. At rallies, Hamilton's complaints demonstrated how the klan's appeals to Christian morality were tightly interwoven with an ideology of white supremacy:

> [I am] fed up with the government and what goes on in America that promises to force us to go to school with the niggers and merge us into a society of half-breeds.... It won't be long before young white men and women will be dating and marrying the colored people in the communities if they take away our white public schools that the white people built and paid for all these years.... Let me assure you tonight

> that the Ku Klux Klan is determined not to let this integration succeed in the Carolinas. We have organized to preserve the white race that believes in Jesus Christ and attends the Protestant denomination churches of our land.[31]

During the height of the Hamilton klan's nightriding, Columbus County Sheriff Hugh S. Nance noted that his deputies avoided approaching houses in the rural county at night because so many residents were "armed and jittery." State officials recognized that victims reported only a fraction of floggings to the police, for fear of subsequent klan retribution. But when a group of hooded klan members abducted and beat Dorothy Martin and Ben Grainger for their alleged infidelities, failure to attend church, and involvement in the moonshine trade, they made the mistake of transporting the victims over the nearby state line, a federal crime. The FBI joined the investigation, and the following February arrested ten alleged klansmen.

Less than two weeks later, state police followed the FBI's action by arresting an overlapping group of eleven klan members on kidnapping and assault charges. Even more arrests followed, and throughout 1952, four separate trials were held against the accused. In total, nearly 100 klan adherents faced charges for their involvement in a range of illegal violence. Hamilton himself was among the sixty-three klansmen subsequently convicted. Soon after, while free on a $10,000 bond, he presided over a crowd of 2,000 at a rally in Johnsonville, South Carolina. Two days later, he was sentenced to four years in prison. To prevent further klan activity, the state legislature also passed an anti-masking law, prohibiting members of "secret political societies" from wearing disguises in public or burning crosses on private property without consent of the owner. The *Raleigh News and Observer* proclaimed the Ku Klux Klan "dead in North Carolina." Public officials concurred, as did Horace Carter's *Tabor City Tribune*, which trumpeted the klan's "total eradication" and expressed "doubt that it will ever rise again."[32]

But the white supremacist impulse remained. While Hamilton's klan did indeed fizzle out after a few poorly attended rallies during his prison stint, the Supreme Court's 1954 school desegregation decision provided new impetus for the multiple self-styled klans still in existence across the South.[33] Of these groups, Eldon Edwards's U.S. Klans was the best organized. Edwards, a paint sprayer at an Atlanta-area auto body plant, had been a lieutenant of Samuel Green. He formed his own organization soon after the Supreme Court's *Brown v. Board of Education* decision, drawing his initial membership from the remains of Green's old Association of Georgia Klans. He courted legitimacy by copyrighting his revision of Simmons's rituals and regularly reminded audiences that his was the klan organization with "the official charter." The U.S. Klans' program, according to Edwards, centered on "maintaining segregated schools at any and all cost." He talked tough during a nationally televised interview with Mike Wallace in 1957, vowing that "if the Supreme Court can't maintain our Southern way of life then we *are* going to do something about it."[34]

That same year, Edwards's organization reached North Carolina, under the state leadership of Grand Dragon Thurman Miller. Its second rally in the Tar Heel State, held on a drizzly night in October, attracted an audience of only 150 but drew considerable media attention after Edwards, a featured speaker, was arrested for assaulting a newspaper photographer covering the event.[35] Despite, or perhaps because of, this sort of publicity, U.S. Klans membership in the state remained relatively small, though a number of its state officers and klavern leaders—including Arthur Leonard, W. R. McCubbins, E. H. Hennis, and Bob Jones—would be instrumental in the rise of the UKA six years later.

Post-*Brown* Segregationist Action

Throughout the latter half of the 1950s, U.S. Klans was but one of a number of organizations self-consciously aligned against federally mandated school desegregation efforts. Across the South, the predominant response to *Brown* came from the Citizens' Councils, a chapter-driven organization that often attracted business and civic leaders willing to exert economic pressure against those who defied its banner of "States' Rights and Racial Integrity." Though the Councils' membership numbered, at its 1957 peak, in the hundreds of thousands, the organization failed to make significant inroads in North Carolina.

In 1955, however, a set of Piedmont business elites formed a like-minded segregationist organization, which they called the Patriots of North Carolina. With University of North Carolina Professor Emeritus Wesley Critz George as its president, the group developed a distinctive focus on biological and other scientific defenses of segregation, rather than on more conventional crude red-baiting or anti-Semitic appeals. Despite the pedigree of its leadership—which, as the *Charlotte Observer* noted, included "some of the most respected men" in the state—the group failed to gain a mass following, and it formally disbanded after much infighting in 1958. A similar organization, the

North Carolina Defenders of States' Rights, soon took its place, though it also struggled to win more than a few hundred members statewide. By 1963, it too passed from the scene. The States Rights League of North Carolina, chartered in Charlotte in 1955 to "maintain the purity and culture of the White race and Anglo-Saxon institutions," was even more ineffectual, though several of that organization's officers reemerged later in the decade in klan circles.[36]

Among its predominantly working-class constituency, the U.S. Klans' primary competition for membership came from James "Catfish" Cole's North Carolina Knights of the Ku Klux Klan. Cole was a World War II veteran and popular tent evangelist, a sharp dresser with a penchant for self-promotion. He also had a mean streak, reflected in a police record that included at least five arrests for drunkenness, false statements, resisting arrest, and assault. During one such incident, Cole had punched a police officer in the mouth; he later paid $50 to cover costs for the officer's new teeth.

Banished from U.S. Klans, Cole reemerged as "Grand Wizard" of his self-styled North Carolina Knights. The group held its inaugural rally in 1956 in Shannon, a small town outside of Fayetteville in the state's southeast corner. Other members referred to Cole reverentially as "our minister" and busied themselves passing out membership blanks and copies of "Truth Magazine," a four-page tabloid-sized publication, to an audience of 400 or 500. Cole's speech, titled "God Set a Pattern for Segregation," emphasized the patriotic and Christian nature of his klan, tying those pillars to the racial crisis sparked by the looming communist threat to American values.[37]

These themes were not new in klan circles; nativism, Protestantism, and white supremacy had characterized every incarnation of the KKK since William Simmons's trek up Stone Mountain in 1915. However, in the post-*Brown* world, where the future of Jim Crow-style segregation was far from certain, these values were no longer expressed as a moral code, designed primarily to exert control over sporadic and isolated breaches of the racial status quo. Instead, they became the ideological foundation for grievances based quite concretely in issues that demanded tactical responses. As with Edwards's televised threats, Cole's crude invocations of klan retribution—references to the group's "Smith and Wesson plan," warnings that "a nigger who wants to go to a white swimming pool is not looking for a bath; he's looking for a funeral," and the like—were far from empty. Even when klan adherents lacked the resources, coordination, or will to carry them out, such pronouncements signaled that the North Carolina Knights took a strong stand against outsiders who sought to forcibly alter a way of life. For those who perceived that desegregation efforts posed a threat to their economic, political, and social standings, the appeal of an organization poised to act in defense of Jim Crow was anything but abstract.

Indeed, at more than two dozen rallies in 1957, Cole continued to drive home the theme that "the Klan will not stand for integration, voluntary or any other way." His campaign yielded at least some success. That summer, Cole's associate Garland Martin organized a klavern in Greensboro, aided, he claimed, by the fact that local residents were "really stirred up over the recent decision to let negros [*sic*] enter school this year."[38] Cole's main competition came from the rival U.S. Klans, which stepped up its efforts in the state in the fall of 1957 with a nearly identical core message. In response, Cole banished three members for consorting with U.S. Klans, implored a State Bureau of Investigation (SBI) agent to put a stop to the "black eye" that Edwards's group's violent inclinations gave to "all good honest klansmen," and appealed to the state attorney general to disband the U.S. Klans as an illegal "foreign corporation" (it was chartered in Georgia).[39]

But Cole soon had more pressing concerns. At the start of 1958, he embarked on a campaign in Robeson County, where 30,000 Lumbee Indians lived alongside 40,000 whites and 25,000 African Americans. To uphold the county's strict tripartite system of segregation, with separate schools and other facilities for "Whites," "Negroes," and "Indians," the klan targeted a Lumbee family living in a white neighborhood and a case of purported miscegenation between a Lumbee woman and a married white man. A group of Cole's klansmen burned two crosses to warn the offenders. Soon after, bright orange handbills appeared announcing an upcoming KKK rally in Maxton, a small Robeson County town.

As the rally date approached, rumblings about the potential of Lumbee reprisals increased. Cole requested federal protection, citing parallels to the National Guard's role in recent school desegregation incidents in Little Rock. "If Ike had the right to call out troops for nine burly-heads," he argued, "I see no reason why he can't do the same for us at Maxton." Instead, County Sheriff Malcolm McLeod policed the event by instructing his sixteen patrol officers to "take [their] time" when moving in to defuse any Lumbee attack. Two hundred cars, holding perhaps fifty klan members and a few hundred onlookers, streamed onto the rally site, which consisted of a generator-powered sound system set up in the middle of a field next to a car outfitted with a large white "KKK" banner. The generator also powered a single light bulb, which provided the event's only illumination.

As darkness fell and music boomed out over the speakers, hundreds of Lumbee moved from the outskirts of the field toward the klan group. As taunts flew back and forth, Sheriff McLeod again warned Cole. "I can't control the crowd with the few men I've got," he told the klan leader. "I'm not telling you not to hold a meeting, but you see how it is." A Lumbee shot out the lone light bulb, and a number of his cohorts began firing, mostly into the air. Klansmen and their supporters, also armed but badly outnumbered, quickly fled the scene, suffering only a handful of minor buckshot injuries and a single arrest.[40]

Cole and his followers absorbed significantly greater long-term costs. The embarrassing rout received widespread press coverage, subjecting the tough-talking klan to considerable ridicule. Editorials around the state condemned the klan's provocation of the Lumbee, and the *New York Times* ran an account of the incident on its front page. Newspapers across the country reprinted Arizona columnist Inez Robb's column "There Go the Palefaces—Into the Tall Timber," which was full of inaccuracies and Lumbee stereotypes but decidedly anti-klan. *Life* magazine's coverage included a striking photo of the KKK's captured banner draped triumphantly around Lumbee leader Simeon Oxendine's shoulders. The Anti-Defamation League noted that the Maxton incident "sent a ripple of laughter clear across the country." In North Carolina, Governor Luther Hodges released a statement characterizing the conflict as "an assault on peace and good order and a slur on the good name of the state," and placed blame "squarely on the irresponsible and misguided men who call themselves leaders of the Ku Klux Klan."[41]

From the North Carolina Knights' perspective, most troubling was that in the wake of the media fallout, Sherriff McLeod arrested Cole and Garland Martin for their role in the Maxton debacle. Two months later, in front of the same judge who had presided over Thomas Hamilton's trial in 1952, Cole was convicted and sentenced to an eighteen- to twenty-four-month prison term for "inciting to riot."[42] Media accounts almost unanimously concurred with the Anti-Defamation League's report on the incident: "in North Carolina, the Klan is in its death throes, brought on by its excesses of violence and helped by the Lumbee Indians of North Carolina, who decisively cut the Klan down to size at Maxton in January."[43]

But once again, the reality was not quite so clear-cut. In the wake of Cole's and Martin's arrests and internal conflicts over related financial improprieties, members began to splinter off to other klan alternatives. In one such case, disgruntled klansman Lester Caldwell moved his Charlotte-based klavern into his own incipient rival organization, the National Christian Knights of the

Ku Klux Klan. In February 1958, five of its members were arrested for plotting to bomb a Charlotte school. The suspects also allegedly carried out failed bombing attempts at synagogues in Charlotte and nearby Gastonia. While the National Christian Knights' plots lacked sophistication, police efforts to break the case succeeded primarily because of information provided by an undercover agent who had infiltrated the group.[44]

Police also placed informants within U.S. Klans, which held at least seventeen rallies between May and December of 1958. The group publicized these events aggressively, placing orders with local print shops for 14,000 rally flyers over the course of that year.[45] Crowds were sizable, if not enormous—200 to 300 being typical. The group also expanded its membership as the year moved forward, organizing new klaverns in Greensboro, Winston-Salem, Reidsville, Todd, and Mt. Airy. An existing klavern, in Jamestown, tripled in size during that spring and summer. By fall, the klavern had split in two, in response to conflicts between a younger faction seeking opportunities for "dirty work" and older adherents who preferred to abide by state laws and avoid violence. When the klavern in High Point enjoyed a similar growth spurt, its members used some of their chapter dues to rent their own building in the center of the city's business district for meetings and even installed a neon sign outside to mark their new headquarters.

These klaverns maintained their political activities. Members initiated a campaign to support a sympathetic candidate for Guilford County sheriff and collected $200 in donations to send to Arkansas governor Orval Faubus, "to fight integration or to be used in the private schools" (later, they also followed the national office's mandate to "support with all the means at your command" Richard Nixon's 1960 presidential campaign). They proposed less above-board initiatives as well, most notably campaigns to intimidate black families thinking of sending their children to integrated schools. In other cases, they sought to impose their brand of Christian morality, in one instance targeting a man who repeatedly took his girlfriend's welfare check, leaving her children badly fed and ill-clothed. For these sorts of actions, U.S. Klans members procured unlicensed weapons from a friendly Winston-Salem gunsmith.

At several U.S. Klans rallies, members dealt with unwelcome and unfriendly appearances by Cole's North Carolina Knights. As a downpour forced attendees to scramble for cover during a mid-May rally in Guilford County, U.S. Klans state officer Walter "Dub" Brown found himself surrounded by George Dorsett, Robert Hudgins, and two other belligerent Knights. He managed to avoid a physical confrontation, and U.S. Klans Grand Dragon

Thurman Miller made arrangements for ten members of the group's "Security Committee" to circulate through the following week's rally in street clothes. When Dorsett and his cohorts arrived, speaking loudly and passing out their "Integration News" pamphlet, the security detail surrounded the infiltrators to avert further trouble.

More inter-klan conflict brewed later that summer, when several Knights sought to disrupt the speakers at a U.S. Klans rally in High Point. They were confronted by a visibly drunk Bob Jones—then the U.S. Klans' "Night Hawk," or courier to the North Carolina Grand Dragon—who challenged Cole's men to fight. The following week, Cole himself quietly milled around the fringes of the crowd at a Jamestown rally, hoping to persuade U.S. Klans members to join the Knights, which he described as a "fighting outfit."[46]

Indeed, Cole, who less than a year earlier was marketing his klan as a responsible alternative to the violent troublemakers in U.S. Klans, was actively remaking the Knights' post-Maxton image as a place to "get some action," to "*do* something" about school segregation and other threats to white supremacy. As part of an effort in June 1958 to build support for a klavern in Burlington, a Knights' motorcade rolled through several black neighborhoods and the downtown, with klansman E. W. Luther in the back of a pickup truck in full robes and with a rifle by his side. A group of drunk Randolph County klavern members made plans at a November meeting to burn crosses on the property of families who allegedly crossed the Knights' strictly demarcated color line. Around the same time, a klavern in neighboring Guilford County set up an official "phone committee" to make harassing calls to transgressors.

In some cases, Cole's marketing of the Knights' new aggressive stance succeeded. At a July meeting, the U.S. Klans' Jamestown klavern spent most of an evening debating whether the group's preoccupation with battling Cole harmed their ability to retain members. One faction actively supported Cole, and by the end of that summer, a number of U.S. Klans members—mostly those who complained about being held back from militant action—left to join with the Knights. In September, two black-robed members stationed with shotguns at their sides on the speakers' platform at rallies signaled the Knights' newfound militancy.[47]

Increasingly, however, Cole's legal problems and the overall confusion created by his inconsistent behavior hindered these efforts. Shortly after his Maxton-related conviction in March 1958, Cole appealed and went free on $3,000 bond. The next year, he would lose his appeal and go to prison, but before then he moved the Knights through several transformations. At one point, he announced that the group would move underground, supported by a public apparatus centered on periodic "evangelistic meetings." Soon after, he began scheming with itinerant segregationist rabble-rouser John Kasper to partner in a reincarnated version of the Reconstruction-era Knights of the White Camellia. Cole was slated to be the group's "Great Commander," but the partnership bogged down as Kasper became embroiled in his own legal problems in Tennessee and Cole continued to hold rallies with the Knights through late summer.[48]

Until he didn't. During the fall of 1958, Cole effectively disappeared. The Knights soldiered on, organizing a consistent stream of political action in their leader's absence. Cole lieutenants George Dorsett, Clyde Webster, and E. W. Luther gathered outside a Greensboro high school as the 1958–59 school year opened, waving Confederate and KKK flags and handing out anti–school desegregation literature that Dorsett had composed (soon after, Luther—who had been the Exalted Cyclops of "probably the roughest and most vicious" Knights klavern, in Siler City—became fed up with what he perceived as Cole's financial improprieties and signed on as an informant with the State Bureau of Investigation). In Randolph County, members threw a warning note wrapped around a rock at the home of one man who had been working for a local black resident. A Guilford County–based klavern made plans for a letter-writing campaign to "high state officials," encouraging them to maintain segregated schools and investigate the National Association for the Advancement of Colored People (NAACP). Its members also supported fellow klansman Roger A. Roberts's constable candidacy. At a late October meeting, local officers decided to give Cole one last chance to return before replacing him with another Grand Wizard.[49]

During this period, Cole was rumored to be considering a move to Florida, and at one point William Stephens, a White Camellia officer, offered to organize a rally and cross burning for Cole around Jacksonville. "We sure could use a good man like you," Stephens told Cole. "We are having a hard fight trying to wake the people around here." But those plans too failed to materialize. In early 1959, Cole resurfaced in Florence, South Carolina, where he was arrested with fellow Knights member Reverend James F. Mulligan for posing as a private detective. Cole pleaded guilty and received a thirty-day suspended sentence on that charge; soon after, he began a sixteen-month prison term after his failed appeal on charges tied to the Maxton incident.[50]

Ultimately, Cole's incarceration, along with the unexpected death of U.S. Klans leader Eldon Edwards in 1960, curtailed North Carolina klan members' post-Maxton momentum. The Knights soldiered on with George Dorsett as Grand Wizard while Cole was in prison. However, Dorsett's organizing efforts were hampered by a coordinated effort by the state to impede, as Governor Luther Hodges put it in a 1958 statement, the klan's ability to assemble an "armed gathering" to "intimidate" North Carolinians. By late 1959, informants reporting to the State Bureau of Investigation noted little activity on the klan front, estimating that total membership had dropped to approximately 150 statewide. Joseph Bryant, a close colleague of Cole in the Knights, wrote Cole regularly during his prison stint, at one point imploring him to write a mass letter to all past and present members, to spur future action. In late 1959, Bryant attended a klan summit in Montgomery, Alabama, where, he reported with bittersweet pride, he was the only member representing "the old north state."

Contrary to popular accounts, this cumulative effect of the state's policing efforts, and not public ridicule in the aftermath of the Lumbee attack, drove the KKK's atrophy across the state. Intensive policing of the KKK in 1958 and 1959 destabilized the state's klan leadership. The SBI convinced klan officers to turn state's evidence, initiated raids of known klan gathering spots, and threatened to publicly expose its membership, causing at least some members to worry that klan affiliation was becoming prohibitively dangerous. More overt police strategies had enabled the Maxton fiasco and produced much of the organizational infighting that followed. Though the klan mobilized on a smaller scale in the 1950s than in its earlier waves, its decline was similar to the Reconstruction-era KKK, sparked by the coordinated policing not only of its criminal acts but also its very ability to organize.

Continuity and Change in the KKK

As the 1960s began, North Carolina remained an outlier in klan circles. The state's klan adherents remained mostly on the sidelines as a new KKK organization with national designs, led by Robert M. Shelton, emerged on the scene. A tireless organizer, Shelton had entered the notoriously fractured klan world in 1957, after forty-six-year-old Alvin Horn was forced to step down as the U.S. Klans' top Alabama official due to a scandal involving his marriage to a fourteen-year-old and subsequent jailing for contributing to the delinquency of a minor. Shelton took over Horn's position, but intense and frequent conflicts with the national leadership—mostly tied to allegations of missing funds—led him to form his own competing organization, the Alabama Klan. After U.S. Klans national head Eldon Edwards died in 1960, Calvin Craig, who had led the group's Georgia state operation, brought his followers to another new organization, the United Klans of America. The following year, at a meeting in Indian Springs, Georgia, Shelton's constituency merged with the UKA. Flanked by an eight-man security guard in paramilitary garb, intended as a show of strength, Shelton emerged from the Indian Springs summit as the group's Imperial Wizard.[51]

In an organization that attracted crude and bombastic leaders, Shelton stood out. A wiry, exceedingly serious man, he almost always wore a suit and tie, which he sometimes covered with his purple silk Imperial Wizard robe at rallies. An Anti-Defamation League intelligence report noted his complete dedication to the KKK, concluding that Shelton "has no hobbies, does not indulge in sports and has no other interests." Though soft-spoken, he was not averse to condoning or encouraging violent action by his members; a point of contention in his fractured relationship with the U.S. Klans was Shelton's inability—or unwillingness—to control klan-perpetrated violence. While he of course steadfastly opposed civil rights, he more often ruminated on the "communist-Jew conspiracy" that lay behind the movement and the subversive potential of fluoridation efforts, mental health programs, and the American Red Cross.[52]

Shelton was based in Tuscaloosa, Alabama, but he spent most of his time crisscrossing the South, organizing and speaking at nightly rallies hosted by local klaverns. As the UKA gathered momentum, these gatherings began to look more like large-scale community events, attracting crowds numbering in the hundreds—sometimes the thousands—in cornfields or cow pastures. By 1963 the group could, without exaggeration, claim 9,000 members spread over several hundred klaverns in eight states. In North Carolina, remnants of the U.S. Klans joined the UKA, with a Tar Heel contingent present at Shelton's Indian Springs election ceremony in 1961. But it would be another two years until those klansmen, under Bob Jones's leadership, would gather momentum for their mid-1960s resurgence.[53]

Jones traced that resurgence to a meeting he convened a few months prior to his Veterans' Day run-in with Capus Waynick in 1963. Gathered with eight of his former U.S. Klan cohorts in his living room in Granite Quarry, Jones pledged that this inner circle would reorganize North Carolina's KKK. Soon after, Robert Shelton detached Robert Scoggin, the UKA's South Carolina Grand Dragon, to initiate the process of bringing Jones's group into the United Klans. Within a year, Jones presided over a large, coordinated statewide outfit, becoming the most successful of Shelton's Dragons and helping to raise the KKK's profile to levels not seen since the 1920s.

Historians and journalists frequently denote this civil rights-era growth as the KKK's third "wave," an image consistent with historical accounts that emphasize the klan's ephemeral quality. Construed more as a reaction than a program, the klan's trajectory has consequently been characterized by crests of mass participation followed by stretches of dormancy and subsequent fresh "rebirths."[54] The history of the KKK in North Carolina, however, complicates that view. To claim that the formal origins of the Carolina Klan's civil rights-era resurgence is rooted in meetings at Indian Springs and Granite Quarry has a neat—and, for klan adherents, a near-mythical—"beginning" quality,[55] but in important ways this story's origin precedes Jones's move to the UKA. In the broadest sense, the beginning occurred nearly a century earlier, when the idea of a Ku Klux Klan organization emerged in Pulaski, Tennessee. In the ensuing decades, fueled by nativist anxieties over economic and political instabilities and later the threat of Jim Crow's demise at the hands of a grassroots civil rights movement and new federal policies, the UKA continued to draw on this klan heritage. William Simmons's KKK renewal in 1915 drew directly on a romanticized portrait of the klan's role as defenders of white supremacy during Reconstruction, and throughout the twentieth century the KKK was less a set of discrete mobilizations than a continuous movement—with relatively stable core personnel, resources, and rituals, alongside a peripheral membership that has ebbed and flowed in different periods.

As sociologist Verta Taylor notes, committed action by core leaders in the abeyance periods between social movement waves enables this continuity.[56] A set of longtime klan adherents forged the klan's 1960s resurgence, bridging the latter days of Simmons's "second wave" KKK, subsequent like-minded regional organizations helmed by Samuel Green and Eldon Edwards, self-styled KKK offshoots like Catfish Cole's North Carolina Knights, and—finally—Shelton's UKA. In spite of frequent infighting and organizational tumult, these predecessors nurtured deep connections to klan ideologies and iconography and produced a committed core of devotees who saw their identities bound with the KKK. Many members of this core saw themselves, as Shelton did, as "born into the klan."

Klan recruiting successes owed much to the organizing strategies adopted by these core members. Often, local and national leaders were active in civic life, both inside and outside KKK circles. Thomas Hamilton, for instance, was a local business owner, Mason, and church deacon. Similarly, Catfish Cole originally made a name for himself as a tent evangelist and host of *The Free Will Hour* radio show for "people of all churches." Later, he volunteered with the March of Dimes, and joined the VFW, Military Order of the Cootie, American Legion, and Women's Club of Kinston. His printing company produced gratis programs for conferences sponsored by groups such as the North

Carolina Council of Women's Organizations. An avid ham radio operator, he became heavily involved with the local Helping Hand CB'ers and later formed his own Lenoir County CB Club. (The club's organizational style paralleled that of the KKK, with a similar slate of officers and a Ladies' Auxiliary.) He also contributed to, and in some cases founded, parallel segregationist organizations, including the States Rights League and the Committee for Better Government. For Cole, these other affiliations informed his KKK work but were always subsumed by his identity as a klansman. "The klan is my life," he explained. "Anything else I do is a sideline."[57]

In the early days of the North Carolina UKA, these leaders' civic predilections provided a sort of ready-made klan infrastructure. As George Dorsett noted, while the North Carolina Knights might have receded in a formal sense following Cole's imprisonment, "many groups of us continued on with our family meetings and Sunday services." Likewise, full klaverns from the U.S. Klans, including the group's Rowan County–based Unit No. 1 (home of UKA state officers Bob Jones, Don Leazer, W. R. McCubbins, Fred Wilson, and Arthur Leonard), resurfaced nearly intact as UKA affiliates. The UKA inherited organizing tools as well. The flyers announcing hundreds of the UKA's rallies throughout the 1960s looked nearly identical to those printed by U.S. Klans a decade earlier. Records kept by kligrapps (secretaries) and klabees (treasurers) used facsimiles of previous klan forms. The UKA's official "Constitutions and Laws," ratified in 1964, lifted text verbatim from materials Simmons and Evans had distributed to KKK units in the 1920s (Georgia Grand Dragon Calvin Craig, a UKA co-founder, had proudly inherited Evans's own copy of the original document). In the mid-1940s, Samuel Green's Association of Georgia Klans retained the copyright on the "Kloran," the official klan manual, and those rights ultimately passed down to Shelton's UKA. By investing in these traditional KKK practices, leaders formalized their cultural link to the klan's emphasis on symbol and ritual.[58]

KKK appeals to adherents attracted to nativist, religious, and patriotic defenses of white supremacy resonated in part because of this continuity in the klan's fraternal organizational style and ritualistic practice, encapsulated respectively by a dizzying array of national, state, and local klavern officers and by the klan's nighttime rallies and cross burnings. Many of the klan's core members—those who crossed generations and viewed klan membership as a central part of their identity—cited the group's symbolic cachet as the true meaning of klan affiliation. But the burgeoning civil rights movement created a window of opportunity for klan leaders to recruit from a much larger pool: those who felt aggrieved by impending racial change. "People just won't stand for this Civil Rights stuff," argued Bob Jones. "Somebody has got to organize this state, and I'm the one who's doing it."

The klan's following shifted with the ebb and flow of such threats. However, viewing the klan solely as a "reaction" subject to structural changes and the vagaries of public opinion neglects another dimension of the KKK story: klan organizations challenged, and at times were challenged by, government and police agencies, whose actions also shaped the KKK's fortunes. While popular accounts of Cole's infamous Maxton rally emphasize how the resulting public ridicule dealt the klan a fatal blow, both Cole's North Carolina Knights and the rival U.S. Klans in fact expanded their memberships and accelerated their actions in the months immediately following the rout by the Lumbee Indians. The groups receded only when authorities jailed Cole and infiltrated klaverns over the following year. The decline of Hamilton's Associated Carolina Klans followed a similar trajectory earlier in the 1950s. State and federal officials' mass arrests of Hamilton and other core klan members accomplished what widespread public condemnation of their vigilantism could not. Similarly, congressional anti-KKK action and subsequent mass arrests of klan adherents in the early 1870s sealed the fortunes of the first klan. The KKK's history demonstrates that when authorities take strong steps to suppress klan organizing, they have the capacity to stamp out systematized racist action.

Even during its peak periods, the KKK polarized the white public. Throughout the 1960s, the UKA failed to win widespread mainstream support even in the communities where it recruited large memberships. To varying degrees, local sheriffs, the State Bureau of Investigation and Highway Patrol, the governor's secret anti-klan committee, the FBI, and the House Un-American Activities Committee all sought to suppress the KKK's activities. The strategies and tactics that Jones and others adopted to draw support to the UKA helps to explain how the klan maintained a large grassroots following in the face of significant criticism from civic and political elites. At the same time, the ambivalent and sometimes contradictory manner in which state and federal authorities carried out their anti-klan charge played a central role in enabling the rise and ultimately securing the fall of the civil rights-era KKK. The story of the Carolina Klan thus mirrors that of the Ku Klux Klan generally: a tale both of how racial threat was mobilized at the grassroots and how the policing of vigilantism tempered and shaped that mobilization.

2 THE RISE OF THE CAROLINA KLAN

There is, of course, no question but that the intent and purpose of the Klan is to promote hatred and to incite violence.

—1966 letter from civil rights activist John Salter to North Carolina officials.[1]

Actually, if you want to break it down and analyze it, the klan is several things simultaneously. It can be a rural trade union, a poor man's fraternal lodge. It can be an economic cooperative. You'll see little stickers discreetly posted in the corners of the store windows which say T-W-A-K, "Trade With A Klansman." It can be a number of things. Indeed, it can be a militia.

—JOURNALIST PETER B. YOUNG, reflecting in 1970 on the Carolina Klan.[2]

During the hot North Carolina summer of 1963, it would have been difficult to see the klan as any of these things. That July, the Rowan County Sportsman's Club in Granite Quarry was provisionally chartered as Unit 1 in the UKA's North Carolina "Realm." The move seemed less than auspicious at the time. "A few of us finally decided that we would try to keep on as a national organization and not stay purely as a state group," recalled Bob Jones, who was elected to an inaugural four-year term as the state's Grand Dragon that August.[3] At first, Jones's following did not extend much beyond eight other former members of U.S. Klans, a group that had been moribund since the death of its national leader, Eldon Edwards, in 1960.

But Jones, displaying the drive that would earn him the nickname "Horse" in klan circles, got to work organizing the state for the UKA. After town officials rejected his attempts to secure a site at a park near his home in Granite Quarry, he moved the group's inaugural rally to a farm outside nearby Salisbury. On August 31, an estimated 2,000 spectators attended that event, which Jones proclaimed the start of a "massive" UKA membership drive. "We have the same right as the Negro to demonstrate," Jones told reporters, responding in part to the previous week's March on

Washington, which had attracted an estimated quarter-million civil rights supporters to the nation's capital. "The Catholics have their Knights of Columbus, the Jews have their B'nai B'rith, the Negroes have the NAACP and we have the Ku Klux Klan."

Imperial Wizard Robert Shelton, who a week earlier had sustained a broken arm and other minor injuries when his private plane crashed in South Carolina, gave the keynote speech. He emphasized the "changed image" and civic orientation of the UKA, which he claimed was "striving to get people who would benefit any fraternal organization instead of the hothead, bully type."[4] To build this following, Jones put his small core of Rowan County adherents to work organizing a handful of other rallies that year. They focused mainly on the eastern part of the state, home to the majority of North Carolina's black population. After a modest turnout in Martin County in early November, an estimated 1,100 spectators came out for a rally later that month on the southeastern coast, near the port city of Wilmington.

Cold temperatures temporarily interrupted the UKA's incipient momentum, but the following spring Jones began a more ambitious series of weekly Saturday night rallies, again mostly in eastern counties. These events generally were held in cow pastures, local air strips, or other large fields. They typically were well orchestrated, with arriving cars greeted by robed klansmen selling small rebel flags, handing out free literature, and directing drivers to a nearby parking area. Spectators bought food at a concession stand. Nearby, piled on the hood of the Grand Dragon's car, various pieces of UKA paraphernalia were for sale: copies of the organization's national newspaper, the *Fiery Cross*, for a quarter; segregationist books such as *God Is the Author of Segregation* and *None Dare Call It Treason* for fifty cents each; and a range of UKA bumper stickers and emblems ("The Knights of the Ku Klux Klan Is Watching You," "Be a Man—Join the Klan," and "You Have Been Visited by the Ku Klux Klan" were the biggest sellers). Sometimes other items—TVs, toasters, motor oil, fertilizer, even used cars—were raffled off as well. As the rallies grew, Jones periodically brought in a five-piece string band, Skeeter Bob and the Country Pals, to play "Move Them Niggers North" and their other segregationist tunes. Twenty different records, most featuring the Country Pals, were on sale for a dollar apiece.[5]

While most spectators dressed in overalls or other work clothes, members themselves typically donned the white robes and hoods characteristic of the KKK. In the wake of the rash of floggings perpetrated by Thomas Hamilton's Associated Carolina Klans, the state had passed an anti-masking law in 1953. The ordinance made it illegal for groups to adopt "any disguise whatsoever in the furtherance of any illegal secret political purpose," and consequently UKA members' hoods did not conceal their faces.[6]

The rally itself began and ended with a prayer from a local preacher, and featured speeches by Jones and other klan officials. The nightly climax was the burning of a wooden cross covered in gasoline-doused burlap. The cross burning was a well-orchestrated ritual; robed klansmen would ceremoniously encircle the fiery cross, which could be anywhere from thirty to seventy feet high. The refrain of the popular Christian song "The Old Rugged Cross," played over the makeshift PA system, accompanied the cross lighting:

So I'll cherish the old rugged cross,
Till my trophies at last I lay down;
I will cling to the old rugged cross,
And exchange it some day for a crown.[7]

Rallies and the Organization of the United Klans of America

These elaborate ceremonies furthered both strategic and organizational aims. Their very existence was an expressive tactic, intended as a sort of blunt message to the community, and in particular to local and state officials inclined to capitulate to pro–civil rights forces. The presence of mass public support at each rally, fundamentally unhindered by the police or other authorities, served to reinforce racial hierarchies and intimidate the klan's many enemies. As the centerpiece of each event, the cross lighting was a ritual saturated with terroristic overtones. Klan leaders proclaimed the act a pure expression of Christian virtue—one of the UKA's recordings featured Jones solemnly reciting that cross lightings were in fact "a sign of the Christian Religion sanctified and made holy nearly 19 centuries ago, . . . a constant reminder that Christ is our criterion of character." Such accounts, however, were belied by the hundreds of cases statewide where the klan used burning crosses as a resonant symbol of terror and intimidation.[8]

Organizationally, rallies functioned to recruit new adherents, build solidarity among existing members, and raise funds for the UKA's expanding operation. Following the featured speaker at each rally, donation buckets would circulate through the crowd. Certain members acknowledged that, at least some of the time, UKA shills would be placed around the site, making a big show of their large donations to encourage spectators' generosity. The FBI estimated that by 1965, the Carolina Klan was taking in an average of $229 per rally in donations. Interested spectators could also fill out readily available

UKA membership blanks, and pay a $10 initiation fee to join. Once they did, they were required to purchase klan robes—$10 for cotton or $15 for satin, about double what Jones would pay a local seamstress for manufacture and delivery—and begin contributing $2 for monthly dues. After each rally, a ranking officer would count and sign for the collected donations and fees before transporting them to the state office (dubbed the "Dragon's Den," the office was located in Jones's home in Granite Quarry). There, the UKA secretary was responsible for depositing and maintaining files for each sum, as well as for keeping track of the monthly financial reports submitted by each klavern's kligrapp (secretary).[9]

The resulting tens of thousands of dollars flowing into Jones's state office each month led inevitably to suspicions that the UKA was little more than a lucrative political front organization that functioned primarily to enrich its leadership. One disgruntled former member of Jones's inner circle described the lifestyles of UKA state officers as "first class, rib eye steaks, Cadillacs." And leaders did benefit from their high-status positions in the UKA. In 1965, the group established a "Cadillac Fund" to supply Jones with periodic new cars as he traveled the rally circuit (at the end of 1965, he traded in his "Dragon Wagon," a dark-green and white Cadillac, for a brand new Chrysler New Yorker). An ultimately unrealized campaign throughout the summer of 1965 even sought to raise funds for a personal plane for Jones. State officers also received weekly salaries, ranging up to $150 for Jones and several full-time organizers. Jones's decision to hire his wife Syble—at a weekly salary of $100—as the secretary handling incoming funds at the Granite Quarry state office only aggravated suspicions that monies lined the pockets of the UKA's elite.[10]

But the intense commitment required of the UKA's leadership undermined such accusations. In 1965, George Dorsett—Catfish Cole's former partner in the North Carolina Knights, and later the UKA's Imperial Kludd (national-level chaplain)—suggested to Jones that the klan hold nightly, rather than weekly, rallies. As summer approached, they put into practice this intense schedule, and both Jones and Dorsett spoke at almost every rally that year. By that point, according to Jones, his typical work day was eighteen hours long, fueled by at least fifteen cups of coffee and three packs of cigarettes. "I drive upwards of fifteen hundred miles a week," he explained. "I get up around six a.m.—the phone starts ringing so I'm awake and up, about thirty calls a day come in on various [klan] matters."

The UKA's account with a local printing company illustrated the sheer scale of the group's operation. Between April 1964 and October 1965, the

UKA placed orders for 300,000 membership applications, 175,000 white supremacist flyers, 200,000 political handbills, and as many as 2,000 posters for *each* of the group's daily rallies. If Jones's accommodations were, in a relative sense at least, "first class," they also constituted his entire existence throughout the 1960s. While "klan business" sometimes could be an excuse for a night on the town drinking and womanizing, the UKA generally did not allow for personal vacations or other such escapes from seemingly never ending organizational tasks.[11]

As rallies occurred more frequently, they also became more routinized. Broader responsibility for their commission fell to Boyd Hamby, the UKA's Grand Nighthawk (i.e., the Grand Dragon's formal "courier," charged with administering the UKA's public exhibitions). "I'm supposed to check and see that everything goes off without a hitch—the property leases, the cross, the local Sheriffs," Hamby explained at the time. "I even get the blame for the weather. If anything goes wrong, the responsibility comes back up to me." Indeed, Hamby's tasks included securing a one-day lease for the rally site and locating a suitable power source for lighting and sound. Flyers and posters also needed to be constructed, printed, and distributed throughout nearby communities. For larger rallies, radio ads had to be written, recorded, and scheduled. Staging for the rally itself—a pulpit, public address system, piles of literature and other klan paraphernalia—traveled in a UKA van and needed to be delivered for setup several hours before the event. In preparation for the cross burning—the climax of every klan rally—telephone pole-sized trees had to be felled, smoothed, nailed together, wrapped in four layers of burlap soaked in a gasoline-kerosene mixture, and lifted with a service station wrecker into a four-foot-deep hole.[12]

Crowds varied, with police estimates ranging from 200 to 6,000 at any single event.[13] A number of factors affected a given night's turnout. Most generally, rally attendance followed the arc of UKA membership, growing rapidly through 1964 and peaking the following year. Within any given rally season, the size and initiative of the klaverns that formally hosted each event drove turnouts, as local members publicized the event and recruited attendees. The presence of national UKA leaders—in particular the Imperial Wizard—or a live band and other carnival-like attractions at some rallies could attract larger local audiences. The weather mattered as well; on cold or stormy nights, many adherents stayed home or watched the rally from cars parked on the fringes of the event site.

A closer look at rally attendance underscores subtler organizational features. Nearly every rally drew a core group of longtime klansmen, including

Jones, Bryant, Hamby, Dorsett, and a small group of colleagues from their respective Piedmont communities. Many core members held leadership positions that charged them with recruiting members statewide, making rally arrangements, or giving one of the featured speeches that preceded the cross burning. In most cases, core adherents earned these higher status positions through their long-time dedication to the KKK cause. They often devoted the bulk of their energies to the klan and maintained their commitment across surges and dips in KKK popularity and support. Jones's and Dorsett's tight-knit circle in Rowan and Guilford counties fit this profile. They had persevered through the collapse of the U.S. Klans and North Carolina Knights at the close of the 1950s, and many would continue in one or another KKK organization through the 1970s, long after the UKA's influence had receded.

Surrounding this steady core were larger numbers of more casual klan members and sympathizers, whose commitment ebbed and flowed as conditions that drove klan appeal shifted. As the UKA grew rapidly in 1964, this periphery encompassed the thousands of new members who signed on with local klaverns, as well as the much larger base of sympathizers willing to support the UKA through donations and attendance at nearby rallies. Early on, when formal UKA membership remained small, core members who traveled to individual events drove rally turnouts. The top map in Figure 2.1 depicts the home addresses of participants in a rally held in Williamston on October 5, 1963, and shows a highly localized attendance base—concentrated mostly in the host Martin County and adjoining Bertie County—augmented by a smaller cohort of core members from several counties in the central Piedmont. The latter group traveled significant distances to the rally; the bands on the bottom map in Figure 2.1 show that at least seven carloads of klansmen lived more than 160 miles from the rally site. Many of these members were present at every rally held during this period, regardless of location.[14]

The following year, average rally attendance increased significantly. A typical rally in the fall of 1964, held in Goldsboro on October 10, drew 1,750 attendees, a figure more than three times larger than in Williamston in 1963. As the maps in Figure 2.2 show, the Piedmont-based core membership was again represented in Goldsboro, but in this case local attendance spread across the region. Only the host county attracted more than 10 percent of total attendees; four or more carloads came from eight nearby counties, and the rally drew participants from nine additional counties across the eastern plain. Because of this large and diffuse crowd, the Piedmont-based core made up a much smaller percentage of the total—only 3 percent of cars present at the

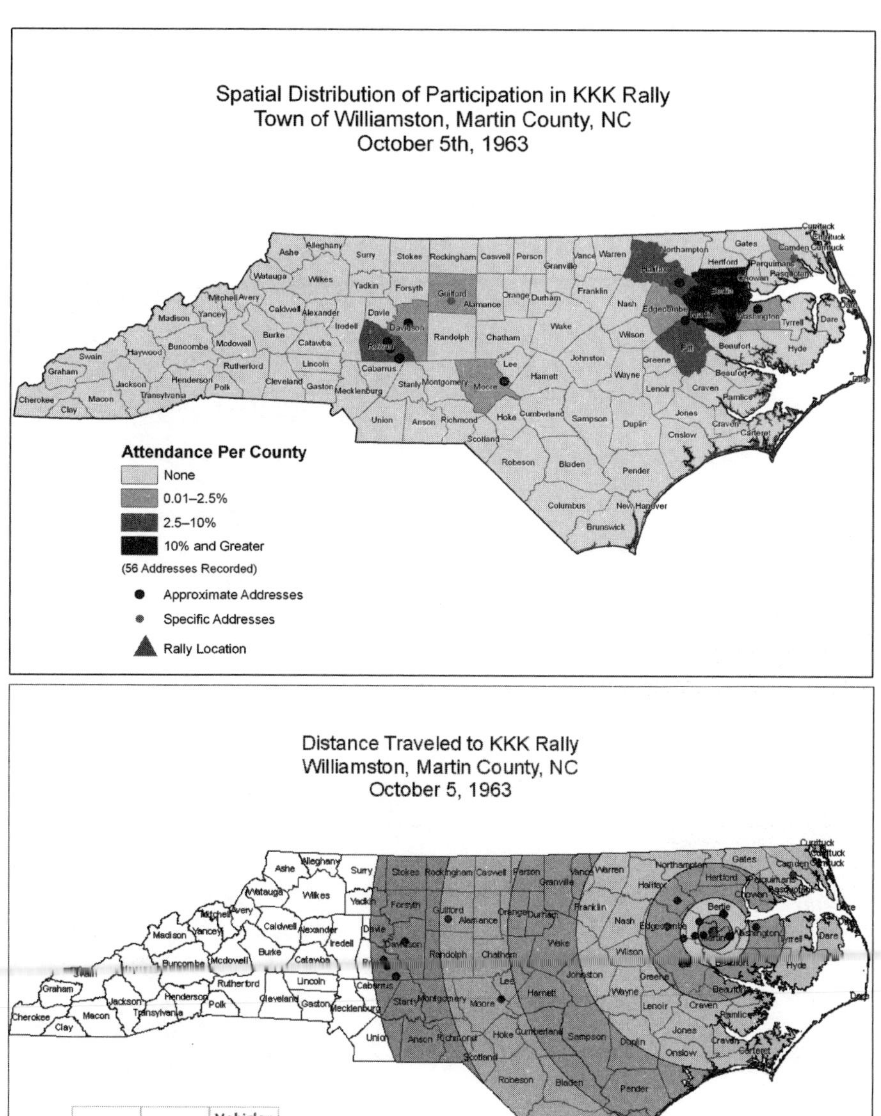

Buffers	Miles	Vehicles Present
	10	27
	20	10
	40	6
	80	1
	120	0
	160	2
	200	5

FIGURE 2.1 Location of attendees and distance traveled, UKA rally in Williamston, NC, October 5, 1963

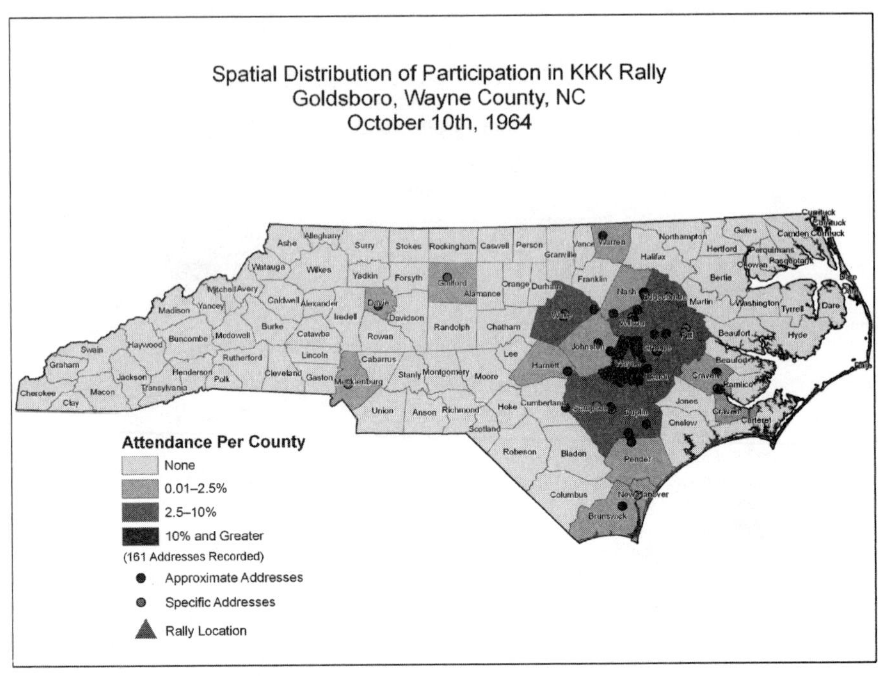

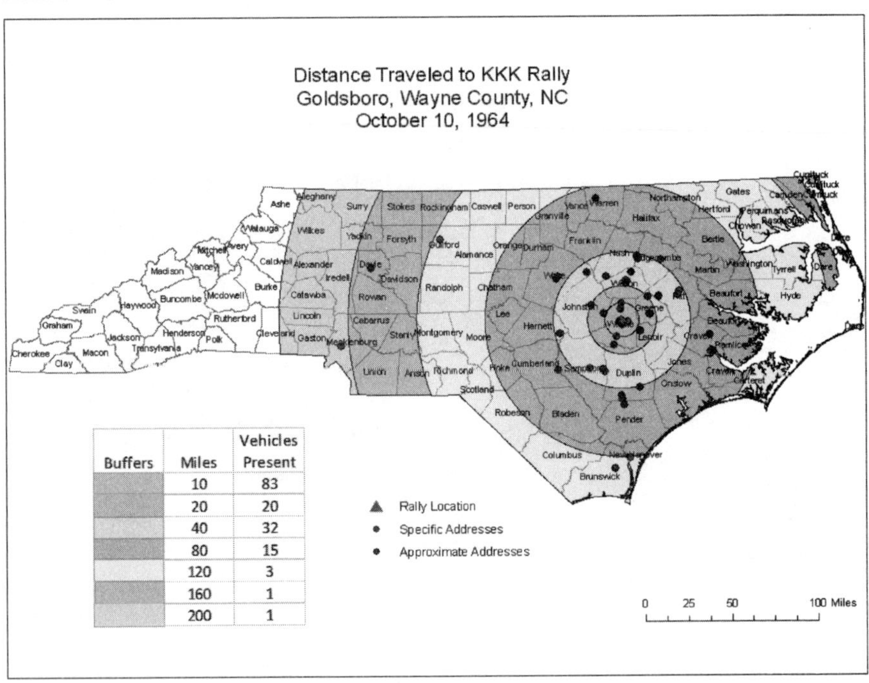

Buffers	Miles	Vehicles Present
	10	83
	20	20
	40	32
	80	15
	120	3
	160	1
	200	1

FIGURE 2.2 Location of attendees and distance traveled, UKA rally in Goldsboro, NC, October 10, 1964

rally traveled more than 100 miles, compared to nearly 14 percent in Williamston the previous year.

These attendance patterns shed light on the nature of threat-based social movements. The growth and spread of UKA support in eastern North Carolina by 1964 aligned with the precarious economic and political conditions of whites across that part of the state. The high proportions of African American residents and fragile agricultural economies in the eastern plain meant that in that region's counties, civil rights reforms would break down traditional white privilege to a degree greater than would occur in the central Piedmont or western mountains. But while such environments were conducive to defensive white supremacist mobilizations, the UKA's growth also required the sustained and intensive efforts of core leaders and organizers. The group's layered membership profile ensured that klan affiliation meant different things to longtime adherents—who often viewed the KKK as a birthright and key fount of political identity—and the bulk of members for whom the UKA provided a more ephemeral outlet. While outer layers of the UKA's membership expanded and contracted along with the group's ability to mobilize anger, frustration, and anxiety associated with encroaching liberal racial policies, the durable commitment of the core membership enabled remarkable continuity in klan ideology and ritual over much of the twentieth century.

Klan Solidarity and the "White Public"

The UKA Security Guard, charged with maintaining order at rallies, was one of the Carolina Klan's distinctive features. The Guard's para-military garb stood out; members each wore work pants, gray-green shirts with plain black ties, white belts, black paratrooper boots with white laces, and white or gold helmets. Grady Mars, a World War II veteran whose service in the military police extended until 1962, joined the UKA in March 1964 and soon after became the group's first security chief. "We provide security not only for the klanspeople but for all of our visitors at any of our rallies," he explained. "Most of our young fellas have had military training and know how to conduct themselves when faced with an emergency.... [They're] only allowed one mistake. If we ever do have trouble with these niggers busting into a rally, we don't want some half-drunk Ku Klux shootin' anybody."[15]

Mars's statement is telling, as while Security Guard members did not openly carry firearms—instead often opting to fill their five-cell flashlights with lead to serve as makeshift clubs—they quickly gained a reputation for belligerence. At times, they directed their actions at rallies toward drunk or otherwise overly boisterous klan supporters. More often they dealt with perceived outsiders, engaging in a precarious balancing act between regulating unwanted visitors and protecting those interlopers from volatile mobs of spectators. At a 1964 rally, for instance, Security Guard members surrounded *Greenville Daily Reflector* reporter Garland Whitaker after suspecting him of recording the event for the FBI. They confiscated his camera film, and after a search revealed no recorder, quickly shifted roles to escort the reporter away from an angry group of bystanders. Whitaker escaped the rally site unscathed, but then, away from the guards' protection, sped home to evade a car in close pursuit.[16]

Others were not as lucky. A group of fifteen Security Guards twice searched a Raleigh minister attending the same rally with his wife and a friend, ultimately confiscating his camera film. After being detained at the rally site against his will during the second search, the minister found two of his car tires deflated, presumably by suspicious klan members. At a later KKK event in Durham County, Security Guard members harassed a group of Duke graduate students when they failed to applaud after speeches. Reacting to the students' long hair and goatees, the Guardsmen accused them of being "white niggers," workers for the Student Nonviolent Coordinating Committee (SNCC), and communists. The scene escalated, and the students were ultimately pushed, hit, and forcibly ejected from the rally.[17] Such confrontations led the *Raleigh News and Observer* to sharply criticize the UKA's openness to outsiders:

> The idea that the general public is invited to Klan rallies is... misleading. These rallies are held only for the purpose of recruiting new members. And the only public wanted is that already filled with a good dose of hatred for Negroes, Catholics, Jews and others who happen to have foreign sounding names. The little man on the back of the truck has something to say to this kind of crowd. He exposes his intolerance without restraint, knowing he has an appreciative audience. It should surprise no one that the Raleigh minister and his friends were spotted as aliens in such a crowd.

Indeed, these kinds of hostilities reinforced klan leaders' strictly bounded conceptions of "whiteness." With Jim Crow increasingly under attack, rally events valued racial separation above all else.

Not surprisingly, in many North Carolina counties, such racial policing had considerable appeal among the "white public." Alongside UKA organizers' efforts to set up new units, rallies contributed significantly to the UKA's continued expansion. The group had organized nearly forty klaverns by the summer of 1964, with most of the new growth occurring in the eastern half of the state. A year later, that total had more than quadrupled; North Carolina's 192 units exceeded those in Georgia, Alabama, and Mississippi combined. By late 1965, the UKA had spread to eighteen states, and its North Carolina membership—estimated at 8,000–10,000—was larger than the joint total in the other seventeen.[18]

UKA bylaws formally required each klavern to maintain a minimum of twenty-five members, with a full slate of officers, including an "Exalted Cyclops" (or "EC," i.e., president), "klaliff" (vice-president), "klabee" (treasurer), "kligrapp" (secretary), "kludd" (chaplain), and so on. This local slate was reproduced at the state level, with state officers denoted by "Grand" preceding their office titles (the only exception was Bob Jones, whose state-level presidential title was Grand "Dragon" rather than "Cyclops"). Between these levels were Provinces, based on state congressional districts. A "Titan" headed up each of North Carolina's eleven Provinces.

Local klaverns each hosted weekly meetings. These meetings could be held on a member's property, though state organizers encouraged klavern officers to purchase abandoned schoolhouses or churches to use as official headquarters. As they grew, some rural units chose to build their own cinder block structures; and in larger towns, places of business owned or leased by a member often served as ad hoc headquarters spaces. In Craven County, one klavern built a space large enough to host indoor rallies attended by more than 200. The Durham klavern, one of the largest in the state, operated a meeting space with seating for more than 500, a reception room, offices, snack bar, and parking for more than 200 cars.[19]

Billboards near many county lines signaled these klaverns' presence. The state office coordinated this process, instructing local klaverns to erect blank signs that Lillington EC Tommy McNeil would then hand-letter. McNeil's work typically incorporated a klansman on horseback, under an announcement that "This is Ku Klux Klan Country." One Greene County klavern preferred a more grandiose message: "Welcome to Klansville, USA."[20]

These kinds of actions aspired to impart a sort of shadow legitimacy to the klan as a political organization. In late May 1964, on the eve of the state's Democratic primary elections, Jones publicly proclaimed a "show of strength," boasting that his members would burn crosses in fifty-five of the state's 100 counties. The actual number fell far short, but the burnings that did occur in more than a dozen counties earned the UKA its most widespread media attention to date. Prior to many rallies, the UKA held more open displays. Klan members gathered in the downtown business district of a nearby community for a "street walk," during which fully robed adherents—accompanied by helmeted members of the UKA Security Guard—marched down the main street. More than a hundred klan members and their families frequently took part, and often the sidewalks filled with spectators.

Like the UKA's rallies, these walks were vehicles for building support. Jones saw them as a way to humanize his followers; he sometimes remarked wryly to reporters that the klan marchers "look just like real people, don't they?" Street walks were also occasions for recruiting new members. Nearly twenty people filled out membership applications following one street walk in Burlington, and spectators sometimes cheered as the participants passed. These events also sometimes drew curious onlookers who might not otherwise travel to a rally. "I've always wanted to see a klansman," a man explained during a 1965 Durham street walk scheduled to counter Vice-President Humphrey's visit to the city. "Well, now I've seen one—plenty of them!"[21]

The public nature of these events and their occurrence in business districts that served as a central space for racial co-mingling added an air of contentiousness that even the UKA's larger rallies often lacked. College students from Duke and NC State University mobilized to jeer the marching klan members during street walks held near their campuses in Durham and Raleigh. And despite Jones's crude claim that "there ain't no niggers around when we march" (UKA flyers advertising upcoming walks were always directed to the "white public"), in larger communities black residents sometimes undermined the klan's intentions by laughing at or otherwise mocking participants. "The KKK don't scare nobody," an African American woman loudly proclaimed to marching klan members in Raleigh. Several hundred black residents more forcefully expressed similar sentiments during a 1965 street walk in Reidsville, a tobacco town near the Virginia border in central North Carolina. Gathering near the end of the march route, they threw rocks at klan members and overturned garbage cans and flower pots to block their path. A month earlier in downtown Salisbury, a thunderstorm interrupted a fist fight between klansmen and black residents following a street walk there.[22]

In addition to these organized events, the UKA earned sustained attention when members sparked or otherwise inserted themselves into various racially charged incidents. In June 1964, an interracial group of teens from Pittsburgh traveled to Elm City, in eastern North Carolina, to assist with the renovation of the First Presbyterian Church, the town's only black place of worship. Soon after their arrival, a group of klan members threatened the visiting students.

Jones claimed that the group "had been living with a bunch of niggers... and the white people were mad as the devil."[23]

Following this confrontation, the students fled the state in the early morning hours, but the conflict escalated when a second, larger group from Pittsburgh, New York, and several North Carolina colleges arrived soon after. Amid continued threats by Jones, 250 klan supporters descended on the small town (population 729). Vowing that the interracial group "will not lay a brush to that church," UKA members offered to finish the job. James A. Costen, the church's minister, quickly rejected the klan's proposal, and following a failed attempt by two klansmen to burn the church, the group commenced its work. In public, Governor Terry Sanford spoke firmly against the klan's intimidation tactics and ordered the State Highway Patrol to reinforce Elm City's two local police officers. Behind the scenes, however, the governor's staff worked to broker a compromise, persuading the Reverend Costen to house the out-of-town group in a hotel rather than in local black residents' homes. This solution addressed the underlying racial transgression—the fact that, in Jones's words, the girls in the group "would be taking black babies back to Pittsburgh"—and enabled the church work to move forward without further incident. But by reinforcing the legitimacy of racial norms, Sanford's approach also provided tacit support for the UKA's stance. This accommodationist dynamic defined state authorities' dealings with the klan through 1965, aiding the Carolina Klan's growth during that period.[24]

1964: Klan Action and State Response

As the UKA made its stand in Elm City, a terrible crime in Mississippi cemented the KKK's notorious national profile. On June 21, 1964, James Chaney, Andrew Goodman, and Michael Schwerner were among the hundreds of young people engaged in voter registration and other civil rights work across the state of Mississippi as part of the Freedom Summer project organized by a coalition of civil rights groups; the three had traveled to Neshoba County, Mississippi, to investigate the burning of a black church. After visiting with a number of locals, they were stopped by Deputy Sheriff Cecil Price for speeding and, improbably, for "investigation" of their possible role in the church burning. By four o'clock that afternoon all three were detained in the county jailhouse. Later that evening, they were released, but never seen alive again.

Their station wagon was found two days later, burned out and submerged in a swamp in the northeast corner of the county. The investigation—one of that year's biggest national news stories—dragged on through the summer. After an intense forty-four-day search, and with the help of a significant payoff to an informant by the FBI, their bodies were found buried in an earthen dam on the other side of the county. The murders were part of a conspiracy involving at least twenty-one people tied to the KKK, including Deputy Price and Neshoba County Sheriff Lawrence Rainey. Edgar Ray Killen, a local preacher, had been the architect of the plot, intended to eliminate Schwerner, whose civil rights work and facial hair had earned him the code name "Goatee" in klan circles.[25]

The crime was tied not to the UKA but to a competing klan organization, the White Knights of the Ku Klux Klan. Based in Mississippi, the White Knights' membership approached 6,000, spread over at least fifty-three units across the state.[26] The group was headed by Sam Holloway Bowers, a forty-year-old World War II veteran and the owner of the Sambo Amusement Company, a vending-machine operation in Laurel, Mississippi. Bowers's organization was more secretive and militant than the UKA, eschewing rallies and street walks for coded communication and covert military-like maneuvers. Its members were frequently implicated in church burnings, beatings, and shootings. "This is an organization of action, no Boy Scout troop," Preacher Killen reportedly emphasized to new adherents. "We're here to do business."[27]

Imperial Wizard Shelton, with an eye toward recruiting members of the White Knights to the UKA, showed up in Neshoba County soon after the boys' disappearance. "These people," he told reporters,

> like to dramatize situations in order to milk the public of more money for their causes. They hope to raise two hundred and fifty thousand dollars for their campaign in Mississippi and I understand that these funds are slow coming in. So they create a hoax like this, put weeping mothers and wives on national television, and try to touch the hearts of the nation. Their whole purpose is just to get more money.[28]

Shelton knew that the boys had been murdered, but also that his claim of a "hoax" was consistent with the worldview of many white Mississippians. The framing of the civil rights movement as a duplicitous front for raising funds, and by extension as a plot by communists and Jews to use the race issue as a wedge to consolidate power, had considerable resonance across the white South. But while in the short run this turn of events, and the looming threat of integration, enabled and enhanced Shelton's appeal, the Freedom Summer murders also had a far-reaching impact on the klan's fortunes. FBI Director J. Edgar Hoover, faced with pressure from President Lyndon Johnson (LBJ) and Attorney General Robert Kennedy to investigate the killings, agreed to open a new FBI field office in Jackson, Mississippi, and quickly ordered the transfer of 153 agents to the state.[29] The FBI also established a broad counterintelligence program against "White Hate Groups," designed to "expose to public scrutiny the devious maneuvers and duplicity" of these targets, as well as to "frustrate," "discourage," and "disrupt" their activities.[30] Over the next five years, this repressive response by the federal government played a central role in the ultimate demise of both the White Knights and the UKA.

But such effects were not yet felt in North Carolina, where during the summer of 1964 momentum from the weekly rallies continued to grow. A crowd estimated at 2,000 came out to an early June rally in Wilson County, and later rallies in the heart of eastern North Carolina were even larger. Over 500 showed up even in tiny Burgaw, located in one of the most sparsely populated counties in the state. By this point, state authorities ordered the State Highway Patrol to monitor each UKA rally. Officers began filing police intelligence reports about the events and their attendees while also managing the streams of traffic that clogged small rural routes before and after each rally, indirectly assisting the UKA's organizing efforts.

The Two Faces of UKA Violence

As the Carolina Klan grew, two other facets of the group's organization began to emerge. The first was its militant underside. In delayed response to the public criticism heaped upon the klan by Governor Terry Sanford during the Elm City incident, klansmen burned a six-foot-tall cross on the lawn of the governor's mansion in Raleigh in mid-August. While the high-profile target was unusually audacious, the tactic itself became increasingly commonplace within the UKA. Reports of at least eighty additional cross-burning incidents—likely representing only a fraction of the statewide total—crossed the governor's desk in the coming months. A later congressional hearing included testimony on thirty-four separate cross burnings perpetrated between late 1964 and early 1965. The minutes from an August 1964 klavern meeting held by the Craven County Improvement Association (most UKA units took on fraternal-sounding cover names; other popular choices were various county "sportsman," "hunting," or "fellowship" clubs) demonstrated the increasingly routine nature of such actions, matter-of-factly stating that members "also decide[d] to burn 3 crosses—one at Oscar Funerl [*sic*] Home, one on Brices

Creek Road, and one in Pamlico County. The meeting was then adjourind [*sic*]. The Klexter [a klavern officer; the term is klan-speak for 'outer guard'] built the cross for us."[31]

A few months later, that particular klavern became the focus of statewide media coverage. Its former Exalted Cyclops, thirty-five-year-old Raymond D. Mills, was well known around the county as a hot-headed segregationist. When he heard that a local police officer planned to vote for Lyndon Johnson in the 1964 presidential election, Mills sought to confront him directly. Finding the officer at a local service station, he pulled out a stack of photos that documented some of the "thieves" in the Johnson administration and pointedly asked whether the officer wanted his children "to go to school with niggers." When the officer told him to stop talking "that old klan stuff," Mills became even more agitated. "Go ahead and vote for Johnson," he challenged. "We have 3,000 [klan] members in the state and a hundred men around here and we will take care of the niggers."[32]

On January 24, 1965, Mills traveled to New Bern, the county seat, with his friend Laurie "Buddie" Fillingame and Buddie's cousin Edward "Bunk" Fillingame. Mills was a sort of mentor to twenty-one-year-old Buddie, to whom he had recently sold his small grocery store. Two days earlier, they had made plans to "cause some trouble for some niggers," and after eating dinner at a New Bern drive-in, the three men drove to St. Peter's AME Zion Church, where 350 people were gathered for a civil rights meeting. Mills earlier had procured several sticks of dynamite, and Buddie tossed some of them under two separate cars parked outside of the church. The three men roared off, returned to the drive-in, and later placed more dynamite behind Oscar's Mortuary, owned by longtime NAACP member Oscar Dove.

The resulting blasts destroyed cars owned by NAACP defense attorney Julius Chambers, who had traveled across the state from Charlotte to speak at the meeting, and Onslow County NAACP chapter president Carolina Chadwick, and caused significant damage to a garage area of the mortuary. FBI agents, likely through an informant's tip, almost immediately suspected Mills and the Fillingames, and after the three men gave seriously conflicting accounts in separate interviews with agents, Buddie Fillingame confessed to the crimes. During the subsequent trial, Fillingame recanted his earlier confession, which allowed Grand Dragon Jones to both acknowledge Mills's klan membership and publicly reaffirm that the UKA did not approve of any form of violence. These dual claims only made sense, of course, if Mills was innocent of the crimes, and Jones pledged that the UKA would defend him "to the very end." To fund his defense, members took up collections at rallies and klavern meetings throughout the state. In early June, however, Mills changed his stance and pled guilty in exchange for a suspended sentence, causing Jones to banish him from the UKA.[33]

The New Bern bombing incident illustrates the general ambivalence that the North Carolina UKA held toward violent militant action. Unlike Bowers's Mississippi White Knights, which drew its power from its secretive underground structure, Shelton and Jones envisioned the UKA as a public vehicle. Its frequent rallies and street walks provided occasions for members and supporters to openly espouse their UKA allegiance. The appeal of the organization and its mission was predicated on its willingness to take a militant public stand, to defend segregation when other institutions preached moderation and the necessity of abiding by federal law.

The place of violence within such a framework was ambiguous. While militance had a clear rhetorical function, attracting aggrieved whites to the klan cause, the violence implied by much of the klan's rhetoric was costly, in several senses. As a matter of organizational process, apparent support for militant action meant that members of local klaverns sometimes felt they had free rein to use terror to respond to ephemeral and idiosyncratic issues. Defending such vigilantism was often strategically difficult for Jones, and providing funds for bail and legal fees sapped much of the UKA's capital. In 1965, Shelton issued an "Imperial Proclamation," assessing klaverns between $200 and $500 each to establish a United Defense Fund. He intended the fund to provide "legal counsel for members of the UKA whose constitutional right [*sic*] are violated as a direct result of his or her activities while promoting, creating or maintaining this Order on orders of his or her superior...that they may be rightly vindicated before the world by a revelation of the whole truth."

Privately, however, the Imperial Wizard had serious reservations about creating such a blanket safety net. As Eddie Dawson, a state officer under Jones, put it, the presence of a defense fund would "give the people the feeling of 'I don't give a damn. I'll go out and shoot a nigger, since I've got a bondsman and can get out right away, and a good attorney.'" Dawson himself felt the concern was valid, admitting that "it was common sense, because we have some people who are not the brightest people in the world, and they would use everything in the book for Klan activity."[34]

This tension between militancy and discipline also played out within the rhetoric espoused at rallies. Local officers were often prone to belligerent talk, sometimes overtly encouraging violence. "If five or more Jews were killed in Charlotte or some other town the same night, the remainder would flee this country," Durham klansman Lloyd Jacobs proclaimed during a rally. "Klansmen are going to have to kill these Jews, Communists, and Negroes that are taking over our country and raping our white women!" Imperial Kludd George Dorsett emphasized similarly violent themes, though for different reasons. Dorsett strategically sprinkled his speeches with militant talk, to fire up the crowd as the donation buckets circulated.

But at the same time, Jones's directives were more measured. While he had no qualms about making "nigger jokes" and offering ominous ultimatums to civil rights activists and moderate state officials during rallies, he would also speak frequently about klan members' "bullets and balance," imploring them to "use the balance." During a 1965 rally in Craven County, Jones took specific aim at the bombings Raymond Mills had abetted in nearby New Bern, proclaiming that the klan would "never tolerate bombings, floggings, or murders." Instead, he argued that the klan's true methodology employed ballots instead of bullets to maintain white supremacy in the South. "The race problem in America will never be solved by crime," Jones argued. "It will be solved by the white folks organizing their voting strength as carefully as the colored folks have done for 20 years." Such claims echoed Imperial Wizard Shelton's proclamation that the UKA would become one of the nation's most powerful voting blocs by 1968. While in most areas of the country this claim seemed a grandiose boast, as Jones and his organizers continued to charter new klaverns in North Carolina, the UKA's growing membership increased its viability as a statewide political force.[35]

Klan ambivalence over ballots versus bullets played out more broadly, and on a national stage, in March 1965. That month, the eyes of much of the nation were fixed on Selma, Alabama, where civil rights marchers had been viciously beaten while attempting to cross Selma's Edmund Pettus Bridge on March 7. In response to the repression of that "Bloody Sunday," Martin Luther King Jr. organized a large-scale Selma-to-Montgomery civil rights march two weeks later. Liberal activists flooded into Alabama to support the marchers. Michigan resident Viola Liuzzo was among the volunteers, tasked with shuttling various participants from the Montgomery airport. A car full of klansmen spotted her and nineteen-year-old black Selma native LeRoy Moton as they returned to Selma after the march. The UKA had been visible throughout the march, at one point organizing an eighty-car motorcade to drive alongside and harass the marchers. But this particular klan car contained a special four-man unit deployed by Alabama Grand Titan Robert Thomas. Its occupants, Collie Leroy Wilkins Jr., Eugene Thomas, William O. Eaton, and Gary Thomas Rowe, were members of Birmingham's Bessemer and Eastview klaverns, two of the roughest units in the state. Liuzzo's green Oldsmobile, with its Michigan plates and mixed-race occupants, was a natural target. After an extended high-speed chase, the klan car pulled alongside the Oldsmobile. Its occupants fired several shots. Moton survived, but the gunfire instantly killed Liuzzo.[36]

To the surprise of many, the FBI apprehended the klan killers the following day. The Bureau's investigation benefited from a key resource: one of the occupants of the klan car, Gary Rowe, had worked as an informant since 1960, and he provided agents with information about the murder soon after his return to Birmingham. Less than twenty-four hours later, President Johnson, with FBI Director J. Edgar Hoover at his side, appeared on national television to announce the arrests, and sharply rebuked the klan in the process. "They struck by night, as they generally do, for their purpose cannot stand the light of day," he said of the KKK, before launching into a more pointed attack:

> My father fought them many long years ago in Texas, and I have fought them all my life because I believe them to threaten the peace of every community where they exist. I shall continue to fight them because I know their loyalty is not to the United States of America but instead to a hooded society of bigots.... So if klansmen hear my voice today, let it be both an appeal and a warning to get out of the Ku Klux Klan now and return to a decent society before it is too late.[37]

Nationally, the brutal crime helped build support for federal civil rights legislation. Following the president's address, NAACP Executive Director Roy Wilkins delivered a telegram to the White House, asserting that "the mood of the country is such that at long last we may be able to make some real progress in controlling these hate groups." Echoing the sentiment, the Providence, Rhode Island, City Council passed a resolution endorsing LBJ's stand on the KKK. Hundreds of letters also poured in to support the president's position.[38]

But the televised response intensified defiance within klan circles. The UKA printed and distributed flyers challenging the president to

> bring on [his] investigations.... We have nothing to fear, for we know that ours is a just cause. Our fight is for racial integrity and Constitutional Government. Are we fighting for too much, Lyndon? The Klan will disband when every Communist and Integrationist is driven from our

> shores. We will fight with every means at our disposal—the ballot box, in the swamps, or in the hills, if necessary, for we shall never surrender! *This is Our Answer!!*

Shelton himself told reporters that "if this woman was at home where she belonged, she wouldn't have been in jeopardy." He featured the three remaining UKA defendants (the fourth, the informant Rowe, was now a sworn klan enemy and in protective police custody) at a rally and street walk in Anniston, Alabama, that May. They marched side by side, Wilkins holding a Confederate flag, past more than 1,500 spectators lining the ten-block parade route. The rally crowd that filled the city auditorium gave them a long ovation. The following week, the trio traveled to North Carolina, where they received a similar enthusiastic reaction from a crowd estimated at 6,000 in Dunn, a small tobacco city near the state's center. In a thinly veiled attempt to avoid outright celebration of murder, Jones and other klan leaders took care to shift the focus of their derision toward the civil rights movement—"masterminded by international Communist banking led by Zionist Jews"—and Mrs. Liuzzo's character, which they painted as irresponsible and whore-like. Klan units began distributing a photo of the civil rights volunteer walking, barefoot, with two black workers, an ostensibly self-explanatory portrait of immorality and subversion.[39]

In Dunn, horrified business and religious leaders released an open letter expressing "regret and shame that the KKK chose our town as a showplace to exhibit three men accused of murder." But in many white communities throughout the state, such sentiments could not compete with the UKA's deft reframing of the issue. While Mrs. Liuzzo's murder clearly contradicted claims that the UKA was a nonviolent political vehicle, Jones and other klan leaders deflected attention to the federal government's lack of concern for rural whites. Raymond Cranford, the head of a large and cohesive klavern in tiny Ormandsville, in rural Greene County, recalled his reaction to LBJ's anti-klan speech:

> That was his message to the white ghetto, and it made us mad as hell. We couldn't remember a President saying anything threatening like that to a whole group of people, like say the Mafia, or the Black Panthers, or the Communist Party. Then, a couple of months later, President Johnson was back on the television, talking to a joint session of Congress, and he had a much different message for the black ghetto: "We shall overcome."

Jones himself, basking in the upsurge in UKA membership, summed up its impetus. "If Lyndon Johnson makes three more speeches," he told a rally crowd in Winston-Salem. "We could quit renting fields and start buying farms."[40]

Individual klaverns reproduced this fragile balance between nonviolent rhetoric and militant action. For the majority of klan members, the group represented "white" political interests against the perceived threats posed by communists and civil rights activists. Weekly meetings, monthly dues assessments, and rallies and other public gatherings imparted some fraternal luster. Members commonly engaged in generalized talk of violence. Stewart Alsop, a journalist who spent two days with Raymond Cranford as part of a *Saturday Evening Post* feature, was most struck by klansmen's incessant boasting about violence and guns. Weapons were a central part of klavern culture, and members spent considerable time passing around and cleaning the guns they acquired, as well as letting fellow members know that they were willing to use them. Klavern spaces sported similarly themed "jokes," such as a doll of a black girl hanging by a noose from a door knob or a sign saying "A Nigger Tried—A Nigger Died."[41]

But this bravado rarely extended to discussions of specific acts of violence. While everyday members might suspect the klavern as a site for plotting more nefarious activities, open conversations about particular cross burnings, beatings, or other acts of intimidation rarely occurred. After reading about a cross burned in the yard of a real estate agent who recently sold a black family a house in the white section of town, one klansman tied the act to a closed-door conference between his Exalted Cyclops and five fellow members following the previous night's klavern meeting. But he never confirmed those suspicions. "They never discussed these things in open meetings," he recalled.[42]

Similarly, Eddie Dawson noted that "nothing was spoken" at klavern meetings. "I observed rapidly that a few people stayed behind after everybody went home," he told an interviewer. "That's what they called the Inner Circle. Fifty people attend the meeting, and 46 of them go home; four of them stay back. And that's the trouble makers.... These people are present at every meeting; they're present at every rally, all activities, street walks, etc." By 1966, the state office formalized this layered membership structure, appointing a handful of core "White Card Members" from each Province to carry out secretive missions. According to an informant developed by the State Bureau of Investigation, these militant squads would "perform any service requested of them... [by] the Titan. This may be the burning of school houses, dynamiting churches, slashing automobile tires, burning crosses, etc."[43]

Insulating core members from everyday adherents provided a means for Shelton, Jones, and other state officers to speak out against violence while simultaneously maintaining the UKA as a vehicle to harshly regulate racial transgressions. When Jones stood up at state meetings and emphatically threatened to "banish" any UKA member who engaged in "violence or disorder," he was not merely putting on a show for reporters or informants in the room. Instead, he was seeking to minimize the unpredictability that resulted when members perceived that the klan provided them with a license to terrorize adversaries. It was not violence per se that Jones opposed, but rather violence that was not strategic. Appropriate militant action, in contrast, was directly tied to goals advanced by the state office and executed secretly to allow for plausible deniability by UKA officers, thus avoiding legal tangles that sapped the UKA's resources.[44]

The tensions created by this ambivalent relationship to violence would, by the later 1960s, contribute to the destabilizing of the UKA's infrastructure. But as the Carolina Klan grew throughout 1964 and 1965, Jones's ability to balance behind-the-scenes strategic violence and more aboveboard activities strengthened the UKA's ability to meet its members' varied needs. While the UKA's militant core—those who, as Dawson noted, were "present at every meeting, . . . every rally, all activities, street walks, etc."—cemented their commitment through violent, often illegal activities under the cover of darkness, thousands of everyday members rooted the klan's appeal in its function as an alternative institution for disaffected white workers and their families.

The UKA's Civic Appeal

"We try to be community leaders," said Clyde Newborn, who in 1966 was a fifty-nine-year-old veteran klansman and father of twelve. Harvey Mickles, who joined a klavern located near the South Carolina border, told with similar pride that he was "a member of the Masons, Moose, and Jaycees, and a church deacon, and can assure you that the . . . klan is as interested in our civic improvement as any of these organizations." George Dorsett, a veteran preacher who served as the UKA's Imperial Kludd, likewise reflected on community and religion in the UKA:

> It takes a lot of ministers to make up our organization—many individual Units have one, and every Province must have an ordained minister. I think it's one of the greatest opportunities, the families are already gathered, and it's almost like accepting a congregation. Many

families in various klans of the same area get together on Sundays and have their own community services and picnic lunches, and I spend right much of my time going around to these meetings.[45]

Such sentiments might be dismissed as empty efforts to elide or apologize for the klan's oppressive character, to explain away white supremacist politics as secondary to more conventional civic functions. Certainly some UKA programs, such as a paternalistic effort to distribute truckloads of groceries to needy families ("making a point to divide the gifts evenly between white and black families") were explicitly at odds with an organization that viewed whites and blacks as anything but equivalent. But disregarding this social side of the klan entirely would miss much of the organization's significance and appeal. Bob Jones and other UKA leaders recognized that a deep sense of alienation from mainstream institutions brought many adherents to the klan. As such, the UKA served not only as a political vehicle, but also as an alternative to that mainstream. The UKA's initiation ritual tellingly asked members to swear to hold the klan above allegiances to the outside, or "alien," world.[46]

In its political stances and actions, the UKA sought to maintain the fidelity of "white" spaces. Rough treatment of outsiders and similar boundary displays simultaneously drew upon and maintained complex racial distinctions, demarcating appropriate participants in the klan world. While the UKA always invited the "white public" to its rallies, liberals were considered "nigger lovers" and therefore not authentically white, regardless of their race. "Just anybody can't join," explained a klan member. "You have to be a white man to join us. And I mean a white man dedicated to what we stand for." Jones's regular instructions to his Security Guard contingent drew upon similar distinctions. "As long as [rally attendees] behave like white people it is ok for them to be here." Jones instructed. "But if they behave like niggers, throw them out." Beyond physiological characteristics, political identity and behavior defined whiteness as something continually enacted through one's clear and consistent allegiance to values centered on racial purity and separation.[47]

Reacting to political and economic elites' clear, if reluctant, accommodation to civil rights reform in the state, UKA leaders frequently framed all mainstream institutions as "behaving like niggers." The klan thus served as a singular "pure white" institution, hostile to the communists, "white niggers," and other enemies that populated its surroundings.[48] The UKA's internal communications reinforced such boundaries. "A good Klansman will avoid becoming overly familiar with non-members," instructed one internal UKA document. "He will be friendly but not too friendly, cordial but not intimate. This condition which is often referred to as 'psychological distance' is not easily explained but it can be very important." Similarly, the "Oath of Allegiance" taken by members focused on fidelity to the "sacred secrets" of the KKK, as well as to the practices of "klanishness" that valued fellow members above all. To cement a sense of solidarity among UKA insiders, members outfitted car windows or lapels with secretive symbols, such as klan-coded "circle within a circle" stickers or tiny "AKIA" ("A Klansman I Am") buttons. When Jones appealed to the state's membership to support a new UKA group hospital insurance plan, he took care to reference mainstream institutions' enmity toward the klan:

> it is practically impossible to get a company to recognize our group.... I could not get any hospital insurance before we got this through and so were a lot of other Klansmen in the same boat with me. Now that we have this, and see the benefit it has already been to our local units, are we going to continue to support people that do not support us or are we going to join this hospital plan and HELP people that helps us. Our North Carolina Group is growing by leaps and bounds and with it we must help keep the ONE COMPANY that is on our side to stay with us.... As you can see NO ONE will support us unless we support them. Klansmen, are we going to lose this group plan or are we going to support and keep a White Man's Company behind us?[49]

Beyond the particular services rendered, these initiatives provided an alternative space for its members, apart from officials and corporations with compromised racial principles. Such efforts extended to klansmen's families as well. While UKA by-laws framed membership as a "manly decision" and restricted formal membership to white men, the group welcomed "klanladies" into a parallel network of Ladies Auxiliary Units. Predominantly comprised of UKA members' wives, these units reproduced the klan's patriarchal orientation. Women members appeared at most rallies, preparing much of the food that was raffled off and sold. Frequently, they pursued charitable works—delivering Christmas gifts to the needy, preparing care packages for soldiers in Vietnam, or holding rummage sales to raise funds for rest home patients.

"Every Klanlady should at all times look and act like a lady," was the motto of the first Ladies Auxiliary State Meeting, held in 1967. Indeed, Auxiliary Units valued genteel behavior, reprimanding women for wearing pants rather than skirts or dresses to rallies. Members described Syble Jones, Bob's wife and the EC of Ladies Unit #1 in Rowan County, as a "lady to the hilt," always wearing makeup and dresses. In the UKA, however, such "ladylike" behavior did not preclude toughness. Doris Mauney, a highly regarded officer in a unit west of Charlotte, delivered floral arrangements, featuring a white cross with "KKKK" (for "Knights of the KKK") in gold letters, to the sick in area hospitals and homes. In her handbag, she also carried a tear gas pencil and pistol, with engraved holster.[50]

Syble Jones herself had a similarly tough reputation. A featured speaker at the majority of UKA rallies, she often gave the most militant talk. Her speeches attacked the usual range of klan targets—communists, the federal government, the "Jewish cabal" that lay behind the civil rights movement—while also directly challenging members' masculinity:

> How much more will you take?...Will your house be destroyed before you realize "this is my problem?"...You tell me "what can I do? I can't buck city hall." You make me sick! *Absolutely sick!*...You know that in Russia, the people live behind an iron curtain. Well, men, let me tell you, I really feel sorry for you because I know a lot of you men who live behind an iron petticoat. And it's pathetic! Men, why don't you step out from behind it and be a man? Women, you don't know how good you would feel if your husband was a man who could stand on his own two feet.

Such rhetoric resonantly reinforced the message on one of the UKA's most popular bumper stickers: "Be a Man—Join the Klan."[51]

Members of the UKA or its Ladies Auxiliary typically attended weekly Tuesday night klavern meetings, as well as assisted with rallies or other klan events in the county. The klan's highly ritualized meetings, activities, and organizational process strengthened and reproduced social boundaries as well. These UKA events, in effect, affirmed members' solidarity to the klan world and rejected the compromised character of other alien institutions. In their rally speeches, both Bob and Syble Jones repeatedly stressed the importance of removing klan children from public schools that complied with federal desegregation orders, and always patronizing "white" businesses (here again, klansmen frequently labeled white-owned commercial enterprises "nigger businesses" if they deviated from segregationist orthodoxy).[52] If a personal tragedy befell a member—when, for instance, a house owned by Garland Martin (whose tenure in the klan stretched back to Catfish Cole's ill-fated Maxton rally a decade earlier) burned in 1968—the UKA newsletter issued pleas for assistance. Families of deceased members could hold a klan funeral ceremony, as outlined in the official UKA funeral service handbook.

United Klans also offered its membership a range of social support programs. In addition to the group hospital insurance discussed earlier, Jones established a "Widows Benevolent Fund" life insurance plan, which paid surviving spouses $995.95. Local klan campaigns collected used toys and clothes, which Ladies Auxiliary Units cleaned, mended, and delivered to needy families. Klan-owned businesses offered members discount toys and car repair deals. In 1967, the state office organized a membership drive, offering prizes that included a transistor radio, 12-gauge shotgun (for men), and "His and Hers Klan ring" (for women).[53]

Klaverns hosted regular social events as well, including turkey shoots, fish frys, and family lunches. Unit #83 in Hickory sponsored a benefit dance, featuring two bands, at the local Dollar-a-Go-Go Club, and Units #44 and 68 in Elizabeth City held a New Year's Eve gathering on a member's property, featuring a midnight cross burning. When B. H. Ingle, a klan member and church pastor, invited the membership to a religious service and barbecue in Raleigh, more than 1,400 showed up. Members of the Country Pals, the UKA's house string band, were frequently available "for personal appearances...for the public and Klanspeople to have a week-end of good country music and wholesome fun." And in 1967, the state office distributed altered lyrics to "'Twas the Night before Christmas," featuring fifteen stanzas of klan-oriented themes (a sample lyric: "'Twas the night before Christmas—When all through the Klavern—Not a Klucker was stirring—Not even the Dragon"), and hosted a Christmas party in Lexington.

Klan members occasionally invited the entire membership to their weddings, some of which were held in klavern halls. In May 1965, a crowd estimated at 5,000 gathered in a plowed cornfield in Farmville for an official UKA wedding. Billed as the first nuptials in twenty-nine years "between a Klansman and Klanswoman married by a Klan preacher on the platform during our rally," the bridegroom wore klan robes and klansmen and Security Guards encircled the couple throughout the ceremony. George Dorsett performed the rite, which he concluded with a prayer: "May this couple be a blessing to the Klan and may the Klan be a blessing to them." As a finale, members burned a forty-foot cross. Periodically, rallies provided other kinds of full-fledged social experiences for members and their families. In 1965, a Wilson-based klavern hosted three days of klan events, including nightly rally meetings, a street walk, and barbecue. Another large-scale rally in Kannapolis featured speeches by Imperial Wizard Shelton and Grand Dragons from four states, along with several string bands, sky diver exhibitions, and carnival booths.[54]

Layered Membership and UKA Attachment

These extensive efforts to connect individuals to the klan provide insight into the remarkably rapid rise of the Carolina Klan during the mid-1960s. As journalist and UKA associate Peter B. Young noted at the start of this chapter, the klan could indeed be many things—a fraternal lodge and economic cooperative as well as a militia. UKA leaders' ambitious efforts to provide a broad array of services while also dealing with thorny questions of violence and militancy signaled the klan's complex political and social functions.

The Carolina Klan's multifaceted role was commensurate with the layered character of its membership. The UKA's mid-1960s upsurge was built around the group's militant core, a critical mass of loyal and highly committed adherents. Core members' long-standing ties to the KKK meant that they tended to view the burgeoning UKA as part of a near-continuous string of klan-related activity rather than as a unique, perhaps ephemeral, boom period. While the overall UKA membership expanded and contracted around them over the course of the decade, members of this core were relative constants, crisscrossing the state to attend most rallies and other klan events. Even as membership plummeted in the later 1960s, the FBI noted that "in practically all instances, the 'hard core' individuals are still Klan members."[55]

With few exceptions, these members had been active in the extensive, if highly marginalized, klan battles fought throughout the latter half of the 1950s. Bob Jones and a number of other U.S. Klans adherents from Rowan County—Arthur Leonard, Don Leazer, and Fred Wilson among them—joined the UKA during its initial North Carolina push in 1963, and all served as state officers during its growth spurt. Other state UKA officials—including George Dorsett, Robert Hudgins, Clyde Webster, and Garland Martin—came from the ranks of Catfish Cole's North Carolina Knights. As with Raymond Cranford, who first joined the KKK in 1938 but preferred to think that he was "born into the klan," UKA affiliation was central to the identity of this critical mass.[56] As these long-standing members bridged distinct "waves" of klan activity, connections within this core group did not coalesce for the first time in 1963 around an intense shared interest in maintaining segregation. Rather, Jones drew upon the durable networks of the broader klan world to recruit those members as a roughly intact bloc. The tight-knit nature of this core network, tied to members' klan identities and largely insulated from cross-pressures exerted by outsiders to the incipient UKA world, enabled these individuals to maintain their commitment to the klan even in the absence of mass support.[57]

Attachment to the group differed for those located in other membership strata, something that the UKA's leadership recognized and perpetuated through its varied strategies to maintain members' commitment over time. New adherents tended to lack a deep connection to the klan in general, and instead viewed the UKA as a vehicle to address race-based anxieties. To the extent that looming civil rights changes posed a threat to the white supremacist status quo, the UKA presented itself as a constituency—perhaps the *only* one—that could resist these seismic shifts. Even when desegregation appeared a near inevitability, the group increasingly focused on its role as an alternative institution—a pure "white" space insulated from various "enemies" in the outside world. Various initiatives available only to the UKA's white adherents (insurance plans, religious services, charitable campaigns, and so on) provided incentives that could be exclusively enjoyed by members. The UKA sought to use such programs to retain an everyday membership willing to continue paying dues, attend klavern meetings, and make other baseline contributions required for the group to survive.

As such, the organization adopted a sort of symbiotic dual structure. Everyday adherents contributed various resources, both material and social, that allowed the UKA to sustain itself and gather the large numbers that might provide it with a measure of political influence. Their presence also provided a sort of cover for more militant action, which was almost always planned and carried out secretly by core members. To sustain this commitment among everyday members, UKA leaders sought to provide programs and resources that could only be enjoyed by insiders. Participation in these programs, in turn, reinforced one's social connections to the organization and thus provided a means for deepening involvement in the klan.

Just as the existence of this dual layered structure explains the emergence of alternative klan institutions, it also provides a means to understand the UKA's complex orientation to the question of violent action. Publicly, Jones and other UKA leaders condemned violence and threatened to banish members who engaged in such acts. His directive was, in part, genuine—Jones did seek to regulate autonomous violence initiated by members. However, other forms of violence were sanctioned by the organization. These acts were strategically oriented—coordinated by state leaders, directed at targets perceived to pose a broad threat to klan goals, and carried out secretively to avoid direct legal culpability. As the UKA grew, the ambiguities inherent in this dual orientation to violence had far-reaching consequences that ultimately contributed to the undoing of the organization.

This discussion of the UKA's infrastructure and functions leaves many questions unanswered, however. While the majority of white southerners publicly supported segregation during this period, their commitments to Jim Crow varied considerably in kind and degree. As historian David Chappell argues, "white people did not stick together in their endorsement (or even in their definition) of racial separation, let alone in their willingness to defend it."[58] Likewise, the pressures exerted by civil rights action differed across communities throughout the South, as did the available means for resisting racial reform. While later chapters focus on these individual and community dynamics, perhaps a more pressing question associated with the rise of the UKA is why the organization enjoyed its greatest success in North Carolina, a state that prided itself on its progressivism and moderation in political and racial matters.

3 "REBIRTH OF KLAN COUNTERS MODERATE ACTION IN STATE"

THE UNITED KLANS OF AMERICA AND SOUTHERN POLITICS

It is important for everyone to realize that the KKK actually represents a very small group that is not providing any leadership in our state, and we are determined that it will not become a threat to the orderly development and growth of North Carolina.

—NORTH CAROLINA GOVERNOR DAN K. MOORE, in response to the 1965 finding by the House Un-American Activities Committee that North Carolina had the nation's largest KKK membership.[1]

I am not in favor of the [Voting Rights] law, but I am in favor of obeying it.

—MALCOLM SEAWELL, North Carolina State Election Board Chair and former State Attorney General, in 1965.[2]

We want enough Klans people at this Rally for the press never again to use the word liberal when they write about the State of North Carolina.

—BOB JONES, in a 1965 letter to the UKA's membership.[3]

In his classic 1949 book *Southern Politics in State and Nation*, political scientist V. O. Key described North Carolina's prevailing mood as "energetic and ambitious." "The citizens are determined and confident; they are on the move," Key observed. "The mood is at odds with much of the rest of the South—a tenor of attitude and of action that has set the state apart from its neighbors." North Carolina's "progressive" orientation, he continued, meant that its citizens exhibited a "willingness to accept new ideas, sense of community responsibility toward the Negro, feeling of common purpose, and relative prosperity." The result was "a more sophisticated politics than exists in most southern states."[4]

Encroaching threats to segregation in the 1950s and 1960s—the *Brown v. Board of Education* court decision, mounting civil rights protests, and the passage of the Civil Rights and Voting Rights Acts—would create significant fissures in this optimistic, forward-looking view. But even through the tumult of this period, North Carolina distinguished itself from many of its southern neighbors for its consistent, moderate course with race relations. Politicians promoting the "massive resistance" techniques that led to closed public schools and intervention by federal marshals in Virginia, Arkansas, Alabama, and Mississippi invariably failed in North Carolina. Instead, the state's public officeholders preached the importance of law and order, centered on a paternalistic orientation toward black residents—"community responsibility toward the Negro," in Key's terms—as well as a grudging willingness to comply with federal desegregation laws.

To the surprise of most observers, this state so widely perceived as a bastion of southern liberalism became a hotbed of Ku Klux Klan activity throughout the mid-1960s. By late 1965, the UKA's North Carolina membership eclipsed that of the entire Deep South, with tens of thousands of the state's residents supporting the klan's activities at rallies and klavern meetings.[5] How can we explain that, as the 1964 *Raleigh News and Observer* headline quoted in this chapter's title trumpeted, the KKK's "rebirth" emerged most fully in the state whose reputation for "moderate action" presumably would best "counter" the klan's militant appeals?[6]

The answer, not surprisingly, is rooted in the state's political, economic, and social makeup. The broad political arena that circumscribed the public articulation of racial interests also shaped the resonance of the klan's racist appeals and militant brand of resistance. State politics were important in two primary ways. First, they defined the degree and tenor of official resistance to civil rights legislation, and by extension the range of institutions willing and able to represent segregationist interests. Second, they determined officials' orientation to political "extremism," which influenced their policing of groups like the KKK.

Across the South, policies developed and advanced through governors' offices shaped reactions to civil rights pressures. Though typically associated with individual officeholders, these policies owed much to the broader political economy, in particular the alignment of political and economic elites and the concerns of the electorate in a given voting cycle. While no state in the South enthusiastically adopted civil rights reforms, social scientists and political observers have distinguished between administrations willing to engage in massive resistance—outright defiance of federal desegregation mandates—and those that resisted more passively. The latter approach could involve a range of policies, bound by a shared recognition of the legitimacy of federal law.

This distinction between massive and passive resistance had significant implications for organized vigilante groups like the KKK. States that militantly defended their sovereign right to self-governance nurtured a broad range of institutions to support and maintain segregation. In places like Mississippi, white residents who feared federal reforms could count on an institutional response—from congressional representatives, school boards, police forces, civic elites, and so on—solidly aligned against desegregation. Precisely because this context provided so many mainstream outlets to preserve segregation, vigilante appeals resonated primarily among those whose faith in their community's institutions withered in the face of encroaching civil rights activity.[7] In contrast, states that adopted a more moderate stance had few outlets for staunch segregationists. In those settings, and especially where whites perceived their economic and political well-being as tied to racial separation, the UKA filled a void, providing in some cases the only organized means for uncompromising resistance to federal policies. Such environments increased the range of potential klan adherents, and also signaled a more expansive social and political role for the KKK in an otherwise-barren hard-line segregationist field.

State officials could also affect KKK organizing directly, by employing policing measures to raise the costs of klan mobilization. While well-known cases of fatal violence against civil rights workers and their supporters in Mississippi and Alabama have fostered a widespread assumption that klan members and other white vigilantes operated with virtual impunity across the South, the reality was much more varied. To be sure, states that engaged in massive resistance often weakly policed KKK members and their activities. At their most extreme, as in the well-known case of police complicity in the murders of three Freedom Summer workers in Neshoba County, Mississippi, officials actively facilitated klan-perpetrated violence. More often, police aided KKK members less directly, by opening space for klan action through hands-off or otherwise unassertive policies.

But in other areas of the South, police limited klan organizing by aggressively policing KKK events and actions, covertly monitoring klan activities, and promoting legislative efforts to criminalize or otherwise limit well-known klan expressions. North Carolina fell somewhere in the middle—Governor Dan Moore and other officials offered strong anti-klan rhetoric, but until 1966 the state's policing of UKA-related extremism was characterized more by ambivalence than consistent, aggressive efforts to limit the group's actions. This ambivalent policing, along with the state's moderate orientation, which undercut most mainstream segregationist outlets, aided the UKA's organizing efforts. State leaders' orientation to civil rights pressures, then, explains much of the paradox posed by the UKA's massive support in "progressive" North Carolina.

The "North Carolina Way"

Over the first half of the twentieth century, North Carolina's progressive image had flourished in spite of its uneasy relationship to Jim Crow. Segregation was a pillar of mainstream North Carolina politics, though one almost always couched in the rhetoric of moderation. With interests largely dictated by what Key, observing the close relationship between the state's business values and political policies, described as an "economic oligarchy," such political moderation was often in the service of economic growth.

Historian Glenda Gilmore notes that prior to 1898's violent Democratic revolution that wrested legislative power from the Fusionists, "questions of racial segregation remained unsettled in North Carolina's towns." The white commercial class at the forefront of the ascendant Democratic Party viewed racial separation as essential for social stability and especially for economic prosperity. Newly empowered legislators argued that the political insurgency and "confused" disorder produced by existing "Negro rule" would scare away investors. Increasingly, these elites deployed white supremacy to advance an economic policy centered on conservative values: low wages, reduced taxation, and limited state spending.[8]

This movement's most prominent mouthpiece was Charles Aycock, who was elected governor in 1900. On the campaign trail, Aycock promoted a state constitutional amendment that would disenfranchise African Americans, shrewdly linking white supremacy to North Carolina's social and economic progress. Disenfranchisement, he contended:

> is both desirable and necessary—desirable because it sets the white man free to move along faster than he can go when retarded by the slower movement of the negro—necessary because we must have good order and peace while we work out the industrial, commercial, intellectual, and moral development of the State.

For Aycock, racial separation would allow both races to flourish, and enable the sort of tranquility that maximized the state's growth. He also emphasized uplift through schooling, and developed a progressive reputation as "the education governor," championing the funding of white and black schools alike.[9]

The wedding of segregation and economic development at the center of Aycock's progressivism endured in the state's politics for decades. In the first half of the twentieth century, North Carolina balanced its traditional emphasis on agriculture with aggressive campaigns to lure industry to the state. Buoyed by the success of those campaigns, southern mills produced two-thirds of the nation's woven cotton goods in 1927, and the Piedmont supplanted New England as the world's premiere textile-producing region. North Carolina's appeal to northern firms hinged both on the state's well of cheap labor, enabled in large part by the exploitation of black workers, and on its leaders' avoidance of defiantly racist public defenses of the Jim Crow system that buttressed its discriminatory dual-wage system. Indeed, "progressive" racial moderation was underwritten by extraordinarily harsh labor practices, as state political leaders consistently allied with industry elites to resist unionization and pro-labor legislation. When textile workers responded to increasingly oppressive mill conditions with a wave of walkouts and work stoppages in 1929 and a general textile strike in 1934, the elite oligarchy responded by harshly, and often violently, suppressing labor conflicts.[10]

The resulting anti-union climate remained strong in the 1960s, and North Carolina continued its aggressive industrial growth. "We were totally a non-union state," longtime political insider and future US Senator Lauch Faircloth recalled. "I mean, from the [1929 strikes] right on, North Carolina and unions did not go together." Spurred by this pro-business orientation, in 1965 the state was home to four of the textile industry's fifteen largest firms and over 30 percent of the nation's cotton-system spindles. Four counties housed major tobacco-manufacturing plants, and North Carolina also became the center of the US furniture industry. The service economy expanded as well, with the state's largest city, Charlotte, developing a national reputation as a banking center.[11]

When threats of racial upheaval followed the *Brown* decision, political leaders continued to invoke Aycock's progressivism. In the mid-1950s, Governor Luther Hodges cited Aycock's "march of progress" in his defense of Jim Crow as a system that both ensured political tranquility and enabled racial uplift. His successor in the state house, Terry Sanford, noted that Aycock famously proclaimed "as a white man, I am afraid of but one thing for my race and that is we shall become afraid to give the Negro a fair chance. The white man in the South can never attain to his fullest growth until he does absolute justice to the Negro race." This framing enabled Hodges, Sanford, and, later, Governor Dan Moore to define the "North Carolina way" in sharp contrast with the racially charged massive resistance rhetoric that defined the approaches of Alabama under George Wallace and Mississippi under Ross Barnett.

This moderate course caused early observers like V. O. Key to view the state as "an inspiring exception to southern racism." Crucially, it operated hand-in-hand with North Carolina's anti-labor stance to advance the state's economic interests. Hodges, Sanford, and Moore approached racial policy by emphasizing tranquility, and thus an intolerance for political contention. These officials placed a high value on law and order, condemning as "extremists" those who threatened North Carolina's "harmonious" race relations by advocating either civil rights or staunch segregation. While racial distinctions could not be elided in the Jim Crow South, where the social fabric was shot through with racial disparity, an Aycock-style progressivist stance emphasized the maintenance of racial separation alongside white elites' moral and civic interest in the well-being of black residents. This interest generally took the form of a pronounced paternalism, which typically enabled powerful white residents to serve as benefactors to their black neighbors, in a sort of patron-client relationship. "It was white people doing something *for* blacks—not with them," explained Charlotte-based Reverend Colemon William Kerry Jr. While often framed as gestures of beneficence and closeness, such acts reproduced inequity and distance. More broadly, this racial order served dominant economic and political interests, as it preserved segregation with a progressive sheen that favored industrial expansion.[12]

Electoral Politics and the Limits of Southern Progressivism

This economic oligarchy, with its interest in generating increased business investment in the state, served as a moderating force in North Carolina's racial politics; however, strong perceptions about the reactionary populist bent of the state's voters created a different sort of boundary on political discourse. In the 1960s, memories of a 1950 primary election for the US Senate remained the most salient touchstone. That race pitted Frank Porter Graham—a newcomer to politics, but well known as the longtime president of the University of North Carolina (UNC)—against Raleigh lawyer Willis Smith. Smith's ability to wrest the election from the popular front-runner Graham served as a warning to future candidates who might see racial justice as part and parcel of their progressivist politics.

In 1949, Graham had been Governor William Kerr Scott's surprise pick to fill the Senate seat vacated by the death of Joseph Melville Broughton. The sixty-two-year-old Graham was an unusual political figure, self-effacing and possessed of what a Greensboro newspaper referred to as a "sweetness of character." He had only reluctantly accepted the Senate post, at the time calling his exit from the UNC presidency the most difficult decision of his life. But as the 1950 elections approached, most expected that there would be no serious challenge to his efforts to win a full term.[13]

Rumblings within the conservative wing of the state's Democratic Party about Graham's "pink-tinted" socialist ties, however, spurred efforts to recruit a formidable challenger.[14] After their most prominent choice, former Senator William B. Umstead, withdrew due to health considerations, these forces settled on Willis Smith, a former speaker of the state House of Representatives and, more recently, a nationally prominent lawyer. From the start, Smith's strategy was clear: he would paint Graham as naïve and susceptible to being duped by subversive interests.

Such attacks also, predictably, extended to the race question. Graham had consistently advanced the white southern liberal position on race relations, couching the issue optimistically within North Carolina's "half century of progress in economics and racial amity."[15] He also endorsed full voting rights for black citizens. More broadly, however, Graham favored handling the issue with his brand of the "North Carolina way," which meant a gradual, voluntary move toward integration, without federal intervention. Graham enjoyed near-unanimous support among the state's African Americans, though his gradualist position on integration meant that most black newspapers offered only a qualified endorsement of his candidacy.

For many white voters, Graham's endorsement of *any* vision of integration was perceived as a serious threat. Smith, who was steadfastly in favor of the traditional racial status quo, moved quickly to exploit that fact, characterizing Graham as a racial zealot. Anti-Graham handbills appeared in many areas of the state; the most popular one depicted black GIs dancing with white women while abroad during World War II, suggesting that Graham favored the same for North Carolina. In many communities, Smith supporters equated Graham with integration. Echoing the brutally racist anti-union campaigns of the 1920s and 1930s, word spread among textile workers in mill towns that "a vote for Graham would mean a nigger at a machine next to a white woman." Less than a week before the election, hundreds of North Carolinians received a fake postcard from the NAACP's "W. Wite" (a reference, presumably, to NAACP executive secretary Walter White) encouraging them to vote for Graham. "You know, just as we [in the NAACP] do," read the card's takeaway message to white citizens, "that 'Dr. Frank' has done much to advance the place of the Negro in North Carolina."[16]

At first, these racist smears appeared ineffectual, as Graham swept to victory in the May 27 primary election. He defeated Smith decisively, by more than 50,000 votes. But the presence of two other minor candidates narrowly prevented him from winning a straight majority, which entitled Smith to request a runoff the following month. In the days leading up to that second primary, driven largely by a widely publicized US Supreme Court decision mandating the admission of a black student to the all-white University of Texas Law School, Smith's racial barbs against Graham took on added resonance.

Smith stepped up his invective, directly attacking Graham's support among black voters in a flyer alleging "block voting by Negroes" in precincts in Raleigh, Durham, Greensboro, and Charlotte. The reverse side reprinted the endorsement of Graham by the *Carolinian*, Raleigh's black newspaper. More incendiary was a set of flyers produced by supporters outside of the campaign. One of those, titled "White People Wake Up," featured a list of things that would happen if Graham was elected: "Negroes working beside you, your wife and daughters, in your mills and factories"; "Negroes eating beside you in all public eating places"; "Negroes teaching and disciplining your children in school"; and so on. Willis Smith, the flyer concluded, instead would "uphold the traditions of the South."[17]

In this climate—which one commentator described as a "full-blown racial panic" and Graham himself likened to an out-of-control forest fire—the runoff results reversed those of the first primary, with Smith taking sixty-one of the state's 100 counties and defeating Graham by nearly 20,000 votes. "The evil genii of race prejudice are out of the bottle," the editor of the *Asheville Citizen* wrote to a colleague. "The chances are that we will not get them back into the bottle in North Carolina for a long time." The *Carolina Times*, a Durham-based black newspaper, declared that "the torch of freedom has been snuffed out in North Carolina and there is a darkness all over the state."[18]

Indeed, the election cast a long shadow, shaping perceptions of voter attitudes and, by extension, the contours of North Carolina's electoral politics for the next two decades. While subsequent commentators note that a number of factors—including resentments associated with Graham's link to the "elitist" University of North Carolina at Chapel Hill, his past association with various liberal international causes, and his ties to the polarizing Governor Kerr Scott—played a role in Smith's victory, the central motivator for many white voters was a lingering sense that Graham represented the looming threat posed by racial mixing.[19]

For most observers, the 1950 election demonstrated the racial politics that would define civil rights-era North Carolina. After Graham's defeat, a more nuanced "North Carolina way"—a politics of progressive moderation that avoided seeming soft on matters of racial separation—was the only viable course to pursue. Racial liberals, no matter how popular their overall personas or how gradualist their platforms, seemed unelectable. Indeed, until the Civil Rights and Voting Rights Acts forced the integration of most public facilities, no major-party candidate dared advocate any form of state-sponsored desegregation.

Politics and Policy in the Age of Civil Rights

While memories of the 1950 election curtailed the politics of integration, the industry-friendly, pro-growth tenor of state politics severely limited the support—financial and otherwise—of strong segregationist candidates willing to militantly defy external challenges to the state's status quo. The politically safe middle ground, which preserved segregation by means other than outright resistance to federal statutes, became increasingly difficult to maintain as legal threats to white supremacy mounted during the 1950s. After the *Brown* decision in 1954, political elites debated how to resist the court's desegregation order without engaging in defiant "massive resistance" schemes. In their deliberations, state officials referenced the "revolt" of white voters against Graham in 1950 as a strong signal of their unwillingness to tolerate integration. Citing concerns about order and civility, they refused to seriously consider accommodating federal mandates and sought a "third way" between capitulation and massive resistance.

In an attempt to maintain that balancing act, Governor Luther Hodges—a former textile executive who had come into office after Governor Scott's successor, William B. Umstead, died of a heart attack in 1954—argued against complying with the Supreme Court ruling, invoking the outrage that lay beneath the move away from Graham several years earlier. Reasoning that "the white citizens of this state will resist integration strenuously, resourcefully, and probably with growing bitterness," he instead endorsed proposals developed by a special Advisory Committee on Education, chaired by State Senator Thomas Pearsall. The Committee's recommendations were transparently segregationist. Race mixing in public schools "could not be accomplished and should not be attempted," its report concluded, and any attempts to meet the requirements of the Supreme Court's decision should be made "without materially altering or abandoning the existing school system." The Committee developed a pupil assignment plan that placed authority over most educational matters with local school boards. Committee members reasoned that this move away from centralized state control over schools would avoid state government involvement in a *Brown*-related lawsuit. Procedurally, the plan also established a long set of non-race-based criteria for student assignment decisions, undercutting black families' ability to challenge segregated schooling.[20]

Hodges signed the pupil assignment plan into law in early April 1955. The following year, an additional set of "safety valves" developed by a second Pearsall-chaired committee bolstered these measures. The resulting bill, widely referred to as the Pearsall Plan, proposed to amend the state constitution to provide local school boards with the authority to hold a public referendum to close any public school in the event of a desegregation order. Students in those districts would then receive tuition aid to attend segregated private schools when, according to the bill, "it was not reasonable and practicable to reassign [them] to a public school not attended by a child of another race." While even the plan's staunchest supporters believed that no schools would ultimately close, the measure allowed Hodges to advance a program of "voluntary" segregation.

Pushing hard to integrate could now lead to the end of public schooling in North Carolina. If this occurred, Hodges repeatedly stressed, the fault would lie with "militant and selfish organizations" like the NAACP. In a stunning inversion of white anxiety over miscegenation, he warned the general black citizenry not to allow the NAACP to make "you ashamed of your color and your history by burying it in the development of the white race." And to both groups he addressed his alternative vision of "voluntary separate school attendance." "I do not agree with the Supreme Court decision [and] I do not favor integration," he declared to rousing applause during a special session of the state legislature, adding that he believed "the majority of white *and Negro* people of the state feel the same way." He promoted similar themes in his radio addresses, and even established a telephone number for parents and school officials to call to obtain assistance in successfully pursuing such voluntary measures.[21]

Not surprisingly, many African Americans criticized the school plan. State NAACP president Kelly Alexander argued that Hodges's plan was "contrary to the law of the land." The state black teachers' association unanimously rejected the governor's proposal, and a Hodges speech at North Carolina A & T College in Greensboro was intentionally interrupted by loud foot shuffling in the student audience. National NAACP executive secretary Roy Wilkins expressed his "disillusionment" with North Carolina, saying that he "had come to believe, as had most of the United States, that your declaration that you were the 'most progressive Southern state with race relations' was true . . . yet on this public school question, Texas and Oklahoma and Arkansas are far ahead of you."[22]

Such criticisms only strengthened Hodges's support among much of the white electorate, and more generally this response to the *Brown* decision proved a highly effective political gambit. While the pupil assignment bill had been modeled on an existing plan in Alabama and the plan's provision to allow citizens to officially close public schools rivaled even the "massive resistance" strategy adopted in Virginia (which had prevented local school districts from desegregating but stopped short of providing a constitutional means of closing public schools), Hodges sustained the impression that North Carolina's approach was the quintessence of moderation. Soon after the Pearsall Plan amendments passed by a 4-to-1 margin in a September statewide referendum, Hodges staked out the state's position:

> Against the background of the violence and turmoil in Tennessee and Kentucky, and some extreme legislative measures taken in other states, North Carolinians can take pride in this solid endorsement of a moderate approach to the explosive problems resulting from the decision of the U.S. Supreme Court.

Fearful that a move toward outright compliance with the *Brown* ruling would result in white working-class revolt, a range of influential voices supported the measure. The *Charlotte Observer* called the plan an ideal mix of "conscience and common sense." Well-known progressive state senator Terry Sanford, who would succeed Hodges as governor in 1960, applauded its "moderation, unity, understanding, and goodwill." Others praised the plan's balance, emphasizing its "flexibility" to allow for gradual desegregation if local (white) voters supported that, and its function as a pressure-valve to diffuse tensions in the event of external efforts to impose integration. Despite this appearance of balance, widespread black opposition, along with an endorsement by the hard-line segregationist North Carolina Patriots (whose spokesman argued that the "fundamental issue is whether the Anglo-Saxon race is to become a mongrel race"), revealed the plan's true leanings. Nevertheless, as historian William Chafe concludes, Hodges had succeeded

> in creating a situation where anything he proposed—short of an outright endorsement of the Ku Klux Klan—could be portrayed as "moderate."...Most important, the Pearsall Plan enabled North Carolina's business and political leaders to continue boosting the state

as a progressive oasis in the South, a hospitable climate for Northern investment, a civilized place in which to live.[23]

A More "Neighborly" Approach

In 1960, the election of Terry Sanford as governor shifted the tone, if not the substance, of the debate surrounding race relations. Known as a southern liberal, Sanford admired Frank Porter Graham's role in building North Carolina's reputation as a forward-looking state, but he also had been a keen observer of Graham's 1950 defeat. Noting the tactics deployed by Willis Smith's supporters, Sanford began keeping a notebook to record ideas about how to avoid Graham's fate if faced with a similar racist campaign.

His 1960 primary campaign, run against arch segregationist I. Beverly Lake, reflected such self-conscious strategizing, balancing criticism of defiant opposition to integration with rhetoric intended to avoid fatal "race mixer" labels. The "tightrope" he walked, Sanford later recalled, expressed support for the Supreme Court alongside criticism of the "force and speed" of its desegregation rulings, to create the contradictory impression that he was "against segregation without getting tagged an integrationist." For Sanford, fears of white voter "revolt" loomed large for good reason—though African Americans were 21.5 percent of North Carolina's voting-age population, racist voter registration policies suppressed their representation in the electorate. In 1960, whites comprised more than 91 percent of eligible voters.[24]

Once in office, Sanford turned his attention to pressing issues of employment and education in the state. Though North Carolina fared poorly in general—ranking no higher than forty-second in housing, per capita income, or literacy—prospects were predictably much worse for African American residents. A 1961 report by the North Carolina Advisory Committee to the US Commission on Civil Rights found a "pattern of significant underutilization of Negro manpower," with fewer than one in twenty firms hiring or promoting any African Americans to supervisory or other skilled white-collar positions. More than a fifth of the state's firms refused to hire black workers at all.

In Sanford's view, this pattern of racial exclusion severely limited the state's productivity and potential. He also recognized the growing threat posed by racial grievances addressed only through civil rights protest. Unlike his predecessor, Sanford actively consulted with black civic leaders, often seeking to emphasize that demonstrations themselves would not yield continued progress. Instead, he urged negotiation, pledging to work for "education, up and down the line and across the board" and "job opportunities for everybody, everywhere, on the basis of ability and training, without regard to race."[25]

As a policy response, Sanford created a network of Good Neighbor Councils (GNCs) to support this vision of interracial negotiation and to encourage reform in racial employment practices. Borrowing the GNC label from a similarly named committee in Texas (which, as part of the legacy of FDR's "Good Neighbor Policy" toward Latin America, welcomed diplomats from that region), he vetted the idea with his "breakfast club"—an informal group of black advisors—and in a speech to a Methodist group west of Charlotte in September 1962. The following January, he formally introduced the GNC in a brief address, establishing its "twofold mission to encourage employment of qualified people without regard to race, and to urge youth to become better trained and qualified for employment." Speaking on the hundredth anniversary of the Emancipation Proclamation signing, Sanford acknowledged the progress made over the past century, but emphasized that North Carolinians must "not merely look back to freedom, but forward to the fulfillment of its meaning.... The time has come for American citizens to quit unfair discriminations and to give the Negro a full chance to earn a decent living."[26]

By the close of that year, thirty-seven communities had formed GNCs. A twenty-four-member state council chaired by David S. Coltrane, who previously had directed state budgets under governors Scott and Umstead, oversaw the network of local bodies. Sanford characterized the program as "voluntary" and "low pressure," and relied on the "conscience of North Carolinians [to] get the job done." Consequently, the GNCs charted a conservative course that included no formal administrative power to prevent racial discrimination in the workplace. The *Durham Morning Herald* referred to the newly created councils as "super cautious" and noted that "quiet and moral persuasion may make life easier for the Council, but they don't promise much for its success.... A committee operating quietly and relying on 'conscience' has never gotten far in this field."

But for precisely the same reasons, the program had broad appeal. More conservative eastern North Carolina newspapers like the *Kinston Daily Free Press* praised its emphasis on patience and gradualism, and others lauded its "fair-minded" avoidance of rigidity. Rather, as the *Winston-Salem Journal and Sentinel* argued, the GNC charted a middle way, helping employers "see the advantage... in lifting the level of economic opportunity for a segment of the population whose lack of buying power holds back the entire state's economy." The *Raleigh Times* noted that while black citizens may be impatient, other constituencies worry that change is coming too fast, and the GNC's role is to urge "the rate of speed and the rate of acceptance which will best serve all the citizens of the state."

Indeed, local GNCs followed this moderate path, primarily by holding community meetings with business leaders to encourage equal employment. When racial tensions bubbled up, the local Council—often the only formal biracial body in the community—negotiated with both sides in an effort to resolve conflicts peacefully. By providing a "reasonable" outlet for racial grievances, the GNC sought to defuse the threat of unrest. GNC heads carefully vetted prospective members—especially the black ones—to ensure that they were respected in the community and aligned with the Council's moderate mission. In one telling case Coltrane resolved a controversy over a New Bern member's past criminal record in the member's favor, primarily to avoid "Negro leadership going to the radical left wing Negro group" if the Council lost his "conservative, moderate" viewpoint.[27]

In some cases, this emphasis on moderation put local GNCs at odds with civil rights groups. After a Council was formed in Statesville, north of Charlotte, NAACP field representative L. B. West noted that it was merely a "rubber stamp organization for the power structure," uninterested in consulting with local people or improving job prospects for black residents. Similar charges of conservatism led many to conclude that the GNCs lacked teeth. William Chafe concurs, concluding that Sanford's GNC initiative "produced little in the way of substantive change in the personnel and policies of state government." But even so, Chafe acknowledges that Sanford's willingness to recognize and, by extension, legitimate African American grievances shifted the contours of the state's politics during the early 1960s.[28]

The significance of this shift was far-reaching. As GNC chairman Coltrane noted in a letter to the state's county commissioners, establishing a local Council would "set an official tone—a public policy signifying that the power structure of the county is concerned and committed to peaceful, rational and affirmative solutions to all racial problems." By bringing business owners and other civic leaders into the fold, the GNC functioned as an analogue to the Citizens' Councils that had achieved widespread support in many southern states. As a staunchly segregationist organization built around local chapters, the Citizens' Councils defiantly mobilized against federally imposed desegregation efforts. With the active support of many business owners and civic leaders, Council chapters brazenly imposed a range of economic sanctions on racial dissenters. Their open deployment of legalized repression had a strong normative function, signaling that upstanding white citizens had a duty to preserve Jim Crow-style white supremacy. In Mississippi, where they were founded and most active, Citizens' Councils were even officially sanctioned by the state, receiving funding through the mid-1960s from the pro-segregationist Mississippi State Sovereignty Commission.

While Citizens' Councils did emerge briefly in a small number of North Carolina cities, the predominant elite emphasis on moderation overwhelmed those efforts.[29] Considered within the broader field of segregationist institutions, the Councils' differing reception in North Carolina and Mississippi lends insight as well into the role played by the KKK in those states. In Mississippi, the Councils' widespread and sustained presence contributed to the state's multipronged, variably coordinated effort to forestall the dismantling of Jim Crow. The KKK was certainly present in many Mississippi counties, with both the UKA and the White Knights battling over members and committing hundreds of acts of terror and intimidation. However, the klan operated in an atmosphere of unambiguous opposition to integration, where the police took decisive action to prevent civil rights activism, the courts consistently refused to prosecute whites for anti-civil rights crimes, business leaders denied loans and jobs to black dissidents, schools expelled young black activists, and the state—through the Sovereignty Commission—surveilled and suppressed suspected transgressions of the racial status quo.

Where the control exerted by these other institutions was strong enough, as in the Mississippi Delta, the klan's presence was minimal, its existence rendered redundant by a myriad of other, less overtly brutal, forms of repression. In those settings, economic threats and various forms of intimidation eased the need for terrorist violence to hold the black community in check. Where elites were most secure in their abilities to subdue civil rights challenges without resorting to vigilantism, they sometimes even invoked the segregationist cause to oppose the klan's presence. "Your Citizens' Council was formed to preserve separation of the races," noted a statement by a Council chapter in Yazoo City, in the corner of the Mississippi Delta, "and believes that it can best serve the county where it is the only organization operating in the field."[30]

In contrast to the matrix of racial control in Mississippi—where a wide range of white-controlled institutions aligned in their efforts to maintain segregation—the prevailing moderate "North Carolina way" ideology produced no coherent multi-ordered resistance to the challenge posed by civil rights interests. Instead, the state pushed conservatively in the other direction, in an effort to set a tone for an integrated future. While the GNCs had no authority to force desegregation in the workplace and often shied away from proclaiming integration as an absolute good, its speeches and published materials consistently adopted a realist position. Desegregation was inevitable, its adherents suggested—a signal of progress that would allow North Carolina to meet its full potential. GNC architects trumpeted a voluntary end to racial discrimination as both a morally and economically sound choice. "We can do this, we should do this, we will do it," proclaimed Governor Sanford in 1963, "because we are concerned with the problems and welfare of our neighbors. We will do it because our economy cannot afford to have so many people fully or partially unproductive. We will do it because it is honest and fair for us to give all men and women their best chance in life."[31]

When, on July 2, 1964, President Johnson signed the Civil Rights Act, making segregation in public facilities illegal, racial discrimination became politically inexpedient as well. In this environment—where, like Mississippi, the suppression of black rights enhanced the status of whites, but where state institutions, in sharp contrast with Mississippi, lacked any coordinated policy to preserve Jim Crow in the face of federal sanctions—the Carolina Klan simultaneously was isolated from mainstream institutions and crucial to the advance of segregationist interests. While throughout the mid-1960s state officials did seek innovative legal means to circumvent federal rulings—mostly in an effort to preserve whites-only public schools—their reluctant acceptance of the Civil Rights Act meant that the UKA was not merely one element in a field of segregationist institutions but rather the central organization devoted to preserving the racial status quo.

Whereas in Mississippi the Citizens' Councils and the KKK differed primarily in their means rather than goals, the North Carolina GNCs and Bob Jones's UKA fell on distant ends of the racial spectrum. "During these days when the Klan preaches hatred and the Good Neighbor Council preaches respect of one man for another," the *Raleigh Times* argued, "the choice between Jones' and [GNC Chair] Coltrane's preaching should be an easy one to make."[32] This distinction underscores a more significant difference between the states. Mississippi's segregationist field was crowded with players, and consequently the KKK occupied a narrow niche, attracting members willing to terrorize civil rights challengers where more "respectable" methods failed. In North Carolina, the UKA presented itself as the only "true" organized segregationist game in town, and consequently the group filled a variety of roles for a larger range of adherents. The Carolina Klan could be dangerous and violent like its Mississippi counterparts, but the group also presented itself as respectable and civic-minded. Its layered membership reflected these different orientations, and so long as Jones and other klan leaders credibly balanced "ballots," "bullets," and community engagement, the group's appeal remained broad.[33]

The UKA and the Election of 1964

The UKA's expansive organizational niche, shaped by North Carolina's moderate political orientation, contributed to the group's overall vitality in the state. That political environment was forged in the crucible of Frank Porter Graham's 1950 defeat, and further defined by Hodges's industry-friendly "North Carolina way" and Sanford's pragmatic southern liberalism. Such lines were most starkly drawn, however, in the 1964 gubernatorial election, where the newly ascendant UKA impacted the tenor and outcome of the campaign. That year's Democratic primary matched three candidates: Richardson Preyer, I. Beverly Lake, and Daniel K. Moore.

Preyer was the most clearly liberal candidate, an heir to Sanford's progressive legacy. A World War II Navy veteran and grandson of the Vick Chemical Company founder, Preyer had spent much of his childhood in Greensboro before entering Princeton and then Harvard Law School. After a stint as a state superior court judge in the late 1950s, he was appointed to a federal judgeship by President Kennedy, a strong Sanford ally, in 1961. With no real experience in electoral politics, he was reluctant to enter the gubernatorial race, but an enormously successful petition campaign initiated by a fellow Greensboro lawyer and strong encouragement from Sanford's forces convinced him to run.

Lake's reputation placed him on the opposite end of North Carolina's Democratic political spectrum. Following a twenty-year career as a professor at Wake Forest Law School, he had served under Governor Hodges as assistant attorney general. In that post, he solidified his segregationist bona fides, defending the state from various integration suits and influencing early versions of the Pearsall Plan legislation. His stances on school integration defined his early identity as a political candidate, as he ultimately broke with the moderate and industry-friendly impulses of the Pearsall Plan to back a controversial brand of massive resistance, involving a shadow system of private whites-only schools supported by a statewide network of nonprofit corporations. By the late 1950s, this position made him the most visible legitimate spokesperson for harder line segregationist forces across the state. Embracing that mantle, he ran for governor in 1960, losing a bitter primary battle against

Sanford. Adopting a similar platform in 1964, he entered the race as the segregationist standard-bearer.

Moore was the self-consciously middle-ground candidate. Like Preyer, he was a World War II veteran and former judge. As a relative political outsider, he had no strong connections to the Hodges or Sanford machines. His primary asset was his ability to convincingly portray himself as a reasonable alternative to "dangerous extremes" represented by Lake's arch segregationism and Preyer's "starry-eyed liberalism."[34]

While other issues certainly arose during the subsequent campaign, including a massive highway bond proposal and an increase in the state minimum wage, matters of race and segregation continually came to the fore. The primary was scheduled for May 30, meaning that the impending passage of the federal Civil Rights Act (which ultimately would be signed into law in early July) loomed large over the campaign proceedings. Despite increasingly heated invective on civil rights, from a policy standpoint there was relatively little difference on the race issue among the candidates. True to the contours laid by the 1950 Graham-Smith election, all three formally opposed any federal civil rights legislation and spoke favorably of continued voluntary "progress" with race relations.

The sharp distinctions that did emerge were mostly rhetorical, as each candidate struck a different tone with his reactions to federal imposition. Lake consistently portrayed himself as the only contender willing to use the courts, and potentially other means, to defy the "unconstitutional" actions emanating from Washington, DC. Preyer, in turn, appealed to the historically progressive orientation of the state's voters, assuring them that he was against national legislation, but also warning of the consequences of Lake-style militancy. To stake out this position, he regularly drew a sharp line between North Carolina and states like Alabama and Mississippi. "We don't want to have anything to do with those whose attitudes would only stir up trouble and result in closed schools, federal troops and violence and encouragement of the Ku Klux Klan," he argued. "The North Carolina way avoids violence and preserves law and order."[35]

Moore played up his role as a law-and-order centrist, savvily painting both other candidates as extremists. Like Preyer, he stressed the potential dangers associated with Lake, emphasizing the importance of keeping North Carolina free from the troubles faced by many other southern communities, and pointedly asking voters if they would "dare put an extremist" in the governor's office "and chance the confusion of emotion with reason." In the time-honored tradition of trumpeting good intentions while upholding white supremacy, he acknowledged that the state's black citizens "deserved" equality, but maintained that such conditions "will not come through violence or civil rights legislation.... You can[not] legislate equality. It must be earned." Though he consistently referred to the Civil Rights Act as a "constitutional mockery," when pressed he conceded that he would enforce such laws as governor, making his position effectively equivalent to Preyer's.

The tight three-way primary election failed to produce a plurality for any candidate, which eliminated the third-place Lake and resulted in a two-way runoff the following month. As that second election drew closer, Moore stepped up his efforts to distance himself from Preyer, actively exploiting many voters' suspicions of his opponent's excessively liberal position on the race question. He accused Preyer of being a "captive of the NAACP and CORE." Behind the scenes, his campaign workers employed Smith-like race-baiting tactics, placing "Negroes Welcome" stickers on Preyer billboards and spreading the word that "a vote for Preyer is a vote for the Nigger." His strongest bid for the segregationist vote came when he successfully procured Lake's endorsement. During a TV appearance soon after, Lake played up his role as a representative of the people in the face of federal tyranny, quoting from William Jennings Bryan's 1896 "cross of gold" speech to suggest that

> the great bulk of Judge Preyer's support in the first primary came from people who had marched and demonstrated for the Civil Rights Bill, who have longed for its adoption, who have praised its authors and who now rub their hands in glee at the thought of how you will suffer when the heavy hand of a cruel, wheeler-dealer administration in Washington presses down this crown of thorns upon your head.[36]

Quietly, Moore also courted the state's rapidly growing klan constituency. Prior to the gubernatorial elections, Bob Jones sought to make the UKA into a political force, calling for his membership to "form a voting bloc to defeat any nigger-loving politician that runs for office." Jones's station wagon sported a Lake bumper sticker, and he and his klan constituency had actively supported Lake's candidacy in the first primary election. But with Lake now out of the running, Moore workers began attending klan rallies, and reporters noted the groups of klansmen that sometimes appeared at Moore's speeches. A week prior to the runoff, police surveillance of a UKA rally west of Charlotte observed that a majority of attendees were wearing "Moore for Governor" buttons, and Jones and other rally speakers called for klan supporters to vote against Preyer. The day before that rally, Jones publicly endorsed Moore, arguing that the decision should be self-evident to klan members, given that "Preyer has the solid support of the Negro bloc."[37]

Moore did little to deflect this klan support. While claiming not to know "the nature of the klan or its membership," he told reporters that he welcomed the support of all responsible groups and complimented Jones's quip that "the state needs *mo(o)re* than Richardson Preyer." Preyer was outraged; he released a statement referring to the klan as "hooded hatemongers" and directly questioned Moore's motives, asserting that he "thought every 10-year-old knew what the klan stood for, and what it did."

The racial attacks were effective. Despite Preyer's late efforts to shift the emphasis of the election toward his industrial expansion plan, Moore won the runoff in a landslide, nearly doubling Preyer's vote totals and capturing ninety-three of the state's 100 counties. Jones triumphantly asserted that the result signified a popular rejection of the racial liberalism of Preyer and, by extension, Sanford. "I think it shows the people want the klan," he told a reporter, and boasted that the outcome demonstrated the UKA's electoral power.[38]

As Democratic candidates enjoyed almost unanimous support in North Carolina, that fall's regular election between Moore and Republican candidate Robert Gavin was almost a foregone conclusion. Given his cushion, Moore backed away from much of his racialized rhetoric, drawing criticism from Jones for his token efforts to solicit support from the NAACP. Even so, NAACP head Kelly Alexander described Moore as "very weak [on] issues close to the hearts of the Negro voter," referencing his "move toward ultra-conservatism" during the primaries. Ultimately, the NAACP state chapter endorsed Moore, though the measure failed to achieve unanimous support among its delegates. Golden Frinks, a prominent local activist with ties to Martin Luther King Jr.'s Southern Christian Leadership Conference, also refused to endorse Moore. "We can't as Negroes understand what happened under the good old Democratic party," Frinks argued, complaining that Moore refused to make himself available to the black community. "How can we talk when we can't even meet the man?"[39]

Policing the UKA

These electoral dynamics underscore how political leaders' moderate orientation to civil rights could paradoxically broaden the appeal of the klan by shrinking the range of institutional outlets for the defense of segregation. But state officials also could directly impact UKA mobilization, through their willingness to tolerate or suppress organized vigilantism. In particular, active and aggressive policing could significantly raise the costs of klan participation and hinder recruitment efforts. Permissive or ambivalent policing, on the other hand, provided political space for the klan to operate and in some cases signaled state complicity in segregationist violence. States that promoted massive resistance almost always failed to exert sustained legal pressure against the KKK,[40] but moderate states varied considerably in their policing of organized anti–civil rights violence.

Florida, for instance, developed a progressive, business-friendly image, centered on tourism and industrial growth. Following the *Brown* decision, its moderate governor, LeRoy Collins, wholly avoided a defiant segregationist stance. He clearly favored maintaining Jim Crow as "custom and law," but his rationale—centered on a paternalistic notion that integration was secondary to raising blacks' housing, educational, and moral "standards"—clearly differentiated Florida from some of its more demagogically minded neighbors. Indeed, Collins strategically viewed "forceful attempts" to maintain segregation as counterproductive, as massive resistance threatened "peace and stability" in the state. At the same time, he cautioned against the disruptive potential of a too-ready acceptance of the *Brown* ruling, instead endorsing a more gradualist response to federal desegregation dictates.[41]

As with Luther Hodges in North Carolina, an assumed white extremist backlash motivated Collins's anxiety about integration's destabilizing tendencies. But rather than employ a safety valve like the Pearsall Plan to assuage those elements, Collins took steps to protect against the "mobs" that would use force to defy either local or federal laws. Such policies were consistent with his long-standing intolerance for political extremism. In 1951, as a state senator, Collins had supported a bill that prohibited klan members from donning masks in public.

As governor, he viewed extremism, either by civil rights activists or militant segregationists, mainly as a policing problem. To guard against the "jurisdictional arrogance" that fueled the unpredictable tendencies of local sheriffs, he centralized policing authority under a Sheriff's Bureau that coordinated and monitored the actions of local officers. He also established a Bi-Racial Advisory Commission, charged with defusing racial problems in the state. As one of its first acts, the Commission developed a comprehensive fourteen-point plan to pro-actively handle racial agitators. When segregationist rabble-rouser John Kasper arrived in Florida in early 1957, Collins enacted the Commission's plan. Working through the Sheriff's Bureau and State Highway Patrol, Collins placed Kasper under surveillance, sought to deny his speech permits, and developed plans to detain him "before he starts any trouble."[42]

Farris Bryant succeeded Collins in Florida's statehouse in 1961. A conservative who developed a reputation in the 1960 election as the "segregation candidate," Bryant in his inaugural address vowed to "oppose with vigor any efforts by the federal government to usurp the proper and lawful prerogatives of the state."[43] But he also shared Collins's concern with racial disorder and maintained the existing centralized policing infrastructure. When a civil rights campaign in the small coastal city of St. Augustine was met by a violent segregationist backlash in 1964, Bryant issued an Executive Order that shifted policing authority from local Sheriff L. O. Davis—who had appointed known klan members as special deputies and encouraged assaults on civil rights demonstrators—to a Special Police Force under the command of State Highway Patrol Major J. W. Jourdan. Under the auspices of this state-controlled force, Bryant moved more than 200 state troopers into St. Augustine and required that Sheriff Davis and other local police officials submit daily reports to their state superiors.

While Davis had allowed white vigilantes to operate freely, the Special Police Force quickly earned the ire of many white locals by cracking down on vigilante elements in the KKK and the associated Ancient City Hunting Club. Soon after the troopers' arrival, they formed a shoulder-to-shoulder wall that "repulse[d] at every turn" a large mob of whites that sought to assault civil rights marchers. The following month, state police arrested five men in connection with the bombing of a recently integrated local motor lodge.[44]

In other Florida communities, local police cooperated with state officials to create a coordinated hostile stance against the KKK. Faced with a 1965 UKA organizing campaign, the Broward County Sheriff developed his own intelligence file on klan supporters, relying on license numbers his deputies recorded at rallies. "If certain people sleep with dogs, they are bound to have fleas," he explained, in response to questions about his broad-brush approach.[45] The governor's Sheriff's Bureau provided support for similarly ambitious anti-klan actions by the Dade County Sheriff's office. In addition to surveilling klan events, Dade County Sheriff T. A. Buchanan worked to pro-actively hinder the UKA's organizing efforts. Buchanan deployed a full complement of uniformed and plainclothes officers to aggressively interview prospective members attending a September klan meeting. "We'll pull a little traffic safety check—inspection stickers, driver's licenses, everything," one of Buchanan's detectives explained, as a pretext for discouraging klan actions. Officers arrested the local Exalted Cyclops (EC) when he was unable to produce a valid driver's license, and the klan meeting broke up within minutes of the police's arrival. "I think we've done what we came to do," the detective concluded.

A month later, police informants learned that Charles "Rip" Riddlehoover, a state-level klan leader and convicted felon, would attend a scheduled klavern meeting. To neutralize Riddlehoover, Buchanan placed his car under "running surveillance" and pulled it over for "careless driving and speeding" following the meeting. Finding a gun strapped to the driver's side door, the police promptly arrested him for illegal firearm possession. "They had this strategy planned," Riddlehoover complained, an assessment that understates the broad sweep of the policing campaign. By the close of the year, state UKA officers complained that a number of klaverns had folded due to the "heat" put on by the Dade County Sheriff's office. To stem the harassment, members suggested wearing masks during rallies and using numbers rather than names to make it more difficult to identify individual adherents.[46]

Meanwhile, Robert Shelton "couldn't quite put his finger on" why the UKA's recruitment efforts in Florida had stagnated. Following the group's organizing successes in North Carolina, Shelton saw the Sunshine State's similarly moderate political climate as fertile ground for the klan. To date, however, he had taken a mostly hands-off approach to the many complaints lobbed at the Florida Realm's extant Grand Dragon, Don Cothran. "We wasn't getting anything out of [the UKA]," one member noted. "They would plan a rally and Cothran would call it off.... They wasn't getting any literature down here or nothing.... it was just a lot of talk." In 1965, Cothran initiated a dizzying array of changes, culminating in a massive edict that divided the state into three Provinces, each responsible for maintaining a new system of organizing rallies, collecting dues and donations, and submitting associated reports. Many members failed to keep up with shifts in state officeholders. In one case, over the course of just a few months, the EC of a local klavern was promoted to Titan of a newly formed state Province, then moved to a state organizer position, and then stripped of his duties altogether.

In the face of growing unrest over this instability, Florida UKA members prepared for a new election at the state meeting on October 10, 1965. Cothran, likely fearing the outcome, canceled the meeting on short notice, but delegates held elections anyway, naming Riddlehoover Grand Dragon. Soon after, Riddlehoover penned a pained letter to Shelton: "Our great organization, United Klans of America, in the state of Florida needs help—and very quickly. The kind of help we need is Leadership. There is no limit to the growth of UKA in this state if we can rid our ranks of this terrible friction and ill will." Members of the state's rank-and-file followed the letter with a petition to "oust" Cothran, citing a number of issues headed by the weighty verdict: "No ability as a leader." With no response from Shelton, Riddlehoover led a meeting on October 24 to "disaffiliate" with the UKA. Those present agreed to reconstitute under the auspices of a new klan group, the United Knights of the Ku Klux Klan.[47]

To quell this growing schism, Shelton finally took a more active interest in the state. Following a successful rally attended by more than 2,000 outside of Fort Lauderdale over the July 4 weekend, he and Jones appeared at a handful of Florida events throughout the fall of 1965. Late that year he decided to replace Cothran with Boyd Hamby and George Dorsett, two of the Carolina Klan's most successful organizers. Hamby and Dorsett set up a new state headquarters near Titusville, hoping to apply the North Carolina model to this new locale.

As in the Tar Heel State, they began by organizing frequent rallies, but the sort of police repression that had neutralized Riddlehoover and other Florida klan leaders hampered their progress. To kick off their 1966 Florida campaign, Hamby and Dorsett organized four January rallies in Cocoa Beach. Local sheriff Leigh Wilson, following the aggressive approach favored by his Dade County colleagues, had first demonstrated his anti-klan proficiency at a rally the previous year in nearby West Melbourne, where his officers issued attendees more than fifty citations for faulty license tag lights. He adopted a similar strategy in Cocoa Beach, announcing to reporters that "we don't want their breed in our county" and setting up roadblocks around the rally site to conduct rigorous "driver's license and safety checks." Hamby himself was cited for faulty brakes, and Dorsett unsuccessfully appealed to the FBI to stop Sheriff Wilson's harassment. Helmeted police officers, some on horseback, monitored the proceedings. By the end of the run of rallies, Dorsett devoted 95 percent of his speech to complaining about the police, and vowed to "declare war" on Sheriff Wilson.

Such tough talk had little impact. Wilson adopted similar harassment tactics at another rally in nearby Scottsmoor, and in April FBI agents coordinated TV news coverage of a police roadblock around a supposedly secret klan meeting. Klan leaders continued to complain about these violations of their right to assemble, and focused at least as much attention on the police as on white supremacy. A frustrated Dorsett asked Shelton whether he might be more effective in Texas. By spring's end, he returned to North Carolina, while Hamby remained as Florida's Grand Dragon. After nearly a year in the state, Hamby continued to struggle with police harassment and the schism created by Riddlehoover's departure. A comprehensive congressional report estimated that by 1967 only 400 dues-paying UKA members remained in all of Florida, while North Carolina maintained nearly twenty times that number. By 1968, Hamby had "semi-retired" and spent most of his time selling "Klean Kars to Kool Kustomers" in a used car lot near Orlando.[48]

Observers typically attributed the UKA's dismal fortunes in Florida to a lack of public support. The klan's strength, however, was never predicated on mainstream approval. In 1965, when the UKA's wave was cresting, only 18 percent of southerners supported the klan, and nearly four times that proportion expressed active opposition. Even in the UKA's eastern North Carolina stronghold, members faced significant public opposition and weathered regular condemnation from ministerial associations and other respected civic bodies. Prior to scheduled UKA rallies, local newspapers often editorialized that the "Community Does Not Need or Want Hooded Hoodlums." When a group of local klansmen attended a high school recital in full robes, the superintendent called them "unwelcome guests," and vowed to "use whatever means are at our disposal to prevent a recurrence." In some counties the klan recruited new members covertly, as open support for the UKA placed many workers' jobs in jeopardy. In the more urbanized Piedmont, bombings targeting four black leaders in 1965 were met with near-unanimous public condemnation, culminating in a city-sponsored fund-raising event in Charlotte's 2,400-seat Ovens Auditorium.[49]

But despite their status as an "unwelcome element," the UKA could still thrive in Tar Heel communities in the absence of coordinated efforts to police their ability to operate. The klan's failure to make inroads in Florida, even with the help of seasoned organizers dispatched from North Carolina, owed much to Florida's aggressive policing efforts. In sharp contrast, North Carolina officials' ambivalent orientation to the klan precluded their consistent policing of UKA activity.

Faced with a mandate to address the state's rapidly growing klan, North Carolina police supplemented normal investigative routines with a passive UKA intelligence-gathering program. In a law enforcement milieu in which many of these agents opposed racial integration, and in the absence of strong directives from high-ranking state officials to pro-actively harass the klan, such measures failed to limit the UKA's ability to organize. Developing a pseudo-collegial "working relationship" with klan leaders, Highway Patrol officers and State Bureau of Investigation agents diligently submitted reports on their rally observations but did little to raise the costs of klan participation. The point is not that these agents would look the other way to allow klansmen to perpetrate violence but rather that they refused to exert control over the group apart from the policing of criminal acts. Higher state officials publicly supported aggressive policing of the KKK, but prior to 1966 they offered no directives to accompany these broad verbal mandates. This laissez-faire approach by centralized police agencies enabled officers' on-the-ground ambivalence toward klan adherents, and created space for the Carolina Klan to use rallies and other gatherings to freely recruit. The state's orientation contrasted both with Florida, where the Sheriff's Bureau enabled aggressive pro-active harassment of klan activities, and with North Carolina's pro-active suppression of civil rights activists.[50]

The Politics of UKA Mobilization

When Dan Moore was sworn in as governor at the start of 1965, the Carolina Klan's rapid ascent continued. Later that year, in Washington, DC, a House Un-American Activities Committee hearing on the KKK exposed North Carolina as far and away the most highly organized klan state in the country. Across the state, officials responded to the news with shock and indignation. A banner headline in the *Raleigh News and Observer* proclaimed that "Tar Heels Reject State's Label of No. 1 for Klan."

But, as sociologist Horace Hamilton observed at the time, the state's political environment "made the atmosphere more conducive for [the klan's mid-1960s resurgence] than it might otherwise have been." The willingness of candidates like Dan Moore to seek votes by painting their competitors as "soft" on the race issue and then to promote a moderate program while in office exacerbated tensions that ultimately bubbled over in the face of a strong civil rights challenge. Hundreds of thousands of segregationist voters swayed by Moore's and Lake's racist appeals who then saw their interests unrepresented by the state's leadership created a constituency that an organized segregationist body like the UKA could reliably draw upon.[51]

Indeed, state leaders' orientation to federal desegregation mandates shaped the politics of klan mobilization. States that valued order over resistance greatly truncated the range of mainstream institutions willing and able to defend Jim Crow, and in the process paradoxically broadened the klan's pool of potential adherents. The UKA eagerly sought to fill this vacuum, presenting itself as an alternative vehicle to address grievances that otherwise fell beyond the pale of institutional politics. When Bob Jones offered his standard justification of the UKA's function—that "everybody's organized except the white Protestant"[52]—his primary intent was not to slyly avoid the obvious fact that white Protestants held virtually every position of power in the state, but rather to make the more incisive point that these white elites did not represent his vision of authentically white interests.

Alongside their willingness to defend Jim Crow against the civil rights movement and related federal incursions, state officials' policing of vigilantism also impacted the viability of the KKK. Locally, police officials' relationships to the klan diverged wildly and often unpredictably. In North Carolina, Wilmington Police Chief Marion Millis made national headlines after he and six of his deputies were exposed as UKA members. A number of other officers across the state joined or otherwise supported the klan as well. But others crusaded against the KKK. In Franklinton, a small town north of Raleigh, the UKA bombed a police officer's home after he defiantly rented property to a black family whose children planned to enroll in the town's previously all-white school. Greene County's sheriff was besieged with threatening phone calls calling patrolmen "white nigger sons-of-bitches" and had a cross burned on his lawn shortly after UKA leader Raymond Cranford came to his office and told him that if he didn't run his office right, "we will run it for you." Given this varying orientation to the klan among rank and file officers, policing the klan required coordination by centralized state agencies. A state's policing apparatus—by condemning extra-legal resistance by treating the KKK itself, rather than only its members' criminal activities, as undesirable—could significantly raise the costs of klan mobilization.[53]

Considering these state dynamics underscores the divergent political climates within a seemingly unified region. States like Mississippi and Alabama actively opposed civil rights reform, engaging in massive resistance against federal mandates and mostly refusing to police white supremacist violence. In that charged climate, local police often dealt with both civil rights activists and klan members as they saw fit, with state agencies typically reinforcing an anti–civil rights posture. The Mississippi State Sovereignty Commission, for instance, worked to "protect the sovereignty of the state... against the illegal encroachment" of the federal government by investigating those who challenged Jim Crow rather than protecting victims of racial violence. The Alabama legislature empowered a state "Peace Commission" to convene hearings against "known integrationists and subversives," and representatives of the like-minded Alabama Sovereignty Commission traveled around the state instructing registrars how to prevent African Americans from joining the voting rolls.[54] Conversely, Florida adopted a consistently moderate approach, refusing to engage in massive resistance to assuage segregationist constituents and also consistently drawing on a centralized policing infrastructure to eliminate the klan as a threat to law and order. While the state's passive approach toward desegregation mandates isolated the KKK as one of the few outlets for resolute segregationists, the UKA's appeal in that state waned in the face of this coordinated policing action.

North Carolina was an unusual hybrid. Officials' efforts to promote the state as progressive and industry-friendly aligned with a posture presenting its liberal "North Carolina way" as exceptional within the Jim Crow South. For a time, this moderate political course co-existed with officials' efforts to retain the strict racial codes in schools and other institutions.[55] But despite this ambivalently reactionary orientation, by 1964 the state's overriding emphasis on perpetuating an image that was progressive, friendly to business, and unlike the hard-line Deep South precluded any coordinated institutional alignment to protect and preserve Jim Crow at all costs. The failure of state leaders to employ pro-active policing measures to stanch the resulting segregationist furor meant that UKA organizers, prior to 1966, confronted no serious repressive action from state police agencies. As a consequence, Bob Jones and his organizers found the Tar Heel State to be fertile organizing ground.

Though seemingly contradictory, these two dimensions aligned in important ways. The moderation at the heart of the "North Carolina way" became more compelling when its gentility contrasted with strident and unseemly extremes. The presence of contained, but nonetheless visible, forces at both ends of the civil rights spectrum allowed political leaders to reinforce their reasonable, moderate position. Far from "countering" the state's moderate image (as the newspaper headline quoted in this chapter's title contends), the presence of the klan, counterbalanced by civil rights activism, served as a device through which state officials could stake out and legitimize their progressive position. While likely not a driving causal force behind the ambivalence that characterized the state's position vis-á-vis the KKK prior to 1966, a policy that contained the UKA without precluding its ability to organize aligned generally with political leaders' "branding" of the state's unique political orientation.

But while this orientation to policing and the state's overall political culture explains the comparatively broad appeal held by the UKA in North Carolina, *within* the state klan mobilization was highly uneven. To understand how and why the UKA resonated in certain locales, we must look more closely at the communities within which the klan recruited, as well as at the motivations of individual members. The three chapters that follow examine how racial competition in local settings shaped the varying degrees to which the UKA's campaigns garnered support within the state's permissive political environment.

4 KLAN RECRUITMENT IN NORTH CAROLINA COUNTIES

If you want to see a Klan county, come to Greene County. That's Klansville, U.S.A.

—RAYMOND CRANFORD, founder of the UKA's Ormondsville klavern, in 1965.[1]

Some of those that work forces, are the same who burn crosses.

—Rage Against the Machine, "Killing in the Name."[2]

While specific membership figures can be elusive, the United Klans of America (UKA) grew substantially during its initial organizing campaign in North Carolina. Following Bob Jones's first set of rallies in late 1963, the klan expanded from its home base in Rowan County to thirteen klaverns and 525 members by the end of that year. Through the first half of 1964, the UKA chartered at least two dozen additional units, nearly all spread across the eastern coastal plain. At that time, its membership totaled 3,500. A year later, that number had almost tripled, and the UKA's 1965 State Meeting featured representatives from 166 klaverns. By early 1966, the FBI estimated that the Carolina Klan encompassed 10,000–12,000 members in approximately 200 units.[3]

These numbers made North Carolina far and away the UKA's great success story. The klan's appeal *within* the state, however, was far from uniform. The UKA thrived in certain regions—in particular, the east—but its presence was spottier throughout the central Carolina Piedmont and almost entirely absent in the western mountains. Likewise, within these regions, certain counties and communities developed hard-earned reputations as klan hotbeds while others resisted the UKA's appeals. The maps in Figure 4.1 show the boundaries of the state's three key regions, as well as the UKA's presence in each county as of 1966.[4]

The vast majority of white North Carolinians opposed civil rights reform, though their opposition differed in both degree and form.[5] The refusal of the state's political apparatus to militantly

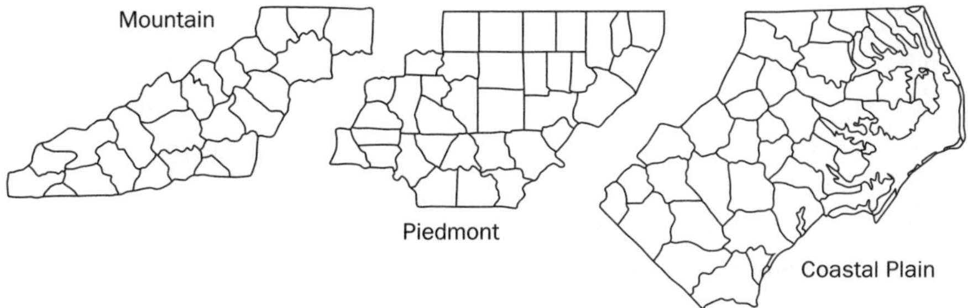

FIGURE 4.1A North Carolina's three regions

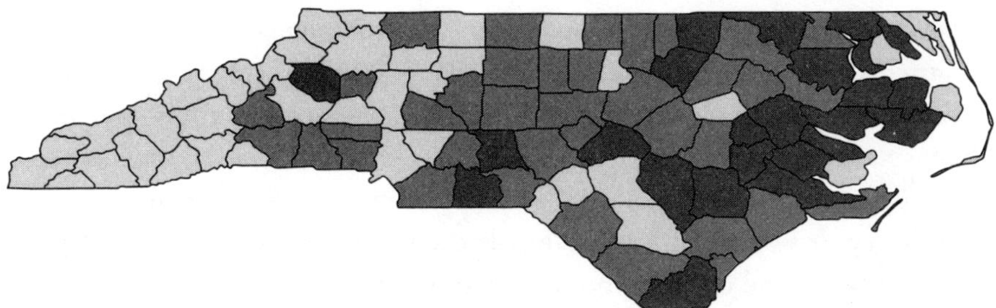

FIGURE 4.1B UKA presence in North Carolina, 1964–1966 (darker shades indicate higher rates of klan presence)

resist federal desegregation pressures contracted the segregationist field and provided added impetus to civic and vigilantist efforts. This intensified sense of political threat provided a primary lens through which communities engaged with racial change, but within a given system of state politics, segregation's collapse meant different things in different places. Locally, UKA recruitment tended to be strongest where large swaths of white residents felt their social, economic, and political standing acutely threatened by civil rights reforms. Desegregation policies, to the extent that they sought to equalize access to jobs, political offices, and other resources, were widely viewed as vehicles for redistributing opportunities. For whites who benefited from unequal access to such opportunities, the fall of Jim Crow meant increased competition for the same resource pool. The degree to which white residents felt threatened by this renewed competition varied, based on the racial makeup of nearby communities, the extent to which African Americans and whites overlapped in the workplace, and the tenor of black political action. Klan recruiters tended to be most successful where their racist appeals intersected with a strongly felt sense that intensified civil rights claims would result in wholesale changes to the social order.[6]

The KKK, of course, was but one of many outlets for whites' racial grievances. The klan's distinctiveness came not from its defense of Jim Crow-style white supremacy, as that goal was pursued in various ways by a range of nonvigilantist bodies across the South. The UKA stood apart from many of these more temperate segregationist vehicles largely because of its militancy, its willingness to engage in terroristic action to preserve the racial status quo. But violence as a motivating force should not be overdrawn. Many klan members claimed sincerely that the UKA's primary appeal was its diagnosis of, and prescription for, the threat that integration posed to freedoms they saw as ordained by the dual pillars of the Constitution and the Bible.

Many southern politicians and conservative commentators drew on patriotic and Christian themes to make their case that federal civil rights legislation infringed upon states' rights.[7] But UKA leaders and recruiters offered an intensified, baldly racist, and conspiratorial version of that argument, centered on grandiose claims about the fragility of whiteness in the face of a revolutionary Jewish- and communist-backed civil rights threat and the discriminatory and unconstitutional actions of the federal government. True Christians and patriots, the UKA line ran, have an obligation to organize to oppose civil rights policies. Further, the klan provided the only authentic "white Protestant" vehicle for defending race, religion, and country. Klan organizers' ability to recruit adherents depended in large part on the resonance of this message in local communities, which in turn had much to do with the demographic, economic, and political composition of those areas.

Demographics

At its base, Jim Crow functioned to control African Americans. In areas where black labor power sustained white-dominated economies and where maintaining white supremacy meant suppressing a large black electorate, segregationist laws and customs were especially salient. The klan, not surprisingly, had greater appeal where African Americans comprised a significant proportion of the local population.

While Bob Jones and his core associates were based in Rowan County, near the western edge of the Piedmont, their first significant recruiting successes occurred in what was generally termed the Black Belt, a seven-county cluster in the northeast corner of the state.[8] Over time, the UKA developed a widespread stronghold across the eastern coastal plain—a region that was approximately 40 percent nonwhite, a figure more than double that in the rest of the state.[9] When asked to explain the ease with which the UKA developed klaverns in the east, a longtime klansman offered a typical response: "There were just a whole lot of colored people."[10]

In the more diverse Piedmont, UKA mobilization was less uniform. Klan presence within the region tended to mirror the concentration of the African American population, with the UKA finding receptive audiences in counties with higher proportions of nonwhites.[11] Such support proved harder to develop in the mountainous western end of the state, which was nearly 95 percent white. In sharp contrast to the UKA's experience to that point, a series of rallies in mountain counties in September 1965 failed to translate into sustained backing of the klan. By the following year, just five of the twenty-three mountain counties were home to a UKA klavern, and fewer than 4 percent of Jones's units were located west of the Piedmont. Jones's and Shelton's grandiose boasts about the UKA's universal appeal among "true" white southerners aside, klan organizers quickly diagnosed the main reason for their failure to gain a foothold in the state's western end. As one frustrated UKA veteran offered bluntly, "there ain't no niggers in the mountains."[12]

The presence of African Americans activated white anxieties in powerful ways. Desegregation would alter the racial order almost everywhere in the South, but such shifts were more evident where white majorities grew thin—or, as in certain Black Belt counties, disappeared altogether. While lifting long-standing racial restrictions ensured that integration would be felt directly in the workplace and in voting booths, behind these material shifts lay the more elusive social dimensions of race mixing. Chief among those were the old fears of miscegenation, which had long motivated Jim Crow's regimented customs. Practices intended to maintain social separation between whites and blacks were near-ubiquitous, but their underlying logic above all protected white women from contact with black men.

"No other way of crossing the color line," wrote Gunnar Myrdal in 1944, "is so attended by the emotion commonly associated with violating a social taboo as intermarriage and extra-marital relations between a Negro man and a white woman."[13] Historically, this aspect of the color line was fiercely guarded, with transgressions (and often even unsupported accusations) a capital offense. Between 1882 and 1930, ninety-seven lynchings of African Americans were recorded in North Carolina, spread across forty-nine of the state's 100 counties. As with the thousands of lynching cases across the South during this period, the ostensible motive in more than a third of those incidents was a claimed violation of sexual norms, almost always involving a white woman and black man.

These lynching cases often directly involved large mobs, with the active or tacit complicity of entire communities. Lynchings also had an intense afterlife, sometimes through the printing of postcard "souvenirs" of the event and always as an oft-repeated cautionary tale. These accounts signaled the lengths to which whites would go to defend threats to white womanhood, and community leaders' willingness to allow vigilantism to trump legal and moral codes against murder. Consequently, in the communities within which racial breaches were harshly regulated, the legacy of racial violence remained strong decades later—even after accounting for all of the demographic, economic, and political factors discussed here, North Carolina counties that suffered lynchings prior to 1930 remained more likely to shelter the UKA and vigilante violence in the 1960s. This effect was significant; the number of klaverns in counties where lynchings had occurred was 78 percent higher than we might expect otherwise. In effect, the willingness to sanction extreme, and often public, violence to uphold racial mores resonated across generations and signaled at least a passive tolerance for informal "justice" in the face of threats posed by civil rights advances.[14]

Racial separation within institutions and public spaces reinforced the resonance of these racial codes. Historian Timothy B. Tyson, writing about his 1960s childhood in Oxford, a tobacco-farming Piedmont city near the Virginia border, describes the depth to which Jim Crow continued to penetrate North Carolina communities during that period. In Oxford, as elsewhere, there was virtually no racial overlap in most jobs—"to say 'black maid' or 'black janitor' would have been entirely redundant," Tyson explains, as "there were no other kinds." This dual labor market reserved high-status positions for whites, and minimized public contact between whites and African Americans. White patrons never encountered black cashiers in stores, or black hostesses or waiters in restaurants. The few jobs held by both whites and blacks—mostly professional positions such as lawyers, doctors, teachers, and sometimes police—reproduced separation, by avoiding occasions in which white professionals would directly provide services to black residents.[15]

Housing in Oxford was strictly segregated—African Americans were confined to a set of neighborhoods that many whites referred to collectively as "niggertown"—as were virtually all public establishments. The downtown movie theater, for instance, allowed black patrons to enter through a separate side entrance, and sit only in the segregated upstairs balcony. The passage of the Civil Rights Act in 1964 had little immediate effect on these arrangements. Faced with federal desegregation mandates in the mid-1960s, city officials chose to close most parks and municipal spaces—including the city's only public swimming pool—rather than desegregate them. When Tyson's own father, a Methodist minister, became the first local clergyman to support an interracial youth social space, a number of his parishioners pressured him to shut it down. And like nearly 95 percent of school districts statewide, Oxford schools remained entirely segregated through the mid-1960s.

Indeed, schools and other youth institutions became especially charged settings for civil rights claims. School desegregation, as Nixon presidential advisor Harry Dent later noted, "dwarfed" all other civil rights–related issues. In 1961, only eleven of North Carolina's 173 school districts had been integrated, and only a small fraction of 1 percent of the state's black students attended white schools. The US Commission on Civil Rights described North Carolina's course of action as "token integration; that is, the admission of a minimum number of Negro children into white schools." As late as 1967, the state commissioned Sutherland, Asbill & Brennan—a law firm based in Washington, DC, that was "sentimentally appreciative" of the state's "problem" with federal civil rights compliance—to defend local school districts against lawsuits stemming from their refusal to meaningfully desegregate. Much of the emotion behind such dogged segregationist efforts centered on white parents' paternalistic fears that any interracial contact among their children could lead to more intimate relationships. Talking with Tyson years later, one Oxford parent reflected on a fear that typified white attitudes toward school desegregation: that her daughter "was going to come home... holding hands with a black boy."[16]

Institutions went to great lengths to minimize such potential contact. Businesses might hire both white and black workers, but "reserve" specific jobs for one or the other race. This separation was often enforced spatially as well as by job, with particular tasks organized in part to physically split racial groups. These controls were especially stringent in informal gathering spaces, where workplace social controls were looser; cafeterias and bathrooms were almost always fully segregated. Such policing was most intense when firms hired white women, who comprised nearly half of the industrial workforce in 1960. Longtime North Carolina NAACP head Kelly Alexander noted that his most rancorous struggles surrounded gains for black textile workers, largely because mills employed so many white women. "The propaganda was that if you let these Negroes be hired on the textile machine line," he explained, "the next thing they'll be marrying your daughters."[17]

Black residents' mere presence, then, created the potential for innumerable breaches in the racial code. Unregulated interracial contact threatened to disrupt the sanctity of whiteness itself, and by extension, the culture and practice of white supremacy. The UKA's recruitment efforts squarely focused on related anxieties. "The Communists are using our schools to start a mongrel race of people," warned a klan handbill, distributed en masse throughout Wake County during the summer of 1965. "If you continue to give in you can expect just what you get. Maybe a Nigger Son-In-Law or Daughter-In-Law." Speeches at UKA rallies similarly preyed on fears of forcible miscegenation, based on apocryphal accounts of "nigrah" sexual assaults on defenseless victims who "could have been your wife or daughter." To anyone who would listen, Raymond Cranford offered his succinct summary of the principle that drew many adherents to the UKA: "These nigger civil rights, they're going to end in the white men's bedroom."[18]

The proportion of African Americans in a given community or county, then, served as a visceral proxy of the threat desegregation posed to Jim Crow status systems. A black community of any significant size virtually guaranteed white resistance to civil rights reforms, though again, this reactionary impulse could take many forms. Culture and tradition alone might push some whites to passively express views opposed to integration—as a significant majority of white North Carolinians did through the 1960s. A more intensive reaction might attribute desegregation policies to a broad communist-Jew conspiracy, or view LBJ's racial policies as a revolutionary affront to the US Constitution. Mobilizing around such extreme positions, by affiliating oneself with a group that militantly defied civil rights policies, represented yet another level of engagement. The demographic makeup of local communities influenced whites' receptivity to these more intense investments in segregation and shaped the UKA's fortunes across the state.

However, while areas with high concentrations of black residents often provided fertile recruiting grounds for the UKA, sustained klan activity was also an organizing achievement, requiring sufficient resources and strategic capacities. The importance of this organizing dimension was evident in many of North Carolina's majority-black counties. Though Bob Jones established some of his earliest klaverns in the northeastern Black Belt, largely by appealing to the dangers of blacks "taking over" areas where they comprised a majority, the UKA's presence in those counties ultimately failed to match their successes across much of the eastern coastal plain. Beyond a certain point, the bump that UKA recruiting efforts received from the looming threat of African American takeover eroded where whites were a minority, as the limited resource base of the klan's key constituencies made it difficult to sustain a sufficient organizing base. In North Carolina, the number of klaverns in a given county increased steadily, from an average of two to almost six, when the proportion of black residents grew from 10 percent to 30 percent. However, when African Americans approached a numeric majority, klavern presence dipped, from six to five in counties where whites and blacks were equally represented, and then to just over three where African Americans made up 60 percent of a county's populace.[19]

But nearly 90 percent of the state's counties maintained white majorities, and here the presence of larger black populations typically aided UKA recruiters' efforts to exploit racial anxieties. Where this baseline demographic threat interacted with other forms of competition, active klan support most reliably emerged. In areas where many whites viewed their jobs or their hold on political power as threatened by civil rights–related changes, their experiences in economic and political arenas sharpened their sensitivities to the dire warnings offered by the UKA.

Economics

In a state where men of working age had, on average, fewer than nine years of schooling, a large number of both white and black workers qualified for many of the same low- and semi-skilled jobs. Jim Crow customs that reserved certain work for whites artificially suppressed interracial competition for many of these jobs. In 1961, a US Commission on Civil Rights report pointed to an overall "pattern of significant underutilization of Negro manpower" in North Carolina. Such racial divisions were strongly entrenched. Even in those firms holding federal government contracts—which provided greater incentive and freedom to deviate from traditional southern employment arrangements—more than one-fifth refused to hire African Americans in any capacity. Those that did hire black workers restricted them almost exclusively to unskilled occupations, and more than half had never promoted a single black employee. Employer recruitment policies also relied heavily on referrals from present workers and reproduced the disparities noted in the Commission's report.[20]

That report focused specifically on North Carolina's manufacturing workforce, but to a large degree its conclusions could be generalized to the labor market overall, which privileged whites by restricting the eligibility of similarly skilled black workers for many positions. Traditionally, the state's predominant agricultural economy, which in the 1960s still flourished mostly in the eastern coastal plain, separated white and black workers by their respective relationships to the land.

Basic farming patterns had become entrenched by the late nineteenth century. A majority of white agricultural workers owned their land, with nearly a quarter serving as landlords and another 36 percent directly overseeing work on their farmland. In contrast, black agricultural workers disproportionately farmed land owned by whites. More than four-fifths of all black farmers either were tenants or sharecroppers on the land that they worked. These patterns were exacerbated in the coastal plain counties, which, despite a population that barely exceeded half of that in the Piedmont, contained almost double the number of male agricultural workers. In the east, only 7 percent of black farmers owned the land they worked.[21]

The experiences of white farmers differed across the state's regions as well. Unlike the Deep South and other areas of North Carolina, the state's eastern Black Belt featured an unusually high number of white families that worked land owned by others. A full two-thirds of white agricultural workers were either tenants or sharecroppers in coastal plain counties. This figure was significantly lower in the Piedmont and mountain regions, where 72 percent and 63 percent, respectively, owned their land. The significant result is that in the east—where black residents made up a higher percentage of the population (39.3 percent in 1960, compared to 15.9 percent in the state's other regions) and overall income levels were relatively low (regardless of race, the average family's income was nearly a third less than in the Piedmont)—white and black farmers were much more likely to compete directly for agricultural work.[22]

For a time, the ascendance of manufacturing provided a sort of racial pressure valve for white workers, offering an alternative source of advantage in the labor market. "If the white man does not farm," noted sociologist Ben F. Lemert in 1933, "he must compete with the Negro for a job and is glad to find an industry which gives the white man preference." Between 1910 and 1930, North Carolina became the nation's leading textile producer. White workers benefited from the racial practices of mill owners, who hired African Americans only into the most menial custodial jobs. Much of the industry's growth occurred across the Piedmont, home to a number of exceptionally large plants. By the 1960s, Burlington Industries, based in Greensboro, was the largest textile company in the nation, employing 83,000 workers, and three other Piedmont textile manufacturers each had workforces that exceeded 10,000.[23] The bulk of the textile economy, however, consisted of smaller plants in rural areas. Eastern North Carolina became home to many small mills, and a growing number of laborers were in fact "worker-farmers," engaged in both agricultural and manufacturing labor at different points throughout the year. By the 1960s, more than half of the state's agricultural workers reported being employed "off-farm" as well.

Entire families, many accustomed to working farmland together, often sought jobs in these rural mills. Mill managers commonly deemed women an appealing surplus labor force to meet seasonal peaks in demand; women comprised more than 35 percent of the manufacturing workforce in 1960. The steady infusion of predominantly poor whites—both urban migrants to the Piedmont and worker-farmers in smaller eastern communities—willing to work for low wages meant that whites held virtually all skilled and semi-skilled positions. Typically, they received preference for lower paid unskilled jobs as well. Commenting on this striking racial compact, Gunnar Myrdal characterized the industry's rise as nothing less than a "civic welfare movement to create work for poor white people."[24]

Buttressed by these arrangements, textile plants prior to 1960 were predominantly white spaces, with the overall proportion of black workers hovering between 3 percent and 4 percent. The presence of white women workers also ensured tightly enforced racial segregation within particular plants. Breaches of that racial code could produce a significant backlash. In rural Northampton County, for instance, a central partition separated white and black employees at the Mylcraft Manufacturing Company plant. When a black employee was placed on the "white" side, her car was vandalized and she and other black employees began receiving threatening phone calls.

Conformity to racial orthodoxy remained largely intact even as the labor market tightened after 1960. Spurred in part by increasing availability of higher paying work in the diversifying industrial sector, manufacturing firms hired African Americans in much greater numbers, though almost always into unskilled or semi-skilled positions that ensured their functional and physical separation from higher status white workers. By 1966, black workers held only 0.6 percent of white-collar positions, but comprised more than a third of the industry's lower-skilled operatives and laborers. "Gains have been made," acknowledged the NAACP, "but Negroes have only touched the outer edges of equal employment in North Carolina."[25]

The situation was similar in the state's two other prominent manufacturing sectors: furniture and tobacco. North Carolina was by far the nation's leading furniture producer, employing 63,000 workers (nearly 14 percent of the national industry total) by the late 1960s. The majority of furniture plants were located in the western Piedmont and mountain counties. The relatively low percentage of African Americans in those areas suppressed to some extent direct racial competition for these jobs. But otherwise, employment patterns within factories mirrored those in textile plants. In 1966, black workers made up 11.6 percent of the overall furniture workforce, but held only 0.7 percent of white-collar positions. In contrast, African Americans filled 37.6 percent of the lowest status blue-collar service positions.[26]

Likewise, the tobacco industry, while a small employer relative to textiles, was traditionally so strictly segregated by task that one could accurately identify the racial and gender roles associated with each specific job within leaf handling, making, packing, and boxing departments. This racial separation held spatially as well, with traditionally "Negro" tasks generally housed on separate floors or in different buildings.

Several of the nation's largest tobacco manufacturers—including American, Liggett & Myers, P. Lorillard, R.J. Reynolds, and Brown & Williamson—operated major facilities across the North Carolina Piedmont. Historically, black workers had been a prominent presence in these plants. In 1930, more than three-quarters of North Carolina's tobacco industry workers were black, though that changed when many of those jobs were eliminated by efficiency measures instituted in reaction to labor strife and legislation, including the 1938 Fair Labor Standards Act, which established a national minimum wage and mandated payment of time-and-a-half for overtime. By 1964, African Americans made up 23.6 percent of the industry workforce and held only 1.5 percent of white-collar positions. Conversely, black workers held nearly 80 percent of low-status blue-collar jobs.[27]

Across these labor market sectors, institutionalized white privilege became increasingly tenuous in the 1960s. Much of the legal debate over the desegregation of public facilities during this period centered on workplace reforms. President Kennedy established a Committee on Equal Employment Opportunity in 1961, which forbade discrimination in hiring by the federal government or its contractors. Title VII of the 1964 Civil Rights Act formalized that association, outlawing discrimination in all larger workplaces.

The Civil Rights Act also created the Equal Employment Opportunity Commission (EEOC). In 1965, the EEOC responded to complaints against segregated facilities in two rural Black Belt manufacturing plants, and two years later held public hearings in Charlotte to investigate general textile employment practices. Local newspaper headlines proclaimed "Hiring Bias Charged in Textile Industry" and "Mills Exclude Negroes as Systematic Policy," and indeed, the hearings attacked many of the industry's traditional and continuing hiring practices. State NAACP head Kelly Alexander declared that the era of textiles as a "closed corporation for employment for whites" was nearing an end, and a comprehensive academic study released soon after noted that "previously unemployed Negroes should find the textile industry a natural source of employment, [as] the same industrial characteristics that made it possible for poor whites to enter the mills as operatives, during 1880 through 1960, are likely to do the same for Negroes in the future."[28]

In different ways and to varying degrees, desegregation threatened the traditional racial organization of these primary labor market sectors. To the extent that industry—which continued to expand through the 1960s, especially in the Piedmont—hired in ways that privileged working-class whites, manufacturing jobs provided a way for whites to enhance their status at the expense of similarly skilled African American workers. Much of the latent threat associated with the presence of black residents thus was bound up in this economic sphere. While opposition to workplace reforms was often expressed as acute anxiety over the social implications of racial mixing within closed industrial environments (particularly where white women were present), the tangible impact of such reforms centered on increased racial competition in a tight labor market that had traditionally guaranteed white workers' advantage.

These economic grievances were clearest in the coastal plain region, where the African American population was proportionately large, white income precariously low, and nonfarming employment in relatively short supply. While rarely articulated directly by klan members themselves, the threat of inter-racial economic competition was a powerful pull for working-class whites. Where African Americans were well-represented in the workforce, the UKA thrived; a 16 percent increase in black manufacturing workers in a county (a figure that roughly approximates the difference in racial makeup between the labor forces in Piedmont and coastal plain counties) translated on average to a 77 percent increase in klan presence. Even after accounting for differences in overall racial demographics and income levels, counties where the manufacturing workforce included higher proportions of African Americans were significantly more likely to be sites of UKA mobilization.[29]

Politics

Regardless of region, these sorts of perceived economic threats tended to resonate most in areas where black residents developed active political organization. At the dawn of the 1960s, North Carolina's black population was the nation's fourth largest, behind only those of New York, Texas, and Georgia. However, North Carolina's "race gap"—the difference in the percentage of registered white versus black eligible voters—was second only to the gap in Mississippi, which blunted black electoral power in the state. In 1965,

96.8 percent of eligible white voters were on the rolls, which exceeded the black registration rate by a full 50 percentage points.[30]

In many counties, especially in the metropolitan areas of the Piedmont, there were relatively few systematic barriers to black voter registration. But in the coastal plain—in particular, the northeastern Black Belt counties—conditions resembled those found in Deep South states. A Student Non-Violent Coordinating Committee (SNCC) worker visiting North Carolina's Black Belt communities observed that "all the usual segregationist tactics are used to keep the black people of this region from exercising their natural and basic rights in determining their own political destiny: violence, intimidation, harassment, fear, economic reprisal, etc." Registrars' record-keeping typically allowed for only a crude estimate of registered voters, and many counties had not purged old names from their rolls in years. Shockingly, in more than half of the state's Black Belt counties, more white voters were registered than were living in the county in 1960.[31]

In 1959 and 1960, thirty-six Black Belt county residents lodged formal complaints with the state advisory committee to the US Commission on Civil Rights. In Bertie County, one registrar refused more than half of the black residents who came before him. Several of those were high school graduates denied on the basis of supposed "misspellings and punctuation" deficiencies on their registration applications. In Franklin County, those rejected claimed they were asked to define "habeas corpus," or to explain "who created the world," along with the meaning of the term "create." In each case, the registrar ruled that their respective answers "didn't satisfy him." Similarly, in Greene County, registrants were asked not only to read, but also to interpret, several provisions in the North Carolina Constitution. The registrar later admitted that he made a point to ask interpretive questions to counter the fact that "most of them could say the constitution by heart. I believe that some of them can go right through it from one end to the other."[32]

Indeed, as in Mississippi and Alabama, the extensive discretion given to registrars was a key mechanism for controlling the registration process. The state's voting statutes contained a literacy provision but no standard method for determining whether registrants were in fact literate. As a result, some counties effectively ignored the provision altogether, others required that registrants read a portion of the State Constitution, and others required them to read aloud from a book or newspaper. Performance was always subjectively assessed. The NAACP had long argued that the literacy policy had been "adopted and designed to permit exclusion" solely on the basis of race, a claim substantiated by the fact that the failure rate due to illiteracy more closely aligned with the proportion of black residents living in a county than with the county's overall educational profile.

In addition, the legally required appeals process for rejectees was unclear and restrictive, with guidelines (almost always unposted) requiring that appeals occur in a twenty-four-hour window. Together, these racist policies enabled seemingly nonsensical election returns. In the 1964 gubernatorial primary, militant segregationist candidate I. Beverly Lake achieved one of his largest victories in majority-black Halifax County. Statewide, Lake's support ran strongest in counties with significant black populations. The truncation of black electoral power produced such counterintuitive results, as black voter registration rates varied inversely with their representation within the overall pool of eligible voters. Understating the issue somewhat, the US Commission on Civil Rights concluded that in the North Carolina Black Belt, "the dice of State politics are loaded in favor of the whites."[33]

By 1968, North Carolina had fewer black elected officials than any other southern state, with no black representation among mayors or state legislators, or in county governance and law enforcement. Only one school board member statewide was black. But despite—or, perhaps, because of—the effectiveness with which black candidates were shut out of office, UKA appeals were less concerned with keeping African Americans from the polls than with building up a powerful, "authentically white" voting base. The klan worldview saw whiteness as requiring the proper Anglo-Saxon background, but also strong, consistent adherence to "one hundred percent American values" centered on segregation and racial purity. As such, klan ideology focused less on preventing the rise of black political candidates than on opposing white officials who would capitulate to federal civil rights pressures.

"If you don't believe in mixing races, we want to vote out all of these nigger lovers that we have in office," Bob Jones told rally crowds during the 1966 election season. "Start voting people in office that will be white men . . . because we need them in office now." When questioned about the UKA's political strategy, Jones would eagerly discuss using "ballots over bullets" to install "good white candidates." The ultimate aim, he argued, was to "form a voting bloc to defeat any nigger-loving politician that runs for office." In 1966 at least thirty UKA members ran as candidates for public office—ranging from state congress, to county commissioner, to constable, to the board of education. In Jones's home county, Carolina Klan members John Stirewalt and James Wayne Davis were elected, respectively, as sheriff and registrar of deeds. The UKA also mounted an ambitious campaign to support conservative congressional candidate John P. East.[34]

Alongside these electoral initiatives, the UKA directed its attention to activist politics, strongly aligning itself against the "radicals" and "agitators" behind the growing challenge to Jim Crow traditions. Chief among those were the several civil rights movement organizations active in North Carolina. In 1962, the Southern Regional Council (SRC) sponsored a Voter Education Project that parlayed support from local and national civil rights groups to conduct a ninety-day registration project in a number of Piedmont and coastal plain communities. The Congress of Racial Equality (CORE), primarily through the efforts of High Point-based minister B. Elton Cox and national leader Floyd McKissick (an Asheville native and Durham resident), sustained a presence in more urbanized areas throughout the Piedmont.[35]

In Wake County, SNCC helped to direct an intensive local voter registration and downtown desegregation campaign in 1963, sponsored locally by the Raleigh Citizens Association. In early 1964, SNCC, in conjunction with the NAACP, CORE, the Southern Conference Educational Fund (SCEF), and the Student Peace Union, organized a number of demonstrations to desegregate public facilities in Chapel Hill. SNCC also initiated a voter registration campaign in Charlotte, but that failed to gain significant momentum. The following year, SNCC worker Eric Morton proposed an ambitious project in northeast Black Belt counties, though the group's subsequent work there suffered from various financial difficulties.[36]

The most visible civil rights presences in the Black Belt were SCEF field organizer John Salter and Southern Christian Leadership Conference (SCLC) field secretary Golden Frinks. Shortly after beginning work with SCEF in late 1963, Salter—an army veteran and self-described "ecumenical socialist"—moved into northeastern North Carolina and established the Halifax County Voters Movement. As a "thoroughly democratic" organization, the movement's officers avoided pronouncements not sanctioned by the overall membership and required no membership fees to join (funding was instead secured mostly through church donations). By 1965, Halifax's successes spread to affiliated voters' movements in neighboring Bertie and Northampton counties, with weekly meetings held in each locale. Beyond voter registration work, these groups also engaged in campaigns to improve the maintenance of roads and other facilities in black neighborhoods, to end racial employment discrimination, to desegregate public facilities, and to improve or close substandard "Negro" school buildings. In a sparsely populated region, these voters' movements were able to draw close to 1,000 attendees to periodic civil rights and anti-poverty "people's conferences."

The UKA was likewise active in the region. Halifax County was home to two klaverns (along with two Ladies' Auxiliary Units), and Bertie and Northampton counties each had one klavern as well. The influence held by the klan's membership increased its impact; twenty-three known or suspected members of the UKA's Northampton unit included a sheriff's deputy, chairman of the county board of elections, a justice of the peace, and the postmaster. Frequently, klan members responded directly to the threat posed by the voters' movements. Multiple cross-burnings occurred on the property of various activists, and Northampton County Voters Movement co-chair Russell Coggins was publicly beaten. Halifax County Voters Movement chairman A.C. Cofield was the target of sustained "night-riding," with objects repeatedly thrown at his house. A recently integrated elementary school was burned to the ground. To counter a voter's movement "people's conference," the UKA mounted a large rally, headlined by Imperial Wizard Shelton.[37]

In Martin and Chowan counties, to the south and east of Bertie, Golden Frinks established like-minded "freedom movements." As creative and flamboyant as his name, Frinks was a former nightclub owner in Edenton who, as secretary of the local NAACP branch, organized his first protests against segregated public facilities in 1959. After Martin Luther King Jr.'s SCLC provided funds to bail him and other Edenton activists out of jail, Frinks began what would become a long association with the organization. In 1963, he formalized this relationship, selling his nightclub to begin work as the SCLC's North Carolina field secretary.

Shortly thereafter, Frinks led a more sustained campaign in Williamston, the Martin County seat. In this small city, where slightly more than half of the nearly 7,000 residents were black, Frinks organized twenty-nine consecutive days of protests beginning in late June 1963. Demonstrators marched regularly on City Hall, where they would sing freedom songs, sometimes for a full hour, before withdrawing. Picketers targeted segregated establishments, including the movie theater, motels, and restaurants. They initiated a sustained boycott against white-owned businesses, and students staged two school walkouts. Another round of protests commenced after the city council instituted a parade ordinance banning unpermitted public gatherings, a measure that Frinks and others considered in defiance of the council's earlier agreement to consider the movement's demands. Police arrested hundreds of demonstrators, and the movement gained wider notice, especially after locals were joined by a group of ministers from New England. The movement's vitality led SCLC leaders to consider Williamston a site to showcase their campaign for national voting rights legislation, before ultimately selecting Selma, Alabama, to center that effort.[38]

Throughout this and subsequent North Carolina campaigns, Frinks was a savvy and sophisticated tactician. Often, he would deftly exploit cross-pressures by highlighting tensions between local and state officials. In Williamston, for instance, Frinks sent a telegram to the governor to demonstrate the complicity of local officials:

> Unlawful elements including Ku Klux Klan threatening security of Civil Rights workers in Williamston. Police Chief out of town. Police Commissioner out of town. Mayor can't be reached. Sheriff without jurisdiction. Community relations committee without authority to act. Local protection inadequate. Request immediate supplementary protection.

The success of such tactics, not surprisingly, drew harsh criticism from much of the white establishment. "The people of Williamston and Martin County," County Commissioner J. H. Thigpen told state officials, "know Frinks as a notorious liar who specializes in spreading hate and damning North Carolina [and] its laws." In October 1964, police used a spurious bad check charge to jail Frinks.[39]

Predictably, the UKA also drew strength from the threat posed by Frinks's campaigns. Local klaverns swelled in size, and the SCLC and klan engaged in a sort of interactive dance. "When the klan marches, we march," Frinks challenged. By August 1965, these tensions came to a head in Plymouth, the Washington County seat, after Frinks initiated a sustained campaign to lift racist restrictions on the voter registration process. Through tip-offs provided by a member of the local police force, klansmen from around the region were twice "called" to Plymouth to counter Frinks's threats that protestors would—in reference to that month's Watts Riots—"make another Los Angeles" out of Plymouth.

On August 26, the UKA held a rally two miles south of town that attracted an estimated 5,000, and afterward a large group of klansmen assaulted civil rights marchers, injuring twenty-seven. Another "call" went out to area klansmen on August 31, and in the face of mounting tensions, Frinks agreed to postpone that night's scheduled march. But as darkness fell, many of the estimated 1,000 klansmen lying in wait outside of town entered the downtown area, where many black would-be marchers had also converged. The situation quickly deteriorated, with scattered violence resulting in one UKA member being stabbed and another sent to the hospital with a bullet wound to the stomach.

Over the next two weeks, tensions remained high, in spite of the presence of more than fifty state troopers with police dogs, the formation of a biracial Human Relations Council, and the passing of an ordinance banning night-time gatherings involving "unreasonably loud…hollering, shouting, screaming, [or] singing." Frinks, after speaking with SCLC head Martin Luther King Jr., agreed to temporarily suspend protest marches while officials considered a set of demands, but he made clear that the black community was "still on the battlefield." On September 13, both sides held dueling demonstrations, with an estimated 5,500 turning out for a UKA rally a mile outside of town while a speech by SCLC vice-president Ralph Abernathy packed Plymouth's largest black church.[40]

These flare-ups occurred in reaction to particular events that posed a threat to the UKA's aims. But more generally, klan conceptions of the statewide civil rights movement centered on a single organization: the NAACP. By far the longest tenured and most widely organized civil rights group in North Carolina, the NAACP chartered its earliest branches in 1917, in Raleigh, Greensboro, and Durham. New branches emerged fairly regularly after that, first based mostly in urban areas but gradually in a number of rural communities as well. The immediate postwar years saw accelerated growth, with the number of branches more than doubling—from twenty-two to fifty—between 1944 and 1946. By 1955, there were eighty-three branches statewide, and as of 1963, North Carolina's 110 branches exceeded the group's presence in any other southern state. The state's NAACP continued to expand, and by the end of 1964 its branch total grew to 183.[41]

Given the group's widespread presence in both urban and rural communities across the state, and its national organization's well-known legal work on desegregation cases, the NAACP was frequently invoked as shorthand for the overall movement. "When [you] come into North Carolina, you find a close-knit [network] of established organized units of NAACP branches throughout the state," NAACP leader Kelly Alexander noted. "When you come into Charlotte, for instance, you're going to meet NAACP leadership. When you go to Winston-Salem, you're going to meet it." The same was true in many smaller communities—rural Greene County, dubbed "Klansville, U.S.A.," also had more than 300 dues-paying NAACP members.[42]

Consequently, for many North Carolina residents, the NAACP, like the KKK on the other pole, functioned as a convenient catch-all for "extremism" in the civil rights struggle. "North Carolinians are sick and tired and fed up with hearing about the Ku Klux Klan and the NAACP," proclaimed Secretary of State Thad Eure in a television interview. Frequently, state officials would echo this view when promoting "moderation," invoking both groups to illustrate that a lack of respect for law and order on either side would not be tolerated.

The UKA itself reproduced that sentiment, often justifying klan actions as countering those of the NAACP. "The only thing that they ever told me [about the klan] was let's get the white people organized," reflected one longtime member. "They said the NAACP was organizing, so at that time I thought that was a good idea." The specter of NAACP organizing also was evident in advertisements for a UKA rally in Surry County, which prominently noted that the event would be held "near the head of the local NAACP home." When a Raleigh-based klavern initiated a phone harassment campaign in 1964, its first target was Ralph Campbell, the president of the local NAACP branch. Soon after, members of the Wayne County Improvement Association (the cover name of the UKA's Goldsboro klavern) burned a cross to intimidate a particularly active NAACP member, one of a string of retaliatory actions that prompted state NAACP leader Kelly Alexander to call for a "Special Action for Branches" in response to klan terrorism across the state. In November 1965, the houses of Alexander and three other Charlotte-based civil rights leaders were bombed. The perpetrators were never caught, but the actions were widely attributed to the KKK. "I want to make it very clear," Alexander responded firmly, "we in the NAACP are not going to allow any type of race hate group with its intimidation and violent acts to deter our efforts in the implementation of the Civil Rights Act."[43]

The NAACP contributed to UKA mobilization because potential klan members saw its organization as a serious threat to segregationist policies. Klansmen typically referenced the Association as a nebulous symbol of the overarching civil rights establishment rather than as a set of activists posing particular and diverse challenges to the status quo. But this rough-hewn view sharpened somewhat in the early 1960s, as the NAACP grew rapidly. Newer branches—many of them formally designated as Youth or College chapters—disproportionately attracted young people inclined toward direct action. As these fresh NAACP recruits pursued this activist course, the UKA's constituencies began to see the new youth branches as a distinct and acute threat. As the UKA expanded across the state, counties with newly established NAACP branches were significantly more likely to develop a counter-network of klaverns. Accounting for the demographic and economic makeup of counties, an entrenched NAACP presence did not provide the UKA with an additional recruiting bump. However, a newly formed NAACP chapter translated, on average, into a 35 percent increase in local UKA organization.[44]

This pattern related to the NAACP's increasing youth-driven dynamism. By 1966, more than 1,000 of the state's nearly 13,000 NAACP members belonged to Youth Councils. Much of the public strongly associated these NAACP-affiliated youth with the 1960 sit-in movement, which had begun in Greensboro after four North Carolina A&T students demanded service at a downtown whites-only Woolworth's lunch counter. Two of those students, Ezell Blair and Joseph McNeil, were former Youth Council officers, and by the summer of 1960 half of the fifty-eight ongoing sit-in protests across the South were somehow affiliated with NAACP Youth and College chapters. NAACP attorneys represented most of the 1,300 students arrested during sit-in campaigns, and the Association provided bail money as well. In his 1960 address to North Carolina's NAACP membership, Kelly Alexander made it clear that times were changing, challenging the audience to confront a difficult question: "Are we keeping pace with our young people?"[45]

In many places, this youth-inspired activism, on the surface at least, dramatically departed from the NAACP's gradualist and judicially centered civil rights challenges. Many long-established branches had developed predictable relations with white officials and a somewhat conservative orientation to protest activity, and in that context newer chapters were more likely to embody an aggressive push for civil rights. The significance of the shift was clear from Alexander's strained call to more traditional NAACP adherents not to "mistake vitality and vigor for irresponsibility; imaginative thinking for radicalism. These old stereotypes... toward youth must go." Often, the severity of this shift fed white southerners' widely held theories that the impetus for civil rights challenges was not indigenous but was influenced by outside radicals and agitators. Such perceptions of the distinctive political threat posed by NAACP growth drove the UKA's recruiting successes in communities with newly formed NAACP chapters, in particular those with significant youth memberships.[46]

Constructing Racial Threats

In his landmark 1944 study *An American Dilemma*, Swedish social scientist Gunnar Myrdal emphasized the multifaceted and interdependent nature of the South's racial caste system. The maintenance of racial subjugation was undergirded by widely held assumptions of "Negro inferiority," which justified a range of social practices intended to preserve racial purity among white superiors. "Whites have to believe in the system of segregation and discrimination and to justify it to themselves," Myrdal argued. "So the social order perpetuates itself and with it the sentiments and beliefs by which it must be expressed." This cultural face of Jim Crow was evident in the myriad customs intended to eliminate the possibility of intimate relations between black men and white women. As a concern of the highest order, the specter of miscegenation brought to the fore struggles over desegregation in schools, eateries, and recreational facilities, where unregulated close contact was likely.[47]

For Myrdal and others, this contentious dynamic seemed a paradox. While many civil rights activists pushed hardest for gains tied to jobs and political participation, segregationist anxieties often were rooted in efforts to maintain racial separation in social spaces. These concerns were in fact inexorably intertwined, as the ideological systems that buttressed Jim Crow served to justify whites' economic and political advantage through the prism of black inferiority. As a result, segregationist outlets—from conservative newspapers to UKA rallies—railed most frequently against social and cultural threats to racial purity, but generally flourished where racial competition in workplaces and city halls was greatest. Where desegregation would create pronounced change in the economic and political status quo, many whites clung tightly to the assumptions upon which their belief in segregation rested. In that sense, cultural and social fears associated with race mixing were of a piece with economic and political competition.

While the stances of state political elites altered perceptions of the likelihood that integration would meaningfully occur, demographic, economic, and political arrangements defined the degree to which such reforms would alter entrenched patterns of racial inequity. As the regional patterning of klan presence in Figure 4.1b shows, UKA appeals connected most strongly in counties where civil rights reforms posed a significant threat to the prevailing racial status quo. Given the deep-seated complexities of Jim Crow, desegregation would, of course, produce significant change everywhere that blacks and whites co-resided. However, the degree to which those changes would impact long-established white supremacist power structures varied. In general, desegregation posed the greatest threat to the systems of power where African Americans were a proportionately large segment of the population, where their overlap in the labor market placed white and black workers in direct competition for jobs, and where political pressures engendered by civil rights activism were most acute. Under these conditions, the klan tended to thrive.

Perceived threats stemming from demographic, economic, and political arrangements all contributed to the formation of racial grievances and resentments. While the contours of North Carolina's political, economic, and social composition demonstrate that the scale of these threats differed across the state's counties, equally important is how, in any given location, distinct dimensions of "threat" operated in different ways. Whites' concern with the growth of a particular NAACP branch, for instance, tended to register narrowly. While ascendant NAACP branches often spurred klan recruitment within the home county of the chapter in question, there was little "spillover" effect in nearby counties, meaning that klavern support did not benefit from increased Youth Council activity in neighboring communities.[48]

The effect of large local black populations was similarly circumscribed. White residents' estimation of how desegregation measures would impact them socially—typically framed as the potential for cross-race mixing in public spaces such as restaurants, movie theaters, and schools—was governed by a sort of NIMBY ("not in my back yard") effect, with the presence of African American residents in home communities mattering a great deal but the composition of neighboring counties contributing little to perceptions of racial threat. In contrast, anxiety over racial competition within the labor force had a greater geographic reach. Where significant numbers of black workers were poised to compete for newly integrated manufacturing jobs, UKA recruiters often had great success even in counties miles away from the workplaces in question. As workers were willing to travel significant distances for good jobs—especially when the labor market tightened—the threat posed by a large black workforce was not confined to a local area but was felt in neighboring communities as well.[49]

In these varied ways, demographic, economic, and political factors shaped the racial climate of local settings, affecting the UKA's ability to recruit in North Carolina counties. But such conditions capture only one side of the story. Competition for economic and political resources might boost receptivity to klan ideology, but translating that predisposition to UKA membership required an organization that could convince sympathetic individuals of the UKA's value as an outlet for the collective expression of white supremacy. To forge those connections, klan members operated within local communities, attempting to make use of existing racial grievances and convert them into sustained KKK participation.

The group's relationship to particular institutions, however, was far from uniform. While workplaces could serve as a crucible for racial animosity around expanding competition for jobs, and thus as UKA recruitment sites, they also could impede racist militancy. The combustible interplay of class and race, reflected in decades of labor struggles and worker support of New Deal-style populism, meant that white workers did not uniformly reject federal intervention or identify with the UKA. Even among klan sympathizers, KKK affiliations sometimes proved costly. Longtime klansman Dub Brown recalled that "a lot of people were afraid that if they was members they would lose their job," after several local firms made statements to that effect. Brown himself was self-employed, so was freed from those sorts of concerns. "I told everybody that I had joined [the klan] and couldn't see nothing wrong with it," he explained. Some UKA recruiting strategies acknowledged and even exploited this need for secrecy. A Caldwell County klavern sent out letters in 1965, saying that it "has been brought to our attention that you are a sound believer in the 'RIGHTS FOR THE WHITES'" but "due to your business or other reasons, you cannot afford" to join the UKA. As an alternative, the letter requested that the recipient make a "top secret" donation to "your local Klu [*sic*] Klux Klan unit."[50]

While renewed civil rights activity could bolster white anxieties, groups like the NAACP also worked to exacerbate these sorts of cross-pressures, by increasing the costs of klan support. NAACP affiliates would encourage workers to bring legal action against employers who continued to discriminate against black workers, especially in companies known to willingly employ klan members. Kelly Alexander frequently emphasized "black America's collective buying power," and in several communities NAACP adherents organized economic boycotts. When the UKA was allowed to rent a booth at the 1966 State Fair, the NAACP encouraged African Americans to stay away. "We have a perfect right to protest by not spending our money in the presence of the KKK," Alexander argued.[51]

Likewise, other types of institutions could operate, in different contexts, to both enable and limit the UKA's appeal. The group's Christian roots were reflected in the dozens of ministers that filled its membership ranks, some of whom held church placements. Nightly rallies always began with prayer and, in some cases, a sermon by a local "kludd" or preacher, and several klan leaders—including George Dorsett and Catfish Cole—spent time on the evangelizing circuit. At the same time, churches and ministers frequently served as a legitimate moral voice that condemned the KKK, urged nonviolence, and promoted racial justice.[52]

As the civil rights movement gained momentum, it became harder for any community institutions to remain neutral in the struggle. In this charged environment, lines were clearly drawn between the UKA's institutional allies and opponents, and the klan could count both supporters and foes in any given community. All the while, UKA adherents distributed handbills, held street walks, hosted rallies, and sought to persuade friends, family members, neighbors, and co-workers that the klan was the only group that truly represented the interests of patriotic white Protestants. These negotiations mediated the ways in which individuals perceived and sometimes acted on threats constituted by broader economic and political configurations. In short, racial competition within and across counties governed UKA mobilization, but those patterns provide only limited insight into how individuals linked to the UKA. The next chapter explores the social trajectories of would-be klan members, examining how UKA recruitment operated from the perspective of individual adherents.

5 JOINING THE KLAN

The Klan is the most dedicated organization in America....You have to be white, Gentile and born in America to be a member of the Klan. You have to be a *real* American.

—a UKA member, speaking in 1964.[1]

The capacity to feel real emotion for spurious reasons is one mark of the romantic, and the capacity to believe what isn't so is another....With the possible exception of Grand Dragon Jones (who seemed a cool customer), all the Klansmen I met were romantics.

—STEWART ALSOP, writing in the *Saturday Evening Post.*[2]

I don't care what all your sociologists and what all your philosophers and psychologists want to tell you. I'm telling you, I knew these people, I talked to them every day for years, they thought that they were fighting Communism in their own stupid way....You talk about loyalty—these guys were all former GI's...talk about disloyal, that's absurd. They were misguided, ignorant people is what they were.

—DARGAN FRIERSON, FBI Special Agent responsible for developing UKA informants in North Carolina.[3]

"The reason for my joining the Klan in the first place," Bob Jones explained, "I was worried about the 1954 Supreme Court decision on school desegregation—the Black Monday decision." Jones's anxiety was certainly not unusual; the *Brown* decision sent shock waves through nearly all white institutions across the South. But following the lead of segregationist thinkers in Mississippi and elsewhere, he interpreted the landmark court decision and the incipient Civil Rights Movement in the context of cold war fears of communist conspiracies:

> I started checkin' and checkin' close, and found out that it's not the niggers themselves that's in charge of these various civil rights organizations—the niggers do not have the brains or the money to finance this revolution on such a scale. These executive positions of CORE and the

> NAACP—their boards of directors and their policy makers are all white. And a good many of them are now, or have been, associated with the Communist Party. The more these Communists gain control, the more violent these organizations get, and they're getting worse and worse every summer. This country's being torn apart by this civil rights mess—this ain't no small thing that's going on—and these Communists are making all they can out of it.[4]

This outlook shaped, and was shaped by, Jones's work in the KKK. In the latter half of the 1950s, he had found the U.S. Klans a natural outlet for his political concerns. The group understood the world through the same conspiratorial "pseudo-conservative" lens that had informed his investigation of the civil rights movement, which historian Richard Hofstadter famously labeled the "paranoid style." By Jones's own telling, the process of affiliating with the klan was simple: he sought out and connected with like-minded segregationists.

But also crucial were the personal ties that enabled him to connect to a group with a precarious public profile. His father, a railroad worker and KKK member in the 1920s, regularly spoke reverentially about the klan. Years later, Jones worked as an awning salesman for home improvement entrepreneur Arthur Leonard, an early core member of the U.S. Klans. The direct channel provided by Leonard and other co-workers enabled Jones's initial entry into the klan's inner circle.[5]

Like Jones, Eddie Dawson describes his entry into the UKA as a ready-made solution to ever-intensifying racial problems. A New Jersey native, Dawson had been dishonorably discharged from the army after World War II. Moving through a series of jobs, he became increasingly angry about what he saw as African Americans' inappropriate sense of entitlement about civil rights matters and their disrespectful behavior toward women in public. These grievances stemmed in large part from Dawson's experiences in the workplace; he was quick to cite his bitterness toward his black laborer colleagues as well as the black workers that his father hired in his New Jersey–based business. Settling in North Carolina in the early 1960s, Dawson mostly kept these racial resentments to himself until he came across a copy of the *Fiery Cross* while working in Wilmington. He soon began to notice UKA stickers in the windows of various restaurants and gas stations. Feeling that this was an organization serious about defending the racial order, he decided to send in the application he had cut out of the UKA's newspaper. Within two years, he was a state leader in the UKA Security Guard.[6]

The bulk of those entering the UKA during its rapid mid-1960s growth, however, did not pro-actively seek out the klan as an outlet for their own fully formed diagnoses of racial ills. While the perceived threat of integration shaped white southerners' receptivity to the klan's conspiracy-laden strain of segregationist thought, conceptions of those threats did not uniformly align with the klan's worldview or magically translate into UKA affiliation. Instead, most came to the UKA through a gradual process—pushed and pulled by their commitments to jobs, family, and other interests, and under the often-tenuous sway of the UKA's efforts to position themselves as the true defenders of white supremacy.

This chapter considers the processes associated with UKA participation, from the perspective of the individuals who joined the organization. The sections that follow explore a number of factors that shaped individual paths toward, or away from, klan participation. While a sense of vulnerability to civil rights reform could shape one's affinity to the klan, active membership often hinged upon connections to other individuals and groups that could reinforce or compete with the UKA. Klan organizing efforts mattered as well. Rallies, street walks, and civic projects provided opportunities for sympathetic individuals to join their worldviews and personal identities with the klan's collective body. By framing the UKA as an organization working to preserve an increasingly beleaguered "real" white America, and then providing an outlet for members to act collectively in "authentically" white settings, klan recruiters sought to align their aims with those of white southerners threatened by civil rights gains. Depending on how such efforts coincided with individual lives, such recruiting tactics could forge and cement, or alternately deter, the UKA's connections to potential adherents.

Workplace Competition and UKA Membership

The UKA's presence increased in counties marked by high levels of racial competition, but within those counties, how broadly shared was this sense of racial threat? Social scientists have long cautioned against succumbing to ecological fallacies, stemming from inappropriate assumptions that group phenomena provide insight into the behaviors of particular individuals within those groups. Extending that logic, county patterns in klan membership do not necessarily indicate which residents were most likely to join the KKK. Equally important, those broader patterns in themselves fail to explain how the presence of general racial competition translated into mobilization among specific county residents.

Settings that breed competition provide ideal starting points for examining the processes through which racial threat translates into collective action. Temporarily confining our focus to the workplace, we might ask whether white workers increasingly in direct competition with African Americans were most likely to join the klan. Or alternately, did the presence of threat create a climate where white residents in general became susceptible to the UKA's recruiting appeals? In the former case, we would expect to find klan members disproportionately occupying labor market sectors marked by high rates of interracial competition. The latter argument, in which competition creates an overall climate of racial animosity, would lend itself to a more even membership distribution, with the UKA drawing support even from those sectors not subject to high levels of racial threat.[7]

In a 1965 report, the Trend Analyses Division of the Anti-Defamation League (ADL) summarized reporters' and other observers' impressions of the KKK's membership. Its characterization was not flattering. "To a great extent," the report argued,

> the Klan's membership is composed... of those at the very bottom of the social ladder, of fanatics with limited education who have spent most of their lives in rural areas or small towns in the South. For the most part, they are laborers, small farmers, service station attendants, salesmen and others with small businesses. Hoodlums and sadists are also said, by authoritative sources, to be members of the various Klan groups.[8]

Klan leaders regularly contested this portrait. Robert Shelton, for instance, repeatedly emphasized the "widely diversified" activities of the UKA's many "business and professional men." More rigorous academic efforts, however, have largely reinforced the ADL's findings. Multiple studies have concluded that klansmen came predominantly from the "lower and lower-middle classes," typically engaged in either skilled trade or semi-skilled or unskilled manufacturing work. A lesser percentage owned small businesses or occupied "marginal white collar positions," as, for example, store clerks, service-station attendants, and police officers. In contrast, white-collar professionals were only a negligible part of the overall membership. News stories and evidence from congressional hearings generally reaffirm this occupational profile. These sources also emphasize the fragility of the klan's base, due to corrupt, exploitative leadership and the ephemeral commitment of an irresponsible, largely apolitical following.[9]

The accuracy of such profiles remains an open question, however, as most existing accounts have not drawn on a representative sample of the overall membership. Nearly all previous studies have made heavy use of KKK members who appear either in media stories or judicial or congressional hearings, almost certainly biasing these samples toward more central, active, and likely militant adherents. Fortunately, a range of largely untapped sources—including State Bureau of Investigation reports and informant-generated lists—avoid these obvious biases and provide a clearer window into the labor market sectors from which Jones and other UKA leaders drew their support. The resulting membership portrait lends insight into whether the Carolina Klan's appeal fell narrowly within occupations and industries most strongly subject to interracial competition.

Using the categorization scheme from the 1960 US Census, Tables 5.1 and 5.2 report the occupations and industrial affiliations held by 159 members of the Carolina Klan, alongside the makeup of the overall white male workforce in the state, the differential between these klan and overall workforce values (i.e., the degree to which the klan was over- or underrepresented, relative to the overall white employed population), and the degree of racial overlap (i.e., the ratio of black to white workers) in each sector.[10]

Table 5.1 shows that more than a fifth of klan adherents worked as "operators" (e.g., machinists, sheet-metal workers, heavy equipment operators, truck drivers), a proportion similar to what we would expect given the state's overall employment breakdown. "Managers and proprietors" (mostly small business owners), on the other hand, were significantly overrepresented in the UKA. Within higher prestige occupations, klan members were underrepresented among professional, clerical, and technical workers. In general, despite the systematic differences within particular categories, no significant difference between klansmen and the local population existed across all occupational categories. In other words, as a group, klan members did not look substantially different from North Carolina's overall white population.[11]

Table 5.2 mirrors those findings, focusing on workers' industry affiliations. Many of the klansmen employed as operators worked in industries associated with transportation and public utilities. The larger-than-expected small business owner contingent was tied predominantly to repair services as well as wholesale and retail trade. As with the occupational breakdown, the overall pattern of industry employment for the UKA's North Carolina membership did not significantly differ from the state's overall white population.

Some of these findings match the suspicions of journalists and other KKK observers. Klansmen were in fact underrepresented in white-collar

Table 5.1 Occupational distribution of white men in labor force

	NC UKA	Overall NC population	Differential	Racial overlap
UKA overrepresented				
Managers and proprietors (nonfarm)	28.9%	11.0%	***17.9%***	0.028
Service workers (not in private homes)	19.5%	3.3%	***16.2%***	0.846
Operators	20.1%	23.4%	3.3%	0.232
Sales workers	9.4%	7.9%	1.5%	0.029
UKA underrepresented				
Private household workers	0.0%	0.1%	–0.1%	3.354
Laborers (nonfarm)	3.4%	4.3%	–0.9%	1.189
Professional and technical workers	6.0%	7.1%	–1.1%	0.102
Farm laborers	0.0%	2.7%	–2.7%	1.431
Clerical workers	0.0%	5.6%	***–5.6%***	0.070
Craft workers	11.4%	19.8%	***–8.4%***	0.106
Farmers and farm managers	1.3%	10.5%	***–9.2%***	0.327
Occupation not reported	—	4.4%	—	—
Total	100%	100%		

occupations, for instance, and nearly one third of the UKA's membership—significantly more than in the population overall—held blue-collar service or operational jobs. But other aspects of these employment breakdowns seem surprising. The UKA's strength in the predominantly rural eastern plain, along with certain reporters' emphasis on the predominance of overalls and gingham dresses among supporters at rallies, contributed to widespread suspicion that farmers were among the klan's strongest Carolina constituencies. However, Tables 5.1 and 5.2 both show significantly fewer than expected farm and agricultural workers in the klan. While more than a tenth of the state's workers fit within this category, only 1.3 percent of the UKA's membership did. A 1965 Gallup Poll supports this discovery, finding farmers only half as likely as unskilled and semi-skilled service workers to "agree with" the KKK. Similarly, the manufacturing sector, perhaps the most visible site of racial competition in the wake of the Civil Rights Act, contained fewer than expected klan memberships. UKA members most often owned small

Table 5.2 Industry distribution of white men in labor force

	NC UKA	Overall NC pop.	Differential	Racial overlap
UKA overrepresented				
Public administration	18.2%	3.8%	***14.4%***	0.128
Business and repair services	10.7%	2.5%	***8.2%***	0.144
Trade (wholesale and retail)	25.2%	17.8%	***7.4%***	0.169
Transportation and public utilities	12.6%	6.2%	***6.4%***	0.224
Personal services	3.1%	1.8%	1.3%	0.747
Entertainment and recreation services	1.3%	0.5%	0.8%	0.474
Construction	9.4%	9.1%	0.3%	0.266
UKA underrepresented:				
Mining	0.0%	0.4%	–0.4%	0.153
Finance, insurance, and real estate	1.9%	2.6%	–0.7%	0.085
Professional services	2.5%	5.1%	–2.6%	0.347
Manufacturing (durable goods)	4.4%	12.1%	***–7.7%***	0.230
Manufacturing (nondurable goods)	9.4%	21.7%	***–12.3%***	0.152
Agriculture	1.3%	13.9%	***–12.6%***	0.539
Industry not reported	—	2.6%	—	—
Total	100%	100%		

Note: Occupations and industries are sorted by "differential," which represents the degree of KKK over/underrepresentation in each category. Bolded and italicized differential values indicate a statistically significant difference between klansmen and the overall local population (see note 11).

businesses, a surprising finding given that ownership insulated individuals from many of the direct pressures of newly integrated workforces.[12]

This profile is consistent with a more general pattern: the UKA was not primarily comprised of workers whose jobs were subject to high levels of racial competition. The final column of Tables 5.1 and 5.2 lists the ratio of black to white workers within each employment category. In high-overlap sectors, signaling greater opportunities for African Americans to compete directly with whites, workers were no more likely to join the UKA. Instead, the average racial overlap value among occupational categories with negative differentials—those least likely to attract UKA members—was 0.327, more than double the 0.131 figure associated with categories where klan members were overrepresented. This finding held for occupations with the most pronounced overrepresentation of klan members. In sectors with statistically significant positive differentials, the average racial overlap value was 0.437, a figure *lower* than the 0.711 value associated with categories with no significant relationship to klan activity.

These relationships hold for industry categories as well. Sectors with fewer-than-expected klan members had an average racial overlap value of 0.230, a figure higher than the 0.157 value in overrepresented UKA sectors. This pattern held generally: across all industry categories together, UKA membership did not correlate with racial overlap. While the UKA thrived in communities marked by the general presence of racial competition for jobs, the klan's recruits were not necessarily those workers who themselves faced new labor challenges from African Americans.[13]

Networks, Commitments, and Opportunities

One way to reconcile this finding with the central conclusion in Chapter 4—namely, that the UKA was strongest in counties characterized by high overall levels of racial competition—is to view racialized threats posed by civil rights reforms as contributing to an overall climate of racial animosity. In these charged climates, a sense of threat emerged widely both within and across "afflicted" communities. UKA presence across counties signaled this diffuse nature of racial threat; independent of the makeup of any particular county, high levels of racial overlap in *neighboring* counties' labor markets significantly increased the likelihood that the UKA would gain a local foothold.[14] Similarly, the general charged climate created by high levels of economic competition across racial groups aided the recruitment of prospective members, even if the UKA's appeals weren't always answered by the most vulnerable workers themselves.

Klan members' accounts emphasize how, within these environments, personal networks and one's degree of autonomy to act on racial grievances influenced the likelihood of klan participation. UKA members would frequently note that they, or others they knew, lacked this feeling of availability, often due to a fear that klan activity might put their jobs at risk. Dub Brown, who boasted that he had personally recruited "two hundred or some" members to the klan, acknowledged that, as an independent business owner, he felt free to openly express his KKK connections. In contrast, when he sought to recruit textile workers, he found that many worried that klan affiliations might cost them their jobs. Another member noted that his insurance agent—a "great big tall Texan,...could gather me up and half break me in two"—admired the klan but was scared of the professional consequences if he himself joined. Gurney Lovette, a Fayetteville klansman, chose to resign from his klavern in early 1967 to increase his odds of winning a job with the post office. His past criminal record proved to be his undoing, however, and he was rejected for the position. Soon after, he returned to the unit, vowing to "be more active than ever before."[15]

Clearly, the workplace could operate at cross-purposes with the klan. But even those whose wariness over economic retribution caused them to avoid the klan were linked to others—friends, neighbors, family members—freer to act on these sorts of generalized grievances. Thus the UKA attracted a disproportionately high number of small business owners—those who, like Dub Brown, felt an obligation to their brethren in part because they themselves were not subject to the whims of employers. Especially when business owners had strong connections to those in more precarious labor sectors, their ability to act without putting their jobs at risk made these independent operators more available to the UKA's appeals.[16]

The social fabric of families, neighborhoods, and workplaces affected the recruitment process in other ways as well. Even the most committed UKA member held a range of interests and obligations alongside the klan. In some instances, those obligations aligned with the UKA, and the klan's recruiting strategies sought to exploit those personal connections. "Best way to get a new member? Ask him," was a prominent message in the *Fiery Cross* during the summer of 1964, when the UKA was experiencing unprecedented growth. Another UKA bulletin trumpeted the best way to bring any "Joe" into the klan: identify a likely friend or acquaintance and "talk to him":

> Get him interested in the klan. Keep an eye peeled. It does not matter what society, organization, club or civic group he may already belong to just so long as he measures up to the ideals and qualifications as required by the klan.[17]

Personal connections, in particular intensive family bonds, in many cases served to create a broadly shared sense of racial threat and made the klan a powerful draw. Bob Jones's immediate motivation to join the KKK might have been the *Brown* decision, but he also saw membership as a way to honor his parents. He proudly noted his father's membership and that his mother marched in a klan parade in his Salisbury hometown two months before his birth. Jones's mother-in-law, wife Syble, and daughter Sheila frequently traveled the rally circuit with him. Sheila felt a strong closeness to the many family members who would also attend rallies all over the state. "We were so involved in people's lives, it was like an extended family," she recounted.

Similarly, one of George Dorsett's earliest memories involved his father taking him to a rally in Greensboro in the mid-1920s. Years later, he recalled the large audience of mill workers and the robed klansmen who formed a human cross at the event's climax. Dub Brown's father and grandfather were both members in the 1920s, and in the 1950s Dub joined the U.S. Klans alongside his father and brother Ikie. An Alamance County klavern leader likewise "sincerely believe[d] that the klan is right," in large part because of his grandfather's membership in the 1920s. "I've always been taught that way," he explained. And Raymond Cranford would proudly declare that his father's and grandfather's membership meant that he was "born into the klan." His own pre-teen son, who by the mid-1960s had taken to scrawling "KKK" on his schoolbooks, was, according to Cranford, born into the klan too.[18]

This intense cross-generational identification with the klan did not hold as widely among more peripheral members, though in many cases klavern rolls featured two or more members of the same families. The Fillingame cousins who carried out the 1964 bombing of a New Bern church and funeral home co-owned their family grocery store and socialized together during much of their free time. Pete Vinson, an active member of a klavern in Fayetteville, was joined at meetings by his son, and a unit in Franklin County included several members of the Brantley family. In Cherryville, west of Charlotte, the local klavern featured three members each from the Homesley and Mauncey families. Women in both of those households also led Cherryville's Ladies Auxiliary Unit. The overall vitality of the Ladies Auxiliaries in North Carolina—there were thirty-three units statewide—stemmed from the group's ability to mix members' spouses into the men-only UKA and thus integrate family and klan life among the membership.

With striking frequency, members framed the segregationist fight, and thus their klan affiliations, as a defense of family. "I joined the klan *because* I love my wife and I love my two children," declared one member, justifying his participation by reiterating the klan's fundamental devotion to the sanctity of family. "Back when I was fighting," explained another member, a World War II veteran, "I didn't know what I was fighting for. Now I have a wife and children and I know what I am fighting for." Anxiety over the rampant miscegenation that members suspected would result from civil rights reforms motivated these kinds of sentiments. But such ideals also signaled an opposing reality: that in the absence of lofty familial goals the demands of UKA membership could in fact compete with their own responsibilities to kin. Grand Nighthawk Boyd Hamby, who was married with five children, maintained that the klan's fight to maintain segregation, if not fully aligned with his family obligations, spoke to his core principles. "I believe in what I'm fighting for—I believe in White Supremacy political and social," Hamby stated emphatically. It was only because he felt so strongly about segregation, he said, that he spent each night presiding over UKA rallies rather than at home with his family.[19]

In some cases, members openly acknowledged the consequences of klan activity for their family lives. Noting that his "main problem is putting too much time away from home," one former adherent resigned after his wife left him. "It was the klan that sent me on all those long personal trips away," he lamented. In contrast, Eddie Dawson spoke with pride about his wife's approval of the KKK. While she hadn't joined the local Ladies Auxiliary, she would willingly attend rallies. But this enthusiasm waned once Dawson was arrested and jailed for his role in klan terrorism. "My wife was pretty much against the Ku Klux Klan by [that] time," he recounted. "She came up and would say, 'If you hadn't been in the damned klan, I wouldn't be visiting you in prison like this.' And she would get pretty upset about it. I'd calm her down by saying that I was going to quit the klan when I got out." But upon his release, Dawson found himself "sneaking down" to UKA meetings once again.

Betty Hill went one step further. Although not overly enthusiastic about the UKA, she joined a Ladies Auxiliary Unit to support her husband, Robert. She knew that Robert had long admired the klan's stances, as he was prone to proud boasts about his grandfather's membership back in the 1920s. But Betty noted that the secrecy associated with his subsequent UKA involvement placed a strain on their marriage:

> We used to always argue about the klan. He'd go out and not tell me where he was going or nothing and then he would come home at one and two o'clock in the morning. I'd ask him where he'd been and he'd say, 'I can't tell you.' I'd ask him if he had got into any trouble and he wouldn't say. We used to talk a lot before he joined the klan. But we never talked after that. We fought a lot.

After Robert was arrested in 1967 for his role in a series of shootings and burnings intended to prevent the integration of Cabarrus County schools,

Betty convinced him to tell his story to the FBI. The consequent fallout, which included near-constant threats from former UKA colleagues, forced the Hills to leave the county.[20]

Just as family bonds could enable or pose difficulties for klan membership, workplaces had varied effects on klan recruitment. As discussed earlier, a key cost centered on some employers' threats to fire known klan members. Significant obligations associated with work, as with family, also could make klan affiliation prohibitively time-consuming. When Wayne County klansman Joseph DuBois resigned from his klavern in 1966, he cited his inability to attend meetings and rallies. "I still have my mother to support, and my family, and my business to look after," he explained, "and I can't be running all over the country."[21]

Work sites could also have the opposite effect, serving as de facto recruiting centers and informal klan affiliates. Clerks working in a small Wilmington hardware store owned by a longtime klansman, for instance, were widely known as UKA members. In Fayetteville, a leader in the UKA's Unit 89 had three of his employees in the klavern, and the bulk of the klavern's remaining membership clustered within four local firms, including the Pepsi-Cola Bottling Company. Similarly, State Bureau of Investigation (SBI) and State Highway Patrol memos noted with concern that a majority of prison department employees in Asheboro "are members of the Klan or have filed an application for membership."[22]

Work at times fostered other personal connections that could bridge to the UKA. Tommy Reagan, a salesman who worked directly with television repair shops and retail dealers, "had set back and watched for years what was going on," admiring from afar the klan's willingness to organize when nobody else would "step forward and fight this thing." But it was only through a sales contact that he connected with his local UKA klavern. "One day I was sitting home between trips and this ol' boy who I used to sell to, asked me if I would come with him to a klan meeting," Reagan recounted. "I'd been dying to go to one, so naturally I jumped at the chance, you know."

In other cases, this connection to the klan came through friends or chance meetings. Such links were so common that when, as part of the FBI's massive effort to neutralize the UKA, a Charlotte agent proposed that the Bureau fill out and submit fictitious UKA membership applications, his boss noted that "this will probably not cause any great decrease in applications processed, because a large number of applications are received from personal contact by members among their friends and acquaintances." In many areas, ad hoc UKA recruiters regularly approached those enjoying a drink or a meal in certain bars and cafes. Bob Jones himself claimed that periodically, buried in a newspaper over a cup of coffee at a truck stop, he would loudly mutter about how the "niggers are taking over." When other patrons affirmed his complaint, Jones would introduce himself and sign them up. These venues were not random; impromptu recruitment efforts almost always occurred in spaces well known as "seg" hangouts with reliably receptive audiences.[23]

Integrated venues more often spurred racial conflict, and could thus foster "chance" meetings tied to acute grievances. Glenn Twigg, klaliff of a large klavern east of Raleigh in Johnston County, first joined the UKA in 1966, soon after the birth of his first child. The hospital that performed the delivery had recently desegregated by federal mandate, and his wife shared a room with a black woman. Eying the roommate's male visitors, Twigg became increasingly uneasy and demanded that nurses move his wife. After he threatened a doctor, hospital staff called the police to usher him out of the building. The local officer who took the call, however, was himself a member of the UKA. Noting Twigg's belligerent attitude, the officer suggested that he would fit well with the klan, and provided contact information for the local klavern. Twigg joined soon after, and quickly rose to leadership in the unit.[24]

In these varied ways, public spaces enabled local klan members to connect with like-minded prospective recruits. The UKA's many events more deliberately fostered similar bonds. Street walks, and especially rally sites, became prime venues for UKA recruitment. These events had local roots, as one or more nearby klaverns sponsored and promoted each rally. Jones's state office prepared standardized fliers announcing dates and locations. "COME HEAR THE TRUTH," each flyer proclaimed, welcoming the "white public" to listen to "the Grand Dragon of North Carolina and other good speakers." At its peak, the UKA printed 2,000 copies of each flyer on colored paper stock. Klavern members handed them out around town to likely recruits. Residents recall certain service station workers and other business owners eyeballing customers prior to local rallies, sizing up whether they might merit a rally flyer and an invitation. While most klaverns would sponsor only one or two rallies each year, some sustained their outreach by erecting signs on roadsides instructing interested locals on how to make contact with a nearby unit.[25]

"Authentic Whiteness" and the UKA's Paranoid Style

The substance of the rallies themselves provided the UKA with a powerful "pull" factor to attract individuals whose segregationist leanings and social ties had already "pushed" them toward the KKK. The klan's ideology, practices, and public self-presentations strove to construct a resonant sense of collective identity among the "white public." Through these performances of "authentic" whiteness, klan leaders offered up an ideological and social space that allowed receptive individuals to see themselves as fitting with the klan.

The klan's brand of "whiteness" was of course a social construction, offering an idealized racial standard to a white population that in practice was far from monolithic. The UKA's dogmatic racial standard truncated its support base, though the group's alignment with a broad field of Cold War right-wing thought, characterized by a belief in a conspiracy theory of history, aided its resonance. This "paranoid style" most often focused on the dangers posed by an alleged sweeping communist plot to destroy American freedoms, which had gained a new kind of traction in the civil rights-era South.[26] Bob Jones's rationale for joining the klan, centered on "Communist control" of CORE and the NAACP, clearly illustrated this connection. To UKA leaders, integration policy was itself the product of a vast conspiracy, engineered not by African Americans (who in their view were incapable of such ambitious action) but instead by the subversive communist Jews who agitated for America's downfall.

Though the UKA drew from, and contributed to, a wide field of extreme organizations and ideologues, postwar concerns over communist plots were not confined to this far-right fringe. President Truman had mandated a loyalty program for federal civil service employees to ensure their "complete and unswerving loyalty to the United States" in 1947, and the Taft-Hartley Act, which required labor officials to establish under oath that they were not communists, passed the same year. The House Un-American Activities Committee, first established in 1938 and formalized as a permanent congressional body in 1945, was charged with rooting out "un-American" communist operatives operating both in public capacities and as private citizens. In 1953, the US Senate Subcommittee on Investigations, headed by Wisconsin Senator Joseph McCarthy, began a series of hearings that targeted the supposed communist infiltration of a number of government agencies, including the Voice of America and the US Army. The Smith Act, which outlawed individuals or groups from advocating the forceful overthrow of the government, led to the indictment of forty-two Communist Party-USA officials between 1953 and 1956. FBI director J. Edgar Hoover was widely respected as the country's foremost authority on the communist menace, and in 1956 the Bureau initiated a sweeping counterintelligence program designed as "an all-out disruptive attack against the CP from within."[27]

In the South, this anti-communist fervor meshed with segregationist concerns. Advocacy for states' rights to override federal civil rights intervention aligned with conservative principles of individual freedom and the elimination of "Stalinist" centralized government systems. Biblical rationales for racial separation gained added resonance when contrasted with the "godless" communists who ignored such dictates. The longtime support for racial equality offered by the Communist Party and other left-wing organizations provided a ready-made link between those groups' civil rights advocacy and a broader "subversive" agenda. A wide range of conservative organizations buttressed these conspiratorial undertones, drawing upon such paranoid logic to promote, in varying combinations and permutations, countersubversive, anti-Semitic, and racist ends.[28]

Indeed, as Willis Smith's 1950 Senate campaign and the successful suppression of interracial union organizing efforts during the prior decade showed, claims that socialism and civil rights were two sides of the same coin resonated strongly with North Carolina's voters. A decade later, the UKA rode this same wave, drawing on ideas associated with both mainstream and extreme conservative outlets. The seminal conservative magazine *National Review* suggested that it would be "irresponsible" to hand political power to black southerners, and former FBI agent Dan Smoot gained popular traction in the early 1960s after publishing a book that spoke of "a few sinister people... at the top of the invisible government" who "want Americans to become part of a world-wide socialist dictatorship, under the control of the Kremlin." The John Birch Society (JBS), which grew to include several hundred chapters and tens of thousands of members in the mid-1960s, advanced similar conspiratorial ideas. Though its brand of anti-communism largely eschewed anti-Semitic or directly racist theories, the JBS strongly opposed the civil rights movement, on the grounds that it was a communist-controlled plot. Hard-line groups like the American Nazi Party and the National States Rights Party championed a different brand of conspiracism, centered on rabid racism and anti-Semitism. Both framed the civil rights danger as a Jewish-engineered plot. "The negro is not the enemy," argued NSRP founder J. B. Stoner. "The Jew is THE enemy... using the negro in an effort to destroy the White Race."[29]

Operating in this environment, the UKA did not construct its blend of racist, anti-Semitic, and anti-communist thought out of whole cloth. Its publications and rally speeches drew liberally on ideas that overlapped with those of other extreme right groups, and at their rallies the Carolina Klan regularly offered for sale pamphlets and books from the JBS and other anti-communist organizations. When Barry Goldwater, the Republican's 1964 presidential candidate, opposed the Civil Rights Act primarily on conservative constitutional grounds, the UKA threw its support behind his campaign (later, Jones's car sported an "I'm not ashamed, I voted for Goldwater" bumper sticker). At the same time, the klan developed its own unique ideological brand, blending a range of themes to construct its ideal of authentic whiteness. As an organization positioned to fill civic and social as well as political needs, the UKA relied on this racial-cultural construct to unify its membership and bridge to segregationist sympathizers.

As with any form of intense political commitment, forging such connections required a significant emotional investment. At rallies, speakers angrily denounced the federal government and other "white nigger" institutions. Journalist Stewart Alsop proclaimed klan adherents "genuine romantics" after speaking with Grady Mars, one of Jones's early state officers. "I seen grown men with tears in their eyes when they see that burning cross," Mars told Alsop. "You know where those tears come from? They come from here," he said, pointing to his heart.[30] One does not need to deny the legitimacy and power of those emotions to understand the UKA's paranoid style not only as an expressive outlet for such personal feelings, but also as a framework within which the group built the collective consciousness necessary to work to preserve white supremacy. In this sense, Mars's emotion signaled not only his personal connection to the cross itself, but also his—and other klan members'—collective feeling of attachment to the UKA and its political aims.

In their search for new recruits, klan leaders self-consciously engineered this solidarity, deploying "whiteness" as a basis for collective identity. Within the UKA, the "white public" became a heroic constituency, the only line of defense in the face of an increasingly contested racial order. "The Jews have the B'nai B'rith. The Catholics have the Knights of Columbus. And the niggers have the NAACP," railed a Rowan County UKA member to a reporter in 1964. "Tell me what in the hell has a white man got besides the Klan? What has the white Protestant gentile got?" Operating in a state where political elites tended to be racial moderates rather than hard-line segregationists (even if their policies often passively resisted integration mandates), the Carolina Klan strove to carve out a space for a community willing both to enact and to defend genuine whiteness. Under this paradigm, racial authenticity was synonymous with segregation—it required not only an acceptable physiological makeup but also, crucially, a cultural and ideological commitment to white supremacy.[31]

Constructing racial identity in this way helped recruiters to build commitment to the klan, by connecting broad segregationist beliefs to the UKA's specific political program. But even within a seemingly homogenous and sympathetic group of authentic segregationists, crafting this sense of "oneness" could be a tenuous process. As we have seen, the UKA's membership profile was not comprised narrowly of those whose economic status was threatened by civil rights reforms, and devoting oneself to the klan cause in many cases could have significant implications for existing social commitments and duties. To focus a sense of shared grievance among a broad segregationist constituency, klan leaders needed to define and direct the threat posed by integration, by linking personal identities to that of the larger klan enterprise.[32]

At their nightly rallies and other events, UKA leaders dedicated their energies to establishing this connection. Rally speeches served, above all, to politicize the culture of whiteness, by enhancing the salience of a shared "white" identity and demonstrating how race pervaded a range of core beliefs. While most outside observers cited klan leaders' vigilante-style racism as obvious evidence of the group's demagogic appeal, the real power of its ideology lay not in its denunciation of others or its willingness to flout law and order, but rather in its insistence on elevating racial identity as the political, moral, and social center of American citizenship. As historian David L. Chappell argues, more mainstream segregationists failed in their efforts to mobilize the majority of white southerners because of their unwillingness to extend their arguments in ways that might threaten the "respectability on which they believed their authority rested." By rejecting allegiances to any institutions that were not organized entirely around the idea of authentic whiteness, the UKA avoided this conundrum. As a consequence, however, the group held little appeal for classes whose "respectability" resided outside the orbit of white supremacy. Unlike many unskilled and semi-skilled workers, the status of most white professionals did not rely predominantly on racial preferences maintained through segregation. Further, vocal support for white supremacy could harm professional status in the eyes of broader and more racially liberal collegial networks that extended outside the South. Such social class-tinged considerations interacted with competition dynamics to truncate the UKA's potential base.[33]

But for those not subject to such cross-pressures, UKA speeches sought to draw upon existing shared values, weaving them in new ways into the cloth of activist identities. By understanding whiteness as bound to racial separation, individuals were more likely to interpret the law-and-order position taken by the state's political elites, whereby North Carolina would abide by federal civil rights legislation, not merely as a pragmatist compromise. Instead, the UKA maintained that such moderate stances capitulated to subversive interests and contributed to the eradication of American freedoms. Similarly, mainstream church leaders' unwillingness to uphold segregation as biblically ordained, UKA leaders insisted, threatened the nation's moral core. Such substantial logical leaps required that adherents accept several key premises about the relationship between civil rights struggles and core "American" values.

Analysts of social movements have long focused on how movement organizers employ these premises, or frames, to align their ideas with receptive audiences. Through such framing efforts, individuals connect ideologically with movement goals and become potential participants in movement actions.[34] Klan leaders offered a range of frames to present their case for defending segregation, and different audiences digested, accepted, and adopted these frames in different ways, in relation to highly localized interests and experiences. These varied religious, scientific, and political rationales comprised a system of ideas that pointed toward the same broad conclusion, providing the requisite ideological material to construct a clear boundary between whites and various others. While adherents could arrive at this endpoint through distinct ideological routes, the UKA's organizational frames provided a basis for receptive individuals to envision themselves within the bounded world of the authentically white public. Participating in klan rituals, services, meetings, and social gatherings could, in turn, reinforce and cement that connection to the UKA.[35]

The central dualism in klan ideology was between "whites" and "niggers." "There's colored folks and there's niggers, there ain't no Negroes," Raymond Cranford frequently claimed. "White" was a category narrower than skin color, requiring adherence to segregationist principles. Conversely, the "nigger" label signaled much more than race. Cranford's coda was that "if it comes to a fight, the *white* nigger's gonna get killed before the nigger." "White niggers," he explained, had "white skin, and a heart that's pumping nigger blood through his veins." In other words, their loyalties lay not with the preservation of racial purity and separation.[36] "Colored folks" were literally the inverse, with black skin but a tacit acceptance of white supremacy, rooted in a supposedly proper sense of their (separate and second-class) place in the racial order.

The UKA's patriotic rhetoric often subsumed these racial categories. Robert Shelton regularly proclaimed that the UKA stood for "everything that's American." For him, "100 percent Americanism" deeply intertwined with race: both were biologically and ideologically ordained. As historian

Evelyn Rich has argued, suspect individuals could thus fall under two categories: those who were "un-American," or biologically unfit, and those who were "anti-American," or ideologically suspect by virtue of adherence to subversive ideas.[37]

In the eyes of the UKA, how could one remain a patriotic American in the face of federal desegregation mandates? Certainly not by accepting—even grudgingly—integration policies. Doing so would implicitly acknowledge that segregation might be at odds with "American" values. And not by viewing civil rights pressures as engineered by civil rights movement leaders themselves, as that would require African Americans to possess the strategic ingenuity to win such substantial concessions. Instead, resonant klan narratives asserted that authentic white Americans opposed racial integration as part of a broader fight, against the machinations of devious "outsiders" at the root of civil rights activism.

Most often, this threat came from "communists" and "Jews." UKA state officer Bob Kornegay, who would later serve as Virginia's Grand Dragon, announced in 1965 that his fellow klansmen "don't hate the niggers, but we are afraid of Communists. Once you pull them away, the niggers will go back to being colored people." Speakers repeated this sentiment ad nauseam at rallies. Syble Jones encouraged klan parents to teach their sons and daughters to "fight Communistic activities" and "influence other teenagers against the evils of the Communist Doctrine." Police agents observing dozens of North Carolina rallies described the "run of the mill speech" of Imperial Kludd George Dorsett—probably the UKA's most popular regular speaker—as his "usual sermon on the Communist Party infiltrating the churches, schools and the Government." Similarly, state officer E. J. "Junior" Melvin confidently informed rally crowds that "the Communists are behind the race-mixing and agitation—this is confirmed by J. Edgar Hoover."[38]

Melvin's invocation of the longtime FBI director was telling, as the UKA worked to align itself, as Georgia Grand Dragon Calvin Craig put it, with the broader "right-wing political community." One onlooker at an early UKA rally recalled Bob Jones in quiet conversation after the large crowd had dissipated. "I can just feel it," Jones proclaimed, tracing a line in the dirt with a stick. "The country's turning conservative." Mainstream conservatives, of course, found the notion of solidarity with the KKK implausible and, in most cases, offensive. But by making explicit the common ground shared by the UKA and the FBI on the issue of anti-communism, Jones and other klan leaders sought to demonstrate the UKA's patriotic bona fides. Unlike liberals and moderates willing to capitulate on—or worse, support—civil rights issues, conservatives had the conviction to demonstrate that they were not "white niggers."

More generally, invoking conservatism tied the klan's struggle to the founding fathers' efforts to preserve constitutional freedoms. "I've been called a bigot, a demagogue, a racist, and every other name in the book, but that's all right with me," Jones told a reporter in 1965. "They said the same things about Patrick Henry, John Hancock, Ben Franklin, and Governor George Wallace, so I figure I'm in good company." Arguing that even those mainstream Americans who didn't agree with the UKA's views on segregation could not dispute the group's patriotic core, Shelton averred that "I love this country and every principle it was founded upon, and I am doing what I feel to be right in my heart to preserve the idealistic principles of our founding fathers." Similarly, the UKA's founding documents pledged to uphold and defend the American flag "with sacred honor," declaring the organization's purpose "to teach patriotism, to support the Constitution and Laws of the United States,... to maintain the liberty bequeathed to us by our forefathers, and to preserve the American way of life."[39]

These patriotic themes intersected with the UKA's emphasis on preserving the nation's Christian traditions. Each klavern hall prominently displayed a klan altar, generally a table outfitted with nationalistic and religious symbols: bayonet and Bible, US and Confederate flags, sometimes a lighted cross. Posted nearby, usually, was Jones's personal klan motto: "Fight for the right, die if we must, but always remember, in God we trust." When the UKA newspaper the *Fiery Cross* ran a feature on North Carolina rallies, it described the thousands who would gather "to hear the truth about the communistic conspiracy existing in our country today and to hear the true gospel of Jesus Christ our Saviour," and concluded that "Klansmen in North Carolina as Klansmen everywhere believe in the tenets of the Christian religion." George Dorsett would solemnly describe the klan's burning cross as "spreading the light of Jesus," and a popular record sold at most rallies featured Jones reciting the values motivating the UKA's cross-burnings:

> Out of the wonderful story of the sacred pages of this old book divine, comes the Sad Sweet Story of Calvary's rugged Holy Cross. This old Cross is a symbol of sacrifice and service, and a sign of the Christian Religion sanctified and made holy nearly 19 centuries ago, by the suffering and blood of 50 million martyrs who died in the most holy faith. It stands in every klavern in the UKA as a constant reminder that Christ is our criterion of character, his teachings our rule of life,

> blood-bought and holy, sanctified and sublime.... As light drives away darkness and gloom, so a knowledge of Truth dispels Ignorance and Superstition. As fire purifies gold, silver and precious stones but destroys the dross, wood, hay and stubble, so by the fire of the Cross we mean to purify and cleanse our virtues by the fire on His Sword. Who can look upon this sublime symbol, or sit in its Most Holy Light without being inspired with a desire and a determination to be a better man. By this sign we shall conquer.[40]

Such pronouncements were notably distinct from those of mainstream church leaders across the South, who largely avoided unified biblical defenses of segregation. The reticence of church officials stemmed not necessarily from personal moral ambivalence—many ministers, like a clear majority of white southerners generally, preferred segregation—but from a pervasive sense that engaging in "political," and therefore secular, racial issues threatened their professional legitimacy. Finding no strong defense of segregation in the Bible, most prominent conservative white southern clergy chose to view civil rights as beyond their purview.[41]

This separation of politics and religion sharply contrasted with the unified vision offered by klan "kludds" or chaplains. The identity appeal of klan ideology relied on rejecting segregation as a secular policy; within the klan worldview, whiteness and Christianity were inextricably linked. Supporting the ordained basis for the UKA's white supremacism, one of the group's many pious flyers echoed Jones's soliloquy, noting that, at root, "Christ is a Klansman's criterion of character." A Fayetteville klavern sent letters to local preachers that cited a number of specific passages as evidence that "the Bible preaches segregation." Other members referred to the "seven places" in the Bible that called for racial separation. George Dorsett made the point more precisely:

> The Scripture tells us that God is not the author of confusion. He himself through Divine Process made the white species separate from the black, and mankind is trying to force them together and confuse the various characteristics and skin color. In Acts 17:26, in Daniel chapter seven, and Revelation 11:15 and 21:24, all nations are to remain segregated in their own part of the earth. God forbade intermarriage between Israel and all other nations in Exodus 34:12 and Deuteronomy 7:3. The mixing of races caused disunity among God's people, as we learn from Numbers 11.[42]

Through such invocations, the klan constructed a view of America as the rightful home of white Anglo-Saxon Protestants. Within this religious-patriotic framework, Jews possessed a uniquely perilous role. Framed as quasi-racial, they were denied on biological grounds the capacity for authentic whiteness. Also, Jews' failure to accept Christian principles because of a presumed adherence to Zionism precluded their loyalty to America generally. Unlike African Americans—often viewed as benign in their "natural" state as "colored people," lacking the intelligence and ingenuity to pose a real threat to American values—Jews were akin to communists, suspected of working from within to destroy the nation. In many cases, Jews and communists became interchangeable terms. As Evelyn Rich notes, in the klan worldview, Jews' distinct biology "was expressed most clearly through their political ideology."

Klan leaders thus framed Jews as the embodiment of the "nigger" ideal, both biologically tainted and politically subversive. As a result, they occupied the core of the conspiracy that threatened to bring down America. An early issue of the *Fiery Cross*, from November 1961, included the banner headline: "Ku Klux Klan Declares WAR! Against Negro-Jew Communism." Six years later, Lloyd Jacobs echoed the sentiments of nearly all UKA rally speakers when he claimed that "the NAACP was operated by Jews, and . . . the niggers and Jews were behind the Communist conspiracy to do away with the white race." Robert Shelton, both in his written correspondence and public speeches, routinely referenced the "Jewish NAACP" and the fact that "many Jews have been found in the Communist conspiracy." Klan observer Pete Young succinctly summarized how Jews served as the central villain in the UKA's conspiratorial worldview:

> It is no accident when worlds collapse. Somebody has planned it just that way. That "somebody" is not the Negro who, by definition, is an incapable inferior. The somebody behind it all is the Jew, who manipulates the Negro. The Klan thus hitches a ride on the old tradition of Southern Populism which, at the turn of the century, saw its Wall Street enemy in Jewish terms; the Klan then adds the contradictory figure of the Jew as Communist agitator.[43]

This paranoid emphasis on the "nigger"/Jew/communist trinity aided UKA recruitment in two ways. First, it provided unusual flexibility. Klan adherents could frame almost any local or global grievance as engineered by "nigger" interests and, by extension, as an integral component of the subversive communist agenda. When Governor Dan Moore, whom the UKA endorsed in

1964, pledged that the state would abide by the Civil Rights Act, Bob Jones and others began referring to him as a "white nigger" who had betrayed the nation's constitutional principles. They also likewise dismissed reporters critical of the UKA as working for "nigger newspapers" that purposely distorted the "truth" spoken at rallies.

The taint of Communist infection applied gratuitously to anyone not properly aligned with the klan's views. In a single 1967 rally speech, Charlotte-based UKA officer Joe Bryant proclaimed that the federal and state governments were communist and controlled by Jews, that the Anti-Defamation League was a communist organization run at different times by Hubert Humphrey and Bobby Kennedy, that North Carolina's involvement in the liquor business "makes money for the crooked politicians, and further is Communism and a violation of free enterprise," that R. J. Reynolds purchased most of their tobacco from communist Yugoslavia and sponsored a trip for the local school superintendent to study communism in Russia, and that the communist Russian government was itself controlled by Jews. At the same rally, another speaker offered a novel interpretation of the Vietnam conflict, calling it a communist conspiracy to skew the gender ratio in America, resulting in white women getting "so hard up that they would marry and have intercourse with niggers."[44]

The veracity of such claims, of course, was not the point. The klan's paranoid style sought to identify threats to white supremacy and attribute them to a broader conspiratorial system. Despite the strong emphasis on the communist-Jew threat in UKA ideology, its function was mostly intellectual scaffolding, tempering and justifying the hard-line racist ideology that resonated with those whose social standing was threatened by civil rights legislation. This interplay was clear at UKA rallies—while leaders frequently, over the course of individual speeches that often ran a half-hour or more, took great pains to develop elaborate arguments about the overarching conspiracy that lay behind civil rights demands, the largest applause always followed punch lines that squarely targeted African Americans themselves. As Bob Jones well knew, while Shelton and other klan ideologists favored reasoned anti-Semitic and anti-communist tracts, at rallies the "nigger joke" provided the most bang for the UKA's buck.[45]

Even so, such bald racism, on its own terms, did little to promote solidarity with the UKA's mission. The second and most important function of the UKA's paranoid style was as the basis for a coherent racial identity, centered on a vision of purity stemming both from biological status and fealty to segregationist values. By situating klan racism within a broader conspiracist system, UKA recruiters offered a framework explaining why powerful forces

U.S. Klans leader Eldon Edwards speaking at a rally in the 1950s. Several of the group's state leaders stand behind him on the stage, including Alabama's Robert Shelton, second from right. Shelton broke from U.S. Klans in the late 1950s, and became Imperial Wizard of the incipient United Klans of America in 1961. (Image courtesy of the Manuscript, Archives, and Rare Book Library at Emory University.)

U.S. Klan members gathered in full robes at leader Eldon Edwards's funeral. Edwards died unexpectedly from a heart attack in 1960 at the age of fifty-one. Georgia Grand Dragon Calvin Craig helped move the bulk of the U.S. Klans membership to a new organization, the United Klans of America (UKA), soon after. (Image courtesy of the Manuscript, Archives, and Rare Book Library at Emory University.)

James “Catfish” Cole, the North Carolina–based Ku Klux Klan (KKK) leader who gained national infamy after Lumbee Indians routed his group’s 1958 rally in Maxton. His resurfacing in United Klans of America (UKA) circles in 1966 caused considerable controversy within the UKA. Prior to his klan notoriety, Cole worked the South’s evangelistic revival circuit. (Image from the James William Cole Papers [#40], East Carolina Manuscript Collection, J. Y. Joyner Library, East Carolina University, Greenville, North Carolina, USA.)

UNITED KLANS
OF AMERICA, INC.
Will Present a Program
SAT. JUNE 26
8:00 P. M.
U.S. Hwy. 64 West at APEX, N. C.
STREET WALKING IN RALEIGH at 4:30
COME HEAR THE TRUTH
THE WHITE PUBLIC ONLY!
The Grand Dragon of North Carolina and
Other Good Speakers
AUTHORIZED BY THE BOARD OF DIRECTORS THE UNITED KLANS OF AMERICA, INC.
National Office: Suite 401 Alston Bldg. Tuscaloosa, Alabama
N. C. Office: Box 321 Granite Quarry, N. C.

The United Klans of America (UKA) printed up to 2,000 of these flyers to advertise each rally. Members passed them out to likely candidates at service stations, cafes, and other meeting spaces. The standardized flyer format always noted that attendance would be restricted to “the white public only.” (Image courtesy of the National Archives and Records Administration.)

L'ENVOI
To the lovers of Law and Order, Peace and Justice we send greeting; and to the shades of the valiant, venerated Dead we gratefully and affectionately dedicate the Knights of the Ku Klux Klan AMEN!

IMPERIAL PALACE, INVISIBLE EMPIRE

United Klans Knights of the Ku Klux Klan of America, Inc.

To All Who Read and Respect These Lines, Greeting:

WHEREAS, The Imperial Wizard has received a petition [illegible] CRAVEN COUNTY IMPROVEMENT ASSOC. Praying for themselves and others and their successors to be instituted [illegible] number of NEW BERN [illegible] NORTH CAROLINA, and same to be located at NEW BERN, in [illegible] State of NORTH CAROLINA, United States of America, and they having given assurance of their fidelity to [illegible] and their ready willingness to take upon themselves and their successors the duties and responsibilities thereof, and their serious [illegible] privileges and prerogatives conferred on them as such, and be faithful and true in all things committed to them;

NOW KNOW YE, that I, the Imperial Wizard of the Knights of the Ku Klux Klan, on this the FOURTH day of the SIXTH Month of the Year of Our Lord Nineteen Hundred and SIXTY FOUR and on the WONDERFUL day of the DREADFUL week of the HIDIOUS Month of the Year of the Klan [illegible] Cycle of the Seventh Reign of our Reincarnation, under the authority possessed by me, do issue this

Charter

HONOR

to the aforesaid petitioners, their associates and successors, under the name and number aforesaid from the day and date hereon, and same is effective from the date of its acceptance by said Klan as certified below.

THE SAID KLAN is hereby authorized and empowered to do and to perform all such acts and things as are prescribed by the Kloran, Laws, Imperial Decrees, Edicts, Mandates and Usages of the Order, and to enjoy all the rights, privileges and prerogatives authorized by the Constitution thereof; and all Klansmen are strictly enjoined to valiantly preserve and persistently practice the principles of pure patriotism, Honor, Klannishness and White Supremacy, ever keeping in mind and heart the sacred sentiment, peculiar purpose, manly mission and lofty ideals and objects of this Order, a devoted loyalty to their Emperor and their Imperial Wizard, a steadfast obedience to the Constitution of this Order, a faithful keeping of their Oath of Allegiance, and a constant, unwavering fidelity to every interest of the Invisible Empire, to the end that progress, power, purpose and influence of KLANKRAFT be properly promoted, the knowledge of the faithful, self-sacrificing service and noble achievements of our fathers be not lost to posterity, and all those things for which this our beloved Order is founded to do and to perform, and to protect, and to preserve and to perpetuate, be diligently done and scrupulously maintained, and that they be blameless in preserving the grace, dignity and intent of this CHARTER forever.

I SOLEMNLY CHARGE YOU to hold fast to the dauntless faith of our fathers and to keep their spotless memory secure and unstained, and true to the traditions of our valiant sires, meet every behest of duty, in all the relationships of life and living, promptly and properly, without fault, without fail, without fear and without reproach.

THE IMPERIAL WIZARD has and holds the full and unchallengeable authority, right and power to cancel, to suspend or revoke this CHARTER and to annul all the rights, powers, prerogatives and immunities conferred hereby, for the neglect or refusal on the part of the said Klan to conform to and comply with the Kloran, Constitution and Laws of this Order and the Imperial Decrees, Edicts, Mandates, Rulings and Instructions thereof, or its failure to respect the Usages of this Order, as proclaimed by and maintained under the Imperial Authority of same.

IN TESTIMONY WHEREOF, I, the Imperial Wizard of the Knights of the Ku Klux Klan, have caused to be affixed hereon the Great Imperial Seal of the Invisible Empire and do hereunto set my hand and impress my official seal, and same is duly attested,—"NON SILBA SED ANTHAR."

Done in the executive chambers of his Lordship, the Imperial Wizard, in the Imperial Palace in the Imperial City of Atlanta, Commonwealth of Georgia, United States of America, on the day and date above written.

CERTIFICATE OF ACCEPTANCE

THIS CERTIFIES that above CHARTER was read to and duly adopted by above named Klan in session assembled with all stipulations and conditions herein stated or implied on the 4 day of June A. D., 1964 A. K. 99 Signed [signature] EXALTED CYCLOPS of the above named Klan and in behalf of all present and future members thereof.

Witness [signature: James R Jones] Grand Dragon of Realm

BY HIS LORDSHIP [signature]
Imperial Wizard, of the Invisible Empire, United Klans, Knights of the Ku Klux Klan of America, Inc.

ATTEST: [signature]
Imperial Kligrapp

The United Klans of America (UKA) adopted the trappings of a bureaucratic organization. Bob Jones distributed business cards that announced him as Grand Dragon. Each local klavern received a charter from the Imperial Office in Tuscaloosa, Alabama. Note that the Exalted Cyclops of the unit chartered here was Raymond Millis, who perpetrated the 1964 bombings of a local church and funeral home in New Bern, North Carolina. Jones banished him from the UKA after he pled guilty to the crimes. (Image courtesy of the National Archives and Records Administration.)

North Carolina Grand Dragon Bob Jones en route to a rally in his "Dragon Wagon." Nicknamed "Horse" for his tireless organizing efforts, Jones claimed that he drove up to 100,000 miles per year and was a featured speaker at virtually all of the Carolina Klan's nightly rallies. (Image courtesy of Charles Moore, Black Star.)

United Klans of America (UKA) Imperial Wizard Robert Shelton, in jacket and tie, stands with a member of the Security Guard, Bob Jones, and Imperial Nighthawk Boyd Hamby outside a rally in Durham. Observers often noted that Hamby was "half Indian," and also that he was a crack shot. Shelton sent him, along with George Dorsett, to Florida in 1966 in an ill-fated effort to organize the Sunshine State. (Image copyright 1976 Art Rogers/Take Stock/The Image Works.)

An aerial view of a 1965 United Klans of America (UKA) rally in Morganton, North Carolina. (Image courtesy of Don Sturkey.)

Members of the Ladies Auxiliary Units of the United Klans of America (UKA) at a 1965 rally. Women members assisted with many aspects of the UKA's work, including circulating through rally crowds with donation buckets. George Dorsett, in full Imperial Kludd regalia, is at the podium. (Image courtesy of Don Sturkey.)

Bob Jones, sharing a light moment with members of the Security Guard prior to a March 1967 street walk in Pineville, North Carolina. George Dorsett, in helmet and sunglasses, stands immediately to Jones's right. Three days later, Dorsett swore Catfish Cole into the United Klans of America (UKA) without Jones's knowledge, which led to his banishment the following month. Dorsett also informed for the Federal Bureau of Investigation (FBI), and later formed rival klan organization the Confederate Knights with Bureau support. (Image courtesy of Don Sturkey.)

The climax of a 1964 United Klans of America (UKA) rally in Salisbury, North Carolina. Carolina Klan rallies featured the burning of crosses up to seventy feet tall. (Image courtesy of Don Sturkey.)

A United Klans of America (UKA) billboard in eastern North Carolina, welcoming visitors to the "Heart of Klan Country." Local klaverns erected dozens of these signs around the state and paid Tommy Neil, a member from Lillington, $10 to paint the text and graphics. (Image courtesy of Don Sturkey.)

President Lyndon Johnson announcing the capture of United Klans of America (UKA) members suspected of murdering civil rights worker Viola Liuzzo during the 1965 Selma-to-Montgomery march in Alabama. Johnson's speech warned klansmen to "get out of the Ku Klux Klan now and return to a decent society before it is too late." The Federal Bureau of Investigation (FBI) quickly solved the crime, as one of its informants, Gary Thomas Rowe, participated in the plot. FBI Director J. Edgar Hoover (left) and Attorney General Nicholas Katzenbach (right) flank the president. (LBJ Library photo by Yoichi Okamoto.)

United Klans of America (UKA) members stapling their membership cards to a cross burned at a rally in September 1969. At the rally, an estimated half of the UKA's dwindling membership left the organization for Joe Bryant's North Carolina Knights. With Jones and Shelton in prison on contempt of Congress charges, the group never recovered. (Image courtesy of Don Sturkey.)

lodged in Washington, DC, aligned against conservative white southerners. If "white niggers" engineered integrationist efforts, a clear boundary emerged between hypocritical, morally bankrupt "others" and authentically "real" Americans. The UKA, as the main organization in North Carolina willing to champion that boundary at all costs, parlayed its own racial ideology to build solidarity around a clear recognition of how and why klan adherents differed from "outsiders."[46]

As a bounded category, "whiteness" was simultaneously inclusive and exclusive. In theory, the category encompassed any Caucasian persons—rich or poor, urban or rural, from the South or North. But inclusion also required a pronounced cultural commitment to white supremacy. Invoking this exclusive criterion, the UKA related racial anxieties over civil rights legislation to broadly shared values tied to God and country.[47] Just as personal connections to economically vulnerable white workers could draw even those insulated from workplace competition into the klan's orbit, the UKA's racial identity work generalized conceptions of racial threat by clearly underlining the relationship between segregation and moral and patriotic authenticity. By enhancing the salience of racial categories and raising the stakes of the civil rights struggle, the UKA worldview sought—with mixed and ephemeral success—to create a pervasive sense that integration would affect all white North Carolinians, not only those who stood to compete with newly empowered African Americans for jobs and other resources.

Paths to Participation

The key puzzle associated with UKA participation centers on an apparent contradiction: though the klan tended to organize successfully in places marked by racial competition, individuals themselves in direct competition with African Americans in the workplace were not disproportionately likely to join. Explaining this finding requires attention to both "push" and "pull" factors, related to how competition translated into a sense of racial threat, how related anxieties spread unevenly through white communities, and how the klan framed itself as a vehicle to repair segregationist ills.

Recent research on ethnic competition has recognized this paradoxical phenomenon. Sociologist Jochem Tolsma and his colleagues explain that people exposed to a competitive atmosphere are more likely to exhibit antagonism toward other groups, either because of their own experiences of competition or because of the "competition experiences of other members in their social stratum." The latter antagonisms occur, Tolsma explains, because individuals view others' experiences as signaling potential competition for any member of their mutual group.[48]

Evidence from the Carolina Klan points to the empathetic spread of anti–civil rights sentiment within certain segments of the white community. Widespread labor market competition provided the baseline conditions for a generally antagonistic racial climate. However, not every white resident in those communities was equally likely to connect with UKA recruiting appeals. Klan members' own accounts demonstrate the importance of networks, with family, neighborhood, and civic connections providing social conduits through which shared conceptions of threat spread. For those located within such networks—typically defined by their proximity to embattled kin, friends, and work colleagues—freedom from sanctions lowered the costs and risks of UKA membership, which helps to explain the clustering of members within particular sympathetic workplaces and also the disproportionate number of small business owners who ultimately joined. The lack of vulnerability to reprisals facilitated organizing in solidarity with their "authentic white" siblings, neighbors, congregants, and classmates.

These salient networks tended to cleave along class lines. Klan membership clustered in working and lower-middle class sectors. Those in higher status professional positions largely rejected klan appeals, even when displaying personal hostility to civil rights reforms, as they necessarily weighed broader reputational concerns against hard-line support for segregation. This interplay of class position and social location helps to explain the degree to which particular individuals felt compelled to actively mobilize in defense of Jim Crow.

At the same time, klan leaders and recruiters sought to "pull" sympathetic individuals to the UKA, by galvanizing racial sentiments and rhetorically positioning the UKA as the solution to the deteriorating color line. Klan leaders accomplished this, most generally, by offering the KKK as a medium for enacting authentic whiteness, apart from the state's racially compromised political and economic elites. This racial-cultural worldview was reinforced and deepened by the UKA's many rituals and collective practices, which in turn served to align adherents' identities with the klan's collective vision.

This identity work—predicated on integrating racial, patriotic, and religious themes under the broad umbrella of "authentic whiteness"—was effective, but also delicate. The long history of interracial organizing within the state—from Fusionists in the 1890s to unionized food and tobacco workers in the Piedmont during the 1940s—signaled that white workers' fidelity to white supremacy and hostility toward federal intervention was not always fixed and preordained. Indeed, durable class divisions within the white population challenged UKA-style conceptions of a monolithic white culture. Fissures in the racial order also created cross-pressures that competed with local experiences of racial "authenticity." Even Raymond Cranford, a successful tobacco planter and by many accounts North Carolina's most militant klansman, entrusted one of his black employees to oversee his farming operation, causing more than one observer to note that his farm contained more integration than did any of the communities that he policed with the klan. While Cranford's rabid devotion to the KKK enabled him to manage the cognitive dissonance required to continue his klan work, one imagines that in many other cases such practices would divide many whites from the UKA.[49]

Even when the absolutes of klan ideology resonated with adherents, the burdens of authenticity could undo the relationship. Joseph DuBois, a used car salesman from Wayne County, resigned from his klavern after his klan superiors ordered him to refuse to provide requested information to government investigators. Anyone who was true to his or her country should have "nothing to hide," DuBois reasoned, a conclusion that motivated his exit due to an irreconcilable sense that the UKA's mission was at odds with his loyalties to God and nation. Similarly, Roy Woodle, a well-known kludd, broke with the UKA after accusing Jones and other state leaders of betraying the group's supposed Christian foundation. "I had enough," he explained, his voice dripping with sarcasm, "of that great religious organization."[50]

These paths toward and away from klan participation reveal the complex interplay between individual choice and social setting. Where the UKA's identity appeals succeeded, its worldview flourished within and relied upon social spaces that fostered and reproduced racial grievances. At the same time, however, attachments to friends, family members, churches, jobs, and so on could also limit participation in the UKA, by restricting the time, energy, and other resources that individuals could devote to the UKA.[51]

To fully understand how these varied effects operated requires a shift in perspective, to focus on how particular aspects of surrounding communities helped or hindered UKA recruitment. Raymond Cranford was fond of calling his native Greene County "Klansville, U.S.A.," and reporters sometimes referred to Rowan County—Bob Jones's home base—as "Klansville, N.C."[52] While intended mostly as rhetorical flourishes, such labels identified certain communities and counties as klan hotbeds, alongside seemingly similar places that resisted the UKA's appeals. To explain why, the next chapter focuses on the UKA's divergent fortunes in Greenville, Greensboro, and Charlotte, to show how the makeup of each community shaped receptivity to klan organizing campaigns.

6 LOCATING "KLANSVILLE, U.S.A."

Blacks were out of it and didn't even think about it in the east. They were out of it and they knew they were out of it in Greensboro. There's a difference.

—NELL COLEY, Dudley High School English teacher and Greensboro NAACP member.[1]

[Charlotte] responded well. And this is encouraging. Have they begun to realize finally that the money is rolling in because of the end of racial segregation? Perhaps. Some of us told them that ten years ago, that it is *they* who will pick up all the marbles, who will win the racial revolution.

—HARRY GOLDEN, Charlotte-based writer and raconteur.[2]

These differences in emphases could have come as a surprise only to those who conceived of the South as a homogeneous region, united in intransigent resistance to any change in the traditional pattern of segregation of the Negro.

— SOCIOLOGIST MELVIN M. TUMIN, commenting in 1958 about the pronounced variation across southern states and communities in reaction to the *Brown* decision.[3]

"Each community is unique," Bill Johnson wrote to Capus Waynick in the summer of 1963. "They differ economically, culturally, in the ratio of white to Negro citizens, in attitudes that have developed with regard to the racial problem." As a researcher focused on race relations on Governor Terry Sanford's staff, Johnson was offering his best take on the state's civil rights climate for Waynick, the governor's unofficial racial troubleshooter. He concluded with a more general assessment: "I feel that it would be extremely difficult, if not impossible, to establish a rigid program in this [civil rights] area that would be applicable to even a majority of the cities and towns in North Carolina."

Indeed, while retrospective accounts of the civil rights struggle have frequently flattened its contours, on-the-ground observers often emphasized the distinct experiences of local communities. Perhaps the starkest differences existed between the Piedmont and the more rural counties to the east. As SNCC worker Eric Morton observed, "North Carolina's liberal image comes from wide publicity given to events in the large cities of the Piedmont section of the middle third of the state where demonstrations brought about some desegregation and little violence." The region furthest from this model, Morton noted, was the "Black Belt" covering much of the state's eastern coastal plain.[4]

In rural eastern counties, desegregation posed the greatest threat to the economic and political status quo. Whites in the workforce benefited from exclusive access to most of the rising number of desirable industrial jobs. This closed labor market ensured that many black workers remained on farms, maintaining a ready tenant labor force for white landowners. As the majority of North Carolina's African Americans resided in the east—representing more than a third of the region's overall population, and a numeric majority in several northeast counties—white political hegemony required widespread black disenfranchisement. Socially, the intricacies of Jim Crow traditions separated whites, and white women in particular, from their black "neighbors" in both public and private spaces.

To a degree greater than anywhere else in the South, the Ku Klux Klan policed this racial boundary. North Carolina's eastern counties were the UKA's stronghold. Mark their klaverns on a map, George Dorsett quipped, and it looked like the area had the measles. A sweeping congressional inquiry found that ninety-five of the UKA's North Carolina units—nearly 60 percent of the state's overall total—were located there, though the region housed only a third of the state's residents. On a per-capita basis, these units were nearly three times as common as in the Piedmont and over six times more prevalent than in the western mountains.[5]

The klan's presence was most pronounced in the east's economic and social hubs. In the heart of the nation's premiere tobacco-growing region, the many tobacco warehouses where farmers and other rural residents gathered in small cities like Kinston, Wilson, and Greenville served as the backdrop for the most significant klan mobilization in postwar America. Near the center of this regional hotbed was Pitt County, the state's largest agricultural producer and self-proclaimed "King of Tobaccoland." Greenville was the Pitt County seat and the county's only nonrural community. Nineteen tobacco warehouses, with two and a half million feet of collective floor space, were located within the city limits. In 1960, local growers sold nearly 62 million pounds of flue-cured tobacco at auction, grossing nearly $37 million dollars.[6]

In Pitt, a county with fewer than 70,000 residents overall, the UKA organized seven klaverns and a Ladies Auxiliary Unit. In many rural areas, the UKA's presence was astounding. In Grimesland, total population 362, klavern meetings could attract fifty members. The Greenville unit, chartered in late

1964 under the cover name "The Benevolent Association," stood at the center of the klan's local efforts. Membership estimates varied—federal investigators found 340 members on the books in late 1965, though informants reported that at any given time the total was closer to 150—but by all accounts the unit was exceptionally large. Klavern officers included a salesman, mill foreman, two textile workers, service station owner, flooring laborer, glazier, and tobacco picker. Klavern meeting attendance fell during the tobacco harvesting season, as many among the unit's rank-and-file were farmers.[7]

The klavern was also unusually active. Rushed late-night phone calls resulted in five carloads of its members traveling to Plymouth at the height of that city's racial strife in the summer of 1965, and the klavern organized a boycott of Sunbeam Bread after the company fired two local klansmen because of their UKA affiliations. Throughout 1965 and 1966, the unit also hosted at least ten rallies. Several of those attracted crowds in the thousands, with 6,000 showing up for a June 1965 rally in nearby Kinston. The previous month, a Pitt County cornfield hosted a UKA wedding, presided over by Imperial Kludd George Dorsett. More than 5,000 gathered for the rally and nuptials, the bride in a light-blue gown with hooped skirt and the groom in full klan robes and hood. "It was the proper place for it," they explained to reporters. "We believe in the klan."

For George Williams, a former Greenville klavern member who left the UKA shortly after being injured during the unrest in Plymouth, the unit's predilection for cross-burnings and beatings intended to prevent perceived racial transgressions overshadowed such celebrations. "A lot of nights you would see seven to eight members go into the back room," Williams explained, "and later that night or the next day you would hear of a cross burning or other trouble." Williams himself had been part of that elite group at times, taking part in plots to beat a disabled white teen for associating with African Americans (according to Williams, the group ultimately decided to "scare" and "warn" the youth rather than physically assault him), and to whip a local woman who allegedly cavorted with black men in nearby Greene County.[8]

Greenville klan members also had a complicated relationship with the police. While other Pitt County klaverns infiltrated local police forces—police chiefs in both Fountain and Grimesland reportedly were klansmen—Greenville Police Chief Henry F. Lawson at times took a strong anti-klan approach. An Atlanta native who served in the Pacific theater in World War II, Lawson was appointed police chief in March 1965 following a sixteen-year stint on the Greenville force. He emphasized public relations and expressed an unusual desire for "both white and colored . . . to become better acquainted with us and to understand the obligation of the police department to enforce the law without letting 'color get into their eyes.' "

A former detective, Lawson soon employed a member of his force as a klan informant. That practice created some controversy within the klavern; three klansmen were suspended in July 1965 for allegedly funneling details about UKA matters to the police. By that time, the Greenville force was familiar enough with local klan activities to distinguish between klan initiatives—such as an incident in October 1965 when members attached signs reading "Nigger City Limits" on each of the highway signs marking the city's boundaries—from unaffiliated racial incidents. When Robert Joe Carney reported that he was fired upon by three or four men with air rifles, investigating officers determined conclusively that the incident was "Not Klan."[9]

The following year, Pactolus klavern leader Harry Ferguson threatened to sue Lawson after the police chief criticized him publicly during a speech to the local Good Neighbor Council. Lawson also arrested two klansmen for demonstrating without a permit after they drove through Greenville's downtown in a car outfitted with posters proclaiming "Be a Man, Join the Klan." A confrontation ensued, during which Lawson allegedly challenged one of the klan members to an armed standoff, earning him a court hearing for violating the state's 1802 anti-duel law.[10]

At times, the various Pitt County klaverns coordinated their actions, as when they collectively placed a full page "We, the United Klan of America, Inc., Believe" ad in Greenville's newspaper, the *Daily Reflector*. But in other instances, klavern relations weathered serious rifts. In response to the election of a polarizing former Greenville constable as Exalted Cyclops (EC) of the Greenville unit, a group of militants from more rural, neighboring Pactolus broke away and formed their own klavern. Tensions escalated after a Greenville klansman made disparaging remarks about his Pactolus colleagues, which led to an attempted retaliatory assault and eventually a shootout between members of the battling klaverns. After protracted negotiations, including a direct intervention by Grand Dragon Jones, the parties agreed to drop the police charges they each had filed at the height of the conflict.[11]

Distinctive tactics and internal disputes aside, the goals of the UKA often aligned with those of other elements in the community. When a number of black families removed their names from a 1964 petition to desegregate the county's schools, widespread accusations of intimidation followed. F. G. Norcott, the head of the Pitt chapter of the NAACP, explained that several signatories withdrew because of pervasive threats. Landlords told petitioners that they would be "put out" of their tenancies, which meant a loss of work as well as shelter. Many in the black community believed such acts to be a coordinated policy, planned during a meeting of the county's influential white citizens, including members of the all-white board of education.

Conservative associations, many of which overlapped with the UKA, also thrived in larger towns throughout eastern North Carolina. During his time away from the KKK, Catfish Cole was active in organizing some of these groups, such as the Committee for Better Government, in nearby Kinston. Another related effort produced a petition signed by hundreds of citizens from Pitt and surrounding counties attacking the Civil Rights Act and encouraging Governor Moore to "offer his support to Governor George C. Wallace and all other governors who are struggling to maintain the sovereignty of their States."[12]

A virtual perfect storm of racial competition fueled both the UKA and the broader culture of fervent segregationism. With a high percentage of black residents in the county, maintaining white supremacy required the strict enforcement of Jim Crow to suppress African Americans' social, economic, and political power. By the 1960s, the latent threat posed by African Americans had intensified not only because of fissures in the racial status quo exposed by civil rights action, but also due to changes in the area's economy across the middle decades of the century. A long-standing agricultural powerhouse, Pitt generated the largest farm income of any county in the state. As late as 1960, municipal boosters could with a straight face trumpet that "a family in Pitt County which is not deeply and personally concerned about farming is almost a rarity, for farming is really a big business in the county." Traditionally, the bulk of the black labor force worked on white-owned farmland, and by 1964, 86 percent of black farmers still toiled as tenants on others' land. More desirable industrial jobs were in effect reserved for whites.

But this way of life, and its attendant racial demarcations, was cracking. Due in large part to the mechanization of many agricultural tasks, the county's rural farm population fell by 30 percent in the 1950s. New industry recruited to the region took up some of the resulting economic slack, but by 1960, Pitt County's male unemployment rate was double the rate in much of the more urbanized Piedmont. This large surplus labor force, coupled with the related reduction in opportunities available to black agricultural laborers, meant that the removal of Jim Crow controls created an intense threat to the racial status quo in the county's workforce.[13]

In the mid-1960s, policies that disadvantaged the county's black citizens continued to mitigate this threat. Local officials regularly touted the city's "big hopes" to attract more industry and service work to Pitt County.

Beginning in 1959, the Pitt County Development Commission encouraged and supported these efforts through outreach to more than 3,000 American manufacturing firms, yielding $14 million in industrial expansion in the early 1960s. DuPont's Dacron Plant, which opened in 1953 in neighboring Lenoir County, employed 800 Pitt County residents by 1962. The *Daily Reflector* noted that the skilled jobs associated with this new industry had all "drawn on the same general labor reservoir," a delicate reference to the fact that they were, by design, filled by white workers.

The training of whites for such work was supported institutionally. The Pitt County Industrial Education Center (IEC) opened its doors in 1964, enrolling 500 county residents that fall. While the Center's available courses in areas such as welding, power sewing, blueprint reading, electrical code and theory, and internal combustion maintenance matched the skills in demand with area employers, many of these classes in fact enrolled only white workers. Across the state, more than 90 percent of participants in IECs were white, and most centers in eastern North Carolina included no African Americans at all. While segregation was not an official policy, Pitt's IEC refused to accept applicants if they could not produce "assurance of employment" related to the training they were to receive. As most skilled industrial positions had traditionally been held only by whites, this policy placed African American workers in an impossible position: employers had no incentive to open jobs to black workers who lacked suitable training, and public training institutions refused to provide opportunities for such training unless applicants had procured advance promise of employment. This "catch-22" was supported by the State Department of Public Instruction, which advised that training courses should be offered to those "for whom specific job opportunities are available," a policy widely interpreted as excluding African Americans from competing for desirable "white" jobs.[14]

This differential access to training exacerbated the educational inequities endemic to segregated schooling. While segregationist claims of "separate but equal" were fictions everywhere, African Americans fared particularly badly in eastern North Carolina schools. Black adults in the region had completed, on average, only six and a half years of schooling, compared to 7.1 and 7.6 years in the Piedmont and mountains, respectively. In Pitt County, African Americans averaged only 5.7 years of education. Fewer than 5 percent attended college even for a semester, while more than double that proportion reported no formal primary schooling at all.

Beginning in the early 1960s, public high school curricula increasingly reflected the county's diversifying economy. School administrators repeatedly expressed the need to add industrial arts and other vocational offerings to reflect graduates' steady shift from farm to industry. But as with IECs, the quality and types of offerings reflected and reproduced the traditional racial makeup of particular occupational sectors. As local schools employed "freedom of choice" districting plans that maintained only token desegregation for much of the decade, black students continued to find it difficult to receive training that would qualify them for skilled industrial jobs.[15]

Given such limits on black educational opportunity, the relatively poor performance of white students in the eastern region was one of the few factors that attenuated the severity of racial inequity. On average, white adults in Pitt and surrounding counties had significantly less schooling than in the Piedmont. Correspondingly, East Carolina College, the largest postsecondary school in the region and a de facto white institution throughout the 1960s, served a much lower proportion of its local constituents than other schools in the state's university system. While more than half of the students at the University of North Carolina's regional campuses in Greensboro and Charlotte were local, only a fifth of students enrolled at ECC came from Pitt or adjacent counties.[16]

Another attenuating factor was the strong performance of students attending C. M. Eppes, Greenville's "Negro" high school. In 1963, the state allotted funds to hire A. E. Murrell, a longtime Eppes faculty member, as the city's first "Negro supervisor for city schools." Two years later, 80 percent of Eppes graduates reported that they planned to continue on to college, a proportion higher than in any other school—black or white—in the state. While this achievement was tempered by the fact that a large fraction of black students in Greenville had dropped out before entering high school—in 1964, the Eppes graduating class numbered sixty-five, less than 1 percent of the city's overall black population and just over one-quarter of its black seventeen- and eighteen-year-olds—it nonetheless meant that a visible cadre of African Americans would be prepared to compete for higher skilled positions.[17]

For many white residents, these factors contributed to a sense of intensified racial competition. Growing concerns among white workers and city officials centered less on immediate threats of job loss than on whether they could continue to hold the tenuous institutional advantages that insulated them from direct racial competition. In the months leading up to the passage of the Civil Rights Act, as Governor Sanford and Governor Moore indicated that the state would abide by federal civil rights mandates, it became increasingly clear that traditional racial arrangements were in jeopardy. Such arrangements, of course, enabled white privilege in Pitt County and eastern North Carolina generally. In a region with a significant black population, African Americans would be a political force unless disenfranchised, as 83 percent of Pitt County's African Americans were in 1961.[18] In counties with a tight labor market, only Jim Crow tradition blocked black workers from the training required to hold jobs informally reserved for whites. And unless outright intimidation continued to reinforce these segregationist traditions, black parents would surely move to register their children en masse in newly desegregated schools.

In white communities across eastern North Carolina, these conditions intersected, contributing to feelings of acute racial threat. That sense of threat, in turn, reinforced racial boundaries and spurred action to protect the fidelity of those boundaries. Thus the UKA, not surprisingly, achieved its greatest recruiting successes in this region. Attention to this broad pattern, however, allows only a limited understanding of how competition played out within community settings. As the klan's presence in Greenville and elsewhere centered on public struggles over workplaces, schools, restaurants, and city halls, a closer look at those institutions can lend more precise insight into how the makeup of particular communities shaped the construction of racial threats and, in turn, cemented or inhibited white individuals' connections to the KKK.

The sharpest contrast in community orientations to the klan could be found 200 miles west of Greenville, in the heart of the Carolina Piedmont. Far from a uniform UKA stronghold, the relatively urban industrialized Piedmont region often failed to yield the large rally turnouts and klavern memberships commonplace in the east. Conventional explanations emphasized the klan's predominantly rural roots. Federal government memos frequently commented on the "difficulties" posed by rural areas, boiling down their take to "the larger the city, the greater the [civil rights] compliance." Such urban versus rural distinctions were echoed by Melvin Cording, the mayor of Wallace, a small tobacco-auction town (population 2,285) in the southeastern corner of the state, who strongly criticized North Carolina's anti-klan efforts as ill-suited to rural communities "whose problems differ greatly from those in the cities." To Cording and others, the tight-knit nature of small communities meant that efforts to redistribute opportunities without accounting for "personalities rather than numbers" would spark resentment and further entrench racial divides. "In North Carolina," Cording concluded, "deep-seated tradition continues to suggest that rural will not follow where metropolitan leads."

The UKA, of course, preyed on such small-town resentments. Closer examination, however, reveals a more complicated portrait of the ideal "klansville." In 1965, for instance, federal investigators questioned a State Bureau of Investigation (SBI) report that rally attendees were rural "hill people" after a license plate check showed that many came from Raleigh and other urban centers. More obviously, the considerable variation in the klan's appeal across Piedmont cities belied conventional explanations that the UKA's predominance in the east was due simply to KKK resonance in sparsely populated areas. While racial traditions and relationships were, as Mayor Cording put it, "more intense" in small eastern plain communities, examining divergent racial dynamics in Greensboro and Charlotte—North Carolina's two largest cities in the 1960s—highlights how features of communities beyond their degree of urbanization shaped the klan's successes and failures.[19]

Greensboro and its surrounding Guilford County communities were known as traditional klan hotbeds. Three U.S. Klan units were active in the county through the latter half of the 1950s. Leading Guilford County–based members of that group and Catfish Cole's North Carolina Knights—including George Dorsett, Garland Martin, E. H. Hennis, and Clyde Webster—comprised a significant part of the UKA's state leadership during the 1960s. By 1965, Guilford County was home to eight UKA klaverns. While some of these local units were small, drawing adherents from narrow communities, several had more than fifty members. Rallies held in the county typically attracted crowds of several hundred, and in 1965 the Greensboro unit even chartered its own bus to travel to a state UKA rally in South Carolina.[20]

Many local members aggressively pushed their views in public, and the Greensboro membership base mobilized in response to even minor racial incidents. On an August afternoon in 1966, for instance, George Dorsett berated an integrated group as they were leaving a local restaurant, referring to the white women as "tramps" and their black companions as "niggers." Still incensed about the interracial public display, Dorsett notified several units to gather members at the restaurant that night. At least fifty came out and proceeded to mill about and harass any integrated groups that arrived.

Such harassment often significantly impacted its targets. When one of the few black students at UNC-Greensboro in the mid-1960s stopped with some of her white friends at another Greensboro restaurant, a group of klansmen met them outside and harangued them with threatening remarks about "coon-hunting season." "We were afraid for our lives," she recalled years later, noting that it was one of the worst racial experiences she had ever faced.

A lack of recourse compounded the fear, as none of the victims felt that anything could come of reporting the verbal assault.[21]

In other cases, klan action around Greensboro was not confined to verbal threats. Unit 130, whose dual cover names ("Guilford County Booster Club" and "Greensboro Gun Club") captured its parallel predilections, spent the bulk of its funds on three new M-1 Carbine rifles and associated ammunition in early 1966. To stir up the membership, George Dorsett and Clyde Webster frequently boasted of their nightriding plans and encouraged others to join them. Greensboro klansmen physically harassed a number of local residents, including a prominent black minister who moved into a previously all-white neighborhood and a school principal who balked when a set of students attempted to organize a Junior KKK Club.[22]

In many ways, Charlotte and its Mecklenburg County neighbors appeared to have a similar klan pedigree. Located less than an hour from the UKA's Rowan County state headquarters, home to the intensely committed lifelong klansman Joseph Bryant, and the site of multiple KKK-perpetrated bombings in the late 1950s, the city seemed well-positioned to become a UKA stronghold. By 1965, however, only a single klavern existed in all of Mecklenburg County. Prior to a brief growth spurt late in the year, its membership languished below twenty. Local police officials publicly expressed concern over local klan members' "tremendous" recruiting efforts, but even at the group's peak, weekly klavern meetings averaged only thirty members. In an effort to organize an associated Ladies Auxiliary Unit, leaders held a joint meeting of interested men and women members in October 1965, but only a small number of women continued to organize, meeting too irregularly to earn an official UKA charter. A number of rallies held in the county were similarly lackluster—the crowd at a November 1966 event held in a field just north of Charlotte's city limits numbered only 100, and three separate rallies the following year failed even to match that turnout.[23]

This disparity in klan presence across potential segregationist centers characterized the UKA's mixed fortunes in the region. While nowhere in the Piedmont approached the klan's extensive organization in many eastern counties—on a per capita basis, the UKA's presence in Pitt County was four times greater than in Guilford County and thirty-eight times larger than in Mecklenburg—the UKA clearly held greater appeal in Greensboro than in Charlotte. By examining how the internal makeup of these communities shaped their receptivity to the klan, we can better understand the settings within which the UKA operated.

Greensboro

In a 1963 letter to Charlotte mayor Stanford Brookshire, prominent Durham bank executive George Watts Hill reflected on their respective cities' progress in race relations. To underscore his enthusiasm about both places, he contrasted their current outlook with that of the state's second-largest city. "Greensboro," Hill wrote, "has a more difficult problem than either Charlotte or Durham in that the white folks are mad at the Negroes in Greensboro and there are just too many Republicans in that community."[24] Hill's blanket assessment burrowed to the root of Greensboro's struggles: the combustible admixture of pride and anger stemming from the city's status as ground zero for the sit-in movement, and the resulting political conservatism concealed by a veneer of civility.

These same phenomena help to explain why Greensboro became a klan hotbed, a relative oasis of white supremacy in the ostensibly progressive Piedmont. But alongside the city's response to continued civil rights pressures, the story of the KKK's rise centered on how the social fabric of the area created vulnerabilities within the white population and also produced the resources that enabled and sometimes constrained vigilante action. Indeed, the origins of the local civil rights struggle and its strong white supremacist backlash are rooted in the county's economic, political, and social institutions—most prominently its burgeoning textile economy and the intellectual aura that stemmed from its five colleges.

Formed through a legislative act in 1807, Greensboro didn't come into its own until late in the nineteenth century. While fewer than 500 called the city home in 1870, expanding opportunities in the manufacturing sector, enabled by local access to the Southern Railway System, provided the impetus for rapid growth. The city's population first reached 10,000 at the turn of the twentieth century, and in the 1920s it exceeded 50,000.[25]

By mid-century, Greensboro's economy centered on textile manufacturing, and a number of the industry's towering figures resided there. Perhaps the best known were Moses and Cesar Cone, whose involvement in the Piedmont began in the 1880s. Operating through their family's Baltimore-based grocery wholesaling outfit, they first prospered as exclusive sellers for much of the plaid and gingham woven in North Carolina mills. Gradually, they moved toward direct involvement in denim production. They constructed Proximity Mill (named for its location adjacent to both cotton fields and railroad tracks) on the outskirts of Greensboro in 1895. Soon after, they opened the nearby White Oak Mill, which by 1914 had become the world's largest denim-producing plant. By the mid-1960s, the Cone Mills Corporation employed 14,000 overall, with more than 5,000 of those workers spread across the Cones' seven Guilford County mills.

Burlington Industries established roots thirty years after the Cones built Proximity Mill and eventually came to dwarf their competitors' operations. From modest beginnings as Burlington Mills in 1925, the company grew rapidly into the largest textile firm in the world, with 83,000 employees in the 1960s. These manufacturing giants forged Greensboro's industrial reputation, but the area's textile economy was considerably more diffuse. By 1964, seventy-five plants unaffiliated with Cone or Burlington operated across Guilford County. These mills served as the backbone of Greensboro's vibrant manufacturing sector, whose 600 firms employed more than a third of the metropolitan area's workforce.

In practice, the mills bridged the considerable gulf that otherwise separated Guilford County's urban areas—Greensboro and, twenty miles to the southwest, High Point—from the mostly rural communities that dotted much of the rest of the county. Guilford's cities, noted sociologist Melvin Tumin, by the 1950s "exemplifie[d] some of the newest trends in urbanization, modernization, and industrialization in the South." Such areas sharply contrasted with the county's many isolated farm dwellings that, according to Tumin, were "far removed from the amenities of modern urban life and exemplif[ied] certain of the most salient features of depressed agricultural areas." As textile mills spread across densely and sparsely populated areas alike, they increasingly allayed these stark rural-urban divides. As conceptions of the economic changes to be wrought by civil rights reforms crystallized throughout the 1950s and early 1960s, the dominant presence of industry created commonalities in interests and perspectives that otherwise would not have existed across the county's cities and rural areas.[26]

In Greensboro at least, certain of these smaller manufacturing plants and other local businesses had quietly adopted hiring practices with limited regard for race. Such initiatives typically did not respond to federal desegregation mandates but rather resulted from instrumental business decisions or idiosyncratic personal relationships. One small downtown clothing shop, for instance, informally promoted a one-time janitor to a clerk position in the 1940s. A decade later, according to the shop's owner, he was the best salesman on the floor. "A great many white people demand that he wait on them," the owner reported, though that fact did not incline the shop to seek out another black employee. Integrating as a matter of policy "never occurred to me," the owner explained. "This boy came to me... and showed so much ambition and attitude, that I simply let him grow as fast as I could." Traveling around the city, one might also come across a black mechanic at a filling station, or a contractor employing a black draftsman. A 1955 report on the city's racial hiring practices by the American Friends Service Committee (AFSC), a Quaker social justice organization whose regional headquarters was in Guilford County, concluded optimistically: "We are gradually gathering knowledge of where Negroes have waited on the public across the counter for 12, 18, 20 years in one place, right in the heart of Greensboro."

There was considerable incentive for certain business owners to maintain such a practice: the steady flow of skilled black workers from the campus of the nearby black Agricultural and Technical College of North Carolina (better known as A&T), a resource that seemed especially appealing when the labor market tightened. Particularly enticing was the stream of machinists—"as scarce in this area as hen's teeth," an AFSC worker noted—trained by A&T each year. Such hires posed risks, however. When the owner of an engineering company near campus decided to take on black machinists to handle contract work, his foreman and two other full-time machinists promptly quit. Bolstered by his pastor's counsel, he continued running the shop as an integrated workplace, hiring A&T's machine shop instructor as his new foreman. Racial justice was not the goal, the owner maintained; "I was just a businessman trying to run a business."[27]

But doing so as an integrated establishment, regardless of one's motivation, subjected one to significant cross-pressures. A department store manager who promoted one of his black women employees to the sales floor ended up relieving her of her position entirely following conflicts with salesworkers from other nearby shops, along with his own senior employees—including one of the owners of his store. His plan to "weather the whole storm" collapsed, the manager explained, when an "avalanche came down upon him" in which he "hardly had a moment's rest" until he agreed to let the employee in question go. Likewise, a regional automobile association phased out its efforts to integrate its workforce when the presence of black employees made it difficult to hire and retain their white salespeople. When the personnel manager at a Greensboro tobacco manufacturing plant sought an African American chemist, the company's New York–based corporate office blocked the move. "In a new place we do not attempt to set the patterns," he was told. "When we are in Rome, we do as the Romans do."[28]

Most often, businesses followed the cautious tack advanced by the manager of Duke Power Company. Top management was "sympathetic and enlightened," he noted assuringly, but at the end of the day "wouldn't stir that hornet's nest, not for a moment." A survey of Greensboro businesses confirmed that the segregationist status quo held in the vast majority of the city's establishments. Of the more than 400 firms interviewed in 1958, only 13 percent reported a willingness to hire without discriminating by race. Nearly 60 percent said the opposite: race was a factor in their hiring policies for all jobs. And more than four-fifths of firms reported that they would be unwilling even to consider nondiscriminatory hiring in the future. As a result, despite a few success stories, workplace integration in Greensboro remained rare and, even when present, usually incomplete. Several years into a Guilford County–based campaign to promote "employment on merit," an AFSC staffer cautioned that their exemplar cases served mostly to underscore that "so many of our organizations have no integration whatsoever" and noted discouragingly that "to overcome the prejudices of white workers, a Negro on a given job has to be about 10 percent better than the white workers doing the same thing."[29]

Changing hiring practices was often most challenging in large firms, where pressures to retain a "traditional" segregated workforce intensified. These pressures came from both the top and the bottom. Cone Mills operated one diaper-hemming plant staffed entirely by black women and employed virtually no African Americans in traditionally white jobs in its other plants. The company rebuffed efforts to integrate its workforce, and until the passage of the Civil Rights Act it retained overt symbols of racial separation, including "white" and "colored" signs on drinking fountains. Cone executives repeatedly insisted that the company was bound by "local conditions" and that their employees would not tolerate having desegregation policies "rammed down their throats." Burlington Industries head J. Spencer Love had similar misgivings—his behind-the-scenes assurances that "you can depend on us to keep working at this thing until the [race relations] problem is solved" was trumped by fears of a white employee "walk out" if common areas in his plants were desegregated. Such theories were often based on assumption rather than evidence, though when the P. Lorillard tobacco plant, under pressure from federal authorities, desegregated its cafeteria in 1961, white employees did in fact initiate a boycott.

Whatever its source, resistance to desegregation initiatives held across nearly all of Greensboro's large manufacturing firms. When the AFSC pushed the city's large corporations to end traditional hiring practices, only Western Electric pledged to change its employment policies. Even there, executives feared negative publicity as well as "disruption from within." To manage those pressures, they constructed segregated bathroom facilities for its first black clerical workers and refused to allow the AFSC to mention their reforms in a proposed brochure.

This reluctance contrasted with the situation in nearby Winston-Salem, where that city's largest employer, R. J. Reynolds, pro-actively responded to President Kennedy's 1961 Executive Order on equal employment opportunities by opening its new Whitaker Park production facility (then the largest cigarette manufacturing plant in the world) on an integrated basis. In Charlotte, Douglas Aircraft Company adhered to its national policy of employing workers without regard to race and had desegregated its bathrooms and other common facilities in the mid-1950s. When an AFSC representative visited the main plant in 1956, he was surprised to find the President's Committee on Government Contracts nondiscrimination pledge placard on prominent display in Douglas's personnel office. "One sees few of these down south," his report noted, "and this is the only framed one I ever saw."[30]

As federal pressures tied to desegregation intensified, this staunch resistance to change in Greensboro workplaces, ironically, served to exacerbate perceptions of the threat posed by civil rights reforms. The effects of the looming Civil Rights Act were seen as most sweeping within institutions and communities that continued to resist grassroots efforts against formal racial separation. The presence of the city's two black institutions of higher learning—Bennett College and A&T—compounded this threat of wholesale change.

Though intellectuals had never exerted significant influence on its local politics, Greensboro took great pride in the cultural cachet of the city's five colleges, including its two "Negro" institutions. In 1960, more than 90 percent of the city's black population concentrated in a small set of neighborhoods to the south and east of downtown. Near the northern border of these neighborhoods, less than a mile to the east of the city's center, stood North Carolina A&T. One of the state's two land grant colleges, A&T was originally established in Raleigh, on the campus of Shaw University and close to the state's whites-only land grant institution (now North Carolina State University). In 1893, the college moved to Greensboro, and by the 1960s it enrolled more than 3,000 students. Bennett College was a few short blocks to the south. A Methodist black women's school, Bennett grew steadily beginning in the 1920s, building a national reputation both for academic excellence and as a strong force for advancement in the city's black community.[31]

Alongside the city's three white colleges—the Methodist institution Greensboro College, the Quaker-run Guilford College, and Women's College, a local affiliate of the University of North Carolina—these campuses exemplified Jim Crow-style racial separation.[32] But they also provided some of the few venues for meaningful interracial contact. In the 1930s, the Greensboro Intercollegiate Fellowship hosted integrated gatherings, attended by students and faculty from all five area campuses. The Guilford County Interracial Commission sponsored conversations on race relations that attracted a number of campus affiliates. By the 1950s the group became more active, working behind the scenes on a successful campaign to remove much of the Jim Crow signage in downtown public facilities. In the early 1960s, another like-minded organization, the Greensboro Community Fellowship, worked to promote desegregation and confront racial inequities in employment and housing. Two of its early leaders were Cleo McCoy, a black chaplain at A&T, and Warren Ashby, a white professor from UNC-Greensboro. And throughout, a number of controversial but often successful one-off events attracted integrated audiences. During World War II, Bennett College brought Eleanor Roosevelt to deliver a talk attended by both white and black Greensboro grade-school students.[33]

A&T and Bennett also served as the main incubators of Guilford County's exceptionally large skilled black workforce. The two schools attracted a sizable number of black students—in 1964, their combined enrollments totaled 3,818—and their student bodies drew significantly from local communities. Nearly a quarter of all students attending A&T and Bennett hailed from Guilford or adjacent counties, an unusually high figure for black colleges during this period. The academic and vocational training that many received during their time on campus gave them skills that were in considerable demand in the area. A&T dropouts who had completed their drafting requirements were regularly channeled to openings in Western Electric's drafting room. When the AFSC's merit employment efforts produced businesses willing to consider African American candidates for openings as chemists, draftsmen, engineers, or clerical workers, A&T and Bennett became conduits to link to appropriately trained workers. Both campuses hosted a range of programs that exposed black high school students to advanced academic work. In 1959, while A&T schooled 500 4-H students on "career exploration" and other topics, Bennett initiated a National Science Foundation–funded program to enhance promising local youths' math and science skills.[34]

More broadly, African Americans in Greensboro were, in a relative sense, exceptionally well educated. While only 14.7 percent of North Carolina's black adults earned high school diplomas in 1960, a full 32 percent of Greensboro's black population graduated from high school. One study found that black adults in Greensboro had, on average, more schooling than in any other comparably sized city in the South. The percentage of black residents who had attended at least some college similarly dwarfed that of most other southern cities; nearly one in five had done so in Greensboro, a rate nearly four times greater than in cities such as New Orleans; Tampa, Florida; Columbus, Georgia; and Greenville, South Carolina.

The quality of black education in Greensboro was exceptional as well. Two-thirds of Guilford County's African American students attended public schools accredited by the Southern Association of Colleges and Secondary Schools, and more than half of the accredited elementary schools in all of North Carolina were located in Greensboro. Nearly two-thirds of the city's black teachers possessed advanced degrees. Well prior to the 1960s, Dudley High School's guidance staff organized programs to encourage students to train for jobs traditionally closed to African Americans. School administrators also partnered with the AFSC's merit employment program to coordinate site visits to area businesses, provide training for professional positions, and arrange panel presentations by A&T graduates who had become racial "pioneers" in various fields.

Whites in Greensboro, in contrast, had relatively low levels of education. More than a quarter of the city's white residents had fewer than eight years of schooling, and barely half graduated from high school. The majority of white children in Greensboro enrolled in nonaccredited schools, a proportion much higher than in the city's black community. In important ways, whites still enjoyed a significant educational advantage—local black residents averaged only 73 percent of the schooling achieved by whites, and were only 70 percent as likely to possess a four-year college degree. But given the enormity of the barriers limiting black educational opportunities in the region, this racial gap was smaller in Greensboro than nearly anywhere else in the South.[35]

This educational dynamic created a pool of black workers who could compete with local whites for the majority of available skilled positions. In the past, of course, such racial competition was artificially suppressed by Jim Crow policies that reserved many skilled and semi-skilled jobs for whites, especially in the textile industry. Discriminatory practices associated with local and state training opportunities supported such efforts. Despite Dudley High School's national reputation for excellence, stark differences existed in the curricular offerings available to the city's white and black students. When a group of economic boosters produced a television series designed to expose area high schools to industry opportunities around Greensboro, Dudley was not invited to participate. And it was an open secret that the area's broadest based resource for vocational training, the Guilford County Industrial Education Center (IEC), was in fact a white institution.

Opened in 1958, the Guilford County IEC was designed as an interracial training school, with original plans incorporating a "stand-up snack bar" rather than a seated cafeteria to guard against controversies over integrated social spaces. But using the same "catch-22" policy employed in Pitt County and with other IECs in eastern North Carolina, the Center's director upheld a policy in which students would be accepted for training only if they could demonstrate a promise of employment related to that specific skill. Why train Negroes as upholsterers, he reasoned, when not a single area furniture factory would hire them?

When the County Supervisor of Negro Schools inquired in 1958 about finding ways to open the IEC to black students, officials suggested that his office might instead pursue state funding for a separate trade school based at A&T. By 1960, all but two of the 1,212 registered students were white. IEC officials undermined their ostensible open admissions policy by recruiting extensively in the county's white high schools but not at all at Dudley and other black schools (not surprisingly, when an AFSC representative visited Dudley, she found that students knew "absolutely nothing" about the IEC). A persistent Dudley guidance counselor pushed IEC officials on the point, who told her they would be happy to consider "one or two" referred applicants.[36]

The dearth of professional work available to African Americans resulted in many college graduates leaving the area to pursue opportunities in the North or Midwest. But many of those migrants expressed a preference to stay if opportunities opened up. One A&T student estimated that up to 90 percent of his engineering classmates planned to move out of North Carolina. Like many of them, he himself wanted to stay in the state, but "things being the way they are it is impossible." Most of the industries that recruited at A&T came from outside of the South, another student noted, and even if he was able to find work in the area, he doubted that he would have opportunities for advancement in his field equal to those of his white counterparts. "I would love to stay if I could get the type of job that I would desire," he concluded. "It's not the state that I don't like, it's the practices of some of the people."

Those who remained and found work in the Greensboro area frequently were overqualified for their assigned tasks. One Greensboro executive confided that, unlike his experiences elsewhere in the South, there was such a surplus of "high calibre" black workers that many of his smartest and most capable employees were consolidated in low-status departments, in positions reserved for African Americans. Reacting to that same phenomenon, a recent A&T grad lamented: "We have people with Master's degrees driving buses. We have people with B.S. degrees as Postmasters, or even Master's degrees. And I don't think it takes a Master's degree to do this."

Civil rights legislation promised to end such policies. By breaking down institutional supports for segregation in training venues and workplaces, whites in Greensboro would lose their primary means of labor market advantage. No longer could they enjoy near-exclusive access to textile and other skilled work, a change that would provide African Americans with the promise of careers that matched their educational credentials and an added incentive to seek work locally. While in practice civil rights reform would not work out this neatly, in 1964 anxieties over such impending change created a sense of racial threat among many white southerners, enhancing the appeal of the UKA and other reactionary organizations. In Greensboro, the klan's appeal was especially strong, largely because the scale of economic and political change exceeded that in the vast majority of southern communities.[37]

The coalescence of civil rights activism, most visibly the sit-in protests that rocked the city beginning in 1960, reinforced this dynamic. A&T and Bennett provided both the crucial impetus and an infrastructure for those actions. On February 1 of that year, four A&T students made the short walk from campus to the downtown Woolworth's department store. After purchasing several small items, the young men proceeded to sit down at the store's whites-only lunch counter. When, predictably, they were declined service, they refused to give up their seats. The day wore on without incident, and the students left when the store closed. "I'll be back tomorrow with A&T College," one of them remarked as he exited. A half-hour after the store opened the next morning, thirty-one A&T students—twenty-seven men and four women—entered the store, took seats at the counter, and dug in for the showdown, textbooks in hand to productively pass the time.

The scene repeated itself each day that week, with the number of students—including some from Bennett and Dudley, along with four white women from Women's College—swelling throughout. The following week, the sit-ins spread beyond Greensboro when students in Durham and Winston-Salem initiated like events. Soon after, sit-ins were reported in Charlotte, Fayetteville, and Raleigh, and then outside the state: Hampton, Virginia, on February 11 and Norfolk and Portsmouth, Virginia, Rock Hill, South

Carolina, and Deland, Florida, the following day. By April, sit-ins had been initiated in sixty-six southern cities.[38]

The origins of this sweeping movement reflected racialized institutional arrangements in Greensboro generally. Three of the original four demonstrators grew up in the area and had ties to Shiloh Baptist Church, whose minister was a vocal NAACP member. At least two had been active members of an NAACP Youth Chapter.[39] As first-year students at A&T, the four became good friends and developed their resolve during regular late-night "bull sessions." The campus's politicized culture, unusual for black public schools dependent on state legislatures for their funding, supported their move toward direct action. During the sit-ins, administrators refused to penalize or otherwise restrict student involvement. Demonstrators used school facilities to copy protest materials, and many faculty overlooked lapses in class attendance throughout the spring of 1960. Several past campus events remained at the forefront of activist students' consciousness as well. Most prominent was Governor Luther Hodges's infamous 1955 speech at A&T, which had been interrupted by an emphatic student audience after the governor referred to black North Carolinians as "nigras" as part of his harangue against the NAACP.[40]

The sit-ins also provided a window into Greensboro's white community. As the demonstrations mounted, so did the presence of white counter-demonstrators, who taunted and physically harassed student activists and staged their own sit-ins and pickets to counteract civil rights actions. George Dorsett was on the scene most days as a self-proclaimed representative of the KKK—although, or maybe because, both the North Carolina Knights and the U.S. Klans remained at a severe low ebb in membership (Shelton's UKA would not be founded until the following year). Rumors persisted that the klan paid white youths to harass demonstrators, and city officials working to broker an end to the conflict received calls and letters laced with anonymous threats.[41]

White community leaders' response to these sit-in demonstrations, and to a successive wave of protests targeting discriminatory hiring practices and continued segregation in many businesses and public facilities, was ambiguous and weak. The fractured, diffuse nature of political and economic power among the city's elites prohibited strong and coherent responses to demonstrator demands. As a 1963 *Greensboro Daily News* editorial noted, Greensboro "does not have the kind of 'big mule' power structure of some Southern cities.... There is no one group which can press a button and produce miraculous cooperation." As a result, the editorial concluded, business executives needed to "combine their resources to assist the political resources in meeting issues which can no longer be evaded."[42]

This plea would not have been necessary in Charlotte or Durham, where business interests had direct input into everyday political decision making. But Greensboro was different. Since 1921, the city had employed a "city council-city manager" municipal structure. The city manager, who oversaw most of the key day-to-day decisions, was appointed and thus not directly accountable to the electorate. The seven-member city council made general policy decisions and advised the city manager. The mayorship was a relatively weak, largely ceremonial position, one that was not elected directly but rather conferred on the council member receiving the highest number of votes in each election cycle.

In earlier decades, the city council had included many of the city's most successful businessmen, including both Cone brothers, the president of Jefferson Standard Life Insurance Company, and the owner of the newspaper. But by 1960, it was largely detached from those elite economic circles—its members were increasingly second-tier lawyers, real estate or insurance salesmen, and mid-level corporate officials. The corresponding lack of cross-cutting connections across influential political and economic interests hindered the city's ability to effectively engage challenges to segregation. As the sit-ins intensified, Mayor George Roach—himself a realtor and insurance agent—did not bring the issue to the city council, nor was he involved in negotiations in the opening weeks of the protests. Likewise, the Greensboro Chamber of Commerce and leading business executives (most of whom did not see their interests as directly tied to those of the downtown merchants) all felt that the issue fell outside their purview. A Mayor's Committee on Community Relations, chaired by Burlington Industries executive Ed Zane, sought to broker a solution, but neither the mayor nor Burlington Industries head J. Spencer Love exerted significant influence, either in public or behind the scenes.

The department stores finally capitulated in July 1960, though simmering tensions and a resistance to more widespread desegregation of public accommodations would spark subsequent rounds of mass protest in Greensboro throughout the first half of the decade. This disruption posed a threat to the status quo directly through the challenges of civil rights activists, and also because mass protest emboldened and empowered previously marginalized supporters of integration. The AFSC, for instance, had for several years maintained its Employment on Merit (EOM) program, tirelessly visiting Greensboro businesses in hopes of convincing owners of the moral and economic advantages of nondiscriminatory hiring. While tangible gains had been minor, the sit-ins both reenergized AFSC staff and sparked a reconsideration of the organization's mission.

"During the past year employment practices have not changed noticeably with respect to merit hiring," an AFSC staffer noted in the 1960 Annual Report. "It is felt, however, that the student demonstrations which occurred during the year did bring about within the policy-making structure of the business world, an increasing awareness of the problems which arise when any segment of the labor market is denied equal economic opportunity." Project staff seized upon that window of opportunity, framing the movement as "against all discrimination" and emphasizing links between discrimination in employment and other forms of political and civic expression. In the coming months, the AFSC would attempt to broker dialogue between city officials and the black community, expand their ongoing EOM program, and host a workshop on nonviolent direct action for student activists and their adult advisors.

The same sense of urgent optimism sparked a resurgence of Greensboro's NAACP branch. Membership hovered around 1,200 for much of the 1950s, but it nearly doubled following the 1960 sit-ins. Black electoral strength increased as well. A 1963 Voter Registration Project yielded 803 new registrants from five black neighborhoods in Greensboro. Local media extensively covered the initiative; the *Greensboro Record* carried a feature article on the project's student workers, and some of them also appeared in radio spots and on a popular political program aired by a local television station.[43]

UKA mobilization in Greensboro and its surrounding Guilford County communities emerged in this context. A number of reinforcing factors shaped and maintained a climate of racial threat. Racial competition for a large number of semi-skilled manufacturing jobs had to this point been artificially suppressed by customs that reserved those positions for whites. Given their comparatively low levels of education, Greensboro's white workers were, as a group, relatively ill-equipped to compete for many of these positions on a truly open market. The county's relatively highly educated black population, most visible through the large proportion of local students attending Greensboro's black colleges, exacerbated this shrinking labor market advantage. The proximity of those schools to the city's downtown district facilitated formal and informal interracial interactions, which created a looser sense of racial separation than in nearby cities such as Winston-Salem and Charlotte.[44] Bennett and A&T also provided valuable infrastructure for civil rights activism that shook Greensboro after 1960. The sustained contention around the initial sit-ins and subsequent protests over the desegregation of public accommodations created an acute political threat, revitalizing integrationist efforts, enhancing the political efficacy of the city's black community, and in turn fostering a general sense of bitterness in the white community, especially among those whose status was most vulnerable to civil rights reform.[45] Along with the presence of a core of committed klan holdovers from the U.S. Klans and North Carolina Knights, this confluence of factors hindered Greensboro's "readiness"[46] for racial progress and provided an ideal setting for the UKA's rallies and recruiting efforts.

Charlotte

Though only an hour and a half car ride from Greensboro, Charlotte's reputation in terms of race relations seemed at times a world apart. In 1963, while some of the largest mass demonstrations of the civil rights era played out in Greensboro, Charlotte's pioneering approach to desegregation received national attention. "As we have accumulated information about changes in racial practices around the Country," Attorney General Robert Kennedy wrote that June, "we have been particularly impressed by the striking progress which has been made in Charlotte." He credited the city's residents, and especially its "business, social and political leadership," as he promoted Charlotte as a regional model. "It is our hope," Kennedy concluded, "that those who have led and contributed to break-throughs such as Charlotte's will find opportunities to share their experiences with other communities which are anxious—as we believe by far the greater number are—to work similar changes, and which are confronted with the same initial difficulties as those which you had to overcome."[47]

By the end of that year, as accounts of the city's successes appeared in newspapers around the country, scores of communities struggling with difficulties posed by desegregation would request assistance from Charlotte mayor Stanford Brookshire. In North Carolina, inquiries rolled in from officials in Wilmington, Goldsboro, Kinston, Hickory, Lexington, Mooresville, Wadesboro, and Burlington. The Community Advisory Committee in Jacksonville, Florida, solicited advice in hopes of "profiting from [Charlotte's] experience." Similar calls came from communities as diverse as Richmond, Virginia; Little Rock, Arkansas; Omaha, Nebraska; and Jamaica Plain, Massachusetts. Florida's Dade County Community Relations Board, the Mississippi Council on Human Relations, and the US Conference of Mayors all requested information to guide their respective processes. Brookshire was elected chairman of North Carolina's Mayors' Cooperating Committee and reportedly was offered the inaugural directorship of the National Citizens' Committee for Community Relations. The *New York Herald Tribune* published his views on race relations, and Brookshire also received the B'nai B'rith Women's Humanitarian Award, an honorary doctorate from Pfeiffer College, and a silver medallion from the National Council of Christians and Jews. In 1965, the *Charlotte News* named him its "Man of the Year."[48]

As Southern Regional Council information director Pat Watters put it, "Charlotte chose a different way."[49] While in many of the South's cities integration emerged incrementally following a protracted struggle, Charlotte's public officials and private business owners agreed to desegregate well in advance of 1964's Civil Rights Act. Subsequent accolades tended to exaggerate the smoothness of the transition, but Charlotte's race relations progression contrasted sharply with that of Greensboro. While in both cities elites responded to pressures exerted by civil rights activists, Charlotte instituted reforms more rapidly and completely, and with significantly less public confrontation. And while Greensboro served as the UKA's de facto Piedmont recruiting center, organized white resistance was minimal in Charlotte, despite a small number of well-publicized spasms of racial violence.

The UKA's inability to penetrate Charlotte continued a long-standing string of failures by militant white supremacist groups in the city. In September 1957, an incipient Citizens' Council chapter organized by white supremacist rabble-rouser John Kasper was at the center of a hostile crowd that harassed fifteen-year-old Dorothy Counts as she approached the newly integrated Harding High School. The ugly incident sparked opposition to the Council's presence in the local press and, allegedly, a stern closed-door meeting with the Charlotte police chief. Soon after, the chapter, which had attracted only fifteen members in any case, folded. Another segregationist organization, the Patriots of North Carolina, similarly failed to make inroads in Charlotte. The group's leader, Kenneth Whitsett, boasted of support from prominent citizens in Greensboro, while grumbling about the chilly reception he received from Charlotte's city leaders. "They were so busy making money," Whitsett lamented. "Charlotte was too commercial... they were afraid business might be hurt."[50]

Virtually all contemporaneous accounts of the so-called "Charlotte Way" center on these sorts of economic concerns, alongside discussions of how the city's visionary leadership charted a progressive course in which racial change fostered business growth.[51] This ethos did create a climate hostile to the militant defense of white supremacy, though white residents' insulation from a strong sense of racial threat enabled city leaders' progressive policies. Charlotte's pronounced racial inequities, combined with stark patterns of residential and economic separation, reduced the strong sense of inter-racial competition for status and jobs that provided the backdrop for white resistance in Greensboro. Charlotte's governmental practices at times supported and reproduced such inequities, which paradoxically prevented a strong backlash by the city's conservative constituencies following Charlotte's early adoption of civil rights reforms. This absence of meaningful conservative opposition, in turn, hindered the recruiting efforts of the UKA and other hard-line segregationists.

As in Greensboro, approximately a third of Charlotte's population was black. These minority residents, however, concentrated in neighborhoods separated from whites to a degree greater than in most other southern cities. In 1960, neighborhood segregation in Charlotte's metropolitan area was 13 percent higher than in Greensboro. Across the region, Charlotte was more highly segregated than any other city in the Carolina Piedmont or in Louisiana, Arkansas, Georgia, and Alabama. By 1970, only four of the nation's largest 109 cities were more segregated than Charlotte.

More than 90 percent of the city's nearly 60,000 African Americans lived northwest of the downtown central business district. Meanwhile, the most affluent area of the city, comprising ten census tracts in the southeastern quadrant, housed more than 40,000 whites and not a single black family.[52] Throughout the 1960s, the city's ambitious municipal planning projects exacerbated this pronounced residential segregation. The "resume of improvements" trumpeted by city officials during this period included the federally funded construction of I-85, which effectively served as a physical barrier separating historically black and white neighborhoods on the north side of the city.

Other urban renewal projects resulted in the razing of Brooklyn and Blue Heaven, two long-standing black communities, to make way for "redevelopment in uses more appropriate for its central location." The city's "blight survey" of Brooklyn—once Charlotte's premier black commercial district—justified the bulldozing of the area by pronouncing more than two-thirds of the 1,689 buildings in the neighborhood to be in "various states of dilapidation or deterioration." Those displaced had few options for new housing, which meant that racially motivated mortgage policies and realtor actions channeled those residents to the city's increasingly segregated northwestern quadrant. Other efforts to provide public housing options served the same purpose when they relocated families to low-income projects concentrated in black areas of the city. "We are getting a compact Negro community in practically one area of town," argued Fred Alexander, Kelly's brother and Charlotte's first black city council member. "We're building our future Watts right now."[53]

While Greensboro's residential patterns were far from progressive, geographic and social boundaries created by the separation of white and black neighborhoods were significantly more stringent in Charlotte. These clear racial boundaries reduced the anxieties that at times provided recruiting fodder for the klan in more porous Greensboro neighborhoods.[54] Charlotte's highly segregated economy reinforced this relative absence of residentially rooted conflicts. In contrast with Greensboro, where the presence of many semi-skilled jobs reserved for whites tenuously suppressed inter-racial competition in the manufacturing-heavy labor market, Charlotte's economy more pronouncedly partitioned into high- and low-skill jobs. As state NAACP President Kelly Alexander observed, despite the city's location "in the heart of [North Carolina's] textile center, it has never been a manufacturing town, it has always been a service town where the majority of the Negroes worked in domestic service and in laundry work and in menial task operations."

Alexander's take on Charlotte's labor market was telling in two respects. Most generally, it highlighted the city's primary service orientation. Less than a quarter of Mecklenburg County's labor force toiled in manufacturing jobs in 1960, while in Guilford County, the total approached 40 percent. By 1967, that disparity had grown, with Greensboro workers nearly twice as likely as those in Charlotte to be employed by manufacturing firms. With agriculture marginal in both areas, the bulk of remaining jobs involved some sort of service work.

Alexander's statement also points to the strict partitioning of Charlotte's service sector. Charlotte's banking and insurance industries grew rapidly through the middle decades of the century. In the 1950s, *Business Week* characterized the city as "a paper town—because most of its business is done on paper." Indeed, Charlotte held significantly more white-collar service jobs than Greensboro—in 1967, nearly 18 percent of the Charlotte workforce engaged in white-collar service work, versus only 12.8 percent in Greensboro. White workers held the vast majority of these positions, with African Americans typically employed in low-skill service jobs. Only 5 percent of the city's clerical and sales workers were black, and African Americans made up an even smaller percentage of managerial, professional, and technical workers. Black women held fewer than 2 percent of the city's clerical positions, and instead overwhelmingly worked as domestic servants. A similarly high percentage of black men worked as laborers and janitors, or in unskilled or semi-skilled service or craft positions; they were almost entirely absent from management, professional, and sales positions. As a result, in a city dominated by its service economy, black workers occupied the bottom end of a segmented labor market, which effectively precluded racial competition for the majority of positions. Unlike in Greensboro, where black and white workers frequently labored in the same manufacturing plants, separated primarily by informal practices that customarily reserved most desirable jobs for whites, white privilege in the Charlotte labor market was both deep-seated and durable in the face of civil rights legislation.[55]

Pronounced educational inequity reinforced this labor market advantage. While relatively high levels of black schooling alongside a weak white educational profile attenuated inequalities in Greensboro, white Charlotteans were the best educated in the state. The city's black residents, on the other hand, had 37 percent less schooling than their white counterparts and also fared significantly worse than their African American peers in other Piedmont cities. While in Greensboro nearly a third of black adults graduated from high school, only 20 percent earned a diploma in Charlotte. The proportion with four or more years of college was less than half that in Greensboro. Further, Charlotte's black university, Johnson C. Smith, enrolled 1,048 students in 1964, compared to the nearly 4,000 students attending A&T and Bennett that same year. Only 133 of those students hailed from Mecklenburg or adjacent counties, meaning that Smith attracted local black students at a considerably lower rate than did Greensboro's institutions of higher learning. Smith's campus was physically as well as socially distant from the downtown business districts, exacerbating these educational inequities. Unlike A&T and Bennett in Greensboro, both of which bordered on the city's central business district, Smith's Biddleville neighborhood was located on the periphery of the city, separated from even the outskirts of downtown by a highway and a large cemetery. Such geographic barriers largely precluded the sorts of interactions that created informal cracks in Greensboro's segregated labor force. More generally, these severe disparities in education interacted with, and reproduced, the racially segmented character of Charlotte's workforce.[56]

As in Greensboro, the tenor of the city's civil rights struggle reflected these conditions. Given the predominance of business interests in sectors unlikely to produce racial competition for work, civil rights pressures were met not by militant grassroots resistance from white workers but instead by coordinated maneuvers by political and economic elites. Prior to the start of the 1960 Greensboro sit-ins, the NAACP dominated civil rights action in Charlotte.

Lifelong resident Kelly Alexander had served as that organization's state president since 1948, and through the 1950s the NAACP focused largely on what Alexander described as "frontal attacks on discrimination," centered on judicial efforts to challenge segregation. In Charlotte, these legal efforts resulted in a number of notable successes. In 1957, under court order, the city integrated the public Bonnie Brae golf course. As part of an agreement in conjunction with Greensboro and Winston-Salem, token school desegregation began that same year, when five of Charlotte's black students were assigned to formerly white schools. Two years later, under the significant threat of an NAACP lawsuit, the city voluntarily integrated its swimming pools.[57]

However, public accommodations—including restaurants, lunch counters, and theaters—remained fully segregated, a policy that would collapse under the weight of student-organized direct action rather than through the NAACP's judicial activism.

Despite its smaller size, Johnson C. Smith catalyzed the sit-in movement, much like A&T. The initial action against the city's lunch counters occurred on February 9, 1960, eight days after the sit-ins began in Greensboro. Smith students demanded service at eight downtown locations, including the city's two major department stores, Belk's and Ivey's. Over the next several months, the protests continued at various intervals, interrupted by periods of negotiation with Charlotte mayor James Smith and, beginning in April, members of his biracial Friendly Relations Committee. On July 9, Charlotte became the second city in North Carolina—after Winston-Salem—to desegregate its lunch counters.[58]

Limitations in the scope and reach of that initial agreement would spark successive rounds of protest over the next two years, though the presence of Mayor Smith's successor, Stanford Brookshire, tempered somewhat the tone of that contention. A former president of the Charlotte Chamber of Commerce, Brookshire was elected with the strong backing of the business community and little support from black voters. But two years later, after overseeing the desegregation of most city establishments a year in advance of the Civil Rights Act, Brookshire returned to office with overwhelming support from black precincts.[59] How this shift occurred says much about the way the city's political and economic structures shaped the contours of race relations, and constrained the efforts of segregationist elements.

Perhaps the defining characteristic of Charlotte's political system was its traditionally close association with the city's economic leaders. Brookshire's move from the Chamber of Commerce to the mayor's office was a typical trajectory, and he privately acknowledged that the city's business leadership encouraged him to run in part to rebuff other outsider candidates. Among elites, the Chamber enjoyed a long-standing reputation as "the prestige organization" in Charlotte, fueling the city's unabashed economic boosterism. City publications during the Brookshire era typically trumpeted headlines such as "Charlotte: A Middle-Sized City—But Very Big on Business." Aerial shots of the city's gleaming downtown skyscrapers accompanied bylines like "Charlotte: The Big Build-Up." (By the 1970s, the Chamber of Commerce had removed any pretense of subtlety with its new slogan: "Charlotte—A Good Place to Make Money.")

"Anything they back goes over," boasted J. Ed Burnside, Brookshire's successor as the Chamber's president, referencing the Chamber's "extraordinary influence" in the city. As the "most powerful institution in the city," Chamber support aided most successful community initiatives. In 1963, Brookshire leveraged the influence of the city's economic elite in an aggressive push to desegregate public accommodations well in advance of Civil Rights Act mandates. Throughout 1961 and 1962, the Brookshire-appointed Mayor's Community Relations Committee, an expanded version of Mayor Smith's Friendly Relations Committee, handled most negotiations between protestors and business owners. But widespread desegregation of Charlotte businesses occurred only when this body received the strong backing of the Chamber of Commerce.[60]

The primary motor of racial change, of course, emerged from the black community, where protestors engaged in pressure tactics that exerted economic and political costs. Around Charlotte, many believed that in the presence of such pressures in Greensboro and elsewhere, city officials' intransigence had kept away new industry. Brookshire himself recognized the economic leverage that protestors possessed in Charlotte. With racial strife, he argued, "the community's pocketbook is placed in jeopardy, as . . . other cities have learned from experience." Unlike in Greensboro, where the mayor's detachment from the city's economic elites reduced his influence in those circles as well as his impetus to preserve economic interests, Brookshire actively and successfully mobilized the city's economic leadership behind desegregation mandates. On May 2, 1963, while Greensboro suffered through a wave of mass marches, the Executive Committee of Charlotte's Chamber of Commerce passed a resolution recommending that "all businesses in this community catering to the general public be opened immediately to all customers without regard to race, creed, or color." Mayor Brookshire, noting the stature of the Chamber's members, told the *Charlotte Observer* that "I feel the total city will follow this leadership." Ultimately, he was correct.

With the costs of integrating distributed unequally across business owners, according to their perceived stature and clientele makeup, Charlotte's strong city leadership mitigated differing investments in the segregated status quo and created opportunities for progressive action. By setting a tone that lowered anticipated costs, they enabled a small number of establishments to serve as integration "pioneers," which in turn reduced the costs of integrating for others, an effect that rippled through the city's business community. In contrast, Greensboro's lack of coordinated municipal leadership meant that desegregation resulted solely from intolerable pressures imposed by civil rights activists. This removed even the facade of interdependent and voluntary action, intensifying the bitterness of white residents whose personal status in the face of such change was often tenuous.[61]

In Charlotte, the process played out differently across establishments. Hotel and motel owners agreed, as a group, to desegregate, beginning with their dining rooms. To avoid negative attention, they requested no advance public announcement of their intentions and that the first black patrons arrive as guests of the mayor and prominent Chamber members. After a three-day test period sparked no "abnormal public attention," the owners agreed to allow local media to publicize their actions.

The path taken by the city's restaurants was considerably rockier. When contacted by members of the Community Relations Committee, many restaurant owners expressed privately their support for desegregation. Most, however, feared the disproportionate attention and costs borne by early movers. The sort of simultaneous, coordinated action pursued by hotel owners proved unworkable, and a general consensus emerged that the city's restaurants would follow S&W Cafeterias owner Frank O. Sherrill, whose twenty-two upscale establishments in North Carolina, Virginia, and eastern Tennessee were considered industry leaders and, by extension, social barometers. When Sherrill delayed action, a small group of twenty restaurants agreed to desegregate anyway, though the fragile nature of their interdependent decisions became clear when a social event attended by a number of restaurant owners resulted in several pulling out of the agreement after being "chided" by some of their fellow restaurateurs.[62]

Throughout these early negotiations, most of the city's top eateries remained holdouts. Their logic was clear: none would agree to follow the Chamber resolution without assurances that a sufficient number of others would do so as well. James Castanas, the owner of the Epicurean fine dining restaurant (many of the city's best-known steakhouses, including the Epicurean, were owned by a close community of Greek families, each acutely aware of the actions of their cohorts and consequently conservative in their actions), clearly expressed his thought process in a letter to the NAACP's Kelly Alexander. "Of course the Negro should have equal rights," Castanas asserted, but the fact that "a certain percentage of our customers are prejudiced and would not wish to eat in an integrated restaurant" posed a conundrum for a business conceived for "the purpose of profit [and not] social advancement." While Castanas acknowledged that the percentage of business that the Epicurean would lose in the transition was "unknown," it would certainly, he believed, exceed the anticipated gain from its added black and liberal white clientele. Even so, he concluded, "the question of civil rights is of so great an importance that we feel some social responsibility; therefore, if the majority of [Charlotte's seven] specialty houses... record on paper their decision to integrate, we shall also integrate."

Harry Golden, the Charlotte-based writer, raconteur, and publisher of the *Carolina Israelite*, attacked the uncertain assumptions that motivated these restaurants' decisions. "On the one hand you say you do not want to mix in with the racial problem," Golden argued, "but on the other hand you all become amateur sociologists... in the stated fear that some of your customers will leave when a Negro is sitting at one of your tables. How do you know this? You do not know this at all." Golden, playing the sociologist himself, was sufficiently confident that "most of your trade will feel a sense of pride and look upon you with a bit of admiration" to stake his own resources on the outcome. "The next time the Negro students come into your restaurant," he challenged, "I will guarantee you in cash the loss resulting from the white folks who walk out."[63]

Though there remained holdouts, Charlotte made significant progress in the desegregation of public accommodations a full year before the Civil Rights Act forced the hand of most other southern communities. The willingness of Mayor Brookshire, his biracial Community Relations Committee, and the Chamber of Commerce to provide a climate supportive of such progressive changes was key; the actions of Charlotte's interlocking political and economic leadership created a framework within which to view the desegregation of public establishments not as autonomous decisions of individual businesses but rather as expressions of the community's civic will. While economic considerations remained central to business owners' behind-the-scenes calculations, elite action managed the associated risks and thereby reduced the uncertain cost calculus; this allowed a contained and carefully orchestrated desegregation process. These initial actions, in turn, diminished the costs and risks that other businesses would bear, creating a sort of tipping effect that produced an outcome free of the sort of resistance and rancor that characterized parallel struggles in Greensboro.

While the resulting political climate was not always hospitable to civil rights struggles—Charlotte activists battled hard in the intervening years to fully desegregate city hospitals and schools—an important consequence of city leaders' actions was the drastic narrowing of acceptable forms of segregationist resistance. Klan-style violence became clearly out of bounds, a fact underscored by the aftermath of the coordinated bombing of the houses of Charlotte's four most visible civil rights leaders in November 1965.[64]

Miraculously, the bombs injured no one, though the homes of Kelly Alexander and his brother Fred suffered severe damage. The community reaction was telling. While the crimes remained unsolved, and thus never conclusively tied to the klan, residents almost unanimously framed the bombings as KKK vigilantism and directed outrage toward both the perpetrators and the klan generally. This indignation spread well beyond the black community. The Charlotte City Council hastily passed a resolution proclaiming its members "ashamed and horrified by the acts of violence done in the early morning hours today." More than 150 white carpenters, artisans, and business owners volunteered their time and materials to repair damage caused by the blasts. The *Charlotte Observer* offered a reward for information about the perpetrators, and more than 200 individuals and local businesses contributed to an Operation Rebuilding fund to further the city's race relations efforts.

While attention nationally focused on the bombings as a symbol of the city's limited progress with civil rights, many locals viewed the acts as a personal affront. "Vicious acts of this kind are not only individual attacks upon you but also constitute a grave invasion of the health and safety of all the members of our community," noted one telegram. "This is an inexcusable act and should not be tolerated under any circumstance," affirmed a Charlotte architect. "The citizens of Charlotte are indignant that such a thing has happened, and I wanted you, personally, to know how I feel." A white UNC student expressed that, "as a fellow citizen of North Carolina, I hope you will not think it too presumptuous of me to consider the attack made on you as an attack on me too. Presumptuous or not—this is how I feel." And the president of the Charlotte-based North Carolina Bank wrote Kelly Alexander to express his "deep concern," and concluded with a "sincere wish that the citizens of our community can overcome this difficulty and continue to work together in making substantial strides in the field of race relations."[65]

Gazing out in amazement at the city's repair efforts, the editor of the *Observer* noted the hypocrisy that lay behind "our 'best people'" being "aghast when anyone plants a bomb at a Negro's door," while at the same time tolerating less crude and overt forms of bigotry and discrimination.[66] Indeed, these expressions of inter-racial solidarities, for the most part, did not extend to the redress of pronounced inequities in housing, employment, and schooling. But they did affirm clearly that certain forms of white resistance—namely, those associated with the KKK—were not acceptable in Charlotte.

This climate of anti-vigilantism did not, of course, preclude all expressions of support for the militant defense of segregation. But its presence highlights both the paucity of UKA organization around Charlotte and the kinds of settings able to effectively impede large-scale klan action. The actions of Mayor Brookshire and other Charlotte leaders were rightfully portrayed as enlightened given the charged civil rights climate of the time. Less obvious, however, is that while the "Charlotte Way" provided a setting inhospitable to hard-line expressions of white supremacy, the pronounced racial divisions that insulated whites' status in the face of civil rights reforms both enabled and reinforced this progressive action. Charlotte's economy largely partitioned into high- and low-skill service work, with racial competition further truncated by the city's severe educational inequities. High rates of residential segregation across geographically distant neighborhoods minimized interracial contact, and the city's urban renewal programs exacerbated such divisions. Such factors made it difficult for the UKA to gain a foothold in the area, and provided a foundation conducive to successful progressive political action.

Locating Klansville

While the desegregation of public facilities created a seismic shift wherever it occurred, the contours of this change differed based on the extent to which civil rights pressures would alter the overall social landscape of a community. In Charlotte, a social structure that limited opportunities for nonhierarchical interracial contact in neighborhoods, schools, and workplaces contained its reverberations. In places like Greensboro, a much lower degree of racial separation ensured a farther-reaching effect. Whites would no longer be insulated from the racial advantages conferred by segregation, and those residents vulnerable to racial competition felt most strongly the corresponding threat to white identity and status.

Nowhere in the Piedmont was there a larger vulnerable population than in Greensboro. A study commissioned by Charlotte's Community Relations Committee in the early 1970s to assess racial progress in ten southern cities over the preceding decade found that Charlotte had higher than average levels of racial inequity across nearly all standard educational, housing, occupational, and health indices. Greensboro, on the other hand, had the lowest level of inequity on more than half of the indicators, and ranked above Charlotte on all but one.[67] As a consequence, civil rights reform had more far-reaching implications in Greensboro. As an organization with appeals explicitly directed toward maintaining "authentically" white spaces in the face of racial competition, the UKA, not surprisingly, resonated strongly in that community. Its rallies were both more frequent and larger than in the more densely populated Charlotte area. The multiple UKA klaverns that dotted Guilford County, many of which maintained large memberships, demonstrated that these rally appeals translated into deeper engagement with the group, a phenomenon noticeably lacking in Charlotte and its Mecklenburg County surrounds. As in Greenville and other communities in the eastern plain, whites in Greensboro simply had more to lose in the civil rights struggle than those in Charlotte. The klan's resonance was one consequence of that threatened loss.

7 THE FALL OF UNITED KLANS

The Bureau continues its program of penetrating the Klan at all levels, and, I may say, has been quite successful in doing so.

—FBI DIRECTOR J. EDGAR HOOVER, in his 1966 statement before the House of Representatives' Subcommittee on Appropriations.[1]

I had one of my informants one time, that the Klan suspected him, took him out to a tobacco barn, put a rope around his neck and threw it over a rafter, and threatened to hang him, trying to get him to admit he was an FBI informant. And he denied it and got away with it. But you know, you were dealing with... characters prone to do almost anything.

—GREENSBORO-BASED FBI AGENT DARGAN FRIERSON, reflecting on his experience developing UKA informants.[2]

The President will be sorry to hear that though we are bleeding and bruised, we are not beaten. We are still very much in business, and their so-called "investigation" has failed.

—BOB JONES, in his televised response to a 1965 WBTV editorial critical of UKA leaders' repeated invocation of the fifth amendment during HUAC's KKK hearings.[3]

Following two years of spectacular growth, cracks began to show in the UKA's armor as 1965 drew to a close. The klan had always been vulnerable to tensions arising from its ambiguous orientation to violence, infighting over funds, and susceptibility to infiltration. As these pressure points intensified and cumulated, the UKA's fortunes in North Carolina and elsewhere suffered drastically in the latter half of the decade. "The klan [we] knew is gone," lamented Raymond Cranford in 1968. "The units are skeletons. A bunch of 'em turned in their charters. The rallies are down to nuthin'. Most of the real good boys have left. Seems like each one of 'em has gone out to form his own klan.... I'm tellin' ya, it's just awful. The boys need leadership real bad."[4]

Such dispiriting accounts reflected the group's shrinking membership. State and federal officials estimated that the Carolina Klan, which in 1965 boasted somewhere around 12,000 dues-paying members, had shrunk to half that size by the summer of 1966. More than fifty klaverns folded during that time, and at the start of 1967, only 4,300 adherents regularly paid dues. By the spring of 1968, total membership hovered around 3,200, with a third of those delinquent on their dues and the majority failing to attend weekly klavern meetings. The FBI estimated that fewer than 1,000 active klansmen remained. And even those modest numbers were again cut in half by the decade's end.[5]

Beginning in 1966, the UKA's rallies attracted fewer supporters and curious onlookers. Certain events still drew large crowds—observers noted, for instance, that 2,000 or 3,000 came out for an August 1967 event in Rowan County, which featured speeches from Shelton and other national klan leaders, several string bands, sky diver exhibitions, and carnival booths. But overall, average rally attendance fell: from 1,880 in 1965, to 617 the following year, and again to 307 in 1967. According to a police report, a Wilmington rally in the summer of 1967 attracted only half the crowd that a gathering on the same site had drawn on a cold night the previous November. Two months later, a rally in the northeast corner of the state, known as a klan hotbed, was canceled for lack of attendance after only six spectators showed up. Following the UKA's 1967 national meeting, Bob Jones found it difficult to hide his disappointment, complaining to the entire state membership that, for the first time in his four years as North Carolina's Grand Dragon, he felt ashamed of the state's poor showing. By 1969, eroding turnouts led the UKA State Board to schedule rallies only on Saturday nights.

These decreasing turnouts meant fewer dollars for the UKA's klaverns and state office coffers, which compounded the loss of dues revenue as members abandoned the organization. The average take from klan speakers' "pass the hat" appeals, according to FBI tallies, was only $71 in 1967, down from $129 the prior year and $229 in 1965. Jones and his inner circle concocted increasingly desperate schemes to rebuild the UKA's membership and finances. Late in 1966, Jones stopped taking his salary for a time and doubled the percentage of dues that klaverns were required to send to the UKA State Office. The 1968 State Meeting included a resolution to assess each unit $100 to get the UKA "out of the red." By that time, membership requirements and standards had all but disappeared, and officers had moved from gentle appeals to step up recruitment to formalized membership drives. Anyone who signed up or reinstated twenty members earned a six-transistor radio and a place in the grand prize drawing for a 12-gauge shotgun for men and "his and hers" klan rings for women. The campaign did little to stem the exodus.[6]

As with the group's rise, a number of factors contributed to the UKA's precipitous decline in the latter half of the 1960s. Historians and other social scientists highlight the closing window of opportunity for the klan to assert itself as a viable line of resistance against encroaching civil rights initiatives. Accounts by journalists and federal investigators emphasize the debates over finances and organizational strategy that increasingly tore at the group from the inside. Those factors certainly mattered, but as with the KKK's decline in the 1870s and the decimation of Thomas Hamilton and Catfish Cole's respective klan outfits in the 1950s, the fall of the UKA is predominantly a policing story.

While the UKA's growth in 1963 and 1964 occurred mostly in communities beset by high levels of racial competition and consequent resistance to civil rights reform, the klan maintained its appeal only when government officials adopted a laissez-faire orientation toward organized white supremacists. In contrast, in states like Florida, which likewise eschewed massive resistance to desegregation policies, coordinated policing severely limited the KKK's ability to build a following. Unlike the active support for the klan witnessed in much of the Deep South, the ambivalent action of supposedly anti-KKK officials informally maintained less stringent policing in North Carolina. Gradually, however, intensified pressures by the federal government and the consequent commitment by state officials to preserve the state's progressive image overwhelmed such ambivalence.

Shrinking Opportunities and Organizational Strife

By the later 1960s, the UKA clearly faced both a closing window of political opportunity and increasing infighting over resources and tactics. With the passing of the Civil Rights Act of 1964 and the following year's Voting Rights Act, the idea that the klan's militantly defensive posture would preserve Jim Crow became an increasingly hard sell. Massive resistance became less palatable, replaced even in the Deep South by subtler shifts that preserved the color line in less formal ways. While civil rights initiatives certainly made an impact on established southern practices, "white flight" residential migration, token school desegregation policies, gerrymandered voting districts, and the emergence of de facto segregated institutions served to limit interracial contact and maintain white advantage in the labor market and elsewhere. Civil right reforms no longer seemed to pose a fatal threat to established systems of racial privilege.[7]

Such shifts helped to reduce the public's tolerance for the UKA's activities. By 1967, klan leaders had difficulty securing leases for many of their nightly rallies. Increasingly, anti-klan resolutions by mainstream religious and civic associations countered advance rally publicity. The Lee County Ministerial Association's 1966 statement was emblematic; it viewed the arrival of the UKA with "alarm" and condemned the klan's "long record of preaching hate, practicing violence and taking the law into its own hands." Likewise, the Raleigh Ministerial Association denounced the klan as "basically un-American," and Washington County religious leaders released a statement on Christmas Day saying that the KKK made a "mockery of Christianity." The North Carolina Baptist State Convention, which represented 3,423 churches and nearly 1 million members, unanimously passed a resolution "decry[ing] the bigotry, prejudice, intolerance and ill will which characterizes the Ku Klux Klan in its treatment of social and economic problems, and... protest[ing] the Klan's perverted use of the Christian Cross, thus making the symbol of eternal love into a symbol of contemporary hate." A Wayne County klavern was expelled from its rented meeting space when a reporter from the *Goldsboro News-Argus* published an exposé of their activities. After a Sampson County newspaper editor published a like-minded blistering anti-klan attack, Bob Jones defensively complained that he was the victim of discrimination.[8]

In the black community, militant responses to klan hate tactics also became increasingly common. When UKA members rode through a black neighborhood outside of Raleigh throwing out pamphlets and threatening violence, a group of locals gathered at a neighborhood soda shop with shotguns and pistols, splitting up in separate cars in an ultimately unsuccessful search for the klan perpetrators. Another resident who had drawn the klan's ire informed local officials that he "intended to shoot" any klansmen who set foot on his property. On at least two occasions, small bands of black marines stationed in North Carolina's Camp Lejeune attempted to provoke armed battles with the KKK, and in 1968 four black teenagers managed to burn down the building that served as a Johnston County klavern's headquarters.[9]

Klan leaders recognized that this increasingly hostile climate signaled a closing window of opportunity. By 1968, as the stock quote, "It is now or never—the hour is getting late" appeared for the first time under Robert Shelton's signature, even the UKA's letterhead signaled that the time had passed for confident claims that the klan would lead the South's defiant defense of segregation.[10] Unrest within the organization only compounded and deepened this pessimism.

Tensions within the klan came from several sources. Syble Jones exclusively handled the tens of thousands of dollars that poured into the UKA's North Carolina State Office, a system that inevitably lent itself to accusations that the Jones's were misappropriating klan resources. Individual klavern officials suffered similar complaints—and with apparent reason. An officer of one klavern was banished after taking more than $4,000 to pay his delinquent personal tax bill. Higher level indiscretions proved more difficult to resolve. State officer Bob Kornegay was relocated to the UKA's Virginia Realm after being accused of various financial misappropriations. Several state meetings were held in 1966 to debate Grand Dragon Jones's failure to disclose the klan's financial details or hire anyone other than his wife to handle the group's accounting ledger. "Without exception," an informant reported, "each officer that had anything to say was very critical of the way the Grand Dragon had conducted his personal life and also the business affairs of the UKA."[11]

Cleavages also emerged over tactical decisions. Jones generally viewed klan violence as costly to the UKA's growth and stability, and carefully counterbalanced displays of uncompromising toughness with appeals intended to discourage members from engaging in unauthorized actions. Reining in wanton violence allowed many peripheral adherents to believe, for a time at least, in the UKA's devotion to above-board civic expressions of traditional southern values. However, this approach alienated more aggressive segments of the klan's core constituency, who felt betrayed by the Grand Dragon's disingenuous boasts that the UKA would use whatever means necessary to protect its white turf.

More and more, such debates led to serious ruptures. "Me and the boys done got you a Cadillac with three forward gears and one in reverse," Raymond Cranford ceremoniously pronounced during his split with Jones at a 1966 meeting, "and I'll be damned if you ain't been doin' nothin' but backin' up ever since!" Cranford's grievances dated back to the previous summer's unrest in Plymouth. With more than a thousand klansmen en route to the small town, Cranford hatched a plan that would have turned Plymouth into the civil rights movement's bloodiest battleground. Reputedly, the scheme involved Cranford setting up "his boys," many with machine guns, on the roads in and out of town. They would then lay down roadblocks, freeing another set of klansmen to "clean house" in Plymouth's black neighborhoods. Regardless of Jones's feelings about the moral implications of such a massacre, President Johnson had placed army units at Fort Bragg on full combat alert, and the federal response to such klan action would certainly have brought an end to the UKA as a public membership organization. Jones refused to authorize Cranford's plan, and in the process lost the allegiance of a significant cadre of his most committed klansmen.[12]

Policing the UKA

One must consider this inter-organizational strife together with the actions of police officials, who alternately monitored, reacted to, fomented, and exacerbated conflicts within the UKA. Through a series of efforts, marked at times by a gulf between aggressive formal policy and ambivalent action in the field, a range of state agencies—from local police forces, to the State Bureau of Investigation and the governor's office, to the FBI and the White House—increasingly focused their attention and resources on the KKK. In the process, they hastened the UKA's demise.

While North Carolina state police officials formally opposed the klan's cavalier lawlessness, ideological alignment with the UKA's segregationist goals often tempered their dealings with the klan. This ambivalence created a mismatch between the goals espoused by police agencies and the actions of individual agents as they carried out orders.[13] At the local level, police attitudes toward the klan ranged from tacitly supportive to overtly antagonistic. The lack of extensive formal training and uniform professional standards among elected sheriffs at the time contributed to this variation, as did individual histories and predilections. As we have seen, Greenville police chief Henry Lawson aggressively challenged local klan members, with one klansman lamenting in frustration that "the chief is 100 percent against the klan." In communities like Pittsboro, in contrast, it was so widely known that police officials were klan members that Good Neighbor Council chairman Dave Coltrane penned a memo to Governor Moore's office to emphasize that such alliances "should not be tolerated."

Coltrane's view was typical enough to make it costly for local police officials to openly acknowledge their klan sympathies, even in the state's KKK strongholds. Locally, police ambivalence over rising klan activity was strongest where officers had to suppress klan affinities in the face of public condemnation. In one case, when word spread that members of the Wilmington police force, including county sheriff Marion Millis, were part of the New Hanover Improvement Association (the cover name for a thriving local UKA klavern), Millis strenuously denied the claims. Later, he reluctantly acknowledged that he and six of his deputies had joined the group, but only, he claimed, as part of their police work, to obtain "inside information" about the klan's actions and plans. In fact, their involvement had gone much deeper. Millis himself helped to arrange the use of a hall for UKA meetings, one of his deputies later became a UKA state officer, and another used the sheriff's office as a space to maintain the klavern's books and collect dues. Under pressure, the sheriff distanced himself from the klan and insisted that his officers—some of whom he admitted had become "enthused" by the klan—leave the UKA. Under fire from scandalous media exposés and public condemnation by Wilmington's Good Neighbor Council, when he vowed to run for reelection in 1966, he knew that maintaining even a semblance of viability required that he continue to deny KKK involvement.[14]

Ambivalence within State Police Agencies

Ambivalence took on different guises within state and federal police organizations, where agents in the field were subject to orders from a centralized bureaucracy. While formal policy, developed at the top levels of each agency, aimed to suppress KKK activity throughout the state, the latitude that agents possessed on the ground opened up possibilities for mismatches to emerge between organizational goals and the day-to-day actions intended to achieve them. In North Carolina, the State Highway Patrol (SHP) and the State Bureau of Investigation (SBI) coordinated most of the state policing response.

Established in 1929, the SHP had grown steadily with the expansion of the state's highway system. With 622 officers spread among the state's six troops, the Highway Patrol was both decentralized and large enough to preclude highly selective recruitment and selection processes. As a result, as with local police, SHP officers' training and professional status frequently failed to override their personal feelings about civil rights issues and the KKK. "Hell, I'm on their side," an SHP officer noted, chuckling and motioning toward a UKA rally site, within earshot of a federal investigator during the summer of 1965. Such affinity with klan supporters also explained how Bob Jones could "give hell" to the president and vice-president, the FBI, and a range of other state authorities, and then conclude rally speeches by sincerely commending the State Highway Patrol for their handling of the meeting and the associated traffic.

SHP officers crossed paths frequently with klan members and sympathizers. Not long after Jones began using rallies to resuscitate the Carolina Klan in 1963, the SHP established an official presence at each of the UKA's public events. The Patrol's formal charge was to deal with traffic issues created by the large-scale events. But SHP officers, under orders from their superiors, additionally monitored the klan's actions, filing summary reports of the rallies themselves and sometimes compiling a list of attendees' license numbers. While it is unclear how these data were typically used, lists of the relevant cars' owners were sometimes forwarded to the governor's office, and presumably this information could be used in future investigations of racially motivated crimes. In 1968, in an effort to publicly shame rally attendees, the *Raleigh News and Observer* published an SHP license plate list, with tag numbers matched to registrants' names.[15]

Like the SHP, the SBI assigned agents to monitor each rally. Formed in 1937 to "secure more effective administration of the criminal laws of the State, to prevent crime, and to procure the speedy apprehension and identification of criminals," the Bureau coordinated investigations and forensic analyses around the state. In 1955, state legislators extended the SBI's "benefits, duties, authority, and requirements," and presumably that expanded role allowed the Bureau to undertake intelligence work, including the monitoring of UKA proceedings. Typically, its agents would remain on the roadway or parking area for the duration of a rally, close enough to observe and hear the speeches but away from the crowd. When Jones or other klan officials would offer invitations to come in to the rally itself, telling them that "all white people" were invited,[16] they would politely decline.

Agents would compile reports of each rally, which typically included a summary of the speeches, detailed observations of the event and its attendees, and even the size of the cross burned at the climax of the proceedings. In some cases, SBI personnel recorded license plate numbers and taped rally speeches. They made frequent use of informants to glean details about the UKA's plans, actions, and organizational practices. With only a small budget to recruit informants, agents often encouraged recruits to "double dip" by also informing for the deeper pocketed FBI, or else target more vulnerable would-be infiltrators, usually people who could be charged for crimes or aspired to law enforcement heroism.[17]

Despite the overlap in tasks, the SBI's small size and elite status among state law enforcement personnel meant that agents were more likely to view themselves as professionals and thus bound by a charge that superseded their personal political views.[18] More selective hiring practices than those of the SHP made it less likely that SBI agents would be drawn from tenuous working-class settings where the klan had its greatest appeal. In contrast with certain SHP officers' tendencies to openly declare their enthusiasm for the UKA's agenda, SBI agents usually adopted an air of detached disdain for the klan. "This is actually a big week-end for them, to be able to go to a rally," SBI agents would note dismissively. "Wouldn't you think people would have more to do with their time than this?"[19]

But while ideological affinities and fewer professional controls explained the SHP's weak policing of the klan, subtler ambivalences among SBI agents contributed to a similar mismatch between goals and on-the-ground action. Haywood Starling, a longtime agent who later would go on to direct the SBI, described the Bureau as having a "working relationship" with the klan, as their regular contact with UKA leaders who attended each night's rally bred a routinized familiarity that bent toward basic cooperation. Jones regularly provided agents with a list of upcoming UKA meetings and rallies, as well as an open invitation to attend each event. Such contact, in Starling's view, was more important for keeping abreast of the UKA's plans than his informants' intelligence work.

While no evidence exists of active SBI complicity, agents' private interactions with klan leaders and members departed from North Carolina officials' tough-talking public anti-klan stance. "Most [klan members] were harmless, honest, and law-abiding citizens who were misguided in their thoughts and beliefs," SBI agent Robert Emerson explained. "The kluxers knew we had our jobs to do, and I must say that we were treated with respect. There were many times the Grand Dragon of North Carolina would sit in the backseat of my car and talk about sports or current events unrelated to race as another agent and I recorded license numbers."[20]

As a result of this working relationship, the SBI limited investigations to certain kinds of legal violations. Despite the mandate to monitor and expose the UKA's frequent acts of terror and intimidation, the Bureau demonstrated a marked inability to deal with the UKA as an organization. Take, for example, the case of the UKA booth at the 1966 State Fair. Jones and the UKA procured the booth to distribute klan literature, sell its paraphernalia, and broadcast racist comments over their loudspeaker system. In the face of a boycott by the state NAACP, which referred to state officials' willingness to rent a booth to the UKA as "an insult to the Negroes of North Carolina," and klan members' obvious harassment of passers-by, the SBI only placed agents in the vicinity to defuse potential conflicts. Following an argument between UKA officer Herbert Rouse and two white college students, an SBI agent arrested Rouse for possessing a concealed weapon, the only punitive action taken against the UKA that week.[21]

This approach encapsulated the Bureau's broader orientation to the UKA. While the SBI would not intentionally look the other way to allow klansmen to perpetrate violence, the agency refused to exert control over the group apart from the policing of explicit criminal acts, even when they had the support of higher state officials to do so. The Bureau's prevailing orientation to the civil rights struggle was that "extremists" on both sides—the KKK as well as the NAACP—threatened law and order. However, the pervasive culture in the SBI, as in many white institutions, precluded equal treatment of both "extremes." In striking contrast to agents' frequent collegiality toward klan leaders, the actions of the SBI showed a pronounced mistrust of and often demonstrated pro-active hostility toward civil rights activists.

In one SBI report, for instance, John Salter, a prominent civil rights leader and field secretary of the Southern Conference Educational Fund (SCEF), was characterized as "largely responsible for most of the tension"; the report effectively ignored the long string of UKA reprisals against Salter's colleagues. Other state officials involved with the SBI's "specialized investigation" of the KKK demonstrated similar attitudes. After Salter objected to local officials' dismissal of various acts of racial intimidation—including cross-burnings, rock- and brick-throwing, verbal threats, physical beatings, and "efforts to force Negro cars off the roads and... to run down walking Negroes with automobiles"—as teenage pranks, Good Neighbor Council chairman Dave Coltrane responded to a colleague that "Salter is inclined to exaggerate the facts." Similarly, Coltrane noted in 1966 that SCLC field secretary Golden Frinks was currently "in command of the Negroes, but we hope to get him out before too long." A county official agreed, noting that Frinks was "a notorious liar who specializes in spreading hate and damning North Carolina, its laws and its people all over the country." When pressed to explain an upsurge in klan-related activity, SBI officials argued that they were a reaction to a series of civil rights demonstrations supported by visits from Ralph Abernathy and Martin Luther King Jr. For the SBI, these movement leaders were the root cause of racial disturbances in the state.

The SBI saw the UKA's activities as a reaction to civil rights activity, so the attitude that pervaded the Bureau was that the UKA could be hindered most effectively by policing the organized *integrationist* efforts that ostensibly aroused the klansmen's ire. As the Bureau was largely suspicious of and hostile toward the civil rights movement, the state's failure to adopt legal restrictions on the UKA implicitly validated the klan's right to militantly defend the Jim Crow status quo. Indeed, according to one SBI official, the media's criticism of the KKK was "all out of proportion," as the klan needed to be monitored not for its association with segregationist terror but rather because of the presence of "a select few [members] capable of anything." As a result, prior to 1966, the sorts of aggressive policing tactics that stymied George Dorsett and Boyd Hamby's organizing efforts in Florida were more likely to be exercised against civil rights activists than the UKA in North Carolina.[22]

SBI officials' refusal to police the klan in the same manner as they did civil rights demonstrators played out clearly in a number of instances, including a large-scale conflict near the city of Roanoke Rapids. When the UKA scheduled a Sunday afternoon rally in a field adjacent to a black neighborhood, members of the black community, with the support of SNCC, mobilized a counter-protest. SNCC field workers and their allies provided state leaders with advance notice of their intentions, sending multiple letters to North Carolina director of administration E. J. Rankin Jr. and other officials.

Tensions ran high the day of the rally. Robert Lee Vincent, a black Roanoke Rapids resident, approached and exchanged words with a group of klansmen preparing for the event. Vincent announced that he was going to go home, get his gun, and run the klan members off the property. He then returned with a .22 caliber rifle and fired a dozen shots, leaving three klansmen with minor injuries and Vincent in jail. By 4:00 that afternoon, approximately 500 klan members and their supporters had arrived at the rally site. The rally itself featured some militant talk by George Dorsett (later exposed as an FBI informant), who made an appeal for violent retaliation to the shooting. Meanwhile, a group of black residents, some of whom held picket signs, gathered on the opposite side of the highway from the rally site. Dorsett's speech grew in intensity, as he criticized the police for not removing the protestors who were "interfering with a religious service." Without a trace of irony, he shouted to the crowd that the police were "not here to protect us, but"—he gestured emphatically toward the picketers across the road—"them!" He urged his followers to go to the highway and remove the dissenters themselves, and at least 400 complied, rushing toward the pickets. At that point, the police and SBI decided "to arrest all the [civil rights] pickets for walking on the wrong side of the road in violation of the pedestrian law." Despite the clear threat of klan violence against nonviolent protestors who had requested state protection days in advance, and the fact that members of the UKA's Security Guard were armed with shotguns, only one klansman was arrested.[23]

Such policing actions should be viewed within their broader context. While dealing with two dozen civil rights picketers rather than the hundreds of klan adherents who challenged them may be a viable strategy to control a volatile situation, the SBI and SHP firmly supported the UKA. Aware of the threat posed by a large-scale klan rally adjacent to a black neighborhood, the SBI implicitly affirmed the UKA's rights to hold such a provocative event by not attempting to prevent or otherwise deal with it pro-actively. When the picketers arrived, in contrast, state police were quick to warn them to leave, to avoid "trouble." While SHP officers were on hand, according to their usual protocol, only to control traffic, they routinely encouraged local officials to deny permits to civil rights groups who planned similar gatherings.

Disjunctures like this illustrate state agencies' ambivalent orientation to the UKA. Clearly concerned about the klan's capacity for illegality and violence, SBI agents employed informants and physical surveillance to gather extensive intelligence on the KKK's activities. When such efforts provided information tied to a particular criminal act, SBI agents took steps to investigate and arrest individual perpetrators. However, the broader cultural climate within the Bureau precluded the use of this intelligence data to pursue the sort of control over the UKA's actions that marked the organization's orientation to civil rights activism, which they viewed as the root cause of racial strife. Clearly, when seen alongside the state's active hostility toward the civil rights movement, their treatment of the klan failed to contribute to any far-reaching program to provide equal protection from racial conflict to both white and black citizens.[24]

Ambivalence within the FBI

When Mississippi civil rights workers Michael Schwerner, James Chaney, and Andrew Goodman went missing in June 1964, the specter of klan terrorism was splayed across the front pages of newspapers throughout the nation. The political fallout reached beyond Mississippi to Washington, where President Johnson and Attorney General Robert Kennedy demanded that FBI director J. Edgar Hoover make use of all of the resources at his disposal to defuse the possibility of further KKK violence in the South.

Hoover was ambivalent about moving on Mississippi. Committed to systems of law and order, however flawed, he found civil rights activists distasteful for their disdain of the southern justice system that failed to uphold the rights of African Americans. He also felt strongly that the movement, with its purported ties to communist interests, posed a significant security risk. In a very real sense, the FBI allied with the klan's goals, as it had long monitored and attempted to suppress civil rights initiatives through its "racial matters" investigations of prominent civil rights organizations and leaders—including Martin Luther King Jr.—whose purported moral shortcomings and alliances with communist agents made them suspect "subversives."

While he sympathized with certain of the klan's aims, however, Hoover clearly did not favor their means. Prior to taking over as FBI director in 1924, Hoover cut his investigative teeth on a 1922 case against the KKK in Louisiana. From that point on, he considered klan members' contempt for law and order as a personal challenge to the FBI's mission. As a "group of sadistic, vicious white trash," he once remarked off the record, klansmen also offended his sensibilities. So when Hoover saw in the urgency of the White House's demands a significant opportunity for the Bureau, he quickly acted on it.

The opportunity arose from the 1956 decision to expand the FBI's investigative and intelligence-gathering purview to actively harass members of the Communist Party–USA and their socialist allies. The resulting counterintelligence program, dubbed COINTELPRO, was designed to "expose, disrupt, misdirect, discredit, or otherwise neutralize" its targets. Legally controversial, the program blatantly disregarded due process and the constitutional rights of its targets; it commonly resorted to a range of "dirty tricks" and illegal procedures such as "black bag jobs," a Bureau term for break-ins intended to gather information and rattle its victims.[25]

In the White House, Kennedy and Johnson were well aware of the effectiveness of COINTELPRO, which had been approved as a means to act only against "hostile foreign powers" and their agents. If in the wake of the Mississippi murders Hoover could convince his superiors that similar tactics could halt KKK violence, he would not only expand the Bureau's klan-fighting repertoire but also establish a precedent for extending its counterintelligence actions to purely domestic targets. In effect, the FBI would add a powerful covert weapon to its arsenal.

To justify these strained connections between COINTELPRO's established countersubversive mission and the KKK, Hoover turned to William C. Sullivan. An assistant director whose unkempt appearance and zeal for political theory stood out in the button-down Bureau, Sullivan had marshaled much of the FBI's evidence linking the civil rights movement to the Communist Party–USA and also authored the first draft of Hoover's 1958 anti-communist best seller *Masters of Deceit*.

Connecting the klan to communist subversion, however, proved more difficult. Speaking in generalities about the civil rights field, Sullivan argued that the Communist Party was "increasing its activities in the field of racial matters and civil rights, directing more and more of its fire against the KKK and similar organizations to confuse the issue." In an internal memo, he pushed further, working by analogy to argue that the KKK and its allies were "essentially subversive" since their actions were, like those of communists, "inimical to the Constitution." Based on Sullivan's stance, James Gale, another assistant director, drafted a memo seeking formal approval for the counterintelligence program on July 30, 1964. There was no question, Gale concluded, that "the Communist Party now has evidenced a definite interest in the racial problem, is becoming deeply enmeshed therein, and appears to be exploiting it to an ever-increasing extent."[26]

At the end of August, the FBI prepared to roll out COINTELPRO–White Hate Groups. "Our counterintelligence efforts against hate groups will be closely supervised and coordinated to complement our expanded intelligence investigations directed at these organizations," explained Fred Baumgarner, director of the FBI Domestic Intelligence Division, in his memo to agents outlining the new program. "We intend to expose to public scrutiny the devious maneuvers and duplicity of the hate groups; to frustrate any efforts or plans they may have to consolidate their forces; to discourage their recruitment of new or youthful adherents; and to disrupt or eliminate their efforts to circumvent or violate the law."[27]

Each of the FBI's fifty-nine field offices scattered throughout the country reported directly to Bureau leadership in Washington, DC. Hoover instructed the FBI Special Agent in Charge (SAC) of each office to exploit local knowledge to propose "hard-hitting" counterintelligence actions against specified targets. Once approved by the director, these actions would be carried out by field agents, with "tangible results" noted in subsequent progress reports. The jurisdiction of the Bureau's Charlotte office included all of North Carolina.

On October 12, the Charlotte SAC outlined his general approach to neutralizing the KKK. In North Carolina, agents would avoid disrupting klan units that lacked "well-established informant coverage," as such actions would reduce the likelihood that informants could be placed in those klaverns in the future. They would generally avoid negative publicity, a time-tested counterintelligence tactic, as the SAC felt that prospective klan members thrived on a sort of outlaw status and would not be deterred by public criticism. Agents also would avoid "stirring up" klaverns that were "small, inactive, and peaceful." They would instead directly attack the klan's most obvious vulnerabilities: the simmering suspicions that leaders exploited the membership financially, certain members' limited employment prospects, and the fact that more than a few wives of klansmen felt that weekly klavern meetings and dark-of-night UKA missions provided ruses for adulterous activities. As with all Bureau programs, secrecy would be a priority, especially as agents were concerned about alienating themselves from local officials in the many communities where the UKA enjoyed broad support.[28]

Over the next six months, Charlotte and sixteen other field offices initiated thirty-six actions against klan-related targets. Several involved writing anonymous chain letters designed to sow dissension among members. Agents also supplied information to local officials to block UKA permit requests, and to "friendly media sources" to remove newspaper ads for klan turkey shoot fund-raisers. Later proposals involved sabotaging the sound system that the UKA planned to use at a national meeting, arranging fake postal deliveries at supposedly secret klavern meetings, and even creating and conveniently "dropping" FBI address books with false information about purported informants.

Perhaps the Bureau's most successful large-scale effort involved anonymous mailings of FBI-produced postcards to thousands of klan affiliates, threatening recipients to stop "hiding your identity under your sheet" because "somebody knows who you are." When Bob Jones's hold on his Grand Dragon's office became tenuous due to internal strife in 1966, the FBI created a "Klan Joke Book" featuring, among other cartoons, depictions of Jones with women and jugs overflowing with money. Agents mailed the Joke Books from locations strategically selected to suggest the involvement of Virginia Grand Dragon Bob Kornegay and old KKK nemesis Catfish Cole. Planted newspaper articles that emphasized the "big business" of the klan and various perks that trickled up to Jones and other leaders reinforced these images.

In total, between 1964 and 1971, agents carried out 455 actions under COINTELPRO–White Hate Groups.[29] The Bureau's massive informant program supported and bolstered these efforts. Throughout the 1960s the FBI sought to infiltrate a wide range of supposed dissidents—including communists, Black Power advocates, and New Leftists—but their ability to develop informants within the KKK was unparalleled. A few months into the White Hate Groups program, agents boasted that they had recruited infiltrators at an average rate of two per day. By early 1966 their North Carolina coverage extended to hundreds of informants in 165 of the approximately 225 active UKA klaverns in the state, and agents had gathered information on more than a thousand members statewide.

In many cases, those informants operated passively, providing information about klavern membership and plans to their FBI handlers. Such intelligence work itself fostered discontent within many klaverns. "I guess you knew I was here before you left Dunn—you apparently know everything else that's going on," "Peanut" Jackson complained to an agent at a rally in Fayetteville, a county over from Jackson's Dunn home. At least one klavern began identifying members by their card numbers, to prevent "leaks" by concealing as much personal detail as possible.

At times, particular infiltrators carried out specific COINTELPRO actions, such as the spreading of rumors to foster conflicts or chart klavern members on ill-fated courses. Most significantly, a small number of highly-placed informants exerted control over the UKA's top-level decisions. The best known of those valued informants was George Dorsett. As the UKA's "Imperial Kludd," Dorsett served as a national officer in his capacity as UKA chaplain. He was close to Jones and a key part of the Carolina Klan's inner circle. He also was a big draw at almost every North Carolina rally in 1965 and 1966. While Shelton tended to deliver dry and long-winded anti-communist screeds and Jones favored "nigger jokes" over higher minded oratory, Dorsett's passionate evangelizing about the UKA's Christian and patriotic missions most reliably filled the money buckets that circulated at rallies around the state.[30]

Dorsett's work with the FBI contributed directly to the fissures that developed gradually in the UKA. He often needled and challenged Jones, who by the end of 1965 became sufficiently fed up with such antics to send the preacher on a short-lived stint to Florida to help organize that state's moribund UKA Realm. When Dorsett returned from the Sunshine State that spring, his rift with Jones only intensified, especially after he hatched a scheme to bring Catfish Cole into the UKA's fold.

Since Cole's release from prison in 1960, he had been active in a variety of segregationist pursuits and had at least one eye on the klan's resurgence in the state. In early 1966, he tried to bring back the North Carolina Knights, holding rallies in Pitt and Beaufort counties and requesting to speak at the Chowan County Courthouse in advance of a local appearance by Martin Luther King Jr. Those efforts mostly fizzled, drawing only a fraction of the crowd that typically came out for UKA events. But Cole's fortunes changed in June, when Dorsett and Greensboro-based klan cohorts Clyde Webster and Robert Hudgins—all veterans of the North Carolina Knights in the 1950s—called to invite him to join with the UKA.

As Cole mulled the offer, he and Dorsett grew closer, united largely by a mutual opposition to Jones's leadership. While traveling to rallies, Dorsett would constantly bad-mouth the Grand Dragon. Jones was embezzling money from the klan fund, he's a drunkard, he chases women, Dorsett charged, to anyone who would listen. Meanwhile, he and Cole continued to travel together to rallies and street walks, and in early 1967 Cole moved to Greensboro, leaving his wife and longtime home in Kinston. In response to charges that the move was part of a UKA power grab, Cole clarified his sense of his role, insisting that "a leader doesn't seek out people—people seek out a leader." Dorsett concurred. "I think Rev. Cole can be a big help to all of us," he told a reporter. Soon after, following a Virginia event that featured Cole, he asked his UKA cohorts what they thought of Catfish's speech. "He would make a good leader," Dorsett remarked, "wouldn't he?" Despite mounting evidence to the contrary, Dorsett maintained to the broader membership that Cole had "no intention at all of trying to be elected to any office in the klan."[31]

The last straw came at a March 7 meeting in Guilford County, where Dorsett swore Cole into the UKA without Jones's knowledge. Less than a month later, Jones responded by banishing Dorsett, Cole, and Webster, instigating an all-out battle for the UKA's membership. Dorsett sent letters to klaverns around the state, asking for support and insisting that the real problem was Jones's corruption. He vouched for the legitimacy of anti-Jones missives from the UKA's National Intelligence Committee (NIC), supposedly a top-secret klan committee that had undertaken an investigation of the group's leadership but in fact a savvy piece of counterintelligence created by Dorsett and his FBI handler. The first NIC mandate, mailed to members on June 5, had "suspended" Jones, along with Robert Shelton, from their offices for "personal misconduct, malfeasance, and... violating the klan constitution."[32] Dorsett also contacted North Carolina's secretary of state, in search of legal standing for his dubious claim that Shelton maintained illegal authority over the UKA's North Carolina Realm. He appeared on a Greensboro television station to announce plans to form a new klan organization with Cole and Webster, and held a rally in Guilford County to address "The Controversy in the Ku Klux Klan with Their Leaders."

Threats of violence regularly marred events organized by both factions early that summer. The toxic atmosphere worsened in late July, when Cole, en route to a fishing excursion with klan colleague Paul LeClair, died after their car went out of control and plunged down an embankment south of Greensboro. Dorsett complained to reporters that "foul play" must have been involved, noting that he and Cole had been receiving threats from the UKA and that the car's steering column appeared to have been "unscrewed."[33]

Now irreparably estranged from United Klans, and without Cole as a partner, Dorsett formed his own rival organization, the Confederate Knights of the KKK (CKKKK). The move was carried out with the active encouragement of his FBI handlers, who helped draft the group's first recruiting letter. Informants made a strong push to discredit Jones and the UKA and to attract members to the CKKKK, which they billed as an "acceptable" alternative. By 1968, Bureau agents drafted letters designed to urge disgruntled UKA members not to renounce the klan entirely but instead to leave the group for Dorsett's new organization. "[Our] attempt to split UKA in North Carolina and diminish its power was successful," reported the Charlotte FBI office at the start of 1969.

By that point, the CKKKK had more than forty functioning units, while the UKA's membership was down by two-thirds.[34] The COINTEL program's overarching aim was signaled by agents' active support for Dorsett's outfit, and their emphasis on members shifting allegiance from the UKA to the CKKKK. Purportedly designed to hit the UKA with a "death-dealing blow," COINTELPRO–White Hate Groups actions, though frequently "exceeding the Charlotte [field office's] expectations insofar as fostering discontent, dissension, and confusion," were in fact intended to control the klan rather than eliminate the group entirely.

These efforts succeeded because of agents' effectiveness in the field. Most did not fully buy into COINTELPRO architect William Sullivan's claims that the UKA was subversive, as it quickly became clear that the group was fundamentally and transparently reactionary—largely supportive of existing power structures and traditional American values. KKK members tended to view themselves as strongly patriotic and vehemently anti-communist, and as strong opponents to the tactics and goals of the civil rights movement. As such, they had considerable ideological overlap with the FBI, which viewed civil rights organizations as the pawns of a Communist Party that, Hoover believed, was using the idea of integration to dupe black leaders into weakening the state to advance a "red" agenda.[35]

The presence of a number of southern agents in the Charlotte field office heightened this sense of overlap. Dargan Frierson, a Greensboro-based special agent well known for his ability to develop klan informants, made good use of his deep local accent and was quick to relate that his own grandfather—once a slave owner in Sumter, South Carolina—had himself been in the KKK during the 1920s. Recognizing the importance of relatability, Frierson advised his FBI superiors not to "send any Yankees" to work with klan informants. Klan members, in turn, often found FBI entreaties compelling, as many had deep respect for the FBI and law enforcement generally and were thus susceptible to patriotic appeals by agents.[36]

Given the FBI mandate to neutralize the KKK, the very characteristics that made certain agents successful at developing klan sources—their ability to relate well to the UKA's core constituencies—produced considerable ambivalence. Agents' day-to-day approaches, which emphasized actions designed to control rather than to eliminate the UKA, partly reconciled these conflicts. In spite of frequent talk of wiping out the KKK altogether in formal memos, Frierson explained, agents in his field office felt that "the klan itself was perfectly permissible to join—but let's not have violence."

Frierson himself had little trouble establishing a political rapport with many klan members. He openly expressed his lack of enthusiasm about integration and sometimes told klansmen to "cuss LBJ all you want; I don't think any more of him than you do." He would also "look the other way" when his informants were involved with cross-burnings or other actions that, in his view, "wouldn't hurt anyone." To Frierson, working with top-level informants required such latitude. To maintain the trust required to access the klan's inner circles, he reasoned, infiltrators like Dorsett "had to be out there, where it was going on. He had to talk like them, he had to act like them, he had to give fiery speeches."[37]

This focus on controlling the klan permeated Charlotte agents' communication with Hoover. From the program's outset, the Charlotte SAC had emphasized taking care not to disrupt klan units when such action would hinder Bureau efforts to place informants. He also established a laissez-faire policy toward "small, inactive, and peaceful" klaverns. Later proposals increasingly focused on efforts to "hold down membership" and keep existing hard-core members stably within klaverns with significant informant coverage. In late 1967, the Charlotte SAC resisted Hoover's emphasis on actions that would remove Bob Jones from the UKA. The SAC was fearful of Jones's possible replacement, Virginia Grand Dragon Kornegay, who possessed sufficient "charm," "personal magnetism," and leadership ability to "give the state organization a 'shot in the arm' which it now needs to continue as an effective klan group." The presence of Jones, in contrast, would stabilize the UKA, maintaining a climate in which informants could easily control klan actions.[38]

The same desire to control the klan's actions guided the Bureau's extended support of Dorsett's Confederate Knights. Despite the widespread sense that Dorsett's group appealed to klansmen who, like Raymond Cranford, were in search of an option even more aggressively militant than the UKA, agents saw the CKKKK as an "acceptable" alternative as informants largely composed its core. By the close of 1968, the Charlotte office announced that the CKKKK had accomplished its intended results: "to siphon off members of UKA, thereby diminishing the power of UKA."

To explain away the fact that those who shifted allegiances remained attached to the KKK, the Charlotte SAC hypothesized that "there are many members who will join any klan organization in existence. If the CKKKK ceases to function as an organization, these members undoubtedly will return to UKA. This is not desirable." Thus, the ambivalence of FBI agents about the threat posed by the klan—a group perceived as dangerous not because of any subversive ideology, but rather because of its propensity to engage in unpredictable lawlessness—dismissed the Bureau's stated overall goal of eliminating the klan. Instead, the Charlotte SAC channeled members toward acceptable klan alternatives controlled by the FBI itself.[39]

Overcoming Ambivalence: Federal Pressures Mount

While individual policing agencies' ambivalence toward the KKK tempered their ability to fully suppress the UKA and other "white hate" targets, by 1965 mounting federal pressures gave rise to significant, if loosely coordinated, anti-klan actions that cumulatively eroded the UKA's ability to organize. The FBI, through COINTELPRO, knew of the outsize growth of the Tar Heel State's UKA; the disturbing trend became more widely known among federal officials after the *New York Times* published an article in September 1964 under the headline "Big Gains Scored by Carolina Klan." The reporter highlighted Bob Jones's leadership, prompting Hoover to instruct the FBI's Charlotte field office to gather information on Jones's potential vulnerabilities.[40]

Jones remained on federal agencies' radar when, several months later, the brutal murder of Viola Liuzzo by a carload of Alabama klansmen spurred more intensive government involvement in the klan problem. Within hours of the Liuzzo killing, as the March 1965 Selma-to-Montgomery voting rights march continued, LBJ leveraged the crime to aggressively push for passage of his signature Voting Rights legislation. The president made it clear to Hoover that the FBI should be working "around the clock" to solve the crime. By the following morning, the Bureau had done just that, aided by the fact that one of its informants, Gary Thomas Rowe, had been a passenger in the klan car that chased and killed Liuzzo. Hoover remained ambivalent about who was ultimately at fault, telling the president that Liuzzo had "indications of needle marks in her arms where she had been taking dope; that she was sitting very close to the Negro [nineteen-year-old fellow civil rights worker LeRoy Moton] in the car; that it had the appearance of a necking party." But despite the FBI director's backroom reservations, LBJ enlisted Hoover to stand by his side for a nationally televised news conference that afternoon. The president's strongly worded statement betrayed none of Hoover's uncertainty. "If Klansmen hear my voice today," Johnson admonished, "let it be both an appeal and a warning to get out of the Klan now and return to decent society before it is too late."[41]

LBJ's vehemence set other anti-klan initiatives in motion. His televised speech offered support for a congressional investigation of the KKK, and that call was taken up—to the surprise of many—by the House Un-American Activities Committee (HUAC). Months earlier, Georgia Representative Charles Weltner, the sole southern congressman to vote for final passage of the Civil Rights Act, had proposed an inquest into the KKK.[42] Now, the Liuzzo murder provided the political momentum to carry through the proposal. Following the president's speech, the path to legislative action by the HUAC was cleared by statements from Senator Thomas Dodd and Speaker of the House John McCormack likening the KKK to other "subversive" and "conspiratorial" threats.

Despite its purported anti-klan leanings, HUAC remained suspect among civil rights groups. A joint petition filed by SNCC, the SCLC, and three other civil rights organizations condemned the initiative. These groups called instead for an investigation run by an independent presidential body, along the lines of the Warren Commission's inquiry into President Kennedy's assassination. "HUAC's history proves that it is a group that has consistently attacked the same people and movements the Klan has attacked," the petition argued. "It is reasonable to assume that the so-called investigation of the Klan will soon become a new attack on civil rights groups."[43]

Good cause existed for such suspicion, as HUAC's long-standing mission to root out communism in American institutions dovetailed with a strenuous effort by the FBI and others to link civil rights activism to communist subversion. Statements by HUAC's southern members, in particular its chairman Edwin Willis of Louisiana, did nothing to assuage these concerns. "Elimination of the influence of the Klans alone will not bring the peace and order we all desire," Willis told reporters. "There are other racial agitators at work in all parts of the country. The Committee is aware that Communist influence is at work in this field." The KKK hearings, according to Willis and his HUAC colleague, Alabama congressman John Buchanan, should rightfully be part of a broader investigation of extremism, centered on civil rights organizations themselves.[44]

But on the eve of the hearings, support in the national media for government action that finally checked the KKK's reign of terror in the South overshadowed such tensions. "Every indication," the *Washington Post* observed, "is that HUAC plans to probe the Klan with propriety and purpose that could enhance the Committee's image." HUAC opened the public phase of its klan investigation on October 19, 1965. Over the next four months the Committee devoted a total of thirty-seven days to KKK hearings, calling nearly 200 klan members and associates to testify. As part of their voluminous investigation, staffers drew on FBI intelligence files; compiled thousands of pages of investigative records, newspaper clippings, and informant reports; and even headed south to observe KKK rallies and events.

The hearings themselves unfolded oddly. Most of the UKA members subpoenaed refused to provide any substantive testimony. On the first day, Robert Shelton—with Raleigh-based attorney and former Wake County Superior Court solicitor Lester Chalmers Jr. by his side—set the tone. "Sir, I respectively [*sic*] decline to answer that question," Shelton responded to each query, "for the reasons that I honestly feel that any answer might tend to incriminate me in violation of my rights as guaranteed to me by Amendments, 5, 1, 4, and 14 of the Constitution of the United States of America." Conferring frequently with his counsel and under threat of a contempt of Congress charge, Shelton repeated his plea seventy-three times during the opening day of the hearings. When Bob Jones and other UKA leaders took the stand, they followed the same strategy. Investigators posed increasingly long-winded questions to introduce much of the detail that Shelton and other klan leaders refused to provide.[45]

The hearings served as a high-profile venue for airing the government's intelligence data on the KKK, slanted to attack the legitimacy of the klan as a patriotic organization and increase suspicion that klan leaders engaged in financial impropriety. Investigators believed that North Carolina's massive UKA operation provided the Committee with their clearest evidence of graft, and they produced canceled checks, bank documents, and rally collection tallies to demonstrate the "enormous profits" that, they claimed, ultimately lined the pockets of Jones and other klan leaders. Disgruntled former members, such as ex-Grand Kludd Roy Woodle, told of shill games he and others used to extract contributions from unsuspecting rally-goers. Joseph G. DuBois, treasurer of a klavern in Goldsboro, resigned dramatically from the KKK on the stand, saying that his vision of the klan as representing "garden variety Americans" was shaken by UKA leaders' refusal to engage with HUAC questioners. "Only a Communist takes the Fifth Amendment or someone with something to hide," he explained to the Committee, after agreeing to turn over his unit's records.[46] New Hanover County sheriff Marion Millis contritely described how he and his deputies joined a Wilmington klavern to gather "inside information," which underscored the tangled relationship between the klan and local law enforcement.

The reputation of "progressive" North Carolina took a hit as well. During the hearing's opening session, investigators documented that North Carolina was "by far the most active state for the United Klans of America." The next day, that phrase was splayed in newspaper headlines across the state.

Investigators even presented maps with detailed listings of klavern locations, which were dutifully reported by the local media in klan hotbeds like Greenville. "Seven Units of KKK Listed in Pitt County," the *Greenville Daily Reflector* trumpeted in bold the following day.

State officials quickly moved to refute the Commission's finding. "I do not concede that we are No. 1," Governor Moore asserted. "The Klan's membership in North Carolina is very small and changes from week to week. They join and drop out." Ignoring HUAC's detailed membership counts, former state attorney general Malcolm Seawell suggested that the state's characterization was due to Jones's organizing strategy, centered on creating a large number of near-empty klavern "seeds" to inflate the group's presence. And state treasurer Edwin Gill speculated that the state's place at the top of the rankings was a credit to the efforts of its officials, who he suspected provided more data than others to investigators.[47]

This rather weak effort to control damage, largely ignored by the national media, was only the public face of a pronounced shift in the state's efforts to manage the presence of thousands of white hoods in its midst. With the "North Carolina way" under siege, officials moved to transform the state's scattershot and ambivalent orientation to the klan. Indeed, the federal investigation's direct effects on the UKA—bad publicity and the mounting legal fees that strained klan coffers—were dwarfed by its longer term impact on North Carolina officials' policing of the KKK.

As the HUAC hearings continued, Governor Moore began regularly and forcefully speaking out against the KKK. Acknowledging that "certainly this publicity does not help North Carolina from a national standpoint," he vowed repeatedly that "neither the Ku Klux Klan nor any other such organization will impede the progress of North Carolina." When the Baptist State Convention passed an anti-KKK resolution the following month, Moore responded with a telegram "welcoming the assistance of the convention in exposing the nature of the Klan" and praised its condemnation of the "bigotry, prejudice, intolerance and ill will which characterizes the Ku Klux Klan." Behind the scenes, he deliberated with the state attorney general about whether it would be possible to declare the KKK illegal.

Soon after, Jones found himself in the state's cross-hairs. In November, his Cadillac was stopped for speeding in Greensboro, the Grand Dragon's second moving violation of the year. Though he volunteered to attend drivers' school in addition to paying his court-imposed fines, the State Department of Motor Vehicles exercised its discretion and suspended Jones's license for sixty days. Two months later, the SBI charged Jones with perjury dating back to his 1951 divorce trial. During those proceedings, Jones had misrepresented the date of his marriage to his first wife, Violet Sue Moorehead, in order to falsely comply with the state's mandatory two-year separation period. The fact that this misstep came to light fourteen years later signals the lengths to which the state was now going to nullify Jones's organizing.[48]

Actions both large and small characterized the sweep of this anti-klan campaign. For the first time, State Highway Patrol officers removed signs placed by UKA members on public right-of-ways to direct traffic to isolated rally sites. Klansmen complained that police blocked rally entrances and harassed attendees. At the start of 1966, the governor confirmed the existence of a newly constituted "anti-Klan committee," headed by Malcolm Seawell. Later formally dubbed the "Law and Order Committee," it coordinated the activities of various state agencies, including the SBI, the SHP, the State Revenue Office, and the Attorney General's Office. While Moore acknowledged that the state had maintained a "constant vigil" on klan activities in the past, this committee would extend such monitoring to put a halt to the group's actions. In communities around the state, Seawell spoke candidly about the committee's approach. "We're through playing games with the Klan," he noted, and vowed that "every resource will be used in tracking down and bringing to justice persons responsible for violence in North Carolina."[49]

Those resources included judicial action. When Jones announced a UKA rally would be held in late March 1966 in Maxton, the site of Catfish Cole's fateful 1958 rout by local Lumbee Indians, state officials obtained a court order preventing the rally from going forward. The move drew criticism from the ACLU. Moore also cracked down on cross-burning, an act that state and federal police agents had to that point failed to investigate aggressively, even though an anti-terror statute had been on the books since 1953. The resulting threat of fines and prison terms, according to one Johnston County klan officer, ultimately "slowed down" certain UKA units' tendencies toward wanton harassment. Meanwhile, a state superior court judge moved to ensure that klan members would not serve as jurors in his court. And when Shelton, Jones, and five other UKA leaders were indicted on contempt of Congress charges for refusing to turn over records during the HUAC hearings, SBI and FBI agents quickly spread the impression among members that any subsequent klan action could lead to similar subpoenas or jail terms.[50]

Beginning in 1966, arrests for klan-related violence increased significantly. On Thanksgiving night, police arrested four klansmen after they fired from a pickup truck into a crowded Alamance County grocery store. The FBI also arrested twelve UKA members for their part in a spree of shootings, bombings, and burnings in Rowan and Cabarrus counties. "Every time we turn around," Bob Jones lamented, "we get arrested." Though a jury acquitted the dozen Rowan and Cabarrus defendants, the proceedings proved costly to the UKA. "Whenever anything like that happened," klansman Eddie Dawson complained, "guys at the next meeting or rally would say, 'Well, we won that case!' I would say 'No we didn't.... We're going to lose 500 men over that.'" Indeed, following the arrests, membership fell off considerably in the South Rowan klavern that was home to many of the defendants. Remaining members fought over what had become of legal fees that Jones had raised for their defense. Others were almost certainly scared away from an organization exposed as willing to resort to deadly terrorist tactics.

In July 1967, five other klansmen were convicted and sentenced to eighteen-month jail terms for their role in a cross-burning outside of Charlotte. Already in serious financial trouble, UKA leadership in the state office voted not to provide legal support, further harming unity within the group. Soon after, the city of Greensboro filed suit against George Dorsett for a series of "annoying and hazardous" activities—many associated with klan training exercises—in and around his home. Dorsett ally Clyde Webster also received a prison sentence in the summer of 1968 for his part in a cross-burning. Tellingly, the judge had little sympathy for the Carolina Klan. "When you go to the next meeting of your brothers who are robed," he instructed Webster, "I hope you tell them that our government is good, that our system is right, and it is wrong to try people in secret by unidentified accusers."[51]

To that point, the UKA's top-level leadership had remained relatively stable, despite the brewing dissension in the ranks. Beginning in March 1969, Jones's year-long federal prison term for his contempt conviction from the HUAC hearings deprived the Carolina Klan of its Grand Dragon for the first time in its five-year history. Shelton had begun his jail term the prior month, and South Carolina Grand Dragon Bob Scoggin awaited his sentence as well. The legal tangle exacerbated pent-up tensions from the past two years. Bob Jones refused to attend an Imperial Board meeting called by Shelton prior to their sentencing, and Scoggin temporarily resigned from the organization, criticizing its "deterioration on the national level." In North Carolina, syndicated coverage of Jones's sentencing referenced Catfish Cole's prison bid a decade earlier. The parallel was apt; in both cases, the jailing of a key leader contributed to organizational disarray and the eventual collapse of the Ku Klux Klan.[52]

In the short term, the UKA soldiered on in Jones's absence. Longtime klansman Joe Bryant—who, ironically, had been a close associate of Cole in the 1950s—took over as acting Grand Dragon. While respected in klan circles, Bryant generally lacked Jones's "Horse"-like assertiveness. Among the membership, many thought that he, as one close observer put it, was "not really the stuff of which Grand Dragons [were] made." Compounding that deficit, Bryant soon found himself the object of controversy, when a July rally in a small coastal community in Hyde County devolved into a shootout with a group of African Americans who had gathered to protest the klan gathering. Police arrested seventeen klansmen. As historian David Cecelski has noted, both the militance of the black community and the decisive police response cemented the sense that "the era of open-air KKK rallies, public toleration, and racist violence with impunity had ended."

The confrontation brought significant costs. The ensuing court proceedings decimated the UKA's coffers, as acting Imperial Wizard Melvin Sexton exhausted the UKA's United Defense Fund by agreeing to a $12,500 fee to retain prominent lawyer Arthur J. Hanes, a former Birmingham mayor who had recently defended James Earl Ray against charges that he killed Martin Luther King Jr. A national appeal for legal funds, spearheaded by Sexton, intensified accusations of financial impropriety after Bryant charged that money collected for Hanes's legal fees instead paid for Sexton's "alligator shoes and $150 suits." Meanwhile, Bryant himself hired his own lawyer and pled guilty, an act that drew calls for his removal.[53]

With Jones and Shelton still in prison and FBI informants working to exacerbate UKA schisms, the conflict escalated into an irreparable fracture. Bryant, fed up with Sexton's financial acrobatics and under fire for his actions following the Hyde County debacle, began a campaign to split the North Carolina realm from the national UKA organization, winning the support of more than half of the state's klaverns. The UKA labeled Bryant a "provocateur," and on September 7 banished him for "conspiring against the prosperity of the order." The following week he held a rally in which an estimated half of the UKA's remaining adherents nailed their membership cards to a cross and ceremoniously torched them. The event also marked the formation of Bryant's new klan order, the North Carolina Knights. While repudiating the UKA, the group, he claimed, remained loyal to Bob Jones, who would have the option to take over its leadership upon his return from prison.

Jones was released two months ahead of schedule for good behavior, but his arrival in North Carolina was still at least half a year too late. On the eve of his sentencing, Jones had warned his Exalted Cyclopes that "if they got a hundred members now, they better have two hundred members when I come out." Instead, the opposite happened, as the UKA retained only a fraction of its base. The breakaway North Carolina Knights established a reported ten klaverns, and other UKA units waited to follow Jones's lead. FBI informants strenuously tried to exploit the disarray by stoking criticism of the UKA's financial misdeeds and its leaders' attempts to reorganize. Bryant still maintained that Jones would throw in with his newly established North Carolina Knights. Syble Jones, however, remained loyal to Sexton, and after meeting with Shelton the Joneses decided to reject Bryant's faction and stay with the UKA.[54]

As the 1970s dawned, the SBI estimated North Carolina's overall klan membership—now spread over several competing organizations—at fewer than a thousand members. Jones spoke of ambitious schemes for a giant reorganization and membership drive, but even though the attention of police agencies had moved elsewhere,[55] public reception was still hostile, the membership base was tiny, and the bank account was nearly empty—all of which meant that his efforts stood little chance of success. By the 1970s, the KKK had also lost its post-*Brown* raison d'etre. The Jim Crow era had ended and few looked to the klan as a foundation for a parallel whites-only society, which reduced Shelton and his rival klan organizations to focusing on veiled racist causes like urban "dope addiction." Much of its base fled to right-wing political candidates, as in many cases the "southern strategy" pursued by Republican candidates provided institutionalized outlets for their grievances. Few could argue when the *Charlotte Observer* labeled the KKK circa 1970 a "decrepit organization."

Jones rejected an offer to take part in a late-1970 summit to reunite North Carolina's splintered klan, which featured Bryant's North Carolina Knights, Dorsett's Confederate Knights, and James Venable's Georgia-based National Knights. Despite a strained relationship with Shelton—variously attributed to charges of financial impropriety and conflicts over control of the UKA's national operation—Jones continued working with the UKA until he finally resigned for good at an October 1973 meeting in Wilson.

The following year, while the UKA continued to eke out a skeletal existence, Jones worked eighteen-hour shifts as a security guard at a mobile home manufacturing plant. By 1976, his house still littered with klan ephemera, he returned to his pre-UKA work selling lightning rods. In his twenty years in the klan, Jones recounted, he worked his "tail off, night and day, . . . drove more than a million miles and spent a year of my life in jail. I figured it was enough." Echoing Robert Shelton's vow that he would die a klansman regardless of the fortunes of his organization, Jones's tie to the KKK was as much an identity as an affiliation. "If they need me, I'll be available," he promised. "You don't turn the oath I took on and off like a water faucet."[56]

Understanding the UKA's Fall

What explains the dramatic fall that mirrored the Carolina Klan's spectacular rise in 1964 and 1965? While the UKA's successes occurred in areas marked by high levels of racial competition, such settings translated into klan growth only when a broader favorable political climate aided KKK recruiting efforts. North Carolina officials' unwillingness to capitulate to federal civil rights mandates provided a set of opportunities for klan recruiters, and police agencies' failure to seriously crack down on the KKK enabled them to exploit that climate.

By 1966, however, the Carolina Klan's window of opportunity had quickly closed. The passage of the Civil Rights and Voting Rights Acts made militant, line-in-the-sand defenses of Jim Crow less viable. While Bob Jones felt that the klan's fortunes would be ascendant so long as the country continued to "turn conservative," increasingly that conservatism turned toward more mainstream electoral outlets. In 1968, both George Wallace's and Richard Nixon's southern campaigns harmonized with the by-products of racial change—the raw discontent over desegregation felt by large swaths of the region's white population, as well as the economic and demographic shifts that new racial policies set in motion.[57]

More important, while the Tar Heel State, like many of its neighbors, began to gradually desegregate its schools, businesses, and public spaces, federal pressures and increasingly poor publicity spurred its officials to redouble their policing efforts. The FBI and SBI infiltrated UKA units, manipulating members to exacerbate interpersonal conflicts and exploit opportunities to disrupt the group's day-to-day activities. At rallies and klavern meetings, corruption charges and tactical squabbles replaced grand calls to tradition and "100 percent Americanism." Informants also sowed widespread mistrust and occupied the attention of UKA leaders, who sketched out plans to form special committees across the state designed to "ferret out" infiltrators. As an FBI-planted story in the *Charlotte Observer* put it, informers were the "hole in [the] Klan's boat."[58]

These covert efforts were matched by HUAC's exposure of widespread klan improprieties and North Carolina officials' resulting newfound emphasis on visible policing tactics: arrests, harassment, and court actions. These actions forced the klan to organize amid growing financial, social, and political impediments. The HUAC proceedings alone sapped the UKA of $100,000 in legal fees, nearly half of which was raised by klan units in North Carolina. The resulting steady stream of arrests and litigation meant that the UKA's already shrinking pool of funds collected from rallies and member dues would be diverted to meet bail and other legal costs. Arrests and infiltration also made it more likely that the klan's membership rolls would be exposed to the broader public, which in many cases did not sit well with employers, family members, and congregations. While informants often fomented discontent in local klaverns, highly placed operatives such as George Dorsett could engineer breaks in the entire statewide outfit. And negative publicity—much of it created by the attention given to Moore's anti-klan committee and by stories of klan discord planted by the FBI's media sources—made it less and less likely that previously sympathetic constituencies would view the UKA as a viable segregationist vehicle.[59]

In short, this intensification of police action raised the costs of UKA membership. Dedicated, multipronged policing initiatives overcame the often-ambivalent orientation of agents that characterized on-the-ground action against the UKA in 1964 and 1965. During that earlier period, the latitude given to SBI and FBI agents enabled their predominantly passive approach and allowed their day-to-day actions in the field to deviate from the overall aims of their respective agencies. To be sure, procuring intelligence by discussing sports with Grand Dragon Jones in the back of a Bureau car or by openly stating to klan adherents that the UKA was "perfectly permissible to join" was at odds with the organizational mandate of the SBI and FBI to put the UKA "out of business." Such pseudo-collegial routines developed through the autonomy given to agents in the field and provided the foundation for more generally ambivalent orientations toward klan targets.[60]

As federal efforts intensified due to pressures created by civil rights violence in the Deep South, directives from the White House narrowed opportunities for such ambivalent action and heightened the overall official response to klan action. The result was a strong—if not always unified—policing effort that resembled the stifling environment that characterized George Dorsett and Boyd Hamby's ill-fated organizing campaign in Florida. UKA leaders worked to combat these intensified policing measures, and at times their efforts bore fruit. In August 1966, they attracted an overflow crowd at Raleigh's Memorial Auditorium for an event protesting the treatment of klan leaders subpoenaed for their actions during the HUAC hearings. Likewise, a "national rally" held in Durham two months later featuring UKA leaders from across the South drew several thousand supporters.

But overall, rally attendance began to ebb, and increasingly UKA organizers needed to offer special guests, manufactured controversies, and carnival-like attractions to draw crowds. The drop-off continued in 1967 and beyond. Membership fell precipitously as well, and by 1968 a popular newspaper columnist could confidently declare that the Carolina Klan was "on the ropes." Indeed, as shown by the UKA's recruiting failures in Florida and its withering fortunes in North Carolina, even the most ambitious klan organizing campaigns found it difficult to succeed in the face of dedicated efforts by state officials to suppress the KKK.[61]

EPILOGUE

HOW THE CAROLINA KLAN DOES—AND DOESN'T—MATTER IN THE POST-KLAN SOUTH

The UKA's late-1960s fall proved fatal to the fortunes of the Ku Klux Klan. While KKK activity continues and the number of self-proclaimed klan organizations even increases,[1] no group since has come close to matching the mass following of the Carolina Klan. The UKA itself limped along for more than a decade, with Imperial Wizard Shelton driving his van to sparsely attended UKA rallies around the South through much of the 1970s and 1980s, until the horrific lynching of nineteen-year-old Mobile, Alabama, resident Michael Donald put the group out of business permanently.

Targeted at random in 1981 to show the UKA's strength and to discourage African Americans from serving on juries, Donald provided the Southern Poverty Law Center (SPLC) with an opportunity to present a pathbreaking legal claim against the UKA. SPLC founder Morris Dees and his co-counsel, Alabama state senator Michael Figures, argued that the organization should itself be held liable for crimes that members commit in its name. An all-white jury agreed, awarding $7 million in damages to the victim's mother, Beulah Mae Donald. The verdict stunned longtime KKK leader James Venable. "Robert Shelton and the UKA have all but been put out of business," he noted. "I've been in the klan since the 1920s, and I never thought I'd live to see something like that." To settle the case, the UKA signed over the papers to its only significant asset, a 7,200-square-foot lakeside headquarters compound outside of Tuscaloosa. In1987, Shelton folded the organization for good.[2]

In an important sense, the present-day klan threat is no longer about the KKK itself. In this "post-klan" era, the KKK's former constituencies might now reside in a range of white power movements—a field that today includes neo-nazis, racist skinhead, white nationalist, and neo-confederate groups[3]—or support political candidates who draw on residual segregationist sentiment. But understanding the Carolina Klan remains important for at least three reasons. First, the UKA's rise and fall sheds light on the causes of racial extremism generally, lending insight into the kinds of strategies that can effectively curtail organized racism today. Second, UKA organizing in the 1960s shaped political orientations and augured remarkable shifts in electoral politics in the 1970s, in particular the ascendance of a new and powerful wave of conservatism that heralded the South's transition to the Republican Party. Finally, the UKA's penchant for violence and intimidation shaped residents' relationships to their communities to a degree still reflected in the stunted capacity of many of those communities to control and prevent violent crime. Recognizing the UKA's role in these well-documented trends demonstrates how the past predominance of white hoods continues to matter to residents of the Tar Heel State, and more important, how organized racism shaped the trajectories of the South and the nation.

Competition and Racial Extremism

The UKA thrived on racial competition. In 1960s North Carolina, civil rights pressures intensified the threat of competition, promising to break down institutionalized economic, political, and social advantages long enjoyed by the state's white residents. The scope of such change varied from community to community, based on the degree to which racial groups would compete on newly constituted economic and political playing fields.

Ethnic competition theory highlights how the composition of local labor markets, the relative presence of racial minorities, and the skills and political efficacy that those groups possess all shape the extent to which groups compete with each other for resources. As Chapter 4 demonstrates, these kinds of factors matter. However, the presence of competition only rarely translates into organized antagonism, and even when such group conflicts occur, conventional competition theories provide little insight into how they activate. The *mediated competition model* developed in the preceding chapters fills this gap, by revealing how various factors interact with the baseline presence of competition to enable the mobilization of groups around a shared sense of threat.

For the UKA, institutional political dynamics shaped the range of outlets that promoted and aligned with prevailing white racial interests. Klan membership appealed to a narrow base in Mississippi and Alabama, where governors, police, local officials, Citizens' Councils, and varied civic initiatives each deployed different means to maintain Jim Crow. The pronounced moderation of North Carolina's top elected officials—in particular, their unwillingness to defy federal civil rights mandates—confined harder line segregationist positions to extremist groups like the KKK, broadening the appeal of the klan in the state. Such racial moderation paradoxically created an opportunity for the UKA, enabling klan recruiters to target diverse constituents. State officials could negate this opening, however, by consistently and aggressively policing vigilantism and "racial extremism." As Chapter 3 shows, a strong, centralized policing campaign precluded UKA success in Florida, where political leaders had also charted a moderate course. When North Carolina officials intensified their policing in 1966, those efforts similarly damaged the UKA's fortunes in the state.

Klan leaders necessarily operated within the contours of this political climate, but their own organizing tactics also defined short-term successes and failures. Bob Jones's achievements as an organizer resulted in large part from his ability to pioneer nightly rallies, regular street walks, parallel Ladies Auxiliary Units, and a range of social and civic initiatives to diversify the UKA's relationship to its varied constituencies. Such appeals enabled a layered membership structure, allowing the Carolina Klan to become, as one commentator noted, "simultaneously respectable and dangerous."[4] Both in print and through oration at rallies and other UKA venues, the klan's ideological entrepreneurs buttressed these organizing feats, crafting a message of authentic whiteness that wove together racial, religious, and patriotic sentiments and anxieties.

The Carolina Klan's organizing efforts interacted with the external political environment in important ways. The State Highway Patrol's ambivalent, quasi-collegial policing approach, for instance, smoothed the UKA's decision to hold nightly rallies, as patrol officers managed traffic, controlled disorder that might repel more casual supporters, and tacitly conferred a degree of legitimacy to the proceedings. Conversely, so long as klansmen avoided lethal violence, the UKA's presence added legitimacy to state officials' efforts to trumpet the "North Carolina way." Executives and spokespersons for the state regularly equated the presence of the KKK and NAACP. By then distancing themselves from these "extremists" on both ends of the charged racial spectrum, political leaders could more easily make the case for North Carolina's pragmatic and progressive stance.

The mediated competition model advanced here contends that this confluence of factors shapes ethnic mobilization. Significant inter-group competition for resources creates the baseline conditions for group members to feel threatened, but such perceived threats translate into contentious action only when they emerge within a conducive political environment, where regulative policing is minimal or absent, and alongside sufficient material, social, and cultural resources to channel group members' discontent into sustained organization.[5]

Outlining the model in these general, theoretical terms highlights its applicability to ethnic or racial conflict generally. The dynamics of mediated competition demonstrate that organized racism flourishes in the presence of acute racialized threats, under conducive political conditions, and where resources support sufficient organizational capacity. These criteria point to distinct strategic interventions. Pervasive feelings of threat conventionally stem from a sense of vulnerability, when resources are both in short supply and zero-sum. Peter B. Young, the North Carolina–based journalist whose familiarity with the Carolina Klan led to his later work as a consultant with a federal commission focused on the prevention of organized violence, characterized the UKA's constituency in this very way. Young relentlessly advanced the idea that the Carolina Klan drew much of its strength from the social and economic isolation and declining sense of opportunity faced by many of the state's residents. In 1965, after the Watts Riots focused increasing attention on the problems of the "black ghetto," Young labeled the under-resourced rural communities that were rapidly becoming klan hotbeds the "white ghetto."[6] He saw many parallels between the two, including deficits in the skills, capital, and leadership necessary for successful integration into mainstream economic and political life. As a solution, he proposed to create stable, mainstream institutions to counter some of the resource deficits that he felt klan leaders exploited to fuel support for a militantly racist program.

Even in a climate generally supportive of social welfare programs, however, Young found it prohibitively difficult to implement such initiatives. Interventions tied to the other dimensions highlighted within a mediated competition framework have proven more successful. The Carolina Klan case demonstrates the importance of police action that reinforces respected political, civic, and religious leaders' public demonization of extremism. Governors Terry Sanford and Dan Moore, alongside a significant majority of the state's newspaper editors and mainstream religious leaders, consistently attacked the klan's program, ideology, and goals. But such criticism had little effect and may even have enlarged the klan's recruitment base by providing the group with increased visibility among constituencies seeking outlets to oppose the very leaders who condemned the UKA. Instead, the klan's fortunes turned in the state only after police officials engaged in an aggressive campaign to close off available organizing opportunities and thereby raise the costs of klan involvement. As in Florida, North Carolina police did not infringe directly upon UKA members' constitutionally protected freedom of speech or assembly (the governor and his staff consistently rejected various closed-door proposals to declare the UKA illegal),[7] but rather sought to remove tacit supports for UKA initiatives and aggressively police minor legal miscues. Officers removed unpermitted rally signs, actively pursued opportunities to apprehend Jones and other leaders for speeding and various vehicular infractions, and fully investigated cross-burnings and other illegal forms of klan harassment.

Mobilizing support for hate crime legislation and policing accomplishes similar ends and demonstrates the importance of grassroots opposition to organized racism. Research has shown that strong social movements that promote compliance with hate crime policy increase the likelihood that such crimes will be reported and prosecuted.[8] In the UKA case, vibrant civil rights organizing played a significant role in the klan's rise and fall. As Chapter 4 reveals, klan recruiters often derived short-run benefits from NAACP and SCLC campaigns, as they exploited those actions to recruit adherents alarmed by the civil rights threat posed by those groups. However, the actions of civil rights activists also prodded state and federal officials and enabled the official response that eventually triggered the klan's decline. Frequent urgent telegrams and public appeals from John Salter, Golden Frinks, and Kelly Alexander made it difficult for the governor's office to ignore the klan's brutal program of intimidation and harassment. Similar pressures from the civil rights establishment led to the HUAC KKK investigations that ultimately turned the policing tide against the UKA beginning in 1966. In short, active and vigilant anti-racist mobilization shrinks the latitude that extremist groups require to operate.

Similarly, since the 1970s, the novel legal strategy pioneered by the Southern Poverty Law Center has continued to limit hate group activity. First deployed against Shelton and the UKA, the SPLC's approach has spawned a series of similar judgments, including a $2.5 million verdict in 2008 against the Kentucky-based Imperial Klans of America.[9] Holding klan organizations responsible for the actions of individual members limits their tactical choices and ultimately saps resources. As with policing strategies that raise the costs of klan action, reducing the funds available to those groups hinders their ability to translate even the most favorable political climate into sustained organization. As these resources also fuel the insulated social spaces where hate groups dispense hard-line racist ideology prohibited in most mainstream institutions, SPLC-style legal strategies can deprive potential adherents from accessing what sociologists Pete Simi and Robert Futrell term white power groups' "hidden spaces of hate."[10] By conferring analytic attention to the conditions where racist ideas resonate as well as how that resonance translates into racist action, the mediated competition model explains how and why these kinds of approaches have successfully reduced the threat of organized racism.

UKA Legacies I: The Rise of the Republican-Dominated South

The preceding chapters have examined the dynamics of the UKA's rise and fall, but how might we assess the group's legacy? While gauging social movement success by whether groups achieve their stated short-run goals seems straightforward, understanding enduring impacts poses a more difficult challenge.[11] On its face, the UKA failed as a movement, as it did not preserve Jim Crow-style segregation in the South or continue as a racially "pure" shelter from the integrated "alien" world. However, the group's influence endures in lasting and perhaps surprising ways, including in the voting booth.

The ascendance of Republican support across the South, foretold by LBJ's oft-cited remark that the Civil Rights Act would result in Democratic losses in the region for at least a generation, represents the most significant shift in the South's politics since the 1960s. White backlash against federal civil rights policy, however, fails to provide a complete explanation for that shift. Analysts typically focus on two main factors to explain the realignment of southern voting patterns: a top-down Republican "Southern Strategy," through which Richard Nixon and other candidates moved to the right on social issues to win support from aggrieved white southern voters, and a grassroots political realignment driven by metropolitan growth in the Sunbelt South that produced what historian Matthew Lassiter describes as a "convergence of southern and national politics around the suburban ethos of middle-class entitlement."[12] To a significant and as-yet underexplored degree, the legacy of KKK organizing in hundreds of southern communities influenced both of these dynamics.

In indirect and unexpected ways, Bob Jones's frequent claim that the UKA's influence would ultimately be through "ballots" rather than "bullets" has proven true. Jones's emphasis on ballots in 1964 and beyond signaled his ambition to build the UKA into a political machine that could elect its own members to top offices. While Robert Shelton enjoyed direct access to the Alabama State House under governors John Patterson and George Wallace, even those officials could rarely afford to publicly acknowledge their klan ties. In North Carolina, neither Terry Sanford nor Dan Moore maintained any relationship with Jones or other UKA leaders. The Carolina Klan failed as well to build a significant unified voting bloc. Its membership profile reflected significant fissures among white southerners, making any politics based on massive resistance increasingly tenuous as the 1960s wore on. As the group's fortunes correspondingly ebbed, klan outfits increasingly shifted their electoral energies to support "real white" candidates tied to major political parties. As the "7 Point Program" advanced by George Dorsett's Confederate Knights instructed in 1968, klan members should "take an active interest in public affairs—ALWAYS vote in elections [and] get others to vote."

That year, the UKA devoted considerable resources to back former Alabama governor George Wallace's presidential campaign. As one close observer told me, while not every Wallace booster in eastern North Carolina was a klansman, all serious klan supporters stumped for Wallace in 1968. Following the UKA's practice of using its members' cars as ad hoc billboards (at rallies and other klan gatherings, vehicles commonly featured "KKKK" scrawled in tape or klan flyers fastened to hoods, doors, and trunks), many members outfitted their vehicles with paraphernalia supporting Wallace as the election approached.[13]

Wallace ran as a candidate on his own American Independent Party ticket, and he colorfully separated himself from both the Republican and Democratic establishments. "You could put them all in an Alabama cotton picker's sack," he told audiences, "shake them up and dump them out; take the first one to slide out and put him right back into power and there would be no change." His message, which attacked federal interventionism, political dissenters, and proliferating urban disorder and crime, while also retaining populist economic support for "little" (white) men and women, remained popular across the Deep South and also garnered support in the urban Midwest and East Coast. In North Carolina, counties most conducive to klan organizing disproportionately backed Wallace; the UKA's strength in a given county correlated strongly and positively with Wallace voting, signaling the extent to which civil rights upheavals had frayed the traditional alliance between the eastern Black Belt and the Democratic Party.[14] Wallace narrowly lost the state, as Republican candidate Richard Nixon eked out a victory by running well in traditionally Republican pockets in the western Piedmont and mountains.

By 1972, the fracturing of the state's Democratic coalition produced a striking shift in its politics. Just eight years earlier, even following his support of the Civil Rights Act, Democrat Lyndon Johnson won 56.2 percent of the presidential votes cast in North Carolina. That party support fell by nearly half in 1968, when only 29.2 percent of the state's electorate supported

Democratic candidate Hubert Humphrey. Wallace's independent candidacy, which drew nearly a third of the state's overall votes, explained much of that drop-off. In 1972, Richard Nixon won 69.5 percent of the vote, as Republicans successfully secured the vast majority of Wallace's prior share. In predominantly white precincts in booming Piedmont centers like Charlotte, nearly four-fifths of voters cast ballots for Nixon, matching his support among white voters in the South overall. Barely more than a quarter of North Carolinians voted for George McGovern, the Democratic candidate.[15]

The shift toward Republican voting extended to that year's Senate election as well. Unreconstructed Republican Jesse Helms, a relative newcomer, entered the fray as a former Raleigh City Council member and longtime conservative television commentator. For years, his nightly televised "Viewpoints" editorials on Raleigh station WRAL had railed against communist subversion, the immorality of liberals, the tyranny of forced school desegregation, and the general illegitimacy of civil rights claims. In 1966, he supported the UKA's right to hold a contested street walk, equating limitations on the klan's freedom of assembly to a racial double standard that validated black protestors' commission of "mayhem." He painted his opponent, Nick Galifianakis, a fellow upstart who had defeated longtime incumbent B. Everett Jordan in the Democratic primary, as a McGovern liberal and not-so-subtly maligned his Greek-American ethnic heritage. Emphasizing his close ties to Nixon and drawing support from his socially conservative "Viewpoints" base east of Raleigh, Helms overcame a double-digit poll deficit to win the seat.[16]

That year's Republican triumphs in North Carolina and across the region portended a broader dealignment of many southern whites from the Democratic Party. Ronald Reagan's campaigns in the 1980s brought many of these voters more firmly into the Republican fold.[17] On the surface, this shift appeared to signal the triumph of the party's "Southern Strategy," in which Nixon and other candidates moved to the right on social issues to add Wallace's base of disaffected former Democrats to the party's traditional base to win a new Republican majority. But efforts to capture the conservative Wallace vote co-existed uneasily with Nixon's parallel attempts to maintain support in the region's shifting power centers, as the southern economic base moved from the traditional Deep South Black Belt to the more urbanized and moderate Sunbelt South. Wallace's language of racial resistance still resonated in the former, but racial issues played differently in the Sunbelt's more affluent suburban enclaves. Residents of the Piedmont's growing metropolitan areas increasingly emphasized a color-blind discourse of homeownership and access to quality education—an ethos that spurned traditional segregationist sentiments but also opposed government policies intended to repair state-sponsored patterns of residential and institutional segregation. These expanding suburban centers aligned increasingly with conservative Republican bases in the North and West, which Nixon deftly targeted through his populist appeals to the "silent majority." In a 1968 campaign speech in Charlotte, Nixon trumpeted the "new voice" of the "forgotten Americans—people who pay their taxes and go to work and support their churches." "So-called southern issues," he regularly noted, "were the same here as they are in America."[18]

Nixon successfully balanced these Black Belt and Sunbelt constituencies in 1972, capturing Wallace's hard-line segregationist voters and also broad swaths of the increasingly white-collar, moderate Sunbelt suburbs. This accomplishment highlights Republican responsiveness to evolving regional dynamics that increasingly defied traditional conceptions of a South that differed from the rest of the nation. Rejecting the stark southern exceptionalism that more simplistic accounts of Nixon's "Southern Strategy" often embrace, however, risks underestimating the role played by distinctly southern segregationist groups like the UKA. While strong across the Deep South Black Belt, the klan's North Carolina power center extended beyond the state's eastern plain into the Piedmont. Working to organize UKA units in both regions in the mid-1960s, Bob Jones and his klan recruiters confronted a dilemma analogous to Nixon's in 1972. Jones quickly learned that Piedmont communities like Greensboro and Salisbury, marked by high levels of racial overlap and significant competition across white and black workers, contained a base that the UKA could capture with its militant appeals. Those same racial arrangements also produced softer but persistent pockets of racial resistance among the white-collar sectors of those communities. While the klan's reach only rarely extended into those middle- and upper-class neighborhoods, a parallel opposition to civil rights reform that William Chafe characterizes as centered on a culture of "civility" emerged in those locales. Nixon's color-blind appeals to the "silent majority" tapped that same vein, providing a more palatable alternative to white anxieties over desegregation policies.

An important study by sociologist Rory McVeigh more firmly demonstrates how the klan's presence in Sunbelt communities, and not only in rural Black Belt strongholds, contributed in important ways to the Republican ascendancy in the state and region. In a systematic analysis of voting patterns in the South, McVeigh finds that support for Republican candidates in the 1970s and beyond correlates strongly with KKK organizing during the 1960s. This relationship between past klan presence and Republican voting endures today and cannot be reduced simply to the presence of segregationist hard-liners, the sorts of voters who supported Wallace in 1968. While UKA members did directly campaign for Wallace that year, even after taking into account this prior Wallace support, communities with a history of strong UKA organizing remained significantly more likely than other North Carolina locales to solidly back Nixon in 1972.[19]

Why might this relationship between klan presence and Republican support have continued in ensuing decades? McVeigh argues that in communities receptive to the klan's ideas, the UKA's organizational base enabled the group to exert influence, by spreading its message to ideological allies and placing a militant public face on widespread white opposition to residential and school integration. The klan reflected such racist sentiments within communities, but its presence also actively reinforced, consolidated, and intensified such views. And while the UKA's formal organizational impact disappeared with the group's late-1960s decline, traces of its influence lived on in the political activism of many former adherents, as a number of the individual profiles in Chapter 5 indicate.

Additionally, the underlying community conditions that enabled the klan to thrive in the 1960s also supported subtler discourses of civil rights resistance. While Republican platforms would generally avoid the klan's segregationist agenda or Wallace's race-baiting positions, prominent candidates—from Nixon to Jesse Helms, along with later figures like Ronald Reagan—mobilized these conditions in subsequent years, by continuing to draw on themes that intersected with the grievances that fueled the UKA's prior appeal. While former klan constituencies in Wallace's old working-class strongholds might find their support for Republican social conservatism counterbalanced by a sense that the party's economic programs favor more affluent residents, such cross-pressures dissipated in more prosperous locales. Indeed, McVeigh's research reveals that the klan's influence endured most clearly in increasingly affluent communities. Residents of these areas often embraced color-blind racial entitlement, predicated on acknowledging equal rights but resisting policies designed to remediate structural barriers to equal opportunity, including busing and affirmative action. The effect of prior klan presence becomes especially salient in these environments, where the racial preferences of former klan supporters more easily align with the class interests favored by Republican policies. In North Carolina, such communities are most often found in the Piedmont, and the klan's electoral legacy remains strongest in that region.

These findings extend existing conceptions of southern political dynamics in the 1970s and beyond. While nearly all accounts of the civil rights-era

KKK confine the klan phenomenon to the Deep South and view its adherents as quintessential exponents of politically outmoded massive resistance, the UKA's great success in North Carolina offers more complex portraits of the group and the region's politics. Recent historiography has challenged explanations that explain the Republican Party's huge gains across the South in 1972 solely through a top-down "Southern Strategy" that courted segregationist interests centered in the Black Belt. By offering a platform centered on color-blind middle-class entitlement, Nixon and other candidates successfully balanced the interests of the racially conservative backers of segregation and the more socially moderate but economically conservative urbanized Sunbelt South. The UKA's broader influence across the region, including in locales that embraced suburban moderation, highlights the confluence of political forces co-existing in the South throughout this period. The klan's enduring impact on Republican support underscores how the resonance of the UKA and similar organizations cross-cut "Black Belt" and "Sunbelt" interests, and by extension how Republican candidates solidified their hold on the "post-klan" South.

UKA Legacies II: Violence and Community Cohesion

While the UKA's continuing electoral influence reveals the group's impact on "ballots," the klan's emphasis on "bullets" and the trappings of violence represents its most tragic and troubling legacy. Many klan members directly promoted violence during the UKA's mid-1960s heyday, and police reports traced hundreds of acts of intimidation to plots hatched in local klaverns. As the Carolina Klan declined in the late 1960s, the contours of klan violence shifted. Close observers noted that certain core members adopted tactics that promoted semi-autonomous actions detached from those sanctioned by UKA leadership. Raymond Cranford referred to the shift as a new "game of ones," where members would operate independently to promote klan aims. "When one of my boys comes up to me and says, 'EC, what you want us to do about such-and-such?'" explained Cranford, "I say, 'You get yourself a good buddy—I don't wanna know his name, and don't you tell anybody his name—and the two of you decide what you want to do, then go out and do it.'"[20]

Such tactics contributed to the claimed proliferation across eastern North Carolina of what Peter B. Young referred to as "nigger-knocking," or the random killing of black citizens by small cells of klan militants intent on maintaining a climate of racial intimidation. The prevalence of these acts has never been systematically compiled and confirmed, but Young estimated that the tactic claimed the lives of "several hundred" black people across the South in the late 1960s. He also reinforced Cranford's characterization of its pseudo-organizational nature, explaining that he had

> never known a Klan officer to advocate "nigger-knocking," either publicly or privately [though they] are aware that [it] is a frequent occurrence. But they are as helpless as everybody else when it comes to describing the remedy, even when, on occasion, they can make a shrewd guess as to which one of "the boys" was out riding with his carbine the night before.[21]

Such actions point to the terrible desperation of a group founded on racial militancy. They also further highlight its members' contempt for legal standards, political institutions, and social order. In local communities where such lawless entities establish a following, their very presence alters community orientations to legitimate authority, undermining mainstream efforts to maintain a stable social order.

Criminologists emphasize how such cracks in systems of social control can increase the prevalence of violent crime and note the difficulties associated with repairing the frayed relations that produce those illegal acts. Former KKK strongholds demonstrate the enduring power of organized vigilantism on unlawful behavior. Strikingly, even two decades after the UKA's collapse, communities where the group was once active continued to suffer from higher-than-expected rates of violent crime. This association between past klan organization and subsequent elevated lethal crime rates holds even after accounting for other major predictors of criminal behavior in communities, including population size, age profile, economic deprivation, police expenditures, and residential and family stability. Controlling for all of these other factors, prior klan presence in a county produces an average of more than one additional homicide per year. Extended over hundreds of counties and several decades, this figure signals that beyond the thousands of acts of violence and intimidation committed by its members during the 1960s, the civil rights-era KKK's legacy also encompasses more than 10,000 "additional" homicides occurring in its wake within communities unable to recapture the stable social conditions required to regulate lawlessness.[22]

How exactly did the UKA's presence create this strong and lasting susceptibility to crime? To explain what disposes communities to unlawful activity, criminologists conventionally focus on a shortfall of social cohesion among community residents. When cohesion is lacking, residents struggle to uphold a general sense of trust in their neighbors and faith in community institutions. This declining sense of collective efficacy in turn undermines community organization and residents' willingness to engage in projects that affirm solidarity and order.[23]

The UKA, as a vigilante force, challenged the legitimacy of existing authorities by encouraging its supporters to defy any official body that failed to devote its full efforts to maintaining segregation and "racial integrity." As Chapters 2 and 5 both show, by emphasizing and reinforcing strict boundaries based on racial purity and allegiance to segregationist ideology, the UKA exacerbated and politicized divisions across community residents. Its willingness to circumvent official practices to threaten and intimidate its enemies reinforced those boundaries and undercut confidence in police and other officials who proved unwilling or unable to regulate klan members' vigilantism. When UKA adherents criticized and sometimes directly targeted community leaders, they fostered a climate that challenged the legitimacy of local elites. By directly targeting these community leaders and relentlessly criticizing officials in Washington, DC, klan leaders and their supporters damaged residents' trust in local elites and the federal government alike.

In short, while state authorities' failure to preserve Jim Crow in the face of federal pressures produced different forms of backlash in many southern communities, support for the klan challenged the foundations of community order and stability. Klan members' defensive rhetoric about the illegitimacy of authorities who capitulate to outside influences and "agitation" contributed to a general shift in the way that many white residents viewed authority. African Americans in klan strongholds had different, but equally strong, reasons to mistrust authorities as well, as they confronted legal systems that not only failed to uphold their rights but also routinely condoned organized racial violence.[24]

The profound impact of vigilantism on community stability and order demonstrates how the klan's influence on lethal crime outran the efforts of adherents to deploy the KKK toward such ends. While researchers have yet to rigorously identify and explain the broad trajectories of organized vigilante violence, the Carolina Klan case shows how the group's orientation to violence evolved, and how that evolution outlasted the UKA itself. Indeed, while klavern policy and the semi-autonomous actions of klan adherents promoted violence in different ways throughout the 1960s, the resulting elevated crime rates in the 1970s, 1980s, and beyond stem not primarily from the acts of former KKK members and sympathizers, but rather from the ways in which prior klan activism disrupted community cohesion, undermined generalized trust, and challenged the perceived legitimacy of local authority.

Truth, Reconciliation, and the Ku Klux Klan

As this relationship between the klan and subsequent violent crime demonstrates, tears in the social fabric rendered by the civil rights-era KKK continue to harm communities across the South. Recognizing and acknowledging these enduring effects of organized racism points to the need for repair. In the face of this terrible legacy, how might communities productively move forward? By far the most visible efforts to engage with the vestiges of KKK violence are the high-visibility civil rights "cold case" trials that have pursued convictions of mostly unrepentant former klansmen for half-century-old crimes. Beginning with the 1994 conviction of Byron de la Beckwith for the 1963 murder of Mississippi NAACP leader Medgar Evers, nearly two dozen perpetrators of civil rights-era crimes have been brought to justice. Arguably the best-known cold case involved Edgar Ray Killen, who was convicted on manslaughter charges in 2005 for his role as ringleader in the 1964 murders of civil rights workers Chaney, Schwerner, and Goodman in Mississippi's Neshoba County.

Killen's trial highlights both the utility and limitations of courtroom efforts. The national press widely framed the outcome of his high-profile trial as belated justice served, as well as a vehicle for broader closure and redemption for the community. To the extent that criminal proceedings signal the broader values of communities and mark the boundaries of what citizens view as acceptable behavior, the near-unanimous condemnation of klan defendants like Killen signals a lack of tolerance for klan-style extremism. Legal processes can also begin to trace lines of complicity in individual acts. A recent civil suit filed by the families of Charles Moore and Henry Dee, both tortured and killed in 1964 as part of a klan plot in southwest Mississippi to find a suspected cache of weapons, charged that county law enforcement colluded with members of the KKK. The SPLC's 1987 lawsuit put the UKA out of business when lawyers successfully argued that Shelton's organization was responsible for the acts of its individual members.[25]

But courtroom proceedings are limited in their reach. Given that the Freedom Summer murders resulted from a conspiracy that encompassed at least twenty-one people—including the county sheriff, who had openly, and successfully, campaigned on his ability to sternly "cope" with the state's influx of "racial agitators"—voices in the legal activist community have promoted processes that address these far-reaching networks of culpability. While additional trials for others directly implicated in the murder plot could help untangle those networks, such efforts cannot transcend the inherent limitations of the legal system. While criminal convictions ensure some measure of justice by forcing the accused to be accountable for their actions, the redemptive potential of the legal process appears more limited. A criminal trial, by its very nature, focuses narrowly on a standard of proof related to a specific person's involvement in a particular act. Further, by holding up individual perpetrators such as Killen as the only "real" villains, we achieve a facile, and ultimately false, closure. As historian Renee Romano has suggested, klan defendants, when treated as "embarrassing relics of a shameful past . . . become almost like displays in the museum case, to be dusted off for their national display in these trials. By emphasizing how far we've come since [this era] and how very different these men are from 'us,' the trials . . . suggest that the nation has fully reckoned with the racial crimes of the past."[26]

This artificial partitioning between then and now becomes more insidious when perpetrators represent a category (e.g., "the klan") entirely separable from the population at large. As Killen—and by extension the KKK—was consistently painted as an evil redneck disconnected from the prevailing mainstream in Neshoba County or the white South generally, his trial shed little light on the klan's role in the community or the institutional conditions that fostered its appeal during that time. Legal scholar Martha Minow defines a similar puzzle in general terms: "justice may call for truth but also demands accountability. And the institutions for securing accountability—notably, trial courts—may impede or ignore truth."[27] Any attempt to avoid the pitfalls of the judicial system's narrow conception of culpability must, therefore, demand that institutions as well as individuals be accountable. The klan and other organized racist vehicles did not operate in a vacuum; they were instead woven into the fabric of Neshoba County and hundreds of other communities.

Agreement on how—or even whether—to engage such culpability to repair the lasting divisiveness created by past klan mobilization has been difficult to reach. Perhaps the most telling exchanges occurred in the wake of the 1979 "Greensboro Massacre," in which several klansmen (including UKA veteran Eddie Dawson) and their neo-nazi allies confronted a "Death to the Klan" march organized in Greensboro by the Communist Workers Party, killing five of the marchers. Local television news crews captured the exchange, and the ghastly footage clearly showed klansmen, in the absence of any immediate danger of deadly attack, firing on the crowd of demonstrators rather than exiting the confrontation. Despite this seemingly damning evidence, two subsequent criminal trials against the shooters resulted in acquittals. In 1985, a civil trial found the white supremacists and the police jointly liable for one of the killings, resulting in a $350,000 payment by the City of Greensboro to settle the suit.[28]

More than two decades after the tragic shootings, as city leaders refused to acknowledge that the day's events signaled anything about Greensboro itself, grassroots momentum continued to build for alternative strategies to promote dialogue and ultimately reconciliation within the community. A central proponent was the Greensboro Truth and Community Reconciliation Project (GTCRP), which in 2003 gave birth to the Greensboro Truth and Reconciliation Commission (GTRC). In their mandate to the Commission, GTCRP members defined their raison d'etre, suggesting that "there comes a time in the life of every community when it must look humbly and seriously into its past in order to provide the best possible foundation for moving into a future based on healing and hope. Many residents believe that for this city, the time is now."[29]

The GTRC operated in the tradition of previous Truth and Reconciliation Commissions in many areas of the world, including South Africa, Argentina, El Salvador, and East Timor. While the motivation and mandate for such work has differed significantly across commissions, the GTRC was distinct from many previous efforts due to its response to a particular event rather than a pattern of abuses, as well as its lack of state or local governmental sponsorship. In Greensboro, notably, there were no offers of legal amnesty for the confession of politically motivated crimes, which had been a controversial component of the South African TRC. But like its predecessors, the GTRC sought, through the testimonies of victims and perpetrators and the analysis of available data, to provide a forum for justice in the form of a contextualized truth that recognized and identified the intersecting roles played by individuals and community institutions. In contrast with the retributive efforts of the legal system, justice pursued by the GTRC was restorative, providing a structure for those who were harmed to tell their stories and for perpetrators to acknowledge and apologize for their crimes.[30]

Formally convened in 2004, the GTRC itself charged its seven commissioners with the task of examining the "context, causes, sequence and consequence of the events of November 3, 1979." Despite a lack of official support from the Greensboro City Council—dividing along racial lines, the majority-white City Council voted to oppose the process—in 2005 the Commission convened a set of three public hearings. Fifty-four people—including former residents, textile workers, police, labor activists, klan members, civic leaders, reporters, and a number of academic and legal experts—gave statements. This testimony, combined with a rigorous analysis of additional interview and archival records from police, government, civic, and media sources, guided the GTRC's investigation, leading to the release of an extensive final report in May of 2006.

Recognizing that if the community as a whole is pronounced guilty, then no particular individuals or groups are held accountable for their decisions or actions, the GTRC's report acknowledged the "wide range of stakeholders harmed by the events of November 3, 1979" and how various parties' actions produced these harms. Its process also provided a space to assess and evaluate the sorts of social scientific claims advanced here. In its final report, the GTRC was clear that the justice to which it "aspires in its search for the truth" comes "not only from trials, but from addressing the root causes of injustices that often lead to violence that rips apart communities." In addition to offering judgments of responsibility and calls for accountability, the Commission proposed reforms to reduce pervasive institutional inequities—ranging from the establishment of a living wage, to increased funding to agencies serving low-income residents, to leadership training provided by the city of Greensboro to local residents—that provide fertile settings for racial and ethnic contention. Importantly, these recommendations acknowledge that inequalities and conflict are produced by practices that cross-cut racial and class lines in complex ways. Successful social justice policies, the GTRC's report argues, foster understanding across groups and move to eradicate institutional racial disparities, but also attack the root causes of inter-group animosity and conflict, defusing the class-based grievances that groups like the klan exploit to mobilize followers. By holding both individual and institutional actors to account, initiatives such as the GTRC open communities to an ideal of justice that values redemption as well as retribution.[31]

As in Greensboro, nearly a half-century removed from the KKK's civil rights-era peak, calls for justice continue to point to additional cold-case prosecutions but increasingly emphasize extra-legal community responses to past and current racism. The 1898 Wilmington Race Riot Commission has compiled an exhaustive report detailing the mob action described in Chapter 1, which resulted in the killing or exiling of well over a thousand members of the local black community. Residents in Duluth, Minnesota, have erected a memorial commemorating the 1920 lynching of three black men. In Walton County, Georgia, members of the Moore's Ford Committee stage an annual dramatic reenactment of a 1946 lynching. Descendants of Rosewood, Florida, residents have fought for reparations stemming from the razing of the primarily black town following a 1923 rape claim.[32]

In each case, the focus on past events serves as a vehicle to spark conversations and reconsiderations of contemporary forms of injustice in local communities. A logical product of such dialogue is a renewed commitment to programs and policies designed to eradicate the institutional conditions that lead to competition and conflict. The pursuit of justice and reconciliation around KKK-perpetrated civil rights violence requires comprehending the klan itself—the settings within which it thrived, how its tentacles deeply penetrated many communities, and how it operated alongside other institutional efforts to maintain white dominance. Our challenge today is to engage with the social forces that produce individual and especially organized acts of racism, to understand the experiences of those for whom the UKA provided refuge as well as those victimized in ways large and small by the klan's ideas and actions.

The KKK operated under the cover of darkness in more than one sense. While its activities often occurred in the dark of night, the silence that its terror often purposefully engendered has obscured efforts to grapple with its legacy of racial violence. Such silences have often been courageously combated within families, neighborhoods, and communities. Bringing the outcomes of klan terror fully into the open requires a broadening of such conversations. The significance of the civil rights-era KKK encompasses the murders, beatings, and burnings it committed across the South, but also the culture of oppression and division propagated by its presence and worldview. Indeed, its circle of victims extends beyond its conscious targets. The klan's legacy permeates the whole cloth of communities where white hoods and burning crosses defied efforts to recognize the dignity of all citizens. As Natasha Trethewey reminds us, though "nothing really happened," though the flames have dimmed, only by telling—and listening to—the story can we forge a common path.

NOTES

ACKNOWLEDGMENTS

1. See Cunningham (2007, 2008, 2009, 2012); Cunningham and Phillips (2007); McVeigh and Cunningham (2012).

INTRODUCTION

1. Alsop (1966b); Hart (1966); Hatch (1966); "Klan Rally Will Alert N.C. Guard," *Winston-Salem Journal,* August 13, 1966; "Moore Tells Troops to Stand By at Rally," *Charlotte Observer,* August 13, 1966; "Police to Surround Site of Klan Rally," *Durham Morning Herald,* August 14, 1966; "Moderation Is Noted at Rally of Klan," *Winston-Salem Journal,* August 16, 1966; "Klan Chaplain Delivers Most Fiery Talk," *Winston-Salem Journal,* August 15, 1966; "Crowds Jeer in Raleigh as Negroes Meet," *New Bern Sun-Journal,* August 15, 1966.
2. The FBI's census of KKK organizations was included in COINTELPRO–White Hate Groups Memo from Director to seventeen field offices, September 2, 1964. Hoover's thoughts about the UKA were expressed in COINTELPRO–White Hate Groups Memo from Director to Richmond, Atlanta, Baltimore, Birmingham, Los Angeles, and Mobile, November 8, 1966.
3. "Good Preparation for Klan Rally," *Charlotte Observer,* August 16, 1966; "Reader's Views: Sickening Spectacle," *Durham Morning Herald,* August 17, 1966; "Cleric Group Brands Klan as Un-American," *Raleigh News and Observer,* May 12, 1965; "The Klan Surges Back into Open; Wedding Tonight," *Raleigh News and Observer,* May 22, 1965; "Baptists May Flay Klansmen," *Raleigh News and Observer,* November 16, 1964.
4. King quoted in "Scuffle Marks Klan and King Rival Meeting," *New Bern Sun-Journal,* August 1, 1966; Golden quoted in the *Carolina Israelite,* May/June 1966.
5. Jones's letter is reprinted in US House of Representatives (1966: 1747). This study of the UKA in North Carolina serves as an analogue of sorts to civil rights scholars' predominant focus on Mississippi (see, e.g., Andrews 2004; Crosby 2005; Dittmer 1995; McAdam 1986; Payne 1995). Just as Mississippi—the racially oppressive "most southern place on earth"—provides broader leverage for understanding the coalescence of civil rights movement activism generally, the fact that the KKK

flourished in North Carolina, the state arguably most resistant to its ideals, poses both a fascinating puzzle and a window through which to comprehend the complex appeal of the UKA as a whole.

6. See, e.g., Branch (1989, 1999); Cagin and Dray (1988); Chalmers (2003); Crespino (2007); Davis (2004); Dittmer (1995); McWhorter (2001); Morris (1993); Nelson (1993); Whitehead (1970).
7. For conceptualizations of the KKK and other white supremacist groups as "reactive movements," see, e.g., Cunningham and Phillips (2007) and Van Dyke and Soule (2002). Foundational work on ethnic competition theory includes Barth (1969), Hannan (1979), and Olzak (1992). Earlier studies have most commonly conceptualized inter-group competition or threat in economic terms, consistent with the centrality of labor market dynamics in theoretical formulations of ethnic conflict. However, Blalock (1967) and others have emphasized the unique impacts of politically rooted threats, and more recent research has also focused on demographic, ecological, and cultural forms of threat (Bergeson and Herman 1998; Olzak 1990; Wilkes and Okamoto 2002).
8. In a racialized setting such as the civil rights-era South, threat has been captured most commonly by demographic proxies; the percentage of nonwhite residents in a particular spatial unit, for example, provides an estimate of the level of threat faced by whites (Fossett and Kiecolt 1989; Quillian 1995, 1996; Tolnay, Beck, and Massey 1989). Employing a similar competition-based logic, other studies have conceptualized these threats multidimensionally, focusing on perceived or actual economic, political, and social gains by African Americans and other racial or ethnic groups (Beck 2000; James 1988; McVeigh 1999; Olzak 1992; Van Dyke and Soule 2002).
9. Typical ethnic competition analyses tend to operate at the aggregate level, demonstrating how variation in ethnic mobilization relates to overall levels of ethnic heterogeneity or labor market overlap in nations, states, or municipalities (see, e.g., Brown and Boswell 1997; Mousseau 2001; Myers 1997; Olzak 1989; VanDyke and Soule 2002; Wilkes and Okamoto 2002). This tendency holds even when explaining individual action such as voting behavior (Medrano 1994), expressions of ethnic identification (Ono 2002), perceptions of trust in political institutions (Michelson 2003), and the likelihood of holding ethnically centered political attitudes (Aguirre et al. 1989; Belanger and Pinard 1991; Coenders and Scheepers 2008; Hwang et al. 1998; Tolsma et al. 2008). While the relevant political outcomes in these studies are associated with individual attitudes or behaviors, competitive determinants are typically rooted in characteristics associated with the makeup of surrounding states or municipalities. Tolsma et al. (2008), for instance, demonstrate that the likelihood that a given individual will oppose ethnic intermarriage is shaped by aggregate changes in the percentage of ethnic minorities in his or her surrounding community. As a result, competition models are unable to tease out the direct versus indirect effects of competition—that is, whether associated conflicts are initiated by individuals who are themselves in direct competition for resources, or alternately whether they emerge

in a more diffuse manner in areas marked by a generalized competitive climate. They also fail to explain how the presence of ethnic conflict is shaped by the social and spatial organization of associations, which mediate the coalescence of grievances within communities and thus serve as crucial mobilization venues (Cunningham and Phillips 2007). In this sense, the emphasis on narrower units of analysis advanced here is not merely an effort to be still more precise in one's choice of contextual unit, but rather a theoretically distinct call to examine how social settings impact perceptions of inter-group competition. Such perceptions likely have much to do with the presence of out-group members, but also with how those alters relate socially, spatially, and culturally to available resources and mobility structures.

10. For examples of how these segregationist institutions operated in Deep South states, see Crosby (2005), Dittmer (1995), and Jeffries (2009). Also note that in Mississippi, the klan was also competing for members with itself, as the UKA battled with the White Knights of the KKK for the allegiance of like-minded klan types (see Cunningham, forthcoming; Whitehead 1970).

11. Both of the central factors discussed here—that is, the truncation of the segregationist political field (which channeled segregationist constituencies toward the klan) and the failure of police action to suppress KKK organizing—fit neatly within standard conceptualizations of the "political opportunity structure," a central explanatory factor in now-canonical political process accounts of social movement emergence (see McAdam 1999; Meyer and Minkoff 2004; Tarrow 1998). Note that while early political process formulations were motivated in part by widespread dissatisfaction with models that explained social movement activity as phenomena that "magically" appeared through the coalescence of grievances (see McAdam 1999: Ch. 1), prevailing accounts of threat-based movements (which are predominantly, though not entirely, right wing) still mostly hinge on whether broad conditions associated with particular cases are conducive to the production of grievances, and pay little attention to the organizational and strategic aspects of movement mobilization (for exceptions, see Blee 2003; Simi and Futrell 2010).

12. This focus on resources and ideological arguments matches political process models' emphasis on the "mobilizing structures" through which social movement organizations deploy material and social assets, and the "framing processes" through which klan ideas align with broader values shared by its constituencies (see Snow and Benford 2000; Edwards and McCarthy 2004; McAdam et al. 1996; Snow et al. 1986). Understanding such practices through the lens of collective identity links to efforts by many recent analysts to examine the strategic dimensions of identity-building efforts (see, e.g., Bernstein 1997, Hunt and Benford 2004, Pfaff 1996, Polletta and Jasper 2001, Taylor and Whittier 1992), and ties particularly closely to Snow and McAdam's (2004) emphasis on how personal identities fit with a collective, which they refer to as the "problem of identity correspondence."

13. Examples of police officials involved with the UKA include Sheriff Marion Millis of New Hanover County and several of his deputies (see US House of Representatives 1966: 1962–2004), Pittsboro Police Chief Guy McNeil (see NCSA, Department of Administration, Human Relations Council, Direct Correspondence, File, 1960–77, Box 29), Wallace Police Chief Earl Whitaker and Clinton Police Captain Bill Thornton (see memo from McConnon to McNamara, October 18, 1965, HUAC, Box 18, Folder: United Klans-North Carolina Investigative Memos [1 of 4]). For instances of police refusing to take seriously allegations of klan violence, see Eddie Dawson interview with Scott Ellsworth, May 26, 1977, p. 45 (DU, Chafe Oral History Collection, Printed Materials Series, Box 1), and letter from Salter and Cofield to Governor Moore, July 24, 1965 (NCSA, Governor Moore Papers, General Correspondence, 1965, Box 71, Folder: Segregation A-E). For discussion of KKK-oriented stickers posted at business establishments, see memo from McConnon to McNamara, July 1, 1965, HUAC, Box 18, Folder: United Klans-North Carolina Investigative Memos (1 of 4). Greene County had its share of TWAK stickers, but also business owners that actively opposed the klan, prompting Raymond Cranford to remark that "everybody knows" that the latter are "just after the nigger dollar" (Alsop 1966a: 24). For examples of anti-klan proclamations by local ministerial associations, see "Local Clergy Condemn Klan in Statement," *Greenville Daily Reflector*, September 25, 1964; "Klan Is Blasted in New Hanover," *Raleigh News and Observer*, November 8, 1965; "Ministers Denounce Klansmen," *Raleigh News and Observer*, December 26, 1965. An example of a published UKA rally flyer can be found in the July 20, 1964 issue of the *Rocky Mount Telegram* (see also Tyson 2004).
14. Alsop (1966a: 23).
15. Klan observer Pete Young, working as a consultant for the Eisenhower Commission, described his initial experience at a UKA rally in 1964 as akin to stumbling onto the "scene of an awful disaster." See *Task Force Report,* Chapter 4, p. 354, LBJ, Federal Records—Eisenhower Commission, Task Force I, Series 10, Box 1.
16. Cecelski (1997: 15).
17. Trethewey (2006: 41). The reading was in Jackson, Mississippi, as part of the 2009 declaration ceremony for the Mississippi Truth Project.

CHAPTER 1

1. "Charlotte Chief Pledges to Fight Klan," *Raleigh News and Observer*, December 10, 1949.
2. "Klan to Open Chapel Hill Drive 'In about 2 Weeks,'" *Durham Morning Herald*, January 7, 1950.
3. Capus Waynick memo, November 3, 1963, ECU Archives, Waynick Papers, #421.27.e.

4. SBI Report #1 to Law and Order Committee, April 27, 1966, NCSA, Governor Moore Papers, General Correspondence, 1966.
5. Randel (1965: 5–7); Trelease (1971: 3–5). There are many accounts of the origins of the name "Ku Klux Klan"; the one included here is the most commonly accepted. Competing theories suggest that the three components of the name constitute an onomatopoeic representation of a gun being cocked and fired; that the words have their origin in an old Hebrew term, "Cu-Clux Clan;" or that they are derived from "Clocletz," a "phantom Indian chieftain" feared by black residents in parts of the South (see Fry 1975:117–19).
6. These ritualized ruses are featured prominently in D. W. Griffith's iconic film *Birth of a Nation*, which—even more than the KKK's self-mythologizing propaganda efforts—served to spread and maintain the intricacies of klan lore among the broader public.
7. Fry (1975: Ch. 4).
8. Historian Allen Trelease (1971: 8–9) notes that if Pulaski was not located in "the most lawless county in Tennessee in 1866 and 1867, it ranked high on the list."
9. Olsen (1962: 345); Trelease (1971: 199). For discussions of how the threat mobilized in the media and by various southern Democratic leaders centered on the sexual threat posed by black men to white women, see Gilmore (1996) and Whites (1998). Conversely, note that where Republicans had consolidated control of local political offices, the klan struggled to mobilize (see Trelease 1971: 339).
10. Trelease (1971: 68–70); *Charlotte Daily Observer,* August 6, 1899. Membership figures are reported in "North Carolina Klan Organizations to September 1959," May 13, 1965, HUAC Box 17, Folder: Klans—North Carolina. Randel (1965: 55) argues that the Invisible Empire, the White Brotherhood, and the Constitutional Union Guard were so closely related as to be effectively identical. The distinctions among the groups, he argues, was "really a dodge to permit Klansmen to swear, without committing perjury, that they did not belong to the Ku Klux Klan." While this isn't an unreasonable thesis, and klan members in North Carolina did frequently go to great lengths to deny the group's existence, there doesn't appear to be any solid evidence to document that the organizations did in fact exist for this purpose. Regional and temporal variation in the groups' respective memberships (see Trelease 1971: 69) point to an interpretation that they were operating in parallel, with some overlap in membership.
11. Trelease (1971: 190, 212–15). Alongside the KKK, the WB, CUG, and the Invisible Empire rapidly grew during this period as well. In Alamance County, near the center of the state, membership in the White Brotherhood was estimated to be 600 to 700. In 1869 the group was tied to more than 100 acts of violence in Alamance alone. Farther west, Cleveland County had a similar number of klansmen, and membership reached into the thousands in adjacent Rutherford County.
12. Ibid, p. 63.

13. Foner (1988: 440–41); Trelease (1971: 208–11); *Raleigh Daily Standard,* May 23, 1870. There is ample evidence of the significant impact of intimidation during the 1870 election, including that at least two-thirds of the counties that swung from Republican to Democrat were sites of intense klan violence and that Republican voter turnout overall was significantly lower than in the 1868 elections (Olsen 1962: 360; Trelease 1971: 223).
14. Cole (2003: 118–44); Foner (1988: 454–55); Trelease (1971: 385–400).
15. Edwards (1998: 120–24); Tyson and Cecelski (1998: 4–5); Tyson (2004: 159–62, 273); Gavins (1998: 191). Even in the 1960s, the paramilitary siege in Wilmington continued to resonate in Klan circles. Pete Young, a North Carolina reporter who covered the UKA extensively during the 1960s, recalls hearing in the early years of that decade repeated references to Wilmington's "Niggerhead Road." The term was a crude allusion to the heads of various murdered African Americans reputedly placed on stakes lining a main thoroughfare in the aftermath of the 1898 takeover (interview with author, Framingham, Massachusetts, February 5, 2004).
16. *Report of the Joint Select Committee to Inquire into the Condition of Affairs in the Late Insurrectionary States*, Committee Report (1872: 292, 422, 508).
17. *Charlotte Daily Observer*, August 6, 1899; see also Cole (2003: 118–44) and Edwards (1998: 113–15). On October 29, 1920, twenty years after Shotwell's account, the *Raleigh News and Observer* published an account by J. J. Laughinghouse, a Confederate Army captain and self-proclaimed last surviving member of the KKK in North Carolina. Laughinghouse portrayed Reconstruction—or the "complete overthrow of the organic law of the Southern States"—as "the greatest act of infamy," perpetrated by "carpetbaggers and negroes." The klan, on the other hand, was comprised of the "best of the South's citizenship." Its members possessed an "honest and sincere motive to protect the society of the South," and "thought it better to die in defense of a righteous cause than to live in infamy and disgrace brought about by negro and carpet-bagger domination." Such romanticized accounts continued to be regularly repeated in the popular media throughout the first half of the twentieth century (see, for example, Henderson [1939] and Ader [1941]). Until revisionist histories began appearing in the 1960s, scholarly accounts remained consistent with these general perspectives. For a critique of the literature on the Reconstruction-era klan to that point, see Olsen (1962: 340–41). The best-known pre-revisionist general history of the KKK is Horn (1939).
18. This brief account generally follows the "power devaluation model" developed by McVeigh (2009). See also McVeigh (1999) and Rhomberg (2005).
19. Jackson (1967: 10–12).
20. See Jackson (1967); Lay (1992). As always with the klan, accurate membership values are notoriously difficult to determine conclusively. The figure cited here is from Chalmers (1981: 96–97), who relies on a variety of sources but doesn't clearly specify how he calculated this number. Jackson (1967: 237) suggests a much lower value (25,000), though his estimates appear to be very conservative for all states

(e.g., his estimated national membership total is slightly over 2 million, while most estimates are closer to 4 million).

21. Chalmers (1981: 94); "Subpoenas Served on Alleged Head of Fairmont Ku Klux Klavern Requiring Him to Produce Roster of Membership and Record," *The Robesonian,* July 18, 1923.
22. Chalmers (1981); McVeigh (1999).
23. Chalmers (1981: 95–97); *Greensboro Daily News,* May 16, 1926; "North Carolina Klan Splits with Dr. Evans," *New York Times,* February 23, 1927. Among North Carolina adherents, the key issue facing Grady was an alleged misappropriation of $900 collected from members to help miners after a disaster in the Carolina Piedmont town of Sanford. His opposition was strongest in the state's western mountain region; the Asheville klavern first charged Grady and other klan officers with these improprieties, and most other mountain klaverns expressed strong criticism as well. This local conflict was compounded by Grady's falling-out with Evans over the latter's dismissal of a state klan officer and subsequent advocacy of legislation that Grady viewed as "unconstitutional."
24. Key (1949: 421); "Georgia Klansmen Burn Fiery Cross," *New York Times,* October 21, 1945.
25. Hinton (1946a, b); "Inquiries Made into N.C. Klan," *Raleigh News and Observer,* October 11, 1946; Chalmers (1981: 329–33); Kennedy (1990). In 2006, Stetson Kennedy's book (republished in 1990 as *The Klan Unmasked*) came under scrutiny for its alleged inaccuracies. The controversy was sparked by research brought to light by Steven D. Levitt and Steven J. Dubner, whose 2004 book *Freakonomics* had featured Kennedy's undercover klan exploits in one of its chapters. In January 2006, Levitt and Dubner published a follow-up article in the *New York Times Magazine,* detailing accusations that Kennedy had in fact embellished and fictionalized many of the interactions detailed in his book and relied upon an uncredited collaborator to infiltrate the KKK. No one, however, disputes that Kennedy was the source of the information channeled to Drew Pearson and others in the media during the 1940s (see Dubner and Levitt [2006] and Patton [2006]).
26. "2 Georgia KKK Units Set Up Rival Group," *New York Times,* June 30, 1948; "Green, Klan Chief, Dies at His Home," *New York Times,* August 18, 1949; "Georgia Klan Names Ex-Policeman Chief," *New York Times,* August 28, 1949; Chalmers (1981: 335).
27. Jenkins (1952b); Sexton (1949); Shumaker (1952).
28. Shumaker (1952); "Charlotte Chief Pledges to Fight Klan," *Raleigh News and Observer,* December 10, 1949; "Klan in State," *Durham Morning Herald,* October 12, 1949; "Klan to Open Chapel Hill Drive 'In about 2 Weeks,'" *Durham Morning Herald,* January 7, 1950; Andrews (1950).
29. Shumaker (1952); Carter (1991: 9–18).
30. Carter (1991: 23–26, 37–42, 61–63); "N.C. Negro Woman Reports Mob of White Men Beat Her," *Asheville Citizen,* January 23, 1951; *New York Times,* July 23, 1952.

31. Carter (1991: 100); Jenkins (1952a); Shumaker (1952). Note that Early Brooks described entering Hamilton's KKK due to frustration that his police work failed to effectively punish most of the moral offenders in his community, combined with his fond nostalgia for tales told by his grandfather, a Civil War veteran who had been jailed by "blue clad savages" in Richmond. Following the war, Brooks's grandfather joined the original KKK, which by his account redeemed the South from the "carpetbaggers and scalawags who covered the Southland like locusts." When Hamilton began organizing in the Carolinas, "spreading the word that the KKK would again save the South from these carpetbaggers, who were again being influenced by the NAACP so as to push the Negro race upon us," Brooks (1958: 22–23) recounted, "it was no problem to sell me on the idea or the merits of what the KKK could do."
32. "Wave of Floggings Laid to Klansmen," *New York Times,* January 20, 1952; "Klan Case to Test Old N.C. Law," *Raleigh News and Observer,* March 26, 1952; "One Simple Question," *Raleigh News and Observer,* March 29, 1952; "Ku Klux Klan Dealt a Heavy Blow in Columbus," *Raleigh News and Observer,* May 15, 1952; Brooks (1958: 47); Cole (1952); Clay (1964); Carter (1991: 190–91). Among those promoting a hard line against future KKK activity was North Carolina Attorney General William Rodman, who in 1955 gave his "complete approval" to a regional statement of policy presented to the Southern Association of Attorneys General, pledging to coordinate investigations, share information, and use any legal means available to oppose "any clandestine organization based on hatred and committed to violence" ("Anti-KKK Fight Shapes Up," *Raleigh News and Observer,* August 17, 1955).
33. "Doing a Grand Job," *Raleigh News and Observer,* July 26, 1952; Carter (1991: 151, 166).
34. "Eldon Edwards, Klan Chief, Dies," *New York Times,* August 3, 1960; *Concord (N.C.) Tribune,* October 27, 1957; Wade (1987: 304–305); Wallace (2006). During the fall of 1953, Hamilton released a letter to the media, in which he pledged to be "through with the Ku Klux Klan." He apologized for the "suffering and heartaches" that his klan had caused, and called on his "klan friends everywhere to disband wherever you are." Later that year, he was granted parole, and was never again publicly involved in KKK activity (Carter 1991: 194–95).
35. *Concord (N.C.) Tribune,* October 27, 1957; "Klan Chief's Hearing Set Nov. 7," *Charlotte Observer,* October 28, 1958. Note that Miller was replaced, on a temporary basis, as Grand Dragon by C. J. "Click" Plummer in December 1957 (letter from Edwards to membership, December 12, 1957, HUAC Box 20, Folder: US Klans-NC Documents [2 of 2]). Plummer was banished from the organization the following November following charges of treason and disrespect for the U.S. Klans order (letter to Plummer, November 15, 1958, HUAC Box 20, Folder: U.S. Klans—North Carolina documents [2 of 2]).

36. Bartley (1969: 96–97); McMillen (1994: 111–15, 153); Lewis (2004); States Rights League of North Carolina, Inc., "Certificate of Incorporation" (1955), ECU #40.3.a. Note that we should not overstate the separation of the klan from these other segregationist organizations. In addition to the membership overlap in the States Rights League noted above, a small group called the "Black Shirts," headed in the South by Columbia, South Carolina, attorney A.W. Holman and organized locally by expelled U.S. Klans member "Click" Plummer, emerged in 1958. In North Carolina, Plummer's Black Shirts were explicitly affiliated with the Defenders of States' Rights, who intended the group to undertake klan-like vigilante action. Both Plummer and his close associate Cannon Odell would resurface a decade later in the UKA, with Odell receiving a UKA "lifetime membership award" in 1967 (see SBI report on "Black Shirts," prepared by R. H. Garland, February 6, 1959, NCSA). The States Rights League was first incorporated by several known klan members (see "Certificate of Incorporation," ECU #40.3.a). Two other organizations—the Durham-based North Carolina Association for the Preservation of the White Race, Inc. (NCAPWR) and the Constitution of White Men Incorporated (CWMI) had sufficiently short lives in the 1950s that their connections to the broader network of white resistance were unclear (see Lewis 2004: 230–31). Finally, despite the fact that the Citizens' Councils never achieved a sustained presence in North Carolina, a 1958 organizing meeting held by the group in Greensboro included George Dorsett as the featured speaker. Clyde Webster and Robert Hudgins were among the nineteen attendees. All three had been prominent members of Cole's North Carolina Knights and would later resume their klan activity as UKA state officers (see SBI memo from Allen to Anderson, July 20, 1958, NCSA).
37. "New Teeth for the Grand Wizard," *Raleigh News and Observer*, January 24, 1958; flyer for rally in Salisbury, North Carolina, July 20, 1957, HUAC Box 19, Folder: U.S. Klans—North Carolina (note that while HUAC staff filed this flyer under "U.S. Klans," it actually was for a North Carolina Knights rally). While Cole quickly became the face of the North Carolina Knights, note that he joined the group shortly after its founding by Arthur Bryant, a fellow banished U.S. Klansman and former States Rights League founder. Maylon D. Watkins, a Baptist minister from Charlotte, preceded Cole as the Knights' preacher, but fell out of favor with Bryant after being accused of financial improprieties ("North Carolina Klan Organizations to September 1959," May 13, 1965, HUAC Box 17, Folder: Klans—North Carolina).
38. Anti-Defamation League (1957: 3); "'Smear Sheets' Klan Label for Newspapers at Rally," *Raleigh News and Observer,* October 20, 1956; Letter from Garland Martin, July 29, 1957, ECU #40.1.a.
39. Thomas (1957); letters from James W. Cole to Attorney General Patton, October 27, 1957 and October 28, 1957, NCSA, Folder: Segregation, KKK. U.S. Klans organizers in North Carolina were likewise threatened by Cole's group. At a State

Officers Meeting held on September 27, 1958, the U.S. Klans Imperial Wizard issued a decree stating that no U.S. Klansman could belong to Cole's outfit (Minutes of State Officers Meeting, September 27, 1958, HUAC Box 20, Folder: U.S. Klans—North Carolina).

40. "Maxton Rally Plans Unchanged; Klan Cites Protection Rights," *Raleigh News and Observer,* January 18, 1958; "Cole Ignored Sheriff's Warning to Leave Scene," *Durham Morning Herald,* January 20, 1958; "Bad Medicine for the Klan," *Life Magazine,* January 27, 1958; Haas (1963: 122–24); Chalmers (1981: 347–48). McLeod is quoted in Oakley (2008: 61). Garland Martin, charged with drunkenness and carrying a concealed weapon, was the lone klan member arrested.

41. "2 Klansmen Face Charges in Clash," *New York Times,* January 20, 1958; "Indians Back at Peace and the Klan at Bay," *Life Magazine,* February 3, 1958; "Hodges Warns Klansmen Not to Breach N.C. Laws," *Asheville Citizen,* January 31, 1958; *ADL,* "The KKK in Its Present Phase"; Oakley (2008). Robb's column was reprinted in a number of wide-ranging newspapers, including the *Daily Oklahoman* and the *Tucson Citizen.* A sampling of local editorials includes "Unprepared for a Well Advertised Battle," *Durham Morning Herald,* January 20, 1958; "Lumbee Indians on the Warpath," *Asheville Citizen,* January 21, 1958; "The Mask and the Coattail," *Raleigh News and Observer,* January 20, 1958. Apparently Cole cooperated with the *Life* reporter's story, which was highly critical and dismissive of the klan, as he later received a letter of thanks from the magazine, "express[ing] appreciation for your courtesies when LIFE covered recent events in North Carolina" (letter from Barbara Boyd to James Cole, February 13, 1958, ECU #40.1.a).

42. Co-defendant Garland Martin was also convicted and sentenced to a six- to twelve-month prison term. His lighter sentence derived, in part, from his lawyer representing him as a sad case, a financially strapped tobacco worker with children and a chronically ill wife who had been "duped" into helping Cole (Craven 1958). A judge later reduced Martin's punishment to a suspended sentence and a $250 fine. Despite the lawyer's claim that his client had since sworn off the klan "forever," Martin not only joined the UKA during the 1960s, but became one of that organization's most loyal longtime members, even helping to run the UKA State Office after Grand Dragon Jones was sentenced to his own year-long prison term in 1969.

43. "2 in Klan Sentenced," *New York Times,* March 15, 1958; "Klan Making Little Progress in South," *Raleigh News and Observer,* April 7, 1958; "Sentence Is Suspended in Robeson Klan Case," *Raleigh News and Observer,* May 5, 1959; SBI memo from Agent Allen to Director, February 8, 1958, NCSA. Note that this impression endured within klan circles. Informants noted that, as Cole reemerged as a visible and polarizing figure in the UKA in 1966, there remained debate over what actually had happened during the doomed Maxton rally. Former FBI agent Dargan Frierson, who developed close relationships with a number of klan members through his work developing klan informants in the mid-1960s, recalled:

"After the Maxton thing... that group sort of lost interest because of that shootout down there. So there went the enthusiasm for that organization" (Frierson interview with Kathy Hoke, November 10, 1989, http://library.uncg.edu/depts/archives/civrights/detail-iv.asp?iv=5; accessed December 16, 2009).

44. The informant in the Charlotte bombing case was thirty-three-year-old Robert Kinley, who claimed he infiltrated the klan at the request of Charlotte Police Chief Frank N. Littlejohn after the klan group's failed attempt to dynamite a Charlotte synagogue (see "Police Spy Cites Klan Blast Plot," *Raleigh News and Observer,* March 19, 1958). Describing his informant trajectory, Hoyle "Sock" Bostian, who served as North Carolina Grand Dragon for both U.S. Klans and the UKA, claimed that he first joined the KKK in the mid-1950s after being requested to do so as an informant for the local sheriff. In 1965, Bostian reemerged as an informant for HUAC investigators, providing them with a range of original documents and tape recordings (memo from Appell to McNamara, June 21, 1965, HUAC Box X, Folder: Jones, J. R. [Investigative Memos]). See also "Five Klansmen Jailed for School Bomb Plot," *Raleigh News and Observer,* February 17, 1958; "Klansmen on Trial in Blast Case," *Raleigh News and Observer,* March 18, 1958; "3 in Klan Sentenced in a Bombing Plot," *New York Times,* March 21, 1958: 44.
45. See bills from Jones Bros. Printing Co. and Jackson Printing Co., HUAC Box 19, Folder: US Klans-NC Documents.
46. Memos from Allen to Director, SBI (May 25, 1958, and August 10, 1958, NCSA); memo from Minter to Director, SBI (August 18, September 29, 10 and October 25, 1958, NCSA); "National Politics" Bulletin to all U.S. Klans Units, undated, HUAC Box 19, Folder: U.S. Klans—North Carolina.
47. Memos from Allen to Director, SBI, August 24, November 1, 10 and November 30, 1958, NCSA; memos from Minter to Director, SBI, August 31, and September 6, 1958, NCSA; SBI memo, June 29, 1958, NCSA.
48. Memo from Allen to Director, SBI, August 10, 1958, NCSA; memo from Minter to Director, SBI, August 24, 1958, NCSA; "Cole Is Named Head of New Race Group," undated, ECU #40.5.
49. Memos from Allen to Director, SBI, May 25, September 29, 1, 10, and November 30, 1958, NCSA.
50. Letter from William Stephens to James Cole, November 3, 1958, ECU #40.1a; "Cole Draws Suspended Sentence after Guilty Plea at Florence," undated, ECU #40.5.
51. US House of Representatives (1967: 21–22); US House of Representatives (1966: 3922), Chalmers (1981: 366–68); ADL memo from Finger to Ellerin, August 21, 1961, HUAC Box 32, Folder: UKA, Inc. Investigative Memos, Other Memos, Some Photos. Calvin Craig claimed that, following Edwards's death, U.S. Klans split due to "the usual element of non-workers in the Order." In order to "save the Klan," he and I. W. Davidson, Edwards's replacement as Imperial Wizard, split off and formed the UKA, negotiating the merger with Shelton's Alabama Klan soon

after (Craig letter to "Esteemed Klanspeople," April 23, 1968, MARBL, Craig Papers, MSS 612, Box 1, Folder 16). Prior to this split, on November 30, 1960, Davidson and Craig hosted a large U.S. Klans meeting at the Dinkler Plaza Hotel in Atlanta (see various photographs in MARBL, Craig Papers, MSS 612, Box 2, Folder 18).

52. US House of Representatives (1967: 22); Haas (1963: 128); Mikell (1966); "The Ku Klux Klan," ADL Trend Analyses Division, June 1965, p. 4, USM Will Campbell Papers M341, Box 10, Folder 2. Early in his klan career, Shelton was less nuanced in his public presentation of the role of violence in klan affairs. "We don't want no violence," Shelton told a large early 1960s rally crowd in Albany, Georgia, "but we ain't gonna let the niggers spit in our face either" (undated report from Bill Shipp, MARBL, Newsweek, Inc. Atlanta Bureau Records, MSS 629, Box 36, Folder 4).

53. Walker (2009: 73); "North Carolina Klan Organizations to September 1959," May 13, 1965, HUAC Box 17, Folder: Klans—North Carolina; SBI memo, April 17, 1959, NCSA; Letter from Joseph Bryant to Cole, November 5, 1959, ECU #40.1.b; US House of Representatives (1966: 1914); US House of Representatives (1967: 25). Note that, during this klan nadir, Thurman Miller, the U.S. Klans' North Carolina Grand Dragon, was replaced in late September by John W. Younger, who moved the group's state headquarters from Salisbury to High Point and held the office until Edwards's death in 1960. Considered by some in the klan to be a "troublemaker," Younger was succeeded in September 1960 by Hoyle Bostian, who soon after moved away from that group to Shelton's UKA. Bostian was followed as the UKA's North Carolina Grand Dragon by Arthur Leonard, Bob Jones's longtime friend and former employer. Jones, in turn, began his long run as the state's Grand Dragon on August 5, 1963 (interview with Arthur C. Leonard, October 21, 1965, and Executive Testimony of Hoyle S. Bostian, July 21, 1965, HUAC Box X, Folder: Leonard, Arthur; memo from Manuel to McNamara, July 7, 1965, HUAC Box X, Folder: Jones, J. R. [Investigative memos]; memo from Manuel to McNamara, May 13, 1965, HUAC Box 19, Folder: United Klans—NC Investigative memos providing general information).

54. Parker (1966). For accounts of KKK generations or waves, see, for example, Chalmers (1981); Lay (1992); Lipset and Raab (1978); Wade (1987). The mode of thinking is standard enough to provide the organizing structure for historical summaries in many general accounts, including related entries in Wikipedia (see, e.g., http://en.wikipedia.org/wiki/Ku_Klux_Klan; http://en.wikipedia.org/wiki/Women_of_the_Ku_Klux_Klan; accessed December 6, 2010). Building on similar ideas, Rapoport (2004) develops a general analysis of wave-based terrorism.

55. *Charlotte Observer,* August 30, 1964. Sociologist Francesca Polletta (2006) discusses how activist origin stories are not easily understood as straightforward accounts of "what happened." Instead, they often serve as vehicles for the construction and affirmation of resonant collective identities. For instance, Polletta

shows how participants in the 1960 civil rights sit-in movement frequently emphasized spontaneity over the calculated organizational character of the movement, which served to validate a new category of student activist apart from the mold of traditional, and more tactically conservative, civil rights organizations. Bearman and Stovel (2000) also highlight the identity functions of political "becoming" stories.

56. Taylor's (1989) explanation of the continuity of activism across waves of contention focuses on the "abeyance structures" bridging periods of mass mobilization that political scientist Sidney Tarrow (1998) refers to as "cycles of contention." Taylor's seminal conceptualization emphasizes the actions of the critical mass of committed actors that provide key resources for subsequent periods of larger scale mobilization. Specifically, she suggests, such abeyance structures facilitate interwave linkages by "promoting the survival of activist networks, sustaining a repertoire of goals and tactics, and promoting a collective identity that offers participants a sense of mission and moral purpose" (Taylor, 1989: 762). Taylor and others (see Bagguley 2002; Holland and Cable 2002; Ulsperger 2002) have suggested that organizations with highly exclusive memberships, rich political cultures, and centralized structures or diffuse associational networks are most successful in their efforts to retain continuity until external factors enable mass mobilization.
57. See various ephemera in the James William Cole Papers, ECU #40.1.c, #40.2.a, and #40.3.a; letter from NC Council of Women's Organizations to James W. Cole Printing Company, October 27, 1963, ECU #40.1.c; various membership cards in ECU #40.4.a; letter from Lester Maddox to Cole, May 3, 1965, ECU #40.1.c; "Catfish Cole Might Change Complexion of N.C. Klan," *Raleigh News and Observer*, March 30, 1967.
58. Interview with George Dorsett by Tony Crane, in Crane and Young, "Voices from the White Ghetto," p. 15, LBJ, RG283, Task Force I, Series 12 (2 of 2); US House of Representatives (1966: 1907). Craig's copy of Evans' KKK "Constitution and Laws" is included in his archive of papers at Emory University (see MARBL, Craig Papers, MSS 612, Box 1, Folder 17).

CHAPTER 2

1. Letter from Salter to Rankin and Coltrane, November 4, 1966, NCSA, Moore Papers, General Correspondence, 1966, Box 149, folder: SBI Reports 3.
2. Pete Young interview by Will D. Campbell, HU, #386, p. 19.
3. *Winston-Salem Journal*, September 16, 1964. This account follows the standard story repeated often by Jones and other core members of the UKA. As discussed in Chapter 1, however, it is almost certain that the connection between North Carolina's old U.S. Klans and the UKA was forged earlier. During the HUAC hearings in October 1965, Chief Investigator Donald T. Appell suggested that, following Eldon Edwards's death in 1960, "the bulk of the US Klan membership in North

Carolina... went into the United Klans of America," with a core group represented at the UKA's founding "National Klonvocation" in Indian Springs, Georgia, on July 8, 1961. Hoyle "Sock" Bostian and Arthur Leonard—both veterans of the U.S. Klans—preceded Jones as the UKA's North Carolina Grand Dragon (US House of Representatives 1966: 1914; HUAC KKK files, Box 20, folder: US Klans—North Carolina documents [2 of 2]). But the UKA effectively had no public presence in the state prior to Jones's emergence in 1963, which explains the sustained resonance of the standard origin story.

4. Young (1969); "Klan Rally Request Denied," *Raleigh News and Observer*, August 11, 1963; "Tar Heel Klansmen Meet in Salisbury," *Raleigh News and Observer*, August 1, 1963; Raynor (1963); UNCC Scoggin Papers, MSS 335; Box 1, Folder 51.
5. Peter B. Young, "Violence and the White Ghetto: A View from the Inside," LBJ, Federal Records—Eisenhower Commission [RG 283], Task Force I—Assassination; Box 1, Series 10, p. 161; Alsop (1966a: 27); SBI memo from Edwards to Director, May 24, 1967, NCSA, Moore Papers, General Correspondence, 1967, Box 213, folder: SHP & SBI reports. Note that until 1964, the *Fiery Cross* was written largely by Wallace Butterworth, who previously had been a well-known radio personality and record producer in the Philadelphia, Pennsylvania, area. Allegedly an alcoholic and a rabid anti-Semite, Butterworth moved to Alabama in 1961 and served on the UKA's Imperial Board as Public Relations Director. He later forged close partnerships with Georgia-based KKK leader James Venable and Retired Admiral John G. Crommelin, a well-known white supremacist (see ADL memo from Finger to Ellerin, February 8, 1962, and HUAC Memo from Manuel to McNamara, July 13, 1965, both in HUAC, Box 32, Folder: UKA, Inc. Investigative Memos, Other Memos, Some Photos). Butterworth's work with the *Fiery Cross*, as well as his production of various records promoting anti-communist and klan causes, added a sheen of professionalism to the UKA's products.
6. Mitchell (1966: 623–24).
7. SHP memo from Clark to Brown, May 3, 1964, NCSA, Sanford Papers, General Correspondence, 1964, Box 420, folder: KKK; Reynolds (1990: 219–20).
8. Jones's recitation is included in Crane & Young, "Voices from the White Ghetto," pp. 44–45, LBJ, RG283, Task Force I, Series 12 (2 of 2). A UKA flyer featured similar text, explaining that "We do not burn, but lite [*sic*] the Cross to signify that Christ is the light of the world, and light drives out darkness. Fire purifies gold, silver and precious stones, but it destroys dross, wood, hay and stubble. So by the fire of the Cross we mean to purify and cleanse our own virtues by burning out our vices with their own sword" (UNCC Scoggin Papers, MSS 335, Box 1, Folder 46a). George Dorsett also frequently spoke of cross-burnings as spreading the light of Jesus (Dorsett interview with Michael Frierson, recording in Frierson's possession). Beyond the crosses burned at each UKA rally, SHP and SBI files document literally dozens of incidents in which klansmen used lit crosses to intimidate particular citizens. To take just one example, in September 1965, Reidsville resident Clarence

Watkins received threatening phone calls and had a cross burned near his house in an effort to get his (African American) child removed from a previously all-white elementary school. Watkins was a tenant farmer, and the farm owner also received threatening calls to pressure him to force Watkins to move (SBI memo from Minter to Director, September 15, 1965, NCSA, Moore Papers, General Correspondence, 1965, Box 57, Folder: SBI).

9. FBI, COINTELPRO–White Hate Groups Memo from SAC, Charlotte to Director, November 6, 1967; US House of Representatives (1966: 1856, 2049, 2872); HUAC, Box 17, Folder: United Klans—NC Photographs (1 of 2); Dawson interview with Scott Ellsworth, p. 51, DU, Chafe Oral History Collection, Printed Materials Series, Box 1.
10. US House of Representatives (1966: 1857, 2047); Alsop (1966b); SBI Report #8 to Law and Order Committee, NCSA, Moore Papers, General Correspondence, 1967, Box 208, Folder: SBI reports; Boyd Hamby, interview by Tony Crane, in Crane and Young, "Voices from the White Ghetto," LBJ, RG283, Task Force I, Series 12 (2 of 2); SBI report from Allen to Director, October 3, 1966, NCSA; SBI report #8 to Law and Order Committee, NCSA, Moore Papers, General Correspondence, 1967, Box 208, Folder: SBI reports; FBI report, "United Klans of America, Inc., Knights of the Ku Klux Klan (North Carolina)," May 2, 1966, p. 22. Attempts to raise funds for Jones's "four-passenger plane" extended at least from late May, when attendees at a Montgomery County rally were encouraged to contribute trading stamp books to the effort, to mid-August, when the SBI reported that, at a rally in Duplin County, $217 was raised for the airplane (see "Klan Rallies Near Biscoe," *Raleigh News and Observer*, May 30, 1965, and NCSA, Moore Papers, General Correspondence, 1965, Box 72, Folder: Segregation).
11. George Dorsett, interview by Michael Frierson, recording in Frierson's possession; Bob Jones, interview by Tony Crane, in Crane and Young, "Voices from the White Ghetto," p. 3, LBJ, RG283, Task Force I, Series 12 (2 of 2); HUAC, Box 17, Folder: UKA-NC Documents (1 of 2). Author interviews with Glenn Twigg (November 7, 2003, Raleigh, N.C.) and Peter B. Young (February 5, 2004), along with FBI COINTELPRO–White Hate Groups Memo from SAC, Charlotte to Director, December 8, 1964 (which suggested that Jones kept multiple "girl friends" around the state), confirm that "klan business" was at times a front for less-than-business-like activities.
12. "Constitution and Laws of the United Klans of America, Inc.," pp. 41–42, UNCC Scoggin Papers, Box 1, Folder 25; Boyd Hamby, interview by Tony Crane, in Crane and Young, "Voices from the White Ghetto," pp. 9–13, LBJ, RG283, Task Force I, Series 12 (2 of 2); SHP memos to Brown, 3 May and June 28, 1964, NCSA, Sanford Papers, General Correspondence, 1964, Box 420, Folder: KKK; Letter from Jones to UKA membership, May 19, 1965, HUAC, Box X, Folder: Jones, J. R. (Exhibits to Public Testimony October 20, 1965); Justice (1965); Knox (1965).

13. See, for example, various State Highway Patrol reports for 1964 rallies, in NCSA, Sanford Papers, General Correspondence, 1964, Box 420, folder: KKK.
14. Attendance data taken from a list of license plate numbers collected by state police outside of the rally site. The list of license tags, matched with the addresses of residents for the rallies in Figures 2.1 and 2.2, comes from State Highway Patrol memos from Williams to Governor Terry Sanford, October 21, 1963, and October 30, 1964, NCSA, Sanford Papers, General Correspondence, 1964, Box 420, Folder: KKK.
15. "Chain of Command," p. 2, in possession of author; Grady Mars interview by Tony Crane, in Crane and Young, "Voices from the White Ghetto," pp. 6–7, LBJ, RG283, Task Force I, Series 12 (2 of 2).
16. SHP memo from Creech to Mitchell, November 9, 1964, NCSA, Sanford Papers, General Correspondence, 1964; "Newsman Ejected by Greenshirts; Film Is Removed," *Greenville Daily Reflector*, September 28, 1964; phone interview with Garland Whitaker, July 2, 2003.
17. US House of Representatives (1966: 1821–27); "Klan Threatens Raleigh Minister," *Raleigh News and Observer*, July 30, 1964; SBI report from Satterfield to Director, October 5, 1966, NCSA, Moore Papers, General Correspondence, 1966; "Duke Students Seek Relief from Abuse at Klan Rally," *Winston-Salem Journal*, October 4, 1966; "Lesson from the Klan," *Raleigh News and Observer*, October 2, 1964.
18. Klan membership was notoriously unstable, which, combined with the inherent secrecy of organizations like the UKA, makes it difficult to obtain authoritative figures. The FBI, with its dense klan informant network, tends to be the most reliable source. The klavern figures are taken from a HUAC report (US House of Representatives 1967: 62) that drew on FBI intelligence data, including bank records (many klaverns opened their own accounts in local banks). The estimated number of individual adherents comes from an exhaustive report produced by the FBI's Charlotte field office in May 1966 (p. 255; copy in author's possession). Note, however, that other FBI figures differ somewhat from these—for example, the Charlotte report identifies only 165 North Carolina klaverns, but also acknowledges that a klavern roll call during a February 1966 state UKA meeting included 227 klaverns. Note also that the HUAC klavern count includes Ladies Auxiliary Units, which I discuss in more detail later.
19. Crane and Young, "Voices from the White Ghetto," p. 62, LBJ, RG283, Task Force I, Series 12 (2 of 2); Alsop (1966a: 25); SBI memo from Minter to Director, June 29, 1967, NCSA, Moore Papers, General Correspondence, 1967, Box 208, Folder: SBI reports; SHP report from Chadwick to Speed, April 12, 1966, NCSA, Moore Papers, General Correspondence, 1966, Box 150, Folder: SHP; "A Pictorial Salute to North Carolina," *The Fiery Cross* (1969: 12; copy in author's possession). Specific units that constructed their own klavern halls were located in North Wilkesboro (which built a new building in 1968 after its original space collapsed under the weight of snow the previous winter), Fayetteville (which purchased property for a

meeting hall in 1966), Wayne County, Ormondsville, and Elizabeth City. The Keystone Club in Henderson constructed a new building on four acres of land its members purchased in 1966 (see SBI report #4 to the Law and Order Committee, July 28, 1966, NCSA, Moore Papers, General Correspondence, 1966).

20. FBI, COINTELPRO–White Hate Groups Memo from SAC, Charlotte to Director, August 9, 1967; "News from Klansville," April 7, 1967, and October 21, 1967, NCSA, Moore Papers, General Correspondence, 1967.
21. Justice (1965); Jefferys (1965); SBI report from Allen to Director, March 13, 1966, NCSA, Moore Papers, General Correspondence, 1966; "Curious Eye Klan in March," *Raleigh News and Observer*, April 25, 1965.
22. Jefferys (1965); SBI memo from Minter to Director, September 15, 1965, NCSA, Moore Papers, General Correspondence, 1965, Box 57, Folder: SBI; "Klan, Negroes Face-to-Face," *Greenville Daily Reflector*, August 23, 1965; HUAC, Box 18, Folder: United Klans—North Carolina Photographs (2 of 2). In response to the mixed reaction klan members received during street walks, UKA leaders allowed members to opt out of participating in walks held in or near their hometowns. An SBI agent noted that "whenever a street walk or similar event was held in the home territory of a Klan member, that member did not have to actively participate in the event dressed in either Security Guard uniform or robe if he chose not to do so.... The reason for having this option on the part of the Klan was to prevent recognition and possible heckling from bystanders" (SBI memo from Peacock to Director, April 1, 1967, NCSA, Moore Papers, General Correspondence, 1967, Box 213, Folder: SHP & SBI reports).
23. Williams (1964a).
24. Williams (1966a, b); "Crosses Are Burned in Eastern N.C.," *Greenville Daily Reflector*, May 29, 1964; West (1964); Mitchell (1966: 623–24); "Sanford Warns Klan: Leave Church Alone," *Raleigh News and Observer*, July 12, 1964. The arson attempt by two Rocky Mount–based UKA members, Kenneth Wayne Owens and Ronnie W. Howell, failed after a breeze blew out the match the men had thrown onto the gasoline-doused front steps of the church (West 1964).
25. For detailed accounts of the murders and subsequent investigation, see Huie (1965), Cagin and Dray (1988), and Whitehead (1970).
26. US House of Representatives (1967: 46).
27. Killen quoted in the testimony of Delmar Dennis, *Mississippi v. Edgar Ray Killen*, introduced June 17, 2005.
28. Quoted in Whitehead (1970: 80).
29. Cunningham (2004: 72).
30. FBI memo from Fred Baumgardner to William Sullivan, August 27, 1964.
31. A comprehensive list of UKA klavern names in existence between 1964 and 1966 can be found in US House of Representatives (1967: 149–62). The Craven County klavern minutes are reprinted in US House of Representatives (1967: 116). The HUAC list of cross-burnings is from US House of Representatives (1966: 1770).

32. Mills's position as Exalted Cyclops was first revealed when FBI and SBI agents confiscated a UKA charter from his home (King 1964). The incident between Mills and the police officer is recounted in an FBI report by SA John W. Worsham, January 28, 1965, NCSA, Moore Papers, General Correspondence, 1965, Box 73, Folder: Segregation—New Bern bombing.
33. "Grand Dragon Sees Smear Try," *Greenville Daily Reflector*, February 2, 1965; US House of Representatives (1967: 116); NCSA, Moore Papers, General Correspondence, 1965, Box 73, Folder: Segregation—New Bern bombing. The state's take on the legal complications that gave rise to the suspended sentences are detailed in a June 10, 1965, letter from State Attorney Luther Hamilton Jr. to Governor Dan Moore. Note that, prior to Mills's guilty plea, Jones suspended Mills "for his own protection," but took care to note to the membership that Mills had not been banished ("Report on State Meeting of North Carolina United Klan," April 5, 1965, HUAC, Box 18, Folder: United Klans—North Carolina Investigative Memos [1 of 4]). Mills's expulsion came only after he pled guilty. According to Jones, "if [Mills] had been found innocent or freed that would have been something different. But when he pleaded guilty to that mess down there he banished himself from this organization" ("New Bern 'Cyclops' Booted Out of KKK," *Raleigh News and Observer*, June 4, 1965).
34. "Imperial Proclamation," undated (1965), UNCC Scoggin Papers, MSS 335, Box 1, Folder 44; Dawson interview with Scott Ellsworth, p. 72, DU, Chafe Oral History Collection, Printed Materials Series, Box 1.
35. "Klan Chaplain Delivers Most Fiery Talk," *Winston-Salem Journal,* August 15, 1966; SBI memo from Barrett to Director, November 6, 1967, NCSA, Moore Papers, General Correspondence, 1967, Box 149; NCSA, Moore Papers, General Correspondence, 1965, Box 72, Folder: Segregation; Wood (1965b); "Wizard Shelton Claims Klan to Become Major Voting Bloc," *Greenville Daily Reflector*, June 5, 1965.
36. Cunningham (2004: 74); Wade (1987: 347–51).
37. Cunningham (2004: 74–75); May (2005); "Transcript of Johnson's Statement on the Arrests in Alabama," *New York Times*, March 27, 1965.
38. LBJ, HU6 Ideologies—WHCF Box 68; LBJ, White House Central File Gen HU6, Box 70.
39. Wade (1987: 352); "Klansmen Cheer 3 in Liuzzo Case," *New York Times*, May 10, 1965; memo from Manuel to McNamara, HUAC, Box 32, Folder: UKA, Inc. Investigative Memos, Other Memos, Some Photos; "Klan Lawyer Matt Murphy Speaks to Sanford Rally," *Raleigh News and Observer*, May 17, 1965; Alsop (1966a: 25).
40. "Dunn Ministers in Klan Protest," *Raleigh News and Observer*, May 21, 1965 (the Dunn statement was also filed in the Governor's papers; see NCSA, Moore Papers, General Correspondence, 1965, Box 72, Folder: Segregation); "Letter from North Carolina—Quaker to Quaker;" USM, Will Campbell Papers M341, Box 46,

Folder 10; "Klan Raps LBJ, Noted Author," *Raleigh News and Observer*, April 12, 1965.

41. Alsop (1966a).
42. Testimony of Pactolus Hunting Club member George Williams, in US House of Representatives (1966: 2884); Hardee (1966a); Haywood Starling, phone interview with author, September 4, 2003.
43. Eddie Dawson, interview with Scott Ellsworth, pp. 22–23, DU, Chafe Oral History Collection, Printed Materials Series, Box 1; SBI Report #1 to Law and Order Committee, April 27, 1966, and letter from SBI Director Walter Anderson to Malcolm Seawell, April 14, 1966, NCSA, Moore Papers, General Correspondence, 1966.
44. SBI memos from O'Daniel to Director, November 2, 1965 (NCSA, Moore Papers, General Correspondence, 1965, Box 57, Folder: SBI), and March 15, 1967 (NCSA, Moore Papers General Correspondence, 1967, Box 213, Folder: SHP & SBI reports). In his testimony before HUAC, George Williams described an action that clearly illustrated state officers' interest in deniability. During a klavern meeting in August 1965, Williams recalls that Charlie Edwards, a state officer from Greenville, took part in the meeting, selecting eight members to "whip" the mayor of Vanceboro in response to his efforts to "help the colored people get jobs." Edwards gave the order, telling the chosen participants "I don't want to know when you are going... or how you do it, but I want him whipped" (US House of Representatives 1966: 2874). Similarly, in private klavern meetings, Jones would sometimes describe an acceptably secure model for carrying out violence, boasting that he was "ready to go out with any Klansman to handle a job but would go only with one Klansman and that way if any information was later talked about what they had done, he would know who had leaked the information and would kill the other Klansman" (memo from Manuel to McNamara, July 7, 1965, HUAC, Box 18, Folder: United Klans—NC Investigative Memos [1 of 4]).
45. "Klansmen Are Emotionally Attached to Organization," n.d.; UNCC Scoggin Papers, MS 335, Box 1, folder 52; Miekles quoted in the *Charlotte Observer*, n.d.; UNCC Scoggin Papers, MS 335, Box 1, Folder 52; George Dorsett interview with Tony Crane, in Crane and Young, "Voices from the White Ghetto," pp. 16–17, LBJ, RG283, Task Force I, Series 12 (2 of 2).
46. "KKK Joins in Giving Spirit," December 23, 1965, UNCC Scoggin Papers, MSS 335; Box 1, Folder 51; Alsop (1966a: 25).
47. SBI report from Satterfield to Director, October 5, 1966, NCSA, Moore Papers, General Correspondence, 1966; undated report from Bill Shipp, MARBL, Newsweek, Inc. Atlanta Bureau Records, MSS 629, Box 36, Folder 4. As discussed in more detail in Chapter 4, ideas about the activation of racial boundaries in response to perceived threats are central to ethnic competition theory (see Barth 1969; Hannan 1979; Olzak 1992).

48. Alsop (1966a: 24) makes a similar point about the division between the klan and "alien" worlds.
49. "Security," undated UKA document, in author's possession; HUAC KKK files, box X, folder: Webster, Clyde (North Carolina). Secret UKA car decals were discussed during the 1964 Klonvocation (see Klonvocation Minutes, MARBL, Craig Papers, MSS 612, Box 1, Folder 22). AKIA buttons are included among various UKA ephemera in MARBL, Craig Papers, MSS 612, Box 3. Jones's thoughts on the UKA's insurance plan are taken from his undated letter, titled "To Be Read on All Klavern Hall Floors," reproduced in US House of Representatives (1966: 1756; capitalized emphasis in original). Note that this and other UKA insurance programs later became a source of conflict, as UKA members and state officials began accusing the leadership of using these programs to extract funds from adherents. While a likely function of this appeal was thus to generate income, the particular resonant framing employed by Jones is of primary interest here.
50. News from Klansville #7, December 1967, NCSA, Moore Papers, General Correspondence, 1967; SHP report from Speed to Anderson, April 15, 1966, NCSA, Moore Papers, General Correspondence, 1966, Box 150, Folder: SHP; Sheila Baker, phone interview with author, September 2, 2003. For UKA communication that refers to new members' "manly decision to join with us in our Great Work," and the extraordinary "demands of manhood" exerted by the UKA, see Memos to Esteemed Klanspeople, September 11, 1962, and to new members, September 21, 1963, MARBL, Craig Papers, MSS 612, Box 1, Folders 3 and 14. Years later, when the Jones's daughter Sheila convinced her mother to start wearing blue jeans, Syble would insist on ironing them so they would have sharp creases.
51. Syble Jones, UKA rally in Four Oaks, North Carolina, September 1968, LBJ, SRT 7054-CD3a, Commission audiotape 3. The UKA also sought to mobilize children to their cause, though with less success. Ad hoc efforts sometimes involved youth, for example, when a set of Greensboro junior high school students attempted to establish a "Junior Ku Klux Klan" club or when a group of teenage boys in Mt. Airy (which incidentally, as the birthplace of Andy Griffith, is often referred to as the model for Mayberry in "The Andy Griffith Show") became known as "Junior Klan" affiliates of a particular local klavern leader. But formal UKA initiatives never seemed to coalesce. As early as 1961, the UKA newspaper the *Fiery Cross* described a "Junior Klan" for "the boys and girls of Highschool and College age," who will "alert us even before school is dismissed for the day, if any treasonous teacher dares to preach the terrible doctrine of One World, United Nations Government, to replace our pride in glorious American nationalism. That teacher will be hailed before the School Board in 24 hours." No such "hailings," however, appear to have occurred. A 1966 effort to establish units at East Carolina College and North Carolina State University to carry out "research projects" failed as well. Later, UKA members distributed applications for both the "Teenage Royal Knights of the Ku Klux Klan" and the "Klan Youth Corp., Youths of the Ku Klux Klan." At the UKA's

1967 Klonvocation, Shelton gave a speech titled "Klankraft to the American Boy," which proposed a Junior Order, intended to "bridge the gap" for school-age boys. Following up on Shelton's mandate, the following year Jones proclaimed a new youth movement modeled after the Boy Scouts, "with a stress on hunting, physical fitness, and sports activities," as "ready to go." Those efforts fizzled as well. See SBI memo from Minter to Director, June 29, 1967, NCSA, Moore Papers, General Correspondence, 1967, Box 208, Folder: SBI reports; SBI memo from Allen to Director, December 18, 1966, NCSA, Moore Papers, General Correspondence, 1966; *Fiery Cross*, Vol. 1, November 17, 1961, p. 5, in UNCC Scoggin Papers, MSS 335, box 1, folder 38; "Klan Youth Corps application," n.d., UNCC Scoggin Papers, MSS 335, box 1, folder 44; SBI Reports #2 [May 26, 1966] and #6 [September 30, 1966] to Law and Order Committee, NCSA, Moore Papers, General Correspondence, 1966; Robert M. Shelton, "Klankraft to the American Boy," MARBL, Craig Papers MSS 612, Box 1, Folder 14; "Klan Organizing Youth Movement across the State," *Durham Morning Herald*, June 24, 1968. To explain these repeated failures, an Anti-Defamation League memo reported an informant's claim that the UKA has "no real intention of trying to start a [youth] group but they just want to use this as a publicity gimmick" (HUAC, Box 17, Folder: Klans—North Carolina).

52. See, for instance, speeches by Bob and Syble Jones, UKA rally in Four Oaks, North Carolina, September 1968, LBJ, SRT 7054-CD3a, Commission audiotape 3. At that same rally, Third Province Titan E. J. Melvin also referred to the local *Smithfield Herald* as a "nigger paper" after it published articles supportive of painting the klan as "violent." Melvin challenged the owners of the paper to refute his claims, saying "they can't prove they're white, not to me."

53. The January 1968 issue of "News from Klansville" (copy in author's possession) contains blurbs about special deals on toys from Roberts Super Market in Stanley, which was managed by UKA Grand Kludd Jim Strikeleather, and on car repair from an unnamed "klanlady and her husband" in Spencer who had recently opened a radiator shop. Other "News from Klansville" issues discuss the Widows Benevolent Fund (October 20, 1966), workshop (October 21, 1967), and membership drive (October 21, 1967) programs (all copies in author's possession). For the UKA's Funeral Service handbook, see MARBL, Craig Papers, MSS 612, Box 1, Folder 15.

54. Glenn Twigg, interview with author, November 7, 2003, Raleigh, North Carolina; "News from Klansville," October and December 1967, NCSA, Moore Papers, General Correspondence, 1967, Box 213, Folder: SHP & SBI; "Klan Visits Church for Sermon, Barbecue," *Raleigh News and Observer*, September 27, 1965; Wood (1965a); "Klan Marriage Another Step in Sudden N.C. Resurgence," *Raleigh News and Observer*, May 25, 1965; untitled document, NCSA, Moore Papers, General Correspondence, 1965, Box 72, Folder: Segregation. Note that a few months after his klan church service, B. H. Ingle resigned from the UKA because of the negative

publicity the event had afforded him and his church (HUAC, Box 17, Folder: Klans—North Carolina). More generally, while Jones's North Carolina Realm developed the UKA's most fully formed repertoire of social supports, activities like klan fish frys and barbecue dinners predate Jones's membership. Calvin Craig hosted many such events between 1961 and 1963 (see various bulletins and letters in MARBL, Craig Papers, MSS 612, Box 1, Folder 16), and such activities were commonplace in the 1920s KKK (see, e.g., McVeigh 2009: 149–56).

55. FBI COINTELPRO–White Hate Groups Memo from Charlotte to Director, December 28, 1966.
56. Raymond Cranford, interview with Robert Campbell, p. 11, HU #387.
57. More formally, this process demonstrates how the UKA's leadership was able to overcome the classic collective action problem. First outlined by Mancur Olson in the 1960s, the "problem" is ensuring participation: given a goal that can be experienced by participants and nonparticipants alike—in this case, the maintenance of segregation—how can movement organizations ensure that individuals contribute to the cause, rather than "free ride" on the actions of others? To solve this dilemma, a long line of research has focused on how particular types of incentives can encourage individuals to take part in collective projects. My focus here is primarily on the long-standing networks shared by members of the UKA's core, which allowed them to be recruited as a bloc from previous klan organizations. As sociologists Hyo Jung Kim and Peter Bearman argue, the relational identity that follows from affiliation with this tight-knit segment of the population served to insulate its members from "counterpressures" exerted by people outside the klan world. The structure of this core thus provided social, or solidary, incentives for the critical mass to engage in costly and high-risk activity on behalf of the UKA even when few others were willing to participate. See Olson (1965); Kim and Bearman (1997).
58. Chappell (1994: xxii).

CHAPTER 3

1. Quoted in Mitchell (1970: 628).
2. Quoted in West (1965).
3. Letter from Bob Jones to UKA members, July 1965, HUAC, Box 18, Folder: United Klans—North Carolina Investigative Memos (2 of 4).
4. Key (1984: 205, 210).
5. As an illustrative snapshot comparing UKA membership across states, a 1967 congressional report listed North Carolina with 7,500 members across 192 klaverns. Georgia had the next largest state membership, with 1,400 members in 57 klaverns, followed by Virginia (1,250 members in 32 klaverns), Alabama (1,200 members in 40 klaverns), South Carolina (800 members in 50 klaverns), Mississippi (750 members in 76 klaverns), Louisiana (700 members in 30 klaverns), and

Florida (400 members in 27 klaverns) (see US House of Representatives 1967: 62). While these figures are lower than during the UKA's 1965 peak, when membership was an estimated 12,000 in North Carolina alone, the relative differences across states held fairly consistently across the mid-1960s (with Virginia an exception, as that state maintained a small membership until the UKA applied Jones's North Carolina-style organizing tactics there after Raleigh-based Bob Kornegay became Virginia Grand Dragon in late 1965).

6. Oliver (1964c).
7. This point has been made, at least implicitly, in historical accounts of civil rights protest. For instance, Charles Payne (1995: 112–13) observes that in racially repressive areas like the Mississippi Delta, "social distance between Blacks and whites were so great that no one ever needed to be reminded of it, rendering the Klan less necessary and lynchings less common." John Dittmer (1995: 217) notes that in Mississippi, only when less affluent whites were no longer convinced that the Citizens' Councils and "the state's business and professional class would take care of any agitation on the race question" did the KKK gain traction. More generally, Anders Walker (2009: 65) asserts that "precisely because moderate governors attempted to comply with the Supreme Court, outbreaks [of violence] were more likely to occur in moderate states. Conversely, in states that took an early, defiant approach to *Brown*, radicals never felt the need to resort to vigilantism or violence, and peace, more often than not, ensued."
8. Gilmore (1996: 73); Korstad (2003).
9. Haley (1998); Korstad (2003); Prather (1984); Tyson (2004). Aycock is quoted in Leloudis (1999: 138).
10. Hall et al. (1987); Irons (2000); Korstad (2003); Roscigno and Danaher (2004). Roscigno and Danaher (2004: 1) report that "wages in southern mills were approximately one-third of those in the North, even after controlling for the cost of living. In addition, southern mill workers worked longer hours."
11. Rowan (1970: 15, 21); Fulmer (1973: 100); Northrup (1970: 11); interview with Lauch Faircloth, March 22, 1999 (I-0069 in Southern Oral History Program Collection #4007, SHC).
12. Key (1984: 211); Kerry quoted in Leach (1976: 48); Hodges quoted in Walker (2009: 57). Sanford's statement about Aycock is taken from his April 1964 approval of the *North Carolina and the Negro* volume (ECU, Capus Waynick papers, #421.28, Folder: Mayors' Cooperating Committee—Minutes and Miscellany, 1964, n.d.).
13. Pleasants and Burns (1990: 17, 251).
14. *High Point Enterprise*, January 13, 1950.
15. This quote is from a Graham campaign ad, reproduced in Pleasants and Burns (1990: 164).
16. Pleasants and Burns (1990: 96, 162, 227). The "NAACP" postcard is reproduced on page 176. Note that this published material was consistent with Smith's public

denunciations of Graham; both were focused on exploiting the latent anxieties of many white people over Graham's liberalism. The handbills, however, were much more vicious and outwardly racist than the discourse offered directly by Smith and his staff, and they likely were produced independently by supporters formally unaffiliated with the campaign. But despite Smith's behind-the-scenes claims that he was disturbed by this racism, he never made any attempt to publicly denounce the handbills or to stem the tide by reducing the stridency of his own rhetoric.

17. These flyers are reproduced in ibid., pp. 223, 236–37. The Supreme Court ruling was given in *Sweatt v. Painter*.
18. Quoted in ibid., pp. 241, 247, 251. Note that upstart klan leader Thomas Hamilton, exploiting many of the same racial fears that buoyed Smith's campaign, began his reign of terror in southeastern North Carolina within weeks of Smith's primary victory.
19. For discussion of the various factors hypothesized to have contributed to the runoff outcome, see Chafe (1980: 57); Lubell (1956); Pleasants and Burns (1990: 255–73). An assessment of voting patterns across the state bears out the conclusion that racial anxieties were primary to the election outcome. Twenty-five of the sixty-four counties won by Graham in the first primary switched to Smith in the runoff, and those counties were disproportionately in the eastern North Carolina Black Belt, and thus the most likely to have been impacted by the acute racial climate. While the proportion of black residents was highest in this region of the state, a systematic strategy of black disenfranchisement effectively suppressed their electoral power (see Chapter 4 for more detailed discussion of this dynamic). Tellingly, the Smith-Graham voting figures are also significantly correlated with sites of klan mobilization fifteen years later (the Pearson's chi-square value [4.357] associated with the correlation of klavern presence and switch to Smith vote [both coded as bivariate measures] is significant at the .05 level). In both cases, characterized by similar political contexts, the framing of a racialized threat effectively mobilized people to action.
20. Cecelski (1994: 25); Chafe (1980: 50–52); Covington and Ellis (1999: 150); Hodges (1962: 81). The Hodges quote is in Chafe (1980: 52). Chafe (1980: 50) provides clear evidence of the legal motive behind the pupil assignment plan, quoting Hodges as responding to a constituent that the bill would allow officials "to be sure that the state is not involved in any state-wide [desegregation] suit." See also Walker (2009: 55).
21. Waynick et al. (1964: 237). Hodges is quoted in Covington and Ellis (1999: 156, 170, emphasis is mine).
22. Chafe (1980: 54); Covington and Ellis (1999: 156–57, 170).
23. Chafe (1980: 52–60); Covington and Ellis (1999: 170, 176).
24. Terry Sanford, interview with William Chafe, p. 3, DU, Chafe Oral History Collection, Printed Materials Series, Box 2; US Bureau of the Census (1960). The US Commission on Civil Rights (1961: 453–55) noted that only 31.2 percent of

eligible nonwhite voters, compared to 90.2 percent of eligible whites, were registered in North Carolina in 1960. As president of the Young Democrats Club (YDC) in 1950, Sanford had refused to grant Willis Smith's request to have "Dixie" play as he was introduced during a YDC-sponsored rally (see Pleasants and Burns 1990: 107). I. Beverly Lake had first elevated his own statewide profile when, in his capacity as assistant attorney general, he argued that North Carolina should sidestep *Brown* completely by closing its public schools and reopening them as privately run institutions (see Walker 2009: 61–62).

25. US Commission on Civil Rights (1961: 489–91, emphasis in original); Chafe (1980: 103); Terry Sanford, address to "Negro leaders," June 25, 1963, reprinted in Mitchell (1966: 597–99). Tellingly, Sanford's notes from this meeting indicate that "a rejection of his plea was clearly evident in the ensuing discussions, and many Negroes voiced intense dissatisfaction with the state's handling of Civil Rights issues and vowed to continue the demonstration movement."
26. Terry Sanford, interview with William Chafe, p. 5, DU, Chafe Oral History Collection, Printed Materials Series, Box 2; Mitchell (1966: 277, 579–80); Waynick et al. (1964: 256).
27. *Durham Morning Herald*, January 28, 1963; *Kinston Daily Free Press*, January 22, 1963; *Raleigh Times*, April 21, 1954; Waynick et al. (1964: 256–57); *Winston-Salem Journal and Sentinel*, January 20, 1963; memo from Coltrane to Moore, October 27, 1965, NCSA, Moore Papers, General Correspondence, 1965, Box 26, Folder: Good Neighbor Council D-Z.
28. Memo from L. B. West to Julius Chambers, October 15, 1965, UNCC Kelly Alexander Papers, MSS 55, Box 2, Folder 8; Chafe (1980: 106).
29. In the late 1950s, SBI agents identified brief, small-scale Citizens' Council mobilization in Greensboro (see Walker 2009: 187). In 1965, HUAC investigators noted that Citizens' Councils chapters had been formed first in Durham and later in Wilmington. One meeting, in November 1964, drew 150 attendees. In both locations, investigators suspected that the Council chapters were strongly intertwined with the local UKA (see memos from McConnon to McNamara, June 30, 1965, and October 26, 1965, HUAC, Box 18, Folder: United Klans—NC Investigative Memos [1 & 2 of 4]).
30. "Guidelines for the Establishment of County-Wide Good Neighbor or Human Relations Councils," undated (1965), p. 2, NCSA, Moore Papers, General Correspondence, 1965, Box 26, Folder: Good Neighbor Council A-C; Irons (2006); McMillen (1994). The Yazoo City Citizens' Council statement is quoted in Dittmer (1995: 218). The overall argument here closely follows Dirks's (2006) comparative analysis of anti–civil rights activities in two Mississippi communities. Crespino (2007: 25) uses similar reasoning to explain the absence of KKK activity in Mississippi prior to 1963, when he argues that "Mississippians had no need for the Klan" so long as the Councils were perceived to be effective.
31. Sanford quoted in Waynick et al. (1964: 256).

32. *Raleigh Times*, May 2, 1966.
33. The discussion here draws on conceptions of social movement organizations as lodged in "multi-organizational fields," which Curtis and Zurcher (1973: 53) first defined as "the total possible number of organizations with which the focal organization might establish linkages." This application of organizational ecology to SMOs typically views richly populated fields as imparting resources that a given organization can draw upon, or improving the odds that a multi-organizational "movement family" (della Porta and Rucht 1995) will achieve its shared goals. Note, however, that Rucht (2007) usefully contrasts this tacit emphasis on cooperation with a discussion of intra-field competition and conflict.
34. Bartley and Graham (1975); Spence (1968: 41, 57).
35. "Preyer to Maintain N.C. Way on Rights," *Raleigh News and Observer*, May 29, 1964. Note that Preyer, probably in reaction to his vulnerability surrounding his positions on race issues, at times systematically avoided the appearance of support from the black community. Following an early campaign stop in Wilmington, for instance, local black leaders were incensed after Preyer failed to contact or visit with anyone from the black community (memo from Elsie Pitts to Capus Waynick, December 16, 1963, ECU, Capus Waynick Papers, #421.25.e).
36. Spence (1968: 64, 76–78, 92, 104). Lake's statement emphasizing Preyer's overwhelming support within the black community resonated in part because of the anti-Preyer tactics of conservative Raleigh television station WRAL. In a repeat of its partisan efforts in 1950 to defeat Frank Porter Graham, WRAL's coverage of the first primary election—in part orchestrated by then-manager Jesse Helms—repeatedly showed pre-prepared charts demonstrating "block voting" for Preyer within particular Negro precincts. The gratuitous nature of WRAL's biased coverage led Sanford aide Capus Waynick to lodge a complaint with the FCC (Letter from Waynick to FCC, June 8, 1964, ECU, Capus Waynick Papers, #421.27.j). But the station's impact had already been felt. As political observer James R. Spence (1968: 87) commented, "the effect was devastating.... By the time the night was over... there was really no need for a second primary." Note also that the following year, Moore repaid Lake for his endorsement by appointing him to the State Supreme Court when Associate Justice William Rodman retired. In protest, the Halifax County Voters Movement (a local group with ties to the Southern Christian Leadership Conference) sent Moore a telegram, promising to "remember" this during the 1968 election. "While it may be true that Lake swung 200,000 votes for you, it must also be remembered that Negroes too gave you about 200,000," the telegram read. "You would have done well to have taken the Negro vote into consideration in paying off your debt for we will certainly take it into consideration at the polls in 1968." (See "Negro Group Blasts Appointment of Lake," *Raleigh News and Observer*, August 27, 1965.)
37. Clay (1966a); Spence (1968: 91); *Charlotte Observer*, August 30, 1964; NCSA, Sanford Papers, General Correspondence, 1964, Box 420, Folder: KKK. Jones's

support for Lake is noted in a memo dated October 26, 1965, from HUAC investigator B. Ray McConnon to Director Francis J. McNamara (HUAC, Box 18, Folder: United Klans—NC Investigative Memos [2 of 4]). A memo dated June 30, 1965, from the same investigator mentioned Jones's Lake bumper sticker. Note that there were also rumors that Moore workers played a role in a series of coordinated UKA cross-burnings prior to the first primary.

38. Williams (1964b); Clay (1964); Bayer (1964); Inman (1964); "Grand Dragon Says Vote Shows Klan Is Wanted," *Greenville Daily Reflector,* June 30, 1964; *Roanoke Rapids Daily Herald*, May 28, 1964, p. 9; NCSA, Moore Papers, General Correspondence, 1968, Box 351, Folder: KKK.
39. "NAACP Leader: N.C. Vote Choice Troubles Negroes," *Raleigh News and Observer*, October 4, 1964; "NAACP Backs Democrats," *Raleigh News and Observer*, October 11, 1964; "Frinks Asks Negroes to Back Gavin," *Raleigh News and Observer*, October 13, 1964. Capus Waynick reported that a month prior to the general election he met a divided NAACP delegation in Greensboro and argued that "they should stay in the Democratic party where most of their friends were lodged," as "Mr. Gavin had made no forthright bid for their support and that he stood in the shadow of Goldwater" (letter from Waynick to Sanford, November 10, 1964, ECU, Waynick Papers #421.27.Q).
40. The exception would be cases where US officials intervened to preserve federal law, such as with the desegregation of Little Rock's Central High School in 1957 or to intercede while Governor George Wallace made his "stand in the school house door" at the University of Alabama in 1963. This threat of intervention underscores the fragility of massive resistance strategies, and for our purposes defines cases in which segregationist action was strictly policed in the face of state and local resistance.
41. Cobb (2004: 53–54); Walker (2009: 94–95).
42. Wagy (1985); Walker (2009: 95, 106–7). Collins's best-known reference to "mobs" in both the civil rights and segregationist camps was during his televised address on race relations in March 1960. Emphasizing law and order, the governor argued that in Florida, racial issues should not be "decided by the mobs, whether they are made up of white people or whether they are made up of colored people" (quoted in Walker 2009: 115). While this position was consistent with Collins's focus on law enforcement generally, the speech became best known for its progressive focus on the moral dimensions of segregation. "But actually friends, [we] are foolish if we just think about resolving this things on a legal basis," Collins asserted. "And so far as I am personally concerned, I don't mind saying that if a man has a department store and he invites the public generally to come into his department store and trade, I think then it is unfair and morally wrong for him to single out one department and say he does not want or will not allow Negroes to patronize that one department. Now he has a legal right to do that, but I still don't think that he can square that right with moral, simple justice" (quoted in Rabby 1999: 107). He

concluded by announcing that he had formed a biracial committee to address the state's civil rights issues, and, presaging Terry Sanford's network of Good Neighbor Councils in North Carolina, urged local communities to establish their own biracial committees (Rabby 1999: 108).

43. Rabby (1999: 116); Bryant quoted in Rabby (1999: 128).
44. Goodwyn (1965); Bigart (1964); Hartley (1989); Herbers (1964); "5 Whites Accused in St. Augustine," *New York Times,* July 25, 1964. Bryant's Executive Order is reprinted in Garrow (1989: 267–71).
45. "Mitchell Checks Out Cars at Klan Rally," *Fort Lauderdale News*, July 14, 1965.
46. Memos from Lieutenant L. J. Van Buskirk to Sheriff Buchanan, October 29, and November 9, 1965, HUAC, Box 35(8), Folder: United Knights of the Ku Klux Klan (Dade Co., FL); Barry (1965); "Police Discourage Meet of Klansmen," *Huntsville (Ala.) Times*, September 15, 1965.
47. Jack Grantham, interview with Van Buskirk, November 8, 1965, pp. 1–2, HUAC, Box 35 (8), Folder: United Knights of the KKK (Dade Co., FL); letter from Cothran to ECs, September 6, 1965, HUAC, Box 35 (8), folder: United Knights of the KKK (Dade Co., FL). Riddlehoover's letter is reprinted in memo from Appell to McNamara, December 7, 1965, HUAC, Box 35 (8), Folder: United Knights of the KKK (Dade Co., FL). This memo also includes minutes of the October 24, 1965, meeting in which disgruntled UKA members voted to found the United Knights. The petition to oust Cothran is reproduced in US House of Representatives (1966: 3754).
48. Hunziker (1966); *Tampa Tribune*, July 5, 1965; US House of Representatives (1967); Drabble, n.d., "The FBI, COINTELPRO–WHITE HATE, and the Ku Klux Klan in Florida, 1964–1971"; LBJ, Federal Records—Eisenhower Commission, RG 283, Series 14, Task Force I, folder: photographs and phonodisks, photo #11. Note that one other factor that shaped this policing dynamic and the UKA Florida Realm's consequent organizing failures is the simple fact that Shelton made a big push in Florida much later than he did in North Carolina. As the organizing opportunity afforded by acute concerns about the passage of the 1964 Civil Rights Act diminished and anti-klan policing increased everywhere (including in North Carolina— see Chapter 7), the klan's fortunes were in decline in every state in the South by the time of Hamby and Dorsett's move. That said, the Sunshine State's long-standing centralized anti-klan policing efforts differed significantly from policing policy in North Carolina, and even in 1964 it seems reasonable to argue counterfactually that Hamby and Dorsett would not have been able to achieve significant organizing successes in Florida.
49. For an example of how public support was assumed to explain the UKA's relative ineffectiveness in Florida, see US House of Representatives (1967: 29). Gallup poll findings related to KKK support in the South in 1965 are reproduced in Lipset and Raab (1978: 328–29). The "hoodlum" editorial was written by publisher Paul Berwick, and it appeared in all four of his local publications: The *Weekly Gazette* in

LaGrange, the *Greene County Ledger* in Snow Hill, The *Chronicle* in Pink Hill, and the *Town and Country News* in Wayne County (see HUAC, Box 17, Folder: Klans—NC; this same folder contains the account of the school superintendent). For a UKA-penned letter that outlines the group's attempts to solicit covert support, see HUAC, Box X, Folder: Jones, J. R. (Exhibits to Public Testimony October 21, 1965). For detail on reaction to the Piedmont bombings, see "Dan Assails Bombings; Mayor Asks Fund Drive," *Charlotte News*, November 22, 1965, p. 1; "Against Every Home," *Charlotte News*, November 23, 1965; "City Rallies to Help Victims of Bombings," *Charlotte News*, November 23, 1965, p. B1.

50. Chapter 7 more fully develops this conception of "organizational ambivalence" within North Carolina policing agencies. Most generally, a mismatch between organizational culture and organizational goals characterizes such ambivalence (see Cunningham 2009). Among state actors, ambivalence is especially pronounced when the protest targets in question are reactionary in their orientation—that is, they seek to uphold values that are shared by the state, but do so by employing tactics, ideologies, and/or frames that are viewed as inappropriate or even illegal. In such cases, state agents must balance their potentially sympathetic views of targets' goals with the knowledge that their means pose a threat to legal and political structures.
51. The headline and Hamilton quote appear in Clay (1965b). Social movement scholars will recognize that the focus here on external political factors tied to the state and other elite institutions fits within a tradition that views the emergence of political contention as enabled in part by openings in the "political opportunity structure" (McAdam 1999; Meyer and Minkoff 2004; Tarrow 1998). One influential conceptualization of this framework, by political scientist Sidney Tarrow (1998: 19–20), focuses both on political opportunities ("consistent—but not necessarily formal, permanent, or national—dimensions of the political struggle that encourage people to engage in contentious politics") and constraints ("factors—like repression, but also like authorities' capacity to present a solid front to insurgents"). While there has been much debate over the particular dimensions that comprise the political opportunity structure and consequently the utility of the overall concept, there has been general agreement on the importance of state repression and facilitation (Cunningham 2004; Davenport et al. 2005; della Porta and Reiter 1998; Earl 2003, 2005). The focus here on policing approaches, extended in Chapter 7, fits within this tradition. The other key factor here—North Carolina's "passive" orientation to civil rights legislation—also constitutes an external political dimension that impacted the UKA's fortunes in the state.
52. Williams (1964d).
53. For an interesting discussion of the heterogeneity of local policing in the civil rights-era South, see Kryder (2009). For evidence of police joining the UKA, see "N.C. Sheriff Tells of Joining Klan in Effort to Get Information," *Raleigh News and Observer*, October 26, 1965; memo from Coltrane to Governor, NCSA,

Department of Administration, HRC, Direct Correspondence, File, 1960–77, Box 29; SBI memo from Minter to Director, June 29, 1967, NCSA, Moore Papers, General Correspondence, 1967, Box 208, Folder: SBI reports. The Franklinton case is reported in SBI memo from Crocker to Director, February 20, 1967, NCSA, Moore Papers, General Correspondence, 1967, Box 208, Folder: SBI reports. For details on Cranford's actions in Greene County, see SBI memo from Edwards to Director, September 11, 1965, NCSA, Moore Papers, General Correspondence, 1965, Box 57, Folder: SBI.

54. Katagiri (2001: 4); Greenhaw (2011: 101–102).
55. Key (1984: 210); Chafe (1980).

CHAPTER 4

1. "Kluxers Gather to Burn Cross," *Greenville Daily Reflector*, October 18, 1965.
2. This track appeared on the band's eponymous debut album, first released by Epic Records in 1992.
3. Williams (1964c); FBI Charlotte report, "United Klans of America, Inc., Knights of the Ku Klux Klan (North Carolina)," May 2, 1966. This rapid growth was confirmed by State Director of Administration Hugh Cannon in Governor Sanford's administration, who told a HUAC investigator that Sanford's office developed a klan informant as well as contacted and provided information to the FBI after the UKA grew from four klaverns in September 1963 to thirty-four in May 1964 (memo from McNamara to McConnon, August 26, 1965, HUAC, Box 17, Folder: Klans—North Carolina).
4. The most comprehensive mapping of these klaverns, from which the data in Figure 4.1b are drawn, occurred as part of a congressional report filed after the conclusion of several weeks of House Un-American Activities Committee (HUAC) hearings on KKK activity. Drawing on information compiled from FBI informant files and local bank records, the report identified the locations of 192 klaverns formed during the first three years of UKA recruiting in North Carolina. Note that while the HUAC report acknowledges the difficulty of pinpointing klan activity—with klaverns frequently appearing, disappearing, or shifting allegiances to different regional or national organizations—the compilers of the report estimate their error rate at "less than ten percent" (US House of Representatives 1967: 19). As discussed in Chapter 2, the klan was a secretive organization, and many klaverns existed under the guise of hunting or social clubs, making it difficult for outside observers to identify their existence as KKK units. As the FBI had a dense informant network in place by 1965 (Cunningham 2004), the HUAC report appears to be by far the most accurate source of unit locations. The FBI coordinated its North Carolina informants through its field office in Charlotte and a set of local resident agencies placed throughout the state, making it unlikely that klaverns missed by agents would be disproportionately associated with any particular county

or region. Also, note that the observed regional clustering is systematically confirmed by a Moran's I test, which assesses the degree of global spatial autocorrelation across a set of units. The Moran's I value associated with the distribution in Figure 4.1b indicates that the spatial pattern in the figure is nonrandom ($p < .001$), meaning that it is highly unlikely that the clustering evident in the map is due to chance.

5. In a study of Mississippi, Crespino (2007) has similarly uncovered lines of division within the supposedly "solid South." More generally, Sokol (2006) has outlined a broad spectrum of white southerners' reactions to civil rights reforms.
6. As discussed in the Introduction, ethnic competition theory provides the framework for explaining the emergence and spread of the sort of reactive mobilization that defined civil rights-era KKK activity. The theory builds on anthropologist Frederick Barth's emphasis on the socially constructed boundaries through which ethnic groups ascribe difference. Competition, stemming from overlap in the economic activities of multiple ethnic groups, becomes a key mechanism through which particular boundaries are reinforced. This enhanced salience of ethnic divisions, in turn, can contribute to the emergence of ethnic conflict. The basic premise underlying this tradition is that when competing groups occupy similar positions in the labor market, thus exhibiting considerable niche overlap, ethnic solidarities intensify and contribute to increased competition-based conflict (see Barth 1969; Hannan 1979; Olzak 1992).
7. See, for example, Crespino (2007: Ch. 2); Woods (2004).
8. North Carolina's Black Belt was significantly more contained than in Deep South states, as only eleven of the state's 100 counties were majority black, compared to 34.1 percent of Mississippi counties and 22.3 percent of Alabama counties ("Negro Population and Southern Politics," *The New Citizen*, February 9, 1962). The heart of the North Carolina Black Belt includes Hertford, Bertie, Northampton, Halifax, Warren, and Edgecombe counties. See "An Upsurge in Carolina," *The Southern Patriot* (June 1964, pp. 1–2).
9. Unless otherwise noted, the demographic figures cited in this section have been computed from county-level data compiled in US Bureau of the Census (1960). The 1960 Census includes economic and demographic characteristics only for "whites" and "nonwhites" in each county. However, in almost all counties during this period, the number of black versus nonwhite residents is essentially identical. A substantial number of Native Americans resided in a handful of counties, though the local klan generally looked down on both groups when advancing its white supremacist agenda (as evidenced by the North Carolina Klan's ill-fated 1958 Maxton rally, discussed in Chapter 1).
10. Dub Brown, interview with Scott Ellsworth, p. 72. DU, Chafe Oral History Collection, Printed Materials Series, Box 1.
11. Even controlling for economic and political factors, the correlation between proportion nonwhite and UKA klaverns per capita in Piedmont counties is highly

significant statistically ($p < .001$; one-tailed test). Also, with this and other related discussions throughout this chapter, UKA activity is represented by the number of klaverns present in a county (see note 4, this chapter, for data considerations). This measure is preferable to a count of UKA-initiated events for two reasons. First, in a spatial sense, violent or terrorist klan actions in particular communities were only loosely related to the level of mobilization in those communities; klan policy frequently called for adherents from neighboring counties to carry out violent acts to reduce the likelihood that they would be identified by local witnesses. Second, as this discussion focuses on the role of community context in contentious political mobilizations, the ideal focus should be on sustained engagement in specific klan organizations rather than potentially more ephemeral participation in a particular short-lived event. While not every klavern member was highly committed to the group, the presence of a stable klavern in a community meant that a substantial number of klansmen were attending weekly meetings, paying monthly dues, and regularly pledging their allegiance to the UKA itself while also participating in the planning of the large number of rallies put on by the klan each year. At the start of 1966, the mean membership size of North Carolina klaverns was sixty-four, ranging from a presumptive UKA-mandated minimum of twenty-five to a small number of units with over 200 adherents (FBI COINTELPRO–White Hate Groups Memo from SAC, Charlotte to Director, April 1, 1968). While this fairly significant variance in klavern size points to the number of members per county as the ideal measure, such detailed data unfortunately are not available.

12. *New York Times*, September 6, 1964.
13. Myrdal (1944: 606).
14. Tolnay and Beck (1995: Ch. 2). I thank E. M. Beck for sharing his historical lynching data. The 78 percent increase in klan presence in counties with a historical legacy of racial violence is statistically significant at the .01 level (two-tailed test), and holds when controlling for the proportion of nonwhite residents, median white family income, the ratio of nonwhite/white manufacturing workers, and the level of NAACP activity in the counties in question (see Cunningham and Phillips 2007: 801).
15. Tyson (2004: 17–20).
16. US Commission on Civil Rights (1961: 477–79); Wright (1958); "Desegregated Schools Open without Incident," *Charlotte Observer*, September 1, 1961; letter from George R. Ragsdale, Legal Counsel to the Governor, to Sullivan, Asbill & Brennan, December 21, 1966, NCSA, Moore Papers, General Correspondence, 1967, Box 269, Folder: School Desegregation Policies; Tyson (2004: 17). Dent is quoted in Crespino (2007: 226). Depending on the source consulted, in 1961 either 202 or 207 of North Carolina's more than 309,000 black students were enrolled in previously white schools. When making the case six years later to retain Sullivan, Asbill & Brennan, George R. Ragsdale, the governor's legal counsel, noted that "probably 95 percent of the personnel was born in or educated south of

the Mason-Dixon Line. I do not know anybody else in the firm and I do not know whether [the lead lawyer's] professional qualifications render him satisfactory for advice concerning administrative law matters, but at least he is a North Carolinian, and he is in a firm which is large enough to accommodate a request such as ours will be" (memo from Ragsdale to Moore, December 19, 1966, NCSA, Moore Papers, General Correspondence, 1967, Box 269, Folder: School Desegregation Policies). The partnership required a significant outlay of funds; within weeks of retaining the firm, North Carolina's attorney general complained that legal representation was "proving to be much more expensive than the State officials concerned anticipated" (letter from Bruton to Sutherland, March 14, 1967, NCSA, Moore Papers, General Correspondence, 1967, Box 269, Folder: School Desegregation Policies).

17. Thompson (1921); Rowan (1970: 62); interview with Kelly Alexander, p. 7, HU, RJB 399.
18. "Hate Propaganda Distributed Here," *Raleigh News and Observer*, July 1, 1965. Cranford quoted in Alsop (1966a: 23). Rally quote is taken from a speech by Syble Jones, UKA rally in Four Oaks, North Carolina, September 1968, LBJ, SRT 7054-CD3a, Commission audiotape 3.
19. For a full elaboration of this model, see Cunningham and Phillips (2007: 805). Note that the relationships described here are modeled by isolating the effect of demographic composition, holding constant salient economic and political factors. The resulting curvilinear pattern thus represents hypothetical cases in which counties differ only by their proportion of black residents. Hence, particular values reported here refer to "expected" rather than "average" numbers of klaverns. Note also that, as described later, the resources available to white militants were restricted as well by the fact that Black Belt planter elites had both other means to control economically dependent African Americans and reduced incentive to maintain strict racial labor controls in the face of increased mechanization (see Luders 2010).
20. US Commission on Civil Rights (1961: 489–91).
21. *Economic and Social Conditions of North Carolina Farmers*, North Carolina Tenancy Commission, 1922 (available at http://docsouth.unc.edu/nc/index.html; accessed July 22, 2008); Wood (1986: 28–29). In 1960, there were 95,284 male agricultural workers in coastal plain counties, compared to 57,050 in Piedmont counties (US Bureau of the Census 1960). The distinction between tenants and sharecroppers is that tenants made cash payments to rent their land, and sharecroppers furnished the landowner with a share (generally half) of their harvested crop (see Pelo 1933: 10–11). According to Wood (1986: 27), North Carolina was unique among southern states, as prior to 1920 it "abolished" the legal distinction between tenants and croppers.
22. US Bureau of the Census (1960). Writing in 1949, V. O. Key (1984: 217) noted how the pattern of white farm tenancy differed between the Black Belts of North Carolina and Alabama, describing the comparatively large number of white tenants

in North Carolina as "a factor perhaps contributory to the difference in political flavor of the two areas."

23. Roscigno and Danaher (2004); Rowan (1970: 15, 21); Lemert (1933: 47).
24. Wood (1986: 180–81); Myrdal (1944: 285). In 1967, 86 percent of North Carolina's textile jobs were located in nonmetropolitan areas (US Department of Labor 1969: 61). Note also that the racial patterns in North Carolina's twentieth-century textile industry differed markedly from those in the smaller scale textile mills active prior to the Civil War. In this antebellum period, the industry drew predominantly upon black labor, including that of slaves (Myrdal 1944).
25. Flowers (1990: 74–75); Frankel (1991: 105); Perlo (1953: Ch. 9); Rowan (1970: 25, 56–57, 62, 99); Thompson (1921: 106–7); letter from Joseph H. Tieger to Northampton County Sheriff E. Frank Outland, August 12, 1965, SNCC Papers, Reel 40; "Address of Kelly M. Alexander," October 13, 1962, p. 4, UNCC Kelly Alexander Papers, MSS 55, Box 1, Folder 4.
26. Fulmer (1973: 100–102).
27. Korstad (2003); Northrup (1970: 11, 27, 97). Industrial Relations scholar Herbert R. Northrup (1970: 3–5) provides the following racial and gender breakdown of cigarette-production jobs: black men removed tobacco leaf from the auction room; black men fed the leaf into the redrying machine, which was operated by white men; black men packed and stored the redried leaf in warehouses; black women freed the tobacco of "trash," prepared the leaves for the steamer, and then removed and sorted them by size; black men and women stemmed the leaves; black men shredded the leaves; white women operated the "making" machines, with the "made" cigarettes inspected by white men; white women then weighed and counted the cigarettes; black men swept and cleaned the area afterward; and white men and women completed various packing tasks. Note that this entrenched racial separation was accepted and reproduced by the central tobacco labor organization, the Tobacco Workers International Union, which operated separate, racially segregated locals (see Northrup 1970: 17).
28. Buddy and Jeannie Tieger, "Report on N.C.," October 26, 1965, SNCC Papers, Reel 40; interview with Kelly Alexander, p. 7, HU, RJB 399; Rowan (1970: 13, 70); Woods (2007: 393–95); *Charlotte Observer*, January 13, 1967; *Greensboro Record*, January 13, 1967. Another factor that facilitated the hiring of black workers after 1960 was the increasing separation of company and worker lives. Traditionally, many mill owners maintained strongly paternalistic relationships with their workers, providing for many of their needs and housing them in mill communities. In that environment, white workers frequently rebelled against African Americans entering the community, but as mill housing was sold off or torn down beginning in the late 1950s, that particular form of pressure was reduced (see Hall et al. 1987; Lahne 1944; Moreland 1958; Rowan 1970: 64).
29. This effect is significant at the .01 level (two-tailed test). See Table 3, Model 1 in Cunningham and Phillips (2007: 804).

30. "Negro Population and Anatomy of Southern Politics," *The New Citizen*, March 23, 1962; US Commission on Civil Rights (1975: 43). The US Commission on Civil Rights (1961: 453–55) noted an even larger racial gap in 1960, when 90.2 percent of eligible white voters, but only 31.2 percent of eligible nonwhite voters, were registered.
31. Eric Morton, "Proposal for a SNCC Project in NC," SNCC Papers, reel 40; US Commission on Civil Rights (1961).
32. US Commission on Civil Rights (1961: 464–65). One of the Bertie County complainants took her case to the state Supreme Court, which ruled in 1961 that "she should be given another opportunity to register, and that it was unreasonable and beyond the intent of the North Carolina law for her to be required to write a section of the Constitution as it was read to her" (see *Bazemore v. Bertie County Board of Elections*, 254 N.C. 398, 406; quoted in US Commission on Civil Rights 1961: 467).
33. US Commission on Civil Rights (1961: 451–63); letter from North Carolina NAACP to Governor Dan K. Moore, p. 3, NCSA, Moore Papers, General Correspondence, 1965, Box 71, Folder: Segregation A-E. In Halifax, Lake received 39.7 percent of the vote, compared to 31.1 percent for Dan Moore and 29.5 percent for Richardson Preyer (*Roanoke Rapids Daily Herald*, June 1, 1964, p. 1). Across all 100 North Carolina counties, the positive correlation between Lake support and the percentage of black residents is significant at the .01 level (r = .809; two-tailed test). For voting data, see *North Carolina Manual* (1965: 261–62) and Spence (1968: 122–25). Though these dynamics seem nonsensical on their face, strong support for strident segregationist candidates within the southern Black Belt was a consistent trend (see Black 1973; Luders 2010). Conditions for these sorts of electoral dynamics remained in place well into the 1970s. In 1974, federal investigators concluded that "blacks in Halifax County fear disapproval from their employers if they become involved in politics." In that county, Doc Brown—a popular black coach to whom his school's 1974 yearbook was dedicated—was relieved of his duties after his unsuccessful bid to win the Democratic nomination for Halifax County clerk in 1974. Weldon school superintendent Myron L. Fisher Jr. claimed that the dismissal was due to "various dereliction of duty as a coach and friction between Brown and another coach," though many assumed the action stemmed from the way in which, in Brown's words, the "white power structure" viewed him as a threat (US Commission on Civil Rights 1975: 196–97).
34. US Commission on Civil Rights (1975: 50); US House of Representatives (1966: 2896); Clay (1966); SBI Report #2 to Law and Order Committee, May 26, 1966 (in author's possession); Drabble (2003: 34); Hardee (1966b); *Raleigh News and Observer*, May 30, 1966. In 1968, Sheriff Stirewalt courted controversy when he swore Jones in as a special deputy. Under fire for the move, he rescinded the appointment soon after (Ross 1966; Sims 1978; *New York Times*, September 28 and 30, 1968).

35. Connelly (1964); CORE Papers, Reel 23:81. CORE workers were involved in sit-ins in Durham and Chapel Hill in late 1962–early 1963, and had active chapters in most urban Piedmont communities, as well as several campuses, including Johnson C. Smith in Charlotte, Duke University in Durham, North Carolina State in Raleigh, and UNC in Chapel Hill. CORE adherents also connected with unaffiliated civil rights groups on the campuses of St. Augustine's, Shaw, and Women's College in Greensboro. A 1965 SNCC report states that CORE "has never worked in the Black Belt" in northeastern North Carolina, a statement that underscores the competition across these groups, but also CORE's primarily urban Piedmont base. Cox's travel schedule in 1964 and 1965 largely confirms this impression, though CORE did provide "both financial and human resources" in the large-scale protest movement in Williamston, as well as organize active chapters in Kinston, Wilmington, and Onslow County, all of which are in the coastal plain (Waynick et al. 1964: 172; SNCC Papers, Reel 40; CORE papers, Reel 19, 23:81).
36. SNCC Papers, Reels 5.76, 40.228, 40.229; Waynick (1964: 138–43); *Raleigh News and Observer*, May 12, 1963; Robinson, "Report of Raleigh, North Carolina Voter Registration Project," SNCC Papers, Reel 17; Morton, "Proposal for a SNCC Project in North Carolina," SNCC Papers, Reel 40. Morton was removed from the project after he apparently spent $500 in SNCC start-up funds on "non-project items." SNCC workers later provided support to the Halifax County Voters Movement, though in October 1965 SNCC's Buddy and Jeannie Tieger complained that they "hadn't received one goddamned cent from SNCC" and that consequently it would be "dishonest for SNCC to fundraise around anything that has been accomplished" in the area ("Report on N.C.," October 26, 1965, SNCC Papers, Reel 40).
37. US House of Representatives (1967); Buddy and Jeannie Tieger, "Report on N.C.," October 26, 1965, SNCC Papers, Reel 40; Letter from Salter to Pierce, April 29, 1965, NCSA, Moore Papers, General Correspondence, 1965, Box 72, Folder: Segregation S-Z; Salter, John (1979; available at www.hunterbear.org/handling_the_klan_on_easter_sund.htm; http://hunterbear.org/NORTH CAROLINA_OUR SUCCESSFUL BLACK BELT MOVEMENT.htm; accessed June 30, 2009); Telegram from Cofield to Waynick, May 29, 1964, ECU, Waynick Papers, #421.27.Q.
38. Waynick et al. (1964: 166–75); Cecelski (1994: 83–85).
39. Telegram from Frinks to Moore, July 8, 1964, NCSA, Sanford Papers, General Correspondence, 1964, Box 450; Telegram from Thigpen to Moore, NCSA, Moore Papers, General Correspondence, 1965, Box 72, Folder: Segregation S-Z; Cecelski (1994: 85); NCSA, Sanford Papers, General Correspondence, 1964, Box 420, Folder: SBI.
40. FBI Intelligence Report, "Racial Developments and Civil Disturbances," September 3, 1965, p. 3, Declassified Documents Reference System; Clay (1965a); US House of Representatives (1966: 2875–78); Hart (1965); Lewis (1965a, b, c, d); "Racial

Committee Named," *The Roanoke Beacon* (September 8, 1965). The Plymouth Town Council's anti-marching ordinance, passed on August 31, is printed on the front page of the September 1, 1965, edition of *The Roanoke Beacon.*

41. Gavins (1991: 107); UNCC Kelly Alexander Papers, MSS 55, Box 1, Folder 17.
42. Kelly Alexander interview, p. 24, HU, RJB 399. The Greene County membership figure is taken from data sheets in UNCC Kelly Alexander Papers, MSS 55, Box 1, Folder 17.
43. Thad Eure is quoted in "Address of Kelly Alexander," October 14, 1966, p. 15, UNCC Kelly Alexander Papers, MSS 55, Box 1, Folder 4; Dub Brown, interview with Scott Ellsworth, p. 25, DU, Chafe Oral History Collection, Printed Materials Series, Box 1; "News from Klansville," July 1968 (in possession of author); "Ku Klux Klan Activities in the State of North Carolina," May 21, 1965, UNCC Kelly Alexander Papers, MSS 55, Box 24, Folder 20; memo from Manuel to McNamara, June 14, 1965, HUAC, Box X, Folder: Kornegay, Marshall R. (North Carolina); "Dynamite Blasts Hit Four Negro Homes in Charlotte," *Raleigh News and Observer,* November 23, 1965; "A Discussion of Where Do We Go from Here," 1965, p. 1, UNCC Kelly Alexander Papers, MSS 55, Box 1, Folder 4.
44. See Cunningham and Phillips (2007: 802).
45. "Monthly Report of the Youth and College Division," February 1–April 30, 1960, UNCC Kelly Alexander Papers, MSS 55, Box 2, Folder 6; "Address of Kelly M. Alexander," October 14, 1960, p. 6, UNCC Kelly Alexander Papers, MSS 55, Box 1, Folder 4. For discussion of local variation among NAACP branches, see, for example, Gavins (1991: 115) and Tyson (2001).
46. "Address of Kelly M. Alexander," October 13, 1962, p. 3, UNCC Kelly Alexander Papers, MSS 55, Box 1, Folder 4. As described earlier, after accounting for salient demographic and economic factors, there is no significant relationship between the overall number of NAACP branches in each county and subsequent UKA mobilization. However, the presence of *new* NAACP chapters (i.e., those established between 1960 and 1964) is significantly associated with the emergence of klan activity ($p < .01$; two-tailed test) (Cunningham and Phillips 2007).
47. Myrdal (1944: 606). More recently, a number of historians have deepened our understanding of the relationship between gender and Jim Crow. See Gilmore (1996); Hall (1993); Tyson (2004); Whites (1998).
48. This discussion draws and elaborates on the results of the spatial diffusion models presented in Cunningham and Phillips (2007: 799–807).
49. Ibid. Analogously, and akin to the diffuse nature of economic threat discussed here, a legacy of racial violence appears to have an impact that stretched beyond county borders. Controlling for local lynching events, the patterning of such occurrences in nearby counties had an independent positive and highly significant effect on klan mobilization ($p < .01$), with a standard deviation increase in the variable associated with a 109 percent increase in klan activity (Cunningham and Phillips 2007: 804–6). As the events in question occurred thirty or more years prior to the rise of

the civil rights-era KKK, the effect is due less to the lynching events themselves than to the underlying cultural conditions that gave rise to them in a previous era. Still, this finding is consistent with past work showing that racial violence had regulative power that held over both space and time, as word spread over surrounding communities through personal connections and media accounts, and ritualistic violence became etched into individual memories (Ayers 1984; Stovel 2001; Tolnay et al. 1996).

50. Dub Brown, interview with Scott Ellsworth, p. 13, DU, Chafe Oral History Collection, Printed Materials Series, Box 1; UKA handbill, HUAC, Box X, Folder: Jones, J. R. (Exhibits to Public Testimony October 21, 1965) (emphasis in original). For discussions of labor organizing in North Carolina and elsewhere in the South, see Hall et al. (1987); Korstad (2003); Roscigno and Danaher (2004). Luders (2010) also more generally emphasizes how class alignments shaped the calculus of civil rights opposition.
51. Memo from L. B. West to Julius Chambers, October 29, 1965, UNCC Kelly Alexander Papers, MSS 55, Box 2, Folder 8; "Address of Kelly M. Alexander," October 14, 1966, p. 16, UNCC Kelly Alexander Papers, MSS 55, Box 1, Folder 4.
52. See Chapter 2 for discussion of anti-klan statements by ministerial associations across the state, and Chappell (2003) for an important broader discussion of the relationship between religious leaders and segregationist thought.

CHAPTER 5

1. Quoted in Gillette and Tillinger (1965: 138).
2. Alsop (1966b).
3. Dargan Frierson, interview with Kathleen Hoke, November 10, 1989, http://library.uncg.edu/depts/archives/civrights/detail-iv.asp?iv=5 (accessed December 16, 2009).
4. Bob Jones interview with Tony Crane, in Crane and Young, "Voices from the White Ghetto," pp. 1–5, LBJ, RG283, Task Force I, Series 12 (2 of 2). The role of anti-communism in segregationist thought is discussed later in the chapter; see also Crespino (2007: 49–57).
5. Sheila Jones Baker, phone interview with author, September 2, 2003; Bob Jones interview with Tony Crane, in Crane and Pete Young, "Voices from the White Ghetto," pp. 1–5, LBJ, RG283, Task Force I, Series 12 (2 of 2); memo from McConnon to McNamara, October 21, 1965, HUAC, Box X, Folder: Leonard, Arthur C. Note that Leonard had first joined the U.S. Klans in 1953.
6. Eddie Dawson, interview with Scott Ellsworth, DU, Chafe Oral History Collection, Printed Materials Series, Box 1.
7. The latter view is consistent with Blumer's (1958) group position model. Bobo and Hutchings (1996: 956–57), applying that model, write: "Feelings of alienation and threat are the product of social and collective processes that derive from the

long-term experiences and conditions that members of a racial group have faced. These feelings are shaped, as Blumer argued, by an ongoing process of collective social definition that cannot be reduced to the current status of individuals." See also Tolsma et al. (2008).

8. "The Ku Klux Klan," ADL Trend Analyses Division, June 1965, p. 4, USM, Will Campbell Papers M341, Box 10, Folder 2.
9. Chalmers (1981); Kallal (1989); Lipset and Raab (1978); McWhorter (2001); US House of Representatives (1967); Vander Zanden (1960, 1965). Shelton quoted in his UKA press release, November 4, 1965, in author's possession. Sociologist Melvin M. Tumin's influential *Desegregation* study, published in 1958, mirrors both the ADL's portrait and these academic studies. Referencing the KKK and other like-minded segregationist outfits, Tumin (1958: 153) described the "emergent" segregationist leadership that would fill the "vacuum of leadership and power" created by a failure of institutionalized leaders to manage their citizenry's passions. The audience receptive to such appeals, according to Tumin, "consists of the most disinherited and alienated members of the social group. These are the poorest, the socially least-prestigeful, the least educated, the persons for whom obedience to law and order has the least appeal for there is so little for them to lose—at least as they see it."
10. The sample size in Tables 5.1 and 5.2 (n = 159) is bounded by data limitations. The members included in the tables represent the sum total of the individual Carolina Klan members with occupations recorded in the various sources accessed in this work. The utility of the data in the table thus resides in its representativeness rather than its comprehensiveness. While there is no way to establish conclusively the degree to which this sample represents North Carolina's overall UKA membership, the data avoid obvious sources of bias—especially that stemming from a reliance on media sources that disproportionately focus on leaders rather than everyday adherents—that have plagued most previous studies of civil rights-era KKK membership (e.g., Kallal 1989; Lipset and Raab 1978; Vander Zanden 1965). As one strong signal that these data are not systematically biased, after broad differences in the makeup of the overall labor force are accounted for, the portrait overlaps considerably with an earlier study I conducted that draws on a verifiably representative sample of north-central Alabama UKA members active in 1963 and 1964 (see Cunningham 2007). In particular, the proportions of "core" and "peripheral" members as well as the composition of the overall occupational distribution are comparable to the Alabama data.
11. US Bureau of the Census (1960, 1963). With the exception of clerical workers ($p < .01$), the individual findings cited as significant throughout this paragraph all hold at the .001 level. The lack of significant differences in the overall distribution was confirmed by a paired-sample t-test.
12. Eight percent of farmers, compared to 16 percent of unskilled workers and 14 percent of service workers, reported agreeing with the KKK (see Lipset and Raab

[1978: 331]). In Tables 5.1 and 5.2, small business owners were captured by the "managers and proprietors" occupational category and largely confined within the "trade" and "business and repair services" industry sectors. The other sectors in which UKA members were glaringly overrepresented ("service workers" in Table 5.1, and "public administration" in Table 5.2) was almost entirely due to the large number of police officers in the North Carolina sample. While it is notable that a significant number of police officials were tied to the UKA, this finding is almost certainly inflated, as investigators diligently sought to identify the degree of klan penetration in law enforcement. These efforts constituted the only significant source of bias in the profile presented here, as police officials' klan affiliations were disproportionately likely to be reported by informants and subsequently to appear in multiple intelligence files and news accounts (see, e.g., US House of Representatives 1967: 73; *Wilmington Journal*, November 16, 1963; Womble 1965; State Highway Patrol memo from Brown to Lambert, November 18, 1963, NCSA, Sanford Papers, General Correspondence, 1964, Box 420, folder: KKK; SBI memo from Minter to Director, June 29, 1967, NCSA, Moore Papers, General Correspondence, 1967, Box 208, folder: SBI reports). Note, however, that the lack of a significant relationship between racial overlap and occupation/industry categories holds even when we adjust for this bias by eliminating police from the overall sample.

13. The average figures presented here are median values.
14. Cunningham and Phillips (2007: 806).
15. Glenn Twigg, interview with author, November 7, 2003, Raleigh, North Carolina; Dub Brown, interview with Scott Ellsworth, p. 13, DU, Chafe Oral History Collection, Printed Materials Series, Box 1; Tommy Reagan, interview with Pete Young, in "Violence and the White Ghetto, a View from the Inside," p. 155, LBJ, Federal Records—Eisenhower Commission (RG 283), Task Force I—Assassination, Box 1, Series 10. Lovette's account is included in SBI memo from McDaniel to Director, March 15, 1967, NCSA, Moore Papers, General Correspondence, 1967, Box 213, folder: SHP and SBI reports.
16. This discussion draws on social movement analysts' emphasis on the "micromobilization contexts" that govern participants' entry into protest groups. Much of that research focuses on the degree to which potential adherents are "biographically available," or free from constraints that might counterbalance their desire to take part in a worthy collective cause (see McAdam 1986, 2003; Schussman and Soule 2005; Wiltfang and McAdam 1991). From the accounts of individual UKA members described later, it is clear that "availability," dictated largely by their embeddedness in multiple social worlds, had direct and varied effects on their klan participation, refracting personal experiences of racial grievance and shaping the resonance of UKA ideology.
17. *Fiery Cross*, August 1964; bulletin from Calvin Craig to Esteemed Klanspeople, January 12, 1963, MARBL, Craig Papers, MSS 612, Box 1, Folder 16.

18. Van Dyke (1986: 51); Sims (1978); Sheila Jones Baker, phone interview with author, September 2, 2003; George Dorsett, interview with Michael Frierson, in possession of Michael Frierson; Calvin Craig interview, p. 2, HU, RJB 124; Dub Brown, interview with Scott Ellsworth, p. 29, DU, Chafe Oral History Collection, Printed Materials Series, Box 1; Dunn (1974); Alsop (1965: 24). Similarly, Robert Shelton recalls being drawn to the klan as a young boy by the stories his "uncles and aunts and grandparents" would tell. "I can remember when there would be hundreds and hundreds of white robes that would parade in cars," he recalled. "I'd say I was seven or eight years old, and I can remember recognizing some of the vehicles and knowing who they were, some of the neighbors" (Sims 1987: 104–5).
19. "Klansmen Are Emotionally Attached to Organization," n.d.; UNCC Scoggin Papers, MSS 335, Box 1, Folder 52 (emphasis added); *Raleigh News and Observer*, October 22, 1965; Boyd Hamby, interview by Tony Crane, in Crane and Young, "Voices from the White Ghetto," p. 13, LBJ, RG283, Task Force I, Series 12 (2 of 2).
20. Jack Grantham interview by Van Buskirk, November 8, 1965, HUAC, Box 35(8), Folder: United Knights of the KKK; Eddie Dawson, interview by Scott Ellsworth, pp. 29, 63–64, DU, Chafe Oral History Collection, Printed Materials Series, Box 1; Covington (1968).
21. US House of Representatives (1966: 1836).
22. SHP memo from Lambreth to Governor Sanford, February 17, 1964, NCSA, Sanford Papers, General Correspondence, 1964, Box 420, Folder: KKK; SBI memo from O'Daniel to Director, November 11, 1965, NCSA, Moore Papers, General Correspondence, 1965, Box 57, Folder: SBI. This general dynamic was also evident in other areas of the South. Federal investigators noted that the International Paper Company's factory in Natchez, Mississippi, was considered "prime recruiting grounds" for the klan, with nearly half of the area's 200 klansmen employed there in 1964 and 1965 (US House of Representatives 1966: 3003). Note that the causal direction in these cases is unclear, as no one has yet been able to systematically determine whether UKA members hired their klan colleagues, or conversely whether klan membership followed from connections forged in the workplace. Either path seems plausible, and both illustrate how workplaces could play a facilitative role.
23. Tommy Reagan, interview by Tony Crane, in Crane and Young, "Voices from the White Ghetto," p. 20, LBJ, RG283, Task Force I, Series 12 (2 of 2). Jones's truck stop tactics are recounted in Sims (1978: 41–42). For a similar example of an impromptu recruitment effort in a bar, see the account of Alex X. Belahovich, sales manager for Central Foods and Appliance Company in Fayetteville, in SBI Report from O'Daniel to Director, November 5, 1965, NCSA, Moore Papers, General Correspondence, 1965, Box 57, Folder: SBI. Another former UKA member, Jack Grantham, reported that the UKA would leave flyers and membership cards in certain restaurants, in hopes of attracting like-minded adherents (Grantham

interview by Van Buskirk, November 8, 1965, HUAC, Box 35(8), Folder: United Knights of the KKK).

24. Glenn Twigg, interviews with author, September 17, 2003 (phone) and November 7, 2003 (Raleigh).
25. Jamie Long, interview with author, May 18, 2011 (Cambridge, Massachusetts). See also the various rally flyers and printing order invoices included in HUAC, Box 17, Folders: UKA-NC Documents.
26. The term "paranoid style" was first used by Richard Hofstadter in a 1964 essay in *Harper's Magazine*. Hofstadter couched his conception of the paranoid style in a rigid distinction between a politics rooted in interests, tied to "material aims and needs," versus that based on status "aspirations" and other "personal motives." Viewing this "pseudo-conservative" phenomenon as a variant of the latter, he concluded that its politicized worldview was fundamentally motivated by "private emotions and personal problems," a space that "does more to express emotions than to formulate policies" (Hofstadter 1966: 63, 87). However, a close examination of the UKA demonstrates that the organization, like many groups on the far right, in fact sought to mobilize emotions in the service of broader segregationist policy. The fact that these policy aims were often muddled and ultimately unrealized does not of course invalidate them as organizational goals.
27. Berlet and Lyons (2000); Cunningham (2004: 27).
28. For similar arguments, see Crespino (2007: 52); Woods (2004).
29. Berlet and Lyons (2000); Cunningham (2004); Durham (2007: 118); Hart (2010); Rabon (1965a). Smoot quoted in Berlet and Lyons (2000: 180); Stoner quoted in Webb (2010: 162).
30. Alsop (1966b).
31. Quoted in Batten and Walls (1964). Note that Kathleen Blee (2003) also develops in compelling detail the idea that, among hard-line racists, genuine whiteness requires cultural commitment to racist ideals. Focusing on more contemporary hate groups, she shows that "authentic whites" are framed as "race loyalists." Similarly, the contemporary analogue to the UKA's conception of "white nigger" is "race traitor."
32. The importance of this racial identity-construction process is highlighted in recent social movement research, much of which emphasizes the ways in which movement organizations strategically construct and deploy collective identities to enable mobilization around their goals. Sociologists David A. Snow and Doug McAdam (2000) refer to associated "fitting" processes as solutions to the "problem of identity correspondence," in which personal identities expand to incorporate a larger collective into individuals' sense of self. For additional discussion of the strategic components of identity, see Bernstein (1997), Hunt and Benford (2004), Pfaff (1996), Polletta and Jasper (2001), and Taylor and Whittier (1992). Much prior research on identity in social movements focuses on the construction and mobilization of identity among subordinate groups challenging the status quo, focused

on the building of oppositional consciousness within systems of domination (see, e.g., Bernstein 1997; Morris 1992; Taylor and Whittier 1992—for an exception, see Bernstein 2008). As such, certain of these ideas are not neatly applicable to reactive threat-based movements. But the general point that identity can be deployed strategically, to enhance the salience of relevant categories and provide a basis to act on the solidarity produced by these categories, certainly holds for groups like the UKA that seek to defend the status quo.

33. Chappell (2003: 155).

34. Frames are broadly conceptualized as "schemata of interpretation" that enable individuals to organize. While in daily life all social actors draw upon frames to engage in the production and maintenance of local meanings, frame analysts have recognized that the strategic process of frame construction and management is central to the mission of social movement organizations seeking to replace a legitimizing belief system with one that supports contentious collective action. See Cunningham and Browning (2004: 347–48); Gamson et al. (1982: 15); Snow et al. (1986:464); Snow and McAdam (2000: 56).

35. Acknowledging that a range of themes helped to align a sense of collective identity or "one-ness" is not to say that some magical combination of these rationales resonated with the membership as a whole. The discussion here aligns with Platt and Williams's (2002) important critique of models that conceptualize collective identity in social movements as more-or-less unitary. In their language, it is important to recognize that the UKA's following was "multivocal," in the sense that different adherents responded to different conceptualizations of the defense of segregation. Rebecca Klatch (2002), drawing on Mannheim's ideas about historical generations, makes a similar point when she argues that individuals in different social locations can perceive and interpret shared historical contexts in very different ways. However, by emphasizing the boundary-construction function of the *system* of ideas proffered by UKA leaders and members, this chapter highlights how localized, multivocal understandings aligned to create the sense of "one-ness" that distinguished klan adherents from the outside, "alien" world.

36. Quoted in Alsop (1966a: 23), with emphasis added.

37. Robert Shelton, interview by Patsy Sims, quoted in Sims (1978: 116); Rich (1988: 66–67).

38. Rich (1988: 31–32); Rabon (1965b); SBI memo from O'Daniel to Director, November 4, 1965, NCSA, Moore Papers, General Correspondence, 1965, Box 57, Folder: SBI; SBI memo from O'Daniel to Director, March 14, 1966, NCSA, Moore Papers, General Correspondence, 1966; UKA rally in Four Oaks, North Carolina, September 1968, LBJ, SRT 7054-CD3a, Commission audiotape 3.

39. Calvin Craig interview, p. 28, HU, RJB 124; Peter B. Young, interview with author, February 5, 2004, Framingham, Massachusetts; *The Daily Record* (Dunn, N.C.), January 19, 1965; Shelton quoted in Rich (1988: 134); Mikell (1966: 38, 45). Note that prior to the 1968 elections, Jones and other rally speakers were prone to

referring to Governor Moore and other moderate politicians as "white niggers," and advocating a "return . . . to constitutional government [by electing] good white candidates into office" (NCSA, Moore Papers, General Correspondence, 1968, Box 351, Folder: KKK).

40. *Fiery Cross* (1969: 9); George Dorsett, interview with author, February 20, 2005, Asheboro, North Carolina; Crane and Young, "Voices from the White Ghetto," pp. 44–45, LBJ, RG283, Task Force I, Series 12 (2 of 2).
41. Chappell (2003). Studies of southern ministers' inclinations toward civil rights show that, in terms their statements and actions, the majority of church officials did not favor integration (see Ammerman 1981; Wood 1972).
42. Untitled flyer, UNCC Scoggin Papers, MSS 335, Box 1, Folder 46a; letter from Fayetteville klavern, NCSA, Moore Papers, General Correspondence, 1966, Box 150, Folder: SHP; *Durham Morning Herald*, December 29, 1974; George Dorsett, interview with Tony Crane, in Crane and Young, "Voices from the White Ghetto," p. 18, LBJ, RG283, Task Force I, Series 12 (2 of 2).
43. Rich (1988: 71); *Fiery Cross*, November 17, 1961, UNCC Scoggin Papers, MSS 335, Box 1, Folder 38; SBI memo from Barrett to Director, November 6, 1967, NCSA, Moore Papers, General Correspondence, 1967, Box 149; letter from Shelton to Alabama Senator John J. Sparkman, January 5, 1962, UNCC Scoggin Papers, MSS 335, Box 1, Folder 37; Long (1965); Crane and Young, "Voices from the White Ghetto," p. 59, LBJ, RG283, Task Force I, Series 12 (2 of 2). For an insightful discussion of the role played by Jews in KKK ideology, see Rich (1988: 67–77).
43. Rich (1988: 77); NCSA, Moore Papers, General Correspondence, 1968, Box 351, Folder: KKK; UKA rally in Four Oaks, North Carolina, September 1968, LBJ, SRT 7054-CD3a, Commission audiotape 3; SBI memo from Barrett to Director, November 6, 1967, NCSA, Moore Papers, General Correspondence, 1967, Box 149.
44. Many reporters and police observers noted the evident popularity of "nigger talk." Evidence of UKA leaders' self-consciousness about this dynamic comes from author interviews with Peter B. Young (February 5, 2004) and George Dorsett (February 20, 2005). A recording of a 1968 rally in Four Oaks (LBJ, SRT 7054-CD3a, Commission audiotape 3) demonstrates that the audience reaction was significantly more pronounced when speakers focused directly on racial grievances rather than on general theories of communist conspiracy. Both Rich (1988: 76) and Wade (1987: 324) make similar points.
45. This discussion draws on Taylor and Whittier's (1992) conception of "boundary markers." For more on how the drawing of cultural boundaries relates to the salience of identity categories, see McAdam and Paulsen (1993); Stryker (1968); Stryker and Burke (2000).
46. The importance of ideological inclusivity in the mobilization process is highlighted by Platt and Williams (2002: 338): "Ideology's flexible capacity to achieve these

ends is essential to the creation of mass movements. Mobilizing a variety of groups with diverse backgrounds and interests to engage in the same mass movement depends upon shared, yet varying, interpretive constructions of ideological language."

47. Tolsma et al. (2008: 216).
48. For discussion of interracial organizing in North Carolina, see Korstad (2003); Tyson (2004); Tyson and Cecelski (1998). Both Peter B. Young (interview with author, February 5, 2004) and Will Campbell (interview 18, USM Will Campbell Papers M341, Box 29, Folder 14) recount the Cranford story.
49. HUAC testimony from DuBois and Woodle is reproduced in US House of Representatives (1966: 1829–1864). See also "N.C. Klansman Resigning; Puts 'God and Country' before KKK," *Raleigh News and Observer,* October 22, 1965; Parker (1965).
50. The discussion here follows a long line of findings in the social movements literature demonstrating the importance of such relational resources—generally conceptualized as organizational and informal networks—in the mobilization process (Diani and McAdam 2003; Edwards and McCarthy 2004; McAdam 1986, 1999; Morris 1984; Oberschall 1973). While it has addressed, suggestively at least, the important issue of specifying how individuals' links to groups like the KKK impact their engagement, the fact that I am not able to employ equivalent data on similarly aggrieved nonparticipants precludes any systematic causal claims about the relationship between social ties and klan participation.
51. Alsop (1966a); Walls (1966).

CHAPTER 6

1. Quoted in Chafe (1980: 18).
2. Letter from Harry Golden to Ralph McGill, November 29, 1965, UNCC, Manuscript collection 91, Box 51, Folder 1.
3. Tumin (1958: 3).
4. Memo from Johnson to Waynick, July 4, 1963, ECU, Waynick Papers, #421.26.n; Eric Morton, "Proposal for a SNCC project in North Carolina," p. 3, SNCC, Reel 40. This sense of uniformity across southern communities generally holds in discussions of militant white resistance (Sokol [2006] and Crespino [2007] provide exceptions), though a prominent strain of Civil Rights Movement studies has adopted a "bottom-up" approach that emphasizes local variation (see, e.g., Cecelski 1994; Chafe 1980; Crosby 2005, 2011, Moye 2004).
5. Author interview with George Dorsett, Asheboro, North Carolina, February 20, 2005; US House of Representatives (1967).
6. Miller (1964: 7).
7. US House of Representatives (1967); North Carolina Manual (1960: 132); FBI Charlotte Report, pp. 96–99; Greenville City Directory, 1964–65; "United Klans

of America, Report #1," April 21, 1965, HUAC, Box 18, folder: United Klans—North Carolina Investigative Memos (1 of 4). The mobilization rate comparison is based on the number of klaverns per white resident in each county.

8. *Greenville Daily Reflector*, May 24, 1965, and June 5, 1965; *Raleigh News and Observer*, May 24, 1965; Hardee (1966a, d); Vernal Gaskins, police informant reports, August 7, 1965, and August 28, 1965, HUAC, Box 18, Folder: United Klans—North Carolina Investigative Memos (1 of 4). On another occasion, Charlie Edwards, a UKA state officer and former local police chief in the tiny Pitt County town of Grimesland, pulled eight members of the Greenville unit aside during a klavern meeting and asked them to carry out a plot to attack the mayor of Vanceboro, in adjacent Craven County. Though the klan was strongly represented around Vanceboro—and active enough that guards had been posted around the clock at recently desegregated local school buildings to foil suspected bomb plots—they preferred that this job be carried out by members who would not be easily identified by locals. Edwards initially told the group that the target, Mayor Royce Jordan, had been "seen in the company of colored women," but the true motive was more directly political: Jordan was also a leader in the Craven County anti-poverty program and had been "trying to get colored people jobs." For that activity, Jordan had previously drawn the ire of a local klavern, which burned a cross in his yard and a building on his property. Two cars filled with these klan conspirators made the twenty-five-mile trek to Vanceboro but ultimately aborted the mission after Williams emphatically expressed his fears about the likelihood that they could be arrested under kidnapping charges, which carried a much higher sentence than assault (Hardee 1966c; "Tentative Procedure Outline to Assist Law Enforcement Agencies during 1965 Public School Openings," NCSA, Moore Papers, General Correspondence, 1966, Box 150, Folder: State Highway Patrol).
9. Savage (1965); Evans (1965a). Lawson's use of informants was not confined to the KKK. In April 1969, he resigned from the force following a probe into the criminal backgrounds of several men whom Lawson had appointed to serve as undercover narcotics officers and members of a "special police force" designed for use to control civil disturbances (Savage 1969).
10. Vernal Gaskins, police informant reports, August 7, 1965, and August 28, 1965; City of Greenville Police Department Complaint Report, October 10, 1965; City of Greenville Police Department Offense Report, October 27, 1965 (all in HUAC, Box 18, Folder: United Klans—North Carolina Investigative Memos [1 of 4]); US House of Representatives (1966: 2888–89); Hardee (1966e); *Charlotte Observer*, March 20, 1966; *Greenville Daily Reflector*, March 29, 1966.
11. Hardee (1966a); Savage (1966).
12. Chapman (1965a, b); "Committee for Better Government: A Declaration of Policy," undated pamphlet, Roy Hardee personal papers; "A Petition to Governor Dan K. Moore," NCSA, Moore Papers, General Correspondence, 1965, Box 71, Folder: Segregation—general. Intimidation of black families seeking to enroll their

students in all-white schools was widespread across the region. In nearby Lenoir County, for instance, seventy-one of the ninety students who transferred to previously white schools in 1965 returned to their original schools within two months of the start of the school year. Good Neighbor Council head Dave Coltrane noted that "some of the Klan members or sympathizers have boasted that when schools open after the Christmas holidays, there will be no Negro children in the schools north of the Neuse River. Negro tenant farmers whose children signed up for transfer to white schools have, in some cases, been forced to move and others have been denied farm work, but advised indirectly that they will be given work if and when their children return to the Negro schools" (GNC memo from Coltrane to Moore, November 18, 1965, NCSA, Moore Papers, General Correspondence, 1965, Box 26, Folder: GNC—A–C).

13. North Carolina County Yearbook (1960: 349); US Department of Commerce (1964: 307); *Greenville Daily Reflector*, April 19, 1962; US Bureau of the Census (1960).
14. *Greenville Daily Reflector*, April 14, 1964; Howard (1963); Powell (1963); Moore (1963); "Statement of North Carolina Demonstration Leaders Presented to Governor Terry Sanford at Conference in Raleigh, North Carolina," June 25, 1963, ECU, #421.26.a; North Carolina State Advisory Committee (1962: 92–93, 95).
15. Evans (1965b); *Greenville Daily Reflector*, April 19, 1962, March 26 and April 24, 1965. Schooling figures computed from data in US Bureau of the Census (1960). Reported averages are median values. Jack Greenberg of the NAACP Legal Defense Fund called the sorts of freedom-of-choice school desegregation plans favored by the Greenville and Pitt County school districts "phony," noting that they frequently subjected black parents who sought to transfer their children to "possible loss of their jobs, their homes or other reprisals" (*Greenville Daily Reflector*, May 25, 1965).
16. US Bureau of the Census (1960). State university figures computed from data in North Carolina Board of Higher Education (1969). ECC was renamed East Carolina University in 1967. Note that, as of the close of the 1967–68 school year, only four African American students had ever graduated from ECC.
17. *Greenville Daily Reflector*, July 18, 1963, and February 5, 1965; US Bureau of the Census, General Population Characteristics, Table 20 (1960).
18. US Commission on Civil Rights (1961).
19. Sokol (2006: 204); Letters from Melvin G. Cording to Governor Terry Sanford, July 11, 1963, and to Stan R. Brookshire, July 24, 1963, UNCC, Manuscript Collection 101, Box 1, Folder 13; memo from McConnon to McNamara, July 1, 1965, HUAC, Box 18, Folder: United Klans—NC Investigative Memos [1 of 4].
20. FBI Charlotte Report, May 2, 1966, pp. 46, 90, 94, 100–101.
21. SBI Report from Allen to Director, August 20, 1966, NCSA, Moore Papers, General Correspondence, 1966; Author interview with anonymous, November 6, 2007, Wilson, North Carolina.

22. SBI memos from Minter to Director, March 1, 1966, and Allen to Director, December 18, 1966 (both in NCSA, Moore Papers, General Correspondence, 1966, Box 149, Folder: SBI reports); SHP memo from Guy to Moore, July 17, 1967, NCSA, Moore Papers, General Correspondence, 1967, Box 213, Folder: State Highway Patrol and State Bureau of Investigation reports; Chafe (1980: 161–64).
23. Adams (1966); "Klan Growth Worries Mecklenburg Official," *Raleigh News and Observer*, November 6, 1965; FBI Charlotte Report, May 2, 1966, pp. 51–56.
24. Letter from George Watts Hill to Charlotte Mayor Stanford Brookshire, November 20, 1963, UNCC, Manuscript Collection 101, Box 1, Folder 6.
25. Wolff (1970: 74).
26. North Carolina Department of Labor (1964); Tumin (1958: 5).
27. Memos from Behrman to File, January 24, 1955 and May 17, 1955, AFSC, Box: Southeastern Regional Office 1947–56, Folder: Merit Employment Program, Visits to Businesses, Southeastern Regional Office 1955; Chafe (1980: 35).
28. AFSC memos from Behrman to File, September 19, 1955, from Behrman to Babbitt, January 10, 1956, from Behrman to Babbitt, November 30, 1955, and Merit Employment Program Contact Check-List, September 26, 1956, all in AFSC, Box: Southeastern Regional Office 1947–56, Folders: Merit Employment Program, Visits to Businesses, Southeastern Regional Office 1955 and 1956.
29. "Employment Survey in Greensboro, North Carolina: Report to Employers," AFSC, Box: American Section 1958, Folder: Southern Program—High Point R.O. 1958, Projects—Miscellaneous, Community Relations File; memos from Behrman to File, January 27 and 31, 1955, Box: Southeastern Regional Office 1947–56, Folder: Merit Employment Program, Visits to Businesses, Southeastern Regional Office 1955. Note that while the Employment Survey covered more than 400 Greensboro firms, several survey design issues prevented it from capturing a representative portrait of businesses (these are discussed on pp. 1–3 of the report). That said, the results were consistent with the impressions of AFSC staff, who had worked closely in the community for several years at this point. The AFSC deemed the survey sufficiently useful to mail out its results to more than 600 businesses and "friends." Also note that the limited impact of desegregation efforts was apparent even in firms trumpeted as the biggest success stories. Western Electric's receptivity to the AFSC's merit employment efforts resulted in only token hirings and few promotions of its skilled black workers (see Chafe 1980: 108). In a "fully integrated" plant like Reynolds's Whitaker Park facility, job mobility continued to be limited by continuing racial inequities in education and training. Within particular departments, finer grained segregation patterns (i.e., by aisle or other physical area) tended to persist (see Northrup 1970: 62–63).
30. Chafe (1980: 35–36); Langguth (1963); Northrup (1970); Patrick (1964); Waynick et al. (1964: 54); "Voter Registration Project, Second Report," August 24, 1963, p. 5, AFSC, Box: CRD 1963, Folder: Southern Program 1963, High Point,

Summer Project—Voter Registration; Merit Employment Program contact memo, November 3, 1956, AFSC, Box: Southeastern Regional Office 1947–56, Folder: Merit Employment Program, Visit to Businesses, Southeastern Regional Office 1956; memos from Behrman to File, May 9, 1955, and August 8, 1955, AFSC, Box: Southeastern Regional Office 1947–56, Folder: Merit Employment Program, Visits to Businesses, Southeastern Regional Office 1955; Merit Employment Program contact memo, June 4, 1958, AFSC, Box: Southeastern Regional Office 1957–59, Folder: Merit Employment Program, Visits to Businesses, Southeastern Regional Office 1957; "Quarterly Report: Employment on Merit Program," January 1960, AFSC, Box: Community Relations 1960, Folder: Southern Program—High Point R.O. 1960, Employment on Merit, Community Relations file. While providing only anecdotal evidence, the AFSC's oft-cited refutation of the reactionary volatility of white employees comes from an interview with Larry Deans, personnel manager of the Southern Desk Co. In response to AFSC requests to integrate his staff, Deans repeatedly argued that his workers would not stand for it. To underscore his point, Deans called his secretary in to ask her what she might think about working alongside African Americans. Without hesitation, she replied that she wouldn't mind at all, leaving her questioner astonished and embarrassed (see memo from Behrman to File, July 13, 1955, AFSC, Box: Southeastern Regional Office 1947–56, Folder: Merit Employment Program, Visits to Businesses, Southeastern Regional Office 1955).

31. Bagwell (1972: 47); Brown (1961); Chafe (1980: 20–21); Powell (1970); US Bureau of the Census (1972b).
32. Greensboro College was initially established in 1838 as the Greensboro Female College and became a co-educational institution in 1954. The main campus of Guilford College was located outside of the Greensboro city limits, though in 1953 the school opened a Greensboro based "downtown campus" focused on adult education. Despite its Quaker ties, in the early 1960s, Guilford still maintained an admissions policy that barred "members of the Negro race." The first African American student graduated from Guilford in 1966, and even then black students were part of the adult college and did not live on campus (Chafe 1980: 110; Erickson 2007: 36; Payne 2001: 13). In 1960, the Greensboro-based Women's College was one of three branches of the Consolidated University of North Carolina (the campus, now co-educational, is currently known as UNC-Greensboro). Presumably, it had been formally desegregated after the first undergraduate students were admitted to UNC-Chapel Hill in 1955, though in the early 1960s the school effectively remained an all-white institution (www.uncg.edu/campus_links/inside_uncg/inside_history.html [accessed November 30, 2009]).
33. Bagwell (1972: 31); Chafe (1980: 21, 29, 115).
34. North Carolina Board of Higher Education (1969); memos from Herbin to Fairfax, February 27, June 25, and August 10, 1959, AFSC, Box: American Section

1959 Community Relations, Folder: Southern Program, High Point R.O. 1959, Employment on Merit. For examples of AFSC placements of A&T and Bennett graduates, see, for example, "Meeting with counselors at A&T College," AFSC, Box: American Section 1958, Folder: Southern Program—High Point R.O. 1958, Projects—Miscellaneous, Community Relations File; and memo from Herbin to Fairfax, September 3, 1958, AFSC, Box: Southeastern Regional Office 1957–59, Folder: Merit Employment Program, Visits with Community Leaders & Orgs., Southeastern Regional Office 1957.

35. US Bureau of the Census (1960); Bullard and Stith (1974); Ladd (1966: 68–69); North Carolina State Advisory Committee on Civil Rights (1962: 245); Chafe (1980: 18); memo from Herbin to Fairfax, January 8, 1963, AFSC, Box: CRD 1963, Folder: Southern Program 1963, High Point, Employment on Merit; memos from Herbin to Faifax, May 28, 1958, and Catchings to Babbitt, February 19, 1957, AFSC, Box: Southeastern Regional Office 1957–59, Folder: Merit Employment Program, Visits with Community Leaders & Orgs., Southeastern Regional Office 1957. Note that the Southern Association school accreditation process was widely considered to be much more rigorous than that undertaken by the State Department of Public Instruction (see North Carolina State Advisory Committee 1962: 106). Also, the gap between black educational achievement in Greensboro and the state as a whole was not purely an artifact of enhanced opportunities in urbanized areas. In 1960, black adults in Greensboro had an average of 8.8 years of schooling. A sample of twenty-three other southern cities compiled by Ladd (1966) averaged 7.5 years, 15 percent lower than in Greensboro.
36. North Carolina State Advisory Committee (1962: 92); EOM contact memo, April 23, 1958, AFSC, Box: Southeastern Regional Office 1957–59, Folder: Merit Employment Program, Visits to Businesses, Southeastern Regional Office 1957; memos from Herbin to Fairfax, February 4 and October 29, 1958, AFSC, Box: Southeastern Regional Office 1957–59, Folder: Merit Employment Program, Visits with Community Leaders & Orgs., Southeastern Regional Office 1957; memos from Herbin to Fairfax, February 1, 1960, and March 24, 1960, AFSC, Box: Community Relations 1960, Folder: Southern Program—High Point R.O. 1960, Employment on Merit, Community Relations File; memo from Herbin to Fairfax, November 9, 1962, AFSC, Box: Community Relations 1962, Folder: Southern Program, High Point, Employment on Merit.
37. "Minority Report, No. II: Goodbye to Carolina" film transcript, ECU, Waynick Papers, #421.28, Folder: North Carolina Film Board, 1964; EOM Program contact memo, November 13, 1958, AFSC, Box: Southeastern Regional Office 1957–59, Folder: Merit Employment Program, Visits to Businesses, Southeastern Regional Office 1957.
38. Andrews and Biggs (2006: 959); Chafe (1980: 85); Laue (1989: 329–30); Morris (1984); Wolff (1970: 29).

39. Chafe (1980: 81). The assertion that all four original sit-in members had Youth Council ties appears periodically in the literature (see, e.g., Morris 1984: 198) and seems to date back to an uncited statement made in Oppenheimer (1964). I have not been able to find more definite support for that strong claim, however, so include the more conservative figure here.
40. Wolff (1970). Bennett College President Willa Player was similarly supportive of her students' involvement in the demonstrations. By way of explanation of her general approach, she noted: "I didn't tell them that they were supposed to join the protest. I just said to them: you will be expected to practice what you've learned; and that was it.... That reduced any tensions that the students had with me as the chief administrator" (quoted in Chafe 1980: 129). More generally, the college environment is conducive to activism, given many students' "biographical availability" to expend time and energy on protest action. "We have no jobs from which to be fired by people who don't like to see us assert ourselves," noted Ezell Blair Jr., one of the original cadre of demonstrators. "We can speak up loudly now without fear of economic reprisal." Joseph McNeil, another member of the quartet, highlighted the same phenomenon: "we had shelter, we had food, and we could take risks that the others couldn't." McAdam (1986: 70) formally defines biographical availability as "the absence of personal constraints that may increase the costs and risks of movement participation, such as full-time employment, marriage, and family responsibilities." For nuanced considerations of the concept, see Wiltfang and McAdam (1991) and Beyerlein and Hipp (2006), as well as the related discussion in Chapter 5 here.
41. Wolff (1970).
42. *Greensboro Daily News* (June 7, 1963); Wolff (1970: 85).
43. Chafe (1980: 79); "Annual Report," September 1960, and memo from Fairfax to Moffett, July 14, 1960, AFSC, Box: Community Relations 1960, Folder: Southern Program, High Point R.O. 1960, Employment on Merit, Community Relations File; memos from Hartzler to Moffett, February 18, 1960, and from Heirich to Staff, April 8, 1960, AFSC, Box: Community Relations 1960, Folder: Southern Program—High Point R.O., Sit-in Demonstrations; "Voter Registration Project Summary Report," AFSC, Box: CRD 1963, Folder: Southern Program 1963, High Point, Summer Project—Voter Registration.
44. This dimension will be discussed in more detail below, but the key supporting statistic is the Greensboro SMSA's low segregation index (as expressed by the "index of dissimilarity") of 66.9 in 1960. For comparison (with higher values indicating a greater degree of segregation), the index for Charlotte's SMSA was 75.6, and the average value for thirty-three other southern SMSAs was 73.8 (Van Valey et al. 1977).
45. Chafe (1980: 155–56) also notes that the perception that Greensboro's direct action protests had made the city less appealing to new industry provided another source of anger, in this case disproportionately shouldered by white elites.

46. The concept of "readiness" was often invoked as a sense of the general feel of cities' racial climates. A personnel manager for Sears, Roebuck, and Co., for instance, spent much of the 1950s in different southern locales to assess whether communities might be "ready" for black sales clerks. When queried about Greensboro in 1958, he doubted the city's readiness (EOM Program contact memo, December 2, 1958, AFSC Archives, Box: Southeastern Regional Office 1957–59, Folder: Merit Employment Program, Visits to Businesses, Southeastern Regional Office 1957). In contrast, Charlotte was frequently invoked as among the most "ready" cities in the South (see, e.g., Harry Golden's quote at the beginning of this chapter, and EOM Program contact memo, March 10, 1958, AFSC Archives, Box: Southeastern Regional Office 1957–59, Folder: Merit Employment Program, Visits to Businesses, Southeastern Regional Office 1957). The fact that Greensboro, but not Charlotte, was highly receptive to the KKK is the obverse of this issue, and the central puzzle tackled in this chapter.
47. Letter from Robert F. Kennedy to Stanford R. Brookshire, June 24, 1963, UNCC, Manuscript Collection 101, Box 1, Folder 5.
48. Various letters to Stanford Brookshire, in UNCC, Manuscript Collection 101, Box 1, Folders 1, 4, 5, 6, 7, 9, 14; Brookshire (1963); Leach (1976: 183–84); Watters (1964: 7). For a sense of the self-regard that followed from these accolades, after the passage of the 1964 Civil Rights Act Charlotte's Mayor's Community Relations Committee adopted a statement that portrayed the city as "set upon a hill in North Carolina. Our example and our conduct will affect the actions of scores of communities and millions of people around us. We must continue to show the way to better human relations by living up to the rich religious and cultural heritage that is ours" (letter from Cunningham to Brookshire, December 2, 1964, UNCC, Manuscript Collection 101, Box 1, Folder 7).
49. Watters (1964: 6).
50. Douglas (1995: 71–73); Leach (1976: 14, 21–22); McMillen (1971). Another short-lived late-1950s segregationist organization, the Defenders of States Rights, Inc., also was largely rebuffed in Charlotte (Leach 1976: 21).
51. Popular and journalistic accounts in this vein include Waynick et al. (1964), Wright (1963), and a twenty-fifth anniversary retrospective look at Charlotte's Community Relations Committee ("Celebrating Charlotte's 25th Year of Harmony, Progress, and Good Human Relations," UNCC, Manuscript Collection 101, Box 1, Folders 12–13). Helpfully, more recent scholarly accounts have provided a critical assessment of the city's political and racial policies (see Lassiter 2006; Smith 2004), placing local political ideology and policy within a broader socioeconomic context. Lassiter's (2006) analysis notably focuses on conservative mobilizations around the controversial court-ordered plan to employ "forced busing" to desegregate the Charlotte-Mecklenburg County school system in the early 1970s. The account here seeks to root the "discourses of power" at the center of Chafe's (1980) "progressive mystique" and Lassiter's (2006) explication of the "Charlotte Way"

within the social, spatial, and demographic processes that provided a crucial foundation for racialized rhetoric to resonate widely among white residents.

52. Hanchett (1998: 261–62). In 1960, the degree of segregation (as captured by the index of dissimilarity) in Charlotte's metropolitan area was 75.6, versus Greensboro's 66.9. Differences for the central cities were smaller (87.1 versus 84.0), though still higher for Charlotte (Van Valey et al. 1977). Douglas (1995: 55) similarly notes that, in the 1950s, Charlotte was more highly segregated by race than all but thirteen of the nation's 100 largest cities.
53. Douglas (1995); Lassiter (2006: 126–28); Smith (2004: 37–38); "Resume of Improvements during Period 1959–1965" and "Brooklyn Area Blight Study," UNCC, Manuscript Collection 91, Box 40, Folder 12; Notes from NAACP Executive Committee meeting, January 13, 1966, UNCC, Kelly Alexander Papers, MSS 55, Box 2, Folder 8; "Can Charlotte Have a Race Riot?" flyer for Charlotte-Mecklenburg Council on Human Relations public forum, November 8, 1966, UNCC, Manuscript Collection 91, Box 39, Folder 5.
54. A well-known example of residential conflict in Greensboro involved Frank Williams, a black minister at Mt. Zion Baptist Church. When the Reverend Williams moved into a house purchased for him by members of his congregation in a previously all-white neighborhood, a group of klansmen led by George Dorsett engaged in a sustained harassment campaign. During Williams's first two weeks in the house, he was subjected to hurled bricks and bottles, near-constant verbal abuse, and blinding lights flashed in his windows. A pickup truck parked nearby flew a Confederate flag and, at one point, also held a black dummy hanged in effigy. Gathering crowds on several occasions created near-riots, and klan members burned a cross on a nearby property and gave speeches to 200 to 300 onlookers from the back of the outfitted pickup truck. While the public nature of this campaign was unusual, the overall dynamic was anything but exceptional. Several months earlier, a black family that had rented a house in a white Greensboro neighborhood had been subjected to similar harassment, including a message from a klansman that he would "kill this nigger to teach a lesson to all others." See Chafe (1980: 160–61); SHP memo from Guy to Governor Moore, July 17, 1967, NCSA, Moore Papers, General Correspondence, 1967, Box 217, Folder: SHP and SBI Reports.
55. Kelly Alexander, p. 7, interview in HU, RJB 399; US Bureau of the Census (1963, 1972a); Employment Security Commission of North Carolina (1968); Hanchett (1998: 225); Leach (1976: 193–98). This labor market partitioning also meant that Charlotte's black workers were disproportionately vulnerable to retribution by white superiors, a reality frequently confronted by the city's black political leadership (see, e.g., memo from Davis to Alexander et al., "Report on the November 12 Charlotte meeting," AFSC, Box: American Section 1959, Community Relations, Folder: Southern Program—High Point R.O. 1959, Southern School Integration).

56. Bullard and Stith (1974); North Carolina Board of Education (1969); Hanchett (1998: 134–39). Note that this account of Charlotte's black colleges does not include Carver College, which opened in 1949 as a community college intended to serve black residents in parallel with the white Charlotte College. In 1961, Carver was renamed Mecklenburg College and relocated to a new campus, a controversial move in that its de facto function was to reinforce segregated schooling in the post-*Brown* era. Falling enrollments caused the school to close in 1965, and it therefore did not significantly alter the black educational landscape in the period considered here (Leach 1976: 81–90).
57. *Carolina Times* (August 10, 1940), quoted in Leach (1976: 69); Gavins (1991: 107, 109, 117); Leach (1976: 71, 74–79). Note that the school desegregation process largely stalled after the initial push in 1957. In 1960, in a school system with an overall student population of 63,500, only three additional black students had been enrolled in previously white city schools. The following year, twenty-six black students were assigned to four predominantly white schools in the consolidated Mecklenburg County-Charlotte school system (US Commission on Civil Rights 1961).
58. Andrews and Biggs (2006: 759); *Charlotte Observer* (February 10, 1960); Letter from James Smith to Jean Hatcher and Frances Vinroot, March 23, 1960, UNCC, Manuscript Collection 101, Box 1, Folder 1. The other six establishments targeted in the original Charlotte sit-ins were F.W. Woolworth, S.H. Kress Co., W.T. Grant Co., Sears Roebuck, McLellan's, and Liggetts Drug (see J. Charles Jones, "Rock Hill and Charlotte Sit-ins," www.crmvet.org/info/rockhill.htm [accessed December 10, 2009]).
59. Among Charlotte's four predominantly black precincts, Brookshire in 1961 received 15 percent of the vote in the Second Ward, 62 percent in Zeb Vance, 7 percent in Northwest, and 19 percent in Double Oaks. Two years later, 90 percent, 64 percent, 89 percent, and 97 percent of voters in those respective precincts supported Brookshire (Smith 2004: 37). In a May 10, 1963, letter to civil rights activist Reginald Hawkins, Brookshire himself described this shift as "an endorsement of our moderate and constructive approach to peaceful progress in race relations" (UNCC, Manuscript Collection 101, Box 1, Folder 5).
60. *Charlotte* Magazine 2, 5 (February 1965), UNCC, Manuscript Collection 91, Box 36, Folder 17; Smith (2004: 27); Watters (1964: 21); "What Was Done in '61 by Our Chamber of Commerce," UNCC, Manuscript Collection 91, Box 36, Folder 17; Minutes of the Executive Committee of the Mayor's Community Relations Committee, December 1, 1961, UNCC, Manuscript Collection 101, Box 1, Folder 10; Letter from Cunningham to Friendly Relations Committee, May 25, 1961, UNCC, Manuscript Collection 101, Box 1, Folder 4; Douglas (1995: 97). Brookshire's Community Relations Committee included twenty-seven carefully selected individuals, nine of whom were black. White members included the editors of the two Charlotte papers, one member of the City Council, leading

Presbyterian and Methodist ministers, two doctors, an executive with Douglas Aircraft (one of the city's largest employers), and three women active in civic affairs. The black membership included two ministers, a banker, an undertaker, an insurance agent, a doctor, a female teacher, and a Johnson C. Smith professor's wife ("The Mayor's Committee on Community Relations," UNCC, Manuscript Collection 101, Box 1, Folder 5).

61. The argument developed here draws on sociologist Mark Granovetter's (1978) ideas about how "threshold" processes impact the outcomes of collective action. By highlighting the dual facts that individuals' interests in action are distributed unevenly and that the perceived cost of any individual act varies according to the number of other participants, Granovetter demonstrates how the actions of early adopters shift the cost-benefit calculations of others, creating the possibility for radically different outcomes even among similarly interested populations. The emphasis here on business owners' weighing of "disruption" and "concession" costs associated with the decision to desegregate follows Luders's (2006) conception of how the desegregation process was shaped by the broad structure of economic opportunities, and more broadly draws on a tradition of research on the civil rights-era South that emphasizes the pivotal role played by the business community (Cobb 1993; Jacoway and Colburn 1982; Thornton 1991). This emphasis in the established literature is reinforced by observations made by, among others, Curtis Gans (interview with author, May 25, 2005, Washington, DC) and Harry Golden (letter to Ralph McGill, November 29, 1965, UNCC, Manuscript collection 91, Box 51, Folder 1). For an earlier account of how "municipal politics" shaped civil rights contention, see Thornton (1991). While Thornton's analysis focuses mainly on how political interactions shaped the ability of the black community to mobilize, the framework applies as well to the ways in which local politics shaped the capacity of white leadership to contain civil rights contention, and by extension reduce opportunities for klan mobilization.
62. Cramer (1963); Brookshire (1963); Snook (1963); Waynick et al. (1964); Wright (1963); "Greensboro 'Marchers' Stay Orderly," *Charlotte Observer*, May 5, 1963. By August 1963, twenty-two of Charlotte's 217 restaurants had agreed to desegregate. A month later, that number had grown to thirty-eight (see letters from Cunningham to Managers of Charlotte Restaurants, August 20 and September 17, 1963, UNCC, Manuscript Collection 101, Box 1, Folder 6).
63. Letters from the James Castanas Family to Kelly M. Alexander, January 14, 1964, and Harry Golden to Jimmy Kanakos, February 19, 1964, UNCC, Manuscript Collection 101, Box 1, Folder 7.
64. Leach (1976). The bombing targets were Kelly Alexander, his brother Fred, NAACP attorney Julius Chambers, and Reginald Hawkins, the city's most visibly militant proponent of black rights.
65. City Council Meeting Minutes, November 22, 1965, UNCC, Manuscript Collection 91, Box 2, Folder 22; Mayor's Community Relations Committee

resolution, undated, UNCC, Manuscript Collection 101, Box 1, Folder 11; donor list, undated, UNCC, Manuscript Collection 101, Box 1, Folder 9; various letters and telegrams, UNCC, Manuscript Collection 55, Box 20, Folder 2.

66. *Charlotte Observer*, December 6, 1965.
67. See Bullard and Stith (1974). The indicators examined in the report included racial gaps in overcrowded housing, low value owner-occupied housing, median education, unemployment, low occupational status, median family income, infant mortality, and family stability. The one dimension where Charlotte ranked above Greensboro was the prevalence of low-income families, though note that the racial gap associated with that indicator in the two cities differed by only 0.3 percentage points.

CHAPTER 7

1. "1967 FBI Appropriation," HUAC, Box 32, Folder: UKA, Inc. Investigative Memos, Other Memos, Some Photos.
2. Dargan Frierson, interview with Kathleen Hoke, January 9, 1990, UNCG, http://library.uncg.edu/dp/crg/oralHistItem.aspx?i=484 (accessed October 25, 2010).
3. WBTV transcript of Bob Jones editorial, NCSA, Moore Papers, General Correspondence, 1965, Box 71, Folder: Segregation—general.
4. Quoted in Peter B. Young, "The Gun and the Guitar," p. 3, LBJ, Federal Records—Eisenhower Commission [RG 283]; Task Force I—Assassination; Series 12; Box 5.
5. The UKA never publicly disclosed accurate membership information, so estimates necessarily rely on data compiled by the FBI and the North Carolina State Bureau of Investigation, both of whom had developed dense informant coverage. Specific figures listed here come from FBI COINTELPRO–White Hate Groups Memos from Charlotte to Director, April 1 and September 30, 1968, and March 27, 1969.
6. SBI memo from Hunt to Director, August 28, 1967, NCSA, Moore Papers, General Correspondence, 1967, Box 213, folder: SHP & SBI; SBI memo from Allen to Director, October 30, 1966, NCSA, Moore Papers, General Correspondence, 1966; SBI memo from Dunn to Governor Scott and the Attorney General, January 20, 1969, NCSA, Scott Papers, General Correspondence, 1969, Box 125, folder: KKK; FBI COINTELPRO–White Hate Group Memos from SAC, Charlotte to Director, March 13 and November 6, 1967; News from Klansville #35 and October 21, 1967, NCSA, Moore Papers, General Correspondence, 1967. Issues associated with the size versus quality of UKA membership had long dogged the organization. In 1965, a report filed by klan informant and Greenville police officer Vernal Gaskins noted that "a very grave and serious crisis is immenent [*sic*]...due to the very low calibre of the people now being accepted into the KKK and the subsequent poor leadership being

administered in local units. The Ku Klux Klan now seems to be more interested in Quantity rather than Quality in its members. . . . Especially Greenville is faced with possible trouble from the Klan because of its large majority of drunks and people of doubtful character for members" (see memo from Gaskins to Police Chief H. F. Lawson, August 7, 1964, HUAC, Box 18, Folder: United Klans—North Carolina Investigative Memos [1 of 4]). Similarly, according to Bob Jones's daughter Sheila, on the eve of the UKA's 1963 reorganization in North Carolina, Bob had to convince his wife Syble that this organization would attract a higher caliber of member than did Bob's old U.S. Klans outfit (Sheila Jones Baker, phone interview with author, September 2, 2003).

7. The argument here draws on social movement theorists' conception of "political opportunity structures" (see Ch. 3, note 48). The discussion of the shifting form of institutional supports for white privilege mirrors sociologist Jenny Irons's (2010) institutional analysis of the Mississippi State Sovereignty Commission, which over time shifted its goals and language to reflect and defend "acceptable" forms of white supremacy as formal segregation fell away.
8. SBI Report #7 to the Law and Order Committee, October 31, 1966, NCSA, Moore Papers, General Correspondence, 1966; Jack Crum, undated 1966, "A Report on the KKK to the Commission on Christian Social Action and to the Executive Board;" SBI memo from O'Daniel to Director, September 27, 1967, NCSA, Moore Papers, General Correspondence, 1967, Box 213, folder: SHP & SBI; *Raleigh News and Observer*, May 12 and December 25, 1965; undated flyer, Roy Hardee personal papers (in author's possession); Erwin (1965). Another example of an anti-klan resolution came from the Anson County Board of Commissioners in 1967 (see Resolution from Board Chairman Fayette J. Cloud Jr., NCSA, Moore Papers, General Correspondence, 1967, Box 268).
9. SHP Report from Chadwick to Speed, April 12, 1966, NCSA, Moore Papers, General Correspondence, 1966, Box 150, Folder: SHP; SBI Report by O'Daniel, November 15, 1965, NCSA, Moore Papers, General Correspondence, 1965; Cockshutt (1969). Note that Timothy Tyson (2001, 2004), Peniel Joseph (2007), Charles Payne (1995), Emilye Crosby (2011), and other historians have compellingly combated the argument that the direct action tactics associated with the Black Power Movement emerged only in the later 1960s, by showing that instances of organized, militant black resistance existed throughout the long civil rights era. The discussion here is not intended to imply that active resistance to the klan in the black community did not exist prior to 1966, but rather that such actions became both more prevalent and more public at this point.
10. See, for example, letter from Shelton to Frankhouser, April 10, 1968, UNCC Scoggin Papers, MSS 335, box 1, folder 37.
11. SBI memos from O'Daniel to Director, July 18, 1967, NCSA, Moore Papers, General Correspondence, 1967, Box 208, Folder: SBI reports; and July 27, 1967, Moore Papers, General Correspondence, 1967, Box 213, Folder: SHP & SBI

reports; SBI memo from Allen to Director, June 16, 1966, NCSA, Moore Papers, General Correspondence, 1966. Shelton failed to discipline Jones or further investigate members' mismanagement claims, which did little to quell brewing dissension in the ranks.

12. Drabble (2003); Pete Young, "The Gun and the Guitar: White Ghetto Revisited," p. 10, LBJ, Federal Records—Eisenhower Commission (RG 283), Task Force I—Assassination, Series 10, Box 5; Peter B. Young, interview with author, February 5, 2004, Framingham, Massachusetts; SBI memo from Allen to Director, May 24, 1967, NCSA, Moore Papers, General Correspondence, 1967, Box 213, folder: SHP & SBI.
13. This mismatch process is akin to what sociologists Robert Merton and Elinor Barber labeled, in their classic 1963 essay, "sociological ambivalence." Focusing on the relational contexts within which ambivalence emerges, Merton and Barber (1976 [1963]: 5–6) argued that the outcome was "built into the structure of social statuses and roles," arising in settings where such roles contain "incompatible normative expectations." Malin Akerstrom has extended such conceptualizations to understand how workers "do ambivalence" within organizational settings. Akerstrom argues that when faced with policy change dictated from above, workers in bureaucratic organizations enact ambivalence by oscillating between "embracement" and "distancing" practices. As a result, policy innovations emerge not as linearly diffused decrees, but through the enactment of workers' "accommodative rhetoric," which involves "presenting an understanding of and appreciation for the new, while simultaneously expressing reservations" (2005: 57). As such, street-level bureaucrats do far more than implement the policy dictated by their superiors—they define the shape of that policy through the practice of ambivalence. Applied to the KKK case, ambivalence is produced by a mismatch between organizational culture and organizational goals. When police targets seek to uphold values shared by the state, but do so by employing tactics, ideologies, and/or frames that are viewed as inappropriate or even illegal, state agents must balance their potentially sympathetic views of targets' goals with the fact that their means pose a threat to legal and political structures. The presence of organizational ambivalence demonstrates that agencies' actions and outcomes are not necessarily direct products of their mandates and goals, which contrasts with traditional interest-based understandings of state repression as a reaction to protest-based threats (Cunningham 2009).
14. US House of Representatives (1966: 1962–80, 2888–89); Emerson (1998); memo from Coltrane, NCSA, Department of Administration, HRC, Direct Correspondence, File, 1960–77, Box 29; *Wilmington Morning Star*, September 1, 1964; *Raleigh News and Observer*, October 27 and November 8, 1965. Another example of active local police-KKK collaboration was in Montgomery County, where a special sheriff's deputy in Troy, the county seat, and police officers in the nearby town of Biscoe, were known UKA members (see memo from McConnon

to McNamara, June 30, 1965, HUAC, Box 18, Folder: United Klans—NC Investigative Memos [2 of 4]). In another case, Rowan County klansman John Stirewalt pledged to avoid active UKA participation after being elected sheriff in 1966. His efforts to do so were mixed at best, as he was severely criticized two years later for naming Bob Jones a special deputy (Ross 1966; Sims 1978; *New York Times*, September 28 and 30, 1968).

15. Coates (1983); Lynch (1968); memo from McConnon to McNamara, HUAC, July 1, 1965, Box 18, Folder: United Klans—NC Investigative Memos (1 of 4).
16. While the SBI at this time was formally an all-white agency, gradually klansmen came to label its agents as "white niggers" insufficiently invested in the maintenance of segregation.
17. Elizabeth Moss, "Bureau of Investigation," NCSA; SBI memo from O'Daniel to Director, September 28, 1967, NCSA, Moore Papers, General Correspondence, 1967, Box 213, folder: SHP & SBI; memo from McConnon to McNamara, July 1, 1965, HUAC, Box 18, Folder: United Klans—NC Investigative Memos [1 of 4]; Warren Campbell, phone interview with author, July 6, 2003; Haywood Starling, phone interview with author, September 4, 2003.
18. SBI agents were responsible for four to five counties each, and dealt with the full range of "disruptive" groups in those counties (i.e., civil rights demonstrators as well as the KKK). When the governor's office mandated that the SBI establish a Specialized Investigations desk focused on "civil disturbances" perpetrated by the KKK and Citizens' Councils, various civil rights groups, and even the Communist Party, only four agents were assigned to this task, underscoring the SBI's small size and centralized structure. See Emerson (1998); SBI memo from Director, March 16, 1966, NCSA, Moore Papers, General Correspondence, 1966; Warren Campbell, phone interview with author, July 6, 2003.
19. Memos from McConnon to McNamara, undated, HUAC, Box 18, Folder: United Klans—NC Investigative Memos (2 of 4), and July 1, 1965, HUAC, Box 18, Folder: United Klans—NC Investigative Memos (1 of 4). After four black men were accused of killing a State Highway Patrol officer in 1964, Jones would regularly ask whether there was anything he could do to support the SHP.
20. Emerson (1998: 189–90); author interviews with anonymous former SBI agent, Apex, North Carolina, September 1, 2003, and Haywood Starling, by phone, September 6, 2003. For examples of Jones's willingness to provide SBI agents with rally and other details, see SBI memos from Satterfield to Director, September 18, 1967, and from O'Daniel to Director, March 7, 1966, NCSA, Governor Moore Papers, General Correspondence, 1966 and 1967.
21. Kelly Alexander, address at North Carolina State Conference of Branches 23rd Annual Convention, October 14, 1966, p. 16, UNCC Kelly Alexander Papers, MSS 55, Box 1, Folder 5; Emerson (1998: 217); *Charlotte Observer*, October 18, 1966. One SBI agent filed an official report acknowledging that "the records being played and the remarks being made about 'nigger' over the public address system is

intimidating against the Negroes present at the Fair," but took no further action to suppress the klan's activities (see SBI Report from Crocker to Director, October 12, 1966, NCSA, Moore Papers, General Correspondence, 1966).

22. Letter from Coltrane to Branch, August 3, 1964, NCSA, Sanford Papers, General Correspondence, 1964; SBI Report #2 to Law and Order Committee, May 26, 1966; Haywood Starling, phone interview with author, September 6, 2003.
23. SHP Report from Speed to Moore, November 7, 1966, NCSA, Moore Papers, General Correspondence, 1966, Box 150, Folder: SHP; "Shooting Occurs at KKK Rally Sunday," *The Roanoke News*, November 10, 1966; Kern (1966).
24. This dynamic was noted by US Attorney General Ramsey Clark, who used North Carolina's poor record in dealing with civil rights crimes to illustrate the need for tougher federal laws against racial violence (see *Charlotte Observer*, September 23, 1967).
25. Hoover quoted in Powers (1987: 411). For detail on the FBI's "racial matters" investigations, see Garrow (1981), Kotz (2006), and O'Reilly (1989). For more detail on COINTELPRO, see Blackstock (1988); Churchill and VanderWall (1988, 1990); Cunningham (2004); Donner (1980); US House of Representatives (1975).
26. O'Reilly (1989: 130); Powers (1987: 343–44); FBI memo from Gale to Tolson, July 30, 1964. Note that the groundwork for the approval of COINTELPRO–White Hate Groups was laid during a June 1964 meeting between Johnson and Hoover. "I want you to put people after the klan to study it from one county to the next," the president instructed Hoover. "I want the FBI to have the best intelligence system possible to check on the activities of these people." Following this meeting, Hoover's only remaining hurdle was to connect this intelligence mandate to the countersubversive purview of COINTELPRO (see O'Reilly 1989: 199).
27. FBI memo from Baumgardner to William Sullivan, August 27, 1964. At the outset, the program targeted twenty-six groups, including seventeen KKK-affiliated organizations (FBI COINTELPRO–White Hate Groups Memo from Director to seventeen field offices, September 2, 1964). Also note that COINTELPRO–White Hate Groups fell under Baumgardner's purview because, upon establishment of the program, KKK matters were transferred from the General Investigative Division, concerned with criminal matters, to the Domestic Intelligence Division, which focused on dissident and subversive threats.
28. Cunningham (2004); FBI COINTELPRO–White Hate Groups Memo from SAC, Charlotte to Director, October 12, 1964. Between 1964 and 1971, the Charlotte SAC and Director Hoover and his high-level advisors exchanged 240 COINTELPRO–White Hate Groups Memos. Those memos show that agents in the Charlotte field office proposed a total of sixty-seven actions and carried out sixty. The discrepancy between the number of proposals and actions is due to a number of factors: some proposals were rejected by the director, some actions were initiated as part of blanket authorizations in response to proposals offered by

different field offices, and a small number of authorized proposals lent themselves to multiple actions over time.

29. FBI COINTELPRO–White Hate Groups Memos from Birmingham to Director, December 17, 1964; Charlotte to Director and Birmingham, February 25, 1965; Tampa to Director, December 16, 1966; Director to Birmingham and Mobile, August 11, 1966; Griffith to Conrad, April 3, 1966; Baumgardner to Sullivan, April 25, 1966; Director to Charlotte and 16 other SACs, May 20, 1966; Charlotte to Director, April 20, 1967. Planted articles generally involved providing "reliable" reporters with selected FBI intelligence, which would then be used as the basis of a negative article. In one such instance, Charlotte agents furnished *Salisbury Post* reporter Ned Cline with an eight-page report detailing the UKA's revenue streams, which Cline drew upon as the basis for an article chronicling the construction of Jones's new home and headquarters—valued "in the $20,000 range"—and the UKA's reputed $125,000 gross in 1967. Another prominent media source was *Charlotte Observer* reporter Howard Covington (see, e.g., FBI COINTELPRO–White Hate Groups Memos from Charlotte to Director, July 2 and 26 and September 30, 1968). See Cunningham (2004: 243–50) for a complete typology of COINTELPRO–White Hate Groups actions.
30. FBI memo from Director to the Attorney General, September 2, 1965; Cunningham (2004: 131–32); SBI memos from O'Daniel to Director, November 2 and 11, 1965, NCSA, Moore Papers, General Correspondence, 1965, Box 57, Folder: SBI; FBI Charlotte Field Office, "Report on United Klans of America, Inc., Knights of the Ku Klux Klan (North Carolina)," May 2, 1966; FBI COINTELPRO–White Hate Groups Memo from Charlotte to Director, March 10, 1966; Peter B. Young, interview with author, February 5, 2004. Gary Marx (1974) presciently notes that informants can never be entirely passive, as by definition their presence has some effect on the targeted group. The effect is heightened once the group is aware of the possibility of infiltration or other forms of surveillance.
31. SBI memo from Allen to Director, June 16, 1966, NCSA, Moore Papers, General Correspondence, 1966; SHP report, May 9, 1966, NCSA, Moore Papers, General Correspondence, 1966, Box 150, Folder: SHP; *Raleigh News and Observer*, March 30, 1967; Dawson interview with Scott Ellsworth, pp. 50–59, DU, Chafe Oral History Collection, Printed Materials Series, Box 1.
32. Sims (1978); FBI COINTELPRO–White Hate Groups Memos from Charlotte to Director, April 12, 1967, and from Charlotte to Director and twelve SACs, May 31, 1967; Undated memo, NCSA, Moore Papers, General Correspondence, 1967, Box 213, folder: SHP & SBI; Dargan Frierson interview with Michael Frierson (recording in the possession of Michael Frierson). Shelton responded to the NIC mandate by issuing a press release denying the NIC's existence and then lodging a formal mail fraud claim with postal authorities and the FBI. A second NIC letter, defending the "committee's" actions and reiterating its suspensions of Shelton and

Jones, was prepared but never sent, as Hoover ordered Charlotte agents not to proceed until Shelton's mail claim investigation had run its course with postal authorities. Even so, the Charlotte Special Agent in Charge noted that the NIC operation had exceeded expectations, "fostering discontent, dissension, and confusion" among both leaders and the North Carolina rank-and-file. At least three klaverns, the SAC reported, had disbanded as a result of the NIC ruse. See FBI COINTELPRO–White Hate Group Memos from Charlotte to Director, June 28, 1967, from Atlanta to Director, June 15, 1967, from Birmingham to Director, June 14, 1967, from Charlotte to Director, June 14, 1967, and from Director to Charlotte, June 29, 1967.

33. *Raleigh News and Observer*, May 24, 1967; Drabble (2003). Cole organized a rally in Mt. Airy on June 24 amid rumors that UKA elements were planning to attend and "break up the meeting." A month earlier, Shelton had been the featured speaker at a UKA rally in Durham, and a large armed security force was mobilized to ensure his safety. When Dorsett traveled to Virginia soon after for a UKA rally, members of the security guard surrounded and threw stones at his car. "There are a hundred people here who would kill you," one of the assailants yelled, as Dorsett beat a hasty retreat. An SBI informant reported that "Dorsett was lucky to get out of Richmond... without getting hurt. There were several klansmen who really wanted to get [him] for causing all the trouble inside the Klan" (SBI memo from Allen to Director, May 24, 1967, NCSA, Moore Papers, General Correspondence, 1967, Box 213, folder: SHP & SBI reports; NCSA, Moore Papers, General Correspondence, 1967, Box 208, SBI reports; Drabble 2003; Sims 1978: 43; E. H. Hennis, interview with author, November 14, 2006, Greensboro, North Carolina). For detail on Cole's fatal car accident, see "'Catfish' Cole Is Wreck Victim," *Kinston Daily Free Press*, July 28, 1967; "Foul Play Suspected in Death," *Kinston Daily Free Press*, July 29, 1967.

34. Drabble (2003); FBI COINTELPRO–White Hate Groups Memo from Charlotte to Director, January 30, 1969; George Dorsett, interview with author, February 20, 2005, Asheboro, North Carolina. The FBI's involvement in the formation of the Confederate Knights was not their first attempt to siphon members from the UKA by creating new, "acceptable" alternatives. In 1966, agents had created the "National Committee for Domestic Tranquility," a fictive organization that implored recruits to "quit the Klan, and back our boys in Vietnam." Though the NCDT existed only on paper, agents composed and disseminated multiple editions of the organization's bulletin to those "who may be involved in a Klan dispute, and/or who may be considered for an FBI interview in connection with informant development" (FBI COINTELPRO–White Hate Groups Memo from Baumgardner to Sullivan, March 10, 1966). Also note that the CKKKK's success in building units was part of a broader FBI strategy to build a viable alternative to the UKA. Eleven of the group's forty-one chartered units never paid dues, and the majority of the others did so only sporadically (FBI COINTELPRO–White Hate Groups Memo from Charlotte to Director, January 30, 1969).

35. Cunningham (2004); O'Reilly (1991); Powers (1988); FBI COINTELPRO–White Hate Groups Memos from Brennan to Sullivan, August 24, 1967, and Charlotte to Director, June 14, 1967.
36. Schlosser (2007); Cunningham (2004: 157). Similarly, William Dukes, a key handler of klan informants during his time in the Jackson, Mississippi, field office, admitted that his recruiting successes resulted from his persistence and ability to relate to klan members. His rapport was aided by the fact that his father was "probably in the klan" during the 1920s, and he grew up hearing "the Klan of that era spoken of with respect" (Dukes Oral History, USM, Vol. 40, pp. 30, 39).
37. Schlosser (2007); Dargan Frierson interview with Michael Frierson (recording in the possession of Michael Frierson); Dargan Frierson, UNCG, http://library.uncg.edu/depts/archives/civrights/detail-iv.asp?iv=11 (accessed December 16, 2009).
38. FBI COINTELPRO–White Hate Group Memos from Charlotte to Director, October 4 and November 6, 1967, and from Director to Charlotte, November 15, 1967. Note that Hoover disagreed with the Charlotte office's plan to ensure that Jones remained Grand Dragon, arguing that Jones "has been, without any doubt, the most effective leader and organizer in the UKA establishment." The subsequent unfolding of actions to unseat the Grand Dragon was telling, as agents proceeded to ensure that delinquent klaverns send in their UKA dues—even though they recognized that this approach would "plac[e] additional funds at Jones' disposal"—so that informants would be eligible to vote against Jones.
39. *Raleigh News and Observer*, April 5, 1967; FBI COINTELPRO–White Hate Groups Memo from Charlotte to Director, January 30, 1969. Perhaps ironically, given the fact that the FBI's counterintelligence programs against civil rights, Black Power, and New Left targets were *unambiguously* designed to eliminate those groups, the Bureau's efforts against the KKK were far more successful than those undertaken in other COINTELPROs during that period. Because of their ideological overlap with klan members, agents were highly effective developing informants and infiltrating klaverns, which greatly aided their ability to hinder the UKA and other KKK groups (see Cunningham 2004: Ch. 5).
40. *New York Times*, September 6, 1964; FBI memo from Director to Charlotte, October 1, 1964.
41. O'Reilly (1989); Powers (1987: 410); Wade (1987: 351).
42. In 1968, Weltner would withdraw his reelection candidacy to avoid running alongside staunch segregationist Lester Maddox, Georgia's democratic gubernatorial candidate (Goodman 1968).
43. Transcripts of Dodd and McCormack statements, LBJ, White House Central File, Box 68, Ex/HU6 Ideologies 11/22/63-5/13/65; letter from C. T. Vivian to LBJ, October 18, 1965, LBJ, White House Central File, Box 71, Gen/HU6 9/16/65-10/27/65. A week later, Special Counsel to the President Lee White sent a return letter that deflected the petition, on the grounds that "the independence of the Legislative and Executive Branches of the Government make it difficult, if not

impossible, for the Executive to dictate to Congressional Committees on the subject matter of their investigations."

44. Goodman (1968: 489–91). Willis quoted in Woods (2004: 223). Some suspected that another of Willis's goals for the Committee was for its hearings to establish a link between Wallace and the KKK, which would harm the Alabama governor's ability to siphon votes from southern Democrats in the 1968 presidential election (Graham 1965).
45. Baker (1965); US House of Representatives (1966: 1605); Herbers (1965); *Raleigh News and Observer*, October 20, 1965. As part of HUAC's investigation, staff investigator B. Ray McConnon traveled to North Carolina to meet with SBI director Walter Anderson and review the SBI's files. During his visit, he also attended a UKA rally in Apex (memo from McConnon to McNamara, July 1, 1965, HUAC, Box 18, Folder: United Klans—NC Investigative Memos [1 of 4]). In at least one instance, the doggedness of the HUAC investigation stretched ethical and legal bounds. Over a three-week period surrounding the start of the hearings, HUAC staff procured a list of the phone calls made from klan counsel Lester Chalmers's suite in the Congressional Hotel (see memo from Russell to McNamara, HUAC, Box 32, Folder: UKA, Inc. Investigative Memos, Other Memos, Some Photos). The HUAC investigation, summarized in the 1967 volume *The Present-Day Ku Klux Klan Movement*, remains the most comprehensive descriptive portrait of the civil rights-era KKK.
46. KKK members and others on the far right had long criticized so-called Fifth Amendment communists for demonstrating their lack of patriotism through their evasion of HUAC questioners. Adopting such a strategy themselves, not surprisingly, took a significant psychological toll on DuBois and other klansmen. In the most extreme case, Grady Mars, a retired Air Force officer from Warrenton who had risen in the UKA ranks to become North Carolina's Grand Klaliff (state-level security chief), committed suicide less than two months after his HUAC testimony. According to his wife, Mars was "deeply unhappy" about pleading the fifth during the hearings (see Alsop 1965b; *Greenville Daily Reflector*, December 13, 1965). Jones acknowledged the tensions associated with the klan's strategy during the hearings in a televised editorial segment. "It was not easy for any of us to swallow that bitter pill of pleading the Fifth Amendment in Washington," he told WBTV viewers. "But our lawyers and friends finally convinced us that the so-called 'investigation' was stacked against us by a very powerful government that has openly proclaimed its intention to destroy us.... Naturally, we know that our pleading the fifth amendment will hurt us in some circles, but most of our people understand" (WBTV transcript, November 9, 1965, NCSA, Governor Moore Papers, General Correspondence, 1965, Box 71, Folder: Segregation—general).
47. *Raleigh News and Observer*, October 20, 22, 26, and 27, 1965; *Greenville Daily Reflector*, October 20, 1965; Clay (1965b). The FBI, frustrated by these denials, considered furnishing state officials with "information as to membership and possibly

other information regarding location of klaverns, etc." (FBI COINTELPRO–White Hate Groups Memo from Charlotte to Director, January 3, 1966).

48. Yancey (1965); letter from Moore to Bruton, August 1, 1966, NCSA, Moore Papers, General Correspondence, 1966, Box 149, Folder: SBI reports 3; *Raleigh News and Observer*, November 19 and 24, 1965, December 8, 1965, January 13, 1966.

49. *Greenville Daily Reflector*, January 3 and 19, 1966; Jefferys (1966); Clay (1966a); SBI memo from Allen to Director, October 3, 1966, NCSA, Moore Papers, General Correspondence, 1966. Note that a month earlier Moore had undertaken a major reorganization of the State Highway Patrol, including the replacement of the SHP's commander and ranking aide (Johnsey 1965). Also, the extent to which pressures from the Law and Order Committee challenged established SBI routines was evident when a protracted controversy over the SBI's treatment of KKK investigations emerged in the summer of 1966. The controversy was tied to a mandate from the governor to supply the Committee with data to aid its efforts to "expose" and potentially outlaw the UKA as an incorporated organization. Committee chair Malcolm Seawell accused the SBI of withholding data, charges that were reinforced by Committee researcher William O'Quinn, who resigned in protest after being told by SBI director Walter Anderson that the Law and Order Committee was a "vigilante group" rather than a "duly-constituted law enforcement organization," and would thus not have access to certain confidential files (Clay 1966b).

50. *Charlotte Observer*, March 4, 1966; *Durham Morning Herald*, March 12, 1966; *Greensboro Daily News*, November 22, 1966; Barbour (1966); Cooper (1966); Rollins (1966); author interviews with Glenn Twigg, Raleigh, North Carolina, November 7, 2003, and Robert Shelton, Tuscaloosa, Alabama. The 1953 law made it a misdemeanor for "any person to place on the property of another a burning or flaming cross without the permission of the owner" (*Raleigh News and Observer*, December 9, 1966). The threat of arrest, not surprisingly, prevented other acts of klan violence from being committed as well. Pitt County klansman George Williams recounted an occasion in which orders to "beat up" the mayor of Vanceboro were ultimately not carried out, after he successfully convinced "the boys" that "we would be charged with kidnapping and other serious crimes, in addition to assault, and that we should not go through with it" (Hardee 1966c). Note also that the contempt charges levied against Shelton and Jones were, behind the scenes, bids to remove the most effective UKA leaders from the organization. This motive was expressed transparently when FBI agents told Jones that they could make the charges disappear if he renounced the KKK. Jones refused, boasting that he could "hold a bear in a bathtub" for the length of his sentence. Upon his release from prison the following year, some of Jones's followers presented him with a toy tub filled with a fifth of liquor (Sheila Jones Baker, phone interview with author, September 2, 2003).

51. *Durham Morning Herald*, November 26, 1966; Eddie Dawson interview with Scott Ellsworth, May 26, 1977, p. 39, DU, Chafe Oral History Collection, Printed Materials Series, Box 1; SBI memo from Allen to Director, October 30, 1966, NCSA, Moore Papers, General Correspondence, 1966; FBI COINTELPRO–White Hate Groups Memo from Charlotte to Director, March 13, 1967; News from Klansville #35. *Raleigh News and Observer*, July 1, 16, and 19 and September 9, 1967; *Greenville Daily Reflector*, June 2, 1968; Eddie Dawson, interview with Scott Ellsworth, May 26, 1977, DU, Chafe Oral History Collection, Printed Materials Series, Box 1. Jones quoted in Young (1969: 135). For a more detailed discussion of the range of costs imposed by arrests in the policing of protest, see Earl (2005).
52. Letter from Scoggin to the Imperial Board, March 17, 1969, UNCC Scoggin Papers, MSS 335, Box 1, Folder 37; *Raleigh News and Observer*, March 25, 1969. Note that the three jailed klan leaders served their sentences in different prisons—Shelton in Texarkana, Jones in Danbury, Connecticut, and Scoggin in LaTuna, Texas—which made communication more difficult. In May 1969, Acting Imperial Wizard Melvin Sexton penned a letter to Scoggin's wife, telling her that though he had been able to visit recently with Shelton, he hadn't heard anything from Scoggin and didn't know how to contact him (UNCC Scoggin Papers, MSS 335, Box 1, Folder 37).
53. Young (1969: 136); Drabble (2003); Cecelski (1994: 146); *Raleigh News and Observer*, July 16, 1969; *Charlotte Observer*, September 9, 1969; Eddie Dawson, interview with Scott Ellsworth, May 26, 1977, DU, Chafe Oral History Collection, Printed Materials Series, Box 1. Note that the UKA's previous go-to lawyer, Lester Chalmers, attempted suicide in April 1968.
54. Sims (1978); Covington (1969); Young (1969: 135); FBI COINTELPRO–White Hate Groups Memos from Charlotte to Director, December 31, 1969 and January 30, 1970. Proud of its efforts, FBI leadership broke from its usual policy of secrecy and informed the attorney general of how it had managed to split the UKA apart (FBI memo from Director to the Attorney General, September 17, 1969).
55. *Durham Morning Herald* (January 10, 1970). COINTELPRO actions had declined as the UKA splintered in 1970, and the FBI shut down the program entirely after it was publicly exposed in 1971 (Cunningham 2004). The Governor's Law and Order Committee appears to have curtailed its intelligence efforts during Jones's imprisonment as well.
56. *Charlotte Observer*, January 20, 1970; *Winston-Salem Journal*, May 28, 1970; Sims (1978); Robert Shelton, interview with author, Tuscaloosa, Alabama; Sheila Jones Baker, phone interview with author, September 2, 2003; Sims (1978); Jones quote from the *Durham Sun* (October 24, 1974).
57. Carter (2000); Crespino (2007); Lassiter (2006).
58. This article, published on July 22, 1968, and provocatively subtitled "Lately, When 10 Kluxers Get Together, 1 of Them Is a Plant," was surely intended to get klan members to think a second or third time about the possibility of informers in their

midst. The reporter produced it in collaboration with the FBI, as part of its program to work with trusted reporters to spread negative information about COINTELPRO targets.

59. SBI Report #3 to Law and Order Committee, June 24, 1966, NCSA; FBI COINTELPRO–White Hate Groups Memo from Charlotte to Director, January 30, 1969.
60. As della Porta and Reiter (1998: 22) argue, given such space for discretion, police agents "seem to intervene first of all on the basis of their appreciation of the situation, and only secondarily on the basis of rules and regulations." As this chapter's discussion of the SBI and FBI demonstrates, the resulting patterns of organizational ambivalence did not necessarily play out in uniform ways across agencies.
61. Young (1969); Creed (1966); *Charlotte Observer*, August 15, 1966; *Durham Morning Herald*, October 3, 1966; *Greenville Daily Reflector*, June 2, 1968.

EPILOGUE

1. In 2012, the Southern Poverty Law Center identified five KKK organizations active in North Carolina, and more than two dozen unique klan groups nationwide. See www.splcenter.org/get-informed/intelligence-files/ideology/ku-klux-klan/active_hate_groups (accessed January 12, 2012).
2. Moore (1987); Dees (1992); author interview with Robert Shelton, 2002, Tuscaloosa, Alabama; "U.S. Jurors Award $7 Million Damages in Slaying by Klan," *New York Times*, February 13, 1987; "Klan Headquarters Is Given to Black to Settle Lawsuit," *Washington Post*, May 20, 1987; Venable quoted in Douthat (1987). Note that the original verdict against the UKA was for $7 million, and the UKA property was appraised at $250,000. When I contacted Shelton fifteen years later, he agreed to meet with me near his home in Tuscaloosa. Though he still drove a Lincoln Town Car with a "Never" vanity plate, at that meeting he confirmed that his UKA organizing days had ended with the 1987 lawsuit. The longtime Imperial Wizard died in 2003 at the age of seventy-three.
3. See Blee (2003); Dobratz and Shanks-Meile (1997); Simi and Futrell (2010).
4. I thank an anonymous reviewer for this insight.
5. As noted in the Introduction, these analytic factors parallel those defining the now-canonical political process approach to social movement emergence. Political process theory emphasizes the role of political opportunities and constraints, mobilizing structures, and framing processes in contentious mobilizations (see, e.g., McAdam et al. 1996). Such dimensions, however, have rarely been applied consistently to reactive or "threat-based" movements, or to right-wing mobilizations generally (as discussed earlier, these categories are not equivalent). The framework developed here seeks to integrate insights from the political process tradition with ethnic competition theories that identify the contexts within which threat-based mobilizations emerge.

6. Interview with Pete Young, February 5, 2004, Framingham, Massachusetts; Pete Young, "White and Black Ghettos: Similarities and Differences," LBJ, Federal Records—Eisenhower Commission, Task Force I, Series 10, Box 1; LBJ, Audio Recording, Federal Records—Eisenhower Commission, Task Force I, Series 13, Tape 3.
7. See, e.g., letter from Moore to Bruton, August 1, 1966, NCSA, Moore Papers, General Correspondence, 1966, Box 149, Folder: SBI reports 3.
8. See Jenness and Grattat (2002); McVeigh et al. (2003); Nolan and Akiyama (1999).
9. Scherr (2009).
10. Simi and Futrell (2010). Their framework draws on, and extends, conceptions of "free spaces" within which political challengers can operate, at least partially, outside the control of authorities (see Polletta 1999).
11. For discussions of long-range outcomes, see Andrews (1997); McVeigh and Cunningham (2012); and Messner et al. (2005).
12. Lassiter (2006: 3). GOP strategist Kevin Phillips penned the first major formulation of the Republican "Southern Strategy" in his 1969 book *The Emerging Republican Majority*. Subsequent influential studies of the Southern Strategy include Aistrup (1996) and Carter (2000). Lassiter (2006) offers a comprehensive treatment of the suburbanization thesis.
13. "7 Point Program," Confederate Knights of the Ku Klux Klan (brochure in author's possession; emphasis in original). Various photos showing UKA members' cars with klan messages on hoods, doors, and trunks can be found in the Don Sturkey Photographic Materials Collection, UNC, P0070; and HUAC KKK files, Box 17, folder: United Klans-NC Photographs (1 of 2). A photograph of a klan member's car outfitted with Wallace ads, as well as a young child outfitted with a Wallace hat and tie, is included in LBJ, Federal Records—Eisenhower Commission, RG 283, Series 14, Task Force I, folder: Photographs and photodisks. For discussion of Shelton's ties to Patterson and Wallace, see Sims (1978) and Carter (2000).
14. Black and Black (2002); Wallace quoted in Carter (2000: 334). The correlation between UKA presence and Wallace voting is significant at the 0.001 level ($r = .298$, 1-tailed test), and holds when a standardized measure of klan presence (i.e., a logged count of klaverns per 100,000 white residents in each county) replaces the raw klavern count.
15. Bartley and Graham (1978: 171, 382).
16. Link (2008). Helms's portrayals of Galifianakis included newspaper ads referencing the "McGovernGalifianakis ONE AND THE SAME" ticket, and also noting that Helms—and not Galifianakis—was "one of us," widely interpreted as a reference to his opponent's Greek heritage (Link 2008; Luebke 1990).
17. Black and Black (2002: Ch. 7) compellingly demonstrate that these Republican gains were achieved dually, through a "realignment" of formally Democratic southern white conservatives and a "dealignment" of southern white moderates.

While, by 2000, more than 70 percent of the former category identified with the Republican Party (up from 24 percent in 1968), the latter remained more evenly split, with nearly 40 percent identifying as Republican, slightly less as Democrat, and the remaining quarter remaining independent swing voters.

18. Quoted in Lassiter (2006: 5, 137).
19. McVeigh (2011). The relationship between klan presence and the percentage increase in votes for Nixon between 1968 and 1972 in North Carolina counties is statistically significant ($p < .05$) and holds when controlling for racial composition and the percentage of votes cast for Wallace in 1968.
20. Cranford quoted in Peter B. Young, "The Gun and the Guitar: White Ghetto Revisited" (LBJ, Federal Records—Eisenhower Commission [RG 283]; Task Force I—Assassination; Series 10; Box 5; p. 12).
21. Peter B. Young, "Violence and the White Ghetto: A View from the Inside" (LBJ, Federal Records—Eisenhower Commission [RG 283]; Task Force I—Assassination; Box 1; Series 10; pp. 96–98).
22. See McVeigh and Cunningham (2012). The positive association between 1960s klan presence and homicide rates in 1970, 1980, and 1990 is statistically significant ($p < .001$). The full set of control variables includes population size, median age, percentage of African American residents, funds expended on police protection, three measures of economic deprivation (median family income, income inequality, and poverty rate), divorce rate, percentage of owner-occupied homes, and overall indicators of political conservatism (support for Republican candidates as well as support for George Wallace in 1968).
23. Rosenfeld et al. (2001), Sampson (1997), and Sampson and Bartusch (1998) each emphasize the role of generalized trust. Influential formulations of social disorganization theory include Shaw and McKay (1942) and Sampson and Groves (1989). Small (2002) usefully emphasizes the role that culture and local networks play in these community-level processes.
24. McVeigh and Cunningham (2012).
25. The complaint filed by the Moore and Dee families centered on whether Franklin County Sheriff Wayne Hutto and his deputies were in fact aware of the klan plot before the victims were killed. In 2010, the county settled the civil suit for a substantial sum prior to its scheduled 2010 trial date. For a comprehensive account of the crimes and subsequent legal efforts, see the online report produced by Northeastern University's Civil Rights and Restorative Justice Project, available at http://nuweb9.neu.edu/civilrights/?page_id=50 (accessed January 17, 2012).
26. Romano (2006: 121).
27. Minow (1998: 9).
28. The basic chronology of November 3 is described in detail in Wheaton (1987), and the Greensboro Truth and Reconciliation Commission (hereafter GTRC) *Final Report*, Ch. 7, available at www.greensborotrc.org/1979_sequence.pdf (accessed July 9, 2006). Note that while the "massacre" label is commonly used to describe

the killings on November 3, 1979 (see, for instance, http://en.wikipedia.org/wiki/Greensboro_massacre; accessed November 15, 2010), in Greensboro the term is highly charged and loaded, representing a particular perspective on the event. The depiction has been contested by others who viewed the incident as a "shootout" between two armed outsider extremist groups (Cunningham et al. 2010; Wheaton 1987).

29. GTRC, *Seeking Truth, Working for Reconciliation* (2004: 5).
30. Hayner (2001).
31. GTRC, *Final Report*, pp. 14, 21; GTRC, *Final Report: Executive Summary*, pp. 16, 28, 31–36. Both available at www.greensborotrc.org (accessed July 9, 2006). Minow (1998: 82–83) similarly notes that proposing viable means to reduce the material subjugation of victimized parties is essential to the success of a Truth and Reconciliation Commission's mission.
32. The Wilmington Race Riot Commission report is available at www.history.ncdcr.gov/1898-wrrc/report/report.htm (accessed November 23, 2010). A similar state-sponsored effort has occurred in Oklahoma, related to the 1921 Tulsa race riot (see www.okhistory.org/trrc/freport.htm; accessed November 23, 2010). For general discussion of memorialization efforts related to lynching and other forms of racial violence, see Ifill (2007) and Markovitz (2004). For a thoughtful discussion of the Moore's Ford reenactments, see Auslander (2010).

REFERENCES

Adams, Jerry. 1966. "About 100 Turn Out to Hear Klan Leader." *Charlotte Observer* (11 November).

Ader, Paul. 1941. "Capt. John Lea Tells of Death in Court House." *Durham Herald Sun* (21 April).

Aguirre, B. E., Rogelio Saenz, and Sean-Shong Hwang. 1989. "Discrimination and the Assimilation and Ethnic Competition Perspectives." *Social Science Quarterly* 70, 3: 594–606.

Aistrup, Joseph A. 1996. *The Southern Strategy Revisited: Republican Top-Down Advancement in the South*. Lexington: University Press of Kentucky.

Akerstrom, Malin. 2006. "Doing Ambivalence: Embracing Policy Innovation—At Arm's Length." *Social Problems* 53: 57–74.

Alsop, Stewart. 1966a. "Portrait of a Klansman." *Saturday Evening Post* (9 April): 23–27.

Alsop, Stewart. 1966b. "The Loaded Pistol." *Saturday Evening Post* (23 April): 22.

Ammerman, Nancy. 1981. "The Civil Rights Movement and the Clergy in a Southern Community." *Sociological Analysis* 41, 4: 339–50.

Andrews, Kenneth T. 2004. *Freedom Is a Constant Struggle: The Mississippi Civil Rights Movement and Its Legacy*. Chicago: University of Chicago Press.

Andrews, Kenneth T. and Michael Biggs. 2006. "The Dynamics of Protest Diffusion: Movement Organizations, Social Networks, and News Media in the 1960 Sit-Ins." *American Sociological Review* 71: 752–77.

Andrews, Mildred Gwin. 1987. *The Men and the Mills: A History of the Southern Textile Industry*. Macon, GA: Mercer University Press.

Andrews, Simmons. 1950. "City Council Here Adopts Ordinance Outlawing Masks." *Raleigh News and Observer* (4 January).

Anti-Defamation League of B'nai B'rith. 1957. "The North Carolina Ku Klux Klan Revival." New York: Anti-Defamation League.

Anti-Defamation League of B'nai B'rith. 1958. "The KKK in Its Present Phase." *Facts* 13, 1: 111–14.

Auslander, Mark. 2010. "'Holding on to Those Who Can't Be Held': Reenacting a Lynching at Moore's Ford, Georgia." *Southern Spaces* (8 November).

Ayers, Edward L. 1984. *Vengeance and Justice: Crime and Punishment in the 19th-Century American South*. New York: Oxford University Press.

Bagguley, Paul. 2002. "Contemporary British Feminism: A Social Movement in Abeyance?" *Social Movement Studies* 1, 2: 169–85.

Bagwell, William. 1972. *School Desegregation in the Carolinas: Two Case Studies*. Columbia: University of South Carolina Press.

Baker, Robert E. 1965. "Klan's Wizards, Dragons Called in House Probe." *Washington Post* (17 October).

Barbour, Charles. 1966. "Court Blocks Robeson Klan Rally March 27." *Durham Morning Herald* (18 March).

Barry, Bill. 1965. "Klan Dragon Here Protests Arrest." *Miami News*.

Barth, Frederick. 1969. *Ethnic Groups and Boundaries*. Boston: Little, Brown.

Bartley, Numan B. 1969. *The Rise of Massive Resistance*. Baton Rouge: Louisiana State University Press.

Bartley, Numan B. and Hugh D. Graham. 1978. *Southern Elections: County and Precinct Data, 1950–1972*. Baton Rouge: Louisiana State University Press.

Bartley, Numan B. and Hugh D. Graham. 1975. *Southern Politics and the Second Reconstruction*. Baltimore, MD: Johns Hopkins University Press.

Batten, James K. and Dwight Walls. 1964. "KKK and Fiery Cross—A 'Religion' of Poor Whites." *Charlotte Observer* (3 September).

Bayer, Richard C. 1964. "Preyer Warns of Ku Klux Klan Involvement in North Carolina's Political Scene." *Durham Morning Herald* (24 June).

Bearman, Peter S. and Katherine Stovel. 2000. "Becoming a Nazi: A Model for Narrative Networks." *Poetics* 27, 2–3: 69–90.

Beck, E. M. 2000. "Guess Who's Coming to Town: White Supremacy, Ethnic Competition, and Social Change." *Sociological Focus* 33, 2: 153–74.

Belanger, Sarah and Maurice Pinard. 1991. "Ethnic Movements and the Competition Model: Some Missing Links." *American Sociological Review* 56: 446–57.

Benford, Robert D. and David A. Snow. 2000. "Framing Processes and Social Movements: An Overview and Assessment." *Annual Review of Sociology* 26: 611–39.

Bergeson, Albert and Max Herman. 1998. "Immigration, Race, and Riot: The 1992 Los Angeles Uprising." *American Sociological Review* 63: 39–54.

Bernstein, Mary. 2008. "The Analytic Dimensions of Identity—A Political Identity Framework." In *Identity Work in Social Movements*, edited by Jo Reger, Daniel J. Myers, and Rachel L. Einwohner (277–301). Minneapolis: University of Minnesota Press.

Bernstein, Mary. 1997. "Celebration and Suppression: The Strategic Uses of Identity by the Lesbian and Gay Movement." *American Journal of Sociology* 103, 3: 531–65.

Beyerlein, Kraig and John R. Hipp. 2006. "A Two-Stage Model for a Two-Stage Process: How Biographical Availability Matters for Social Movement Mobilization." *Mobilization* 11, 3: 299–320.

Bigart, Homer. 1964. "St. Augustine Aides Say They Cannot Keep Peace." *New York Times* (27 June): 1.

Black, Earl. 1973. "The Militant Segregationist Vote in the Post-*Brown* South: A Comparative Analysis." *Social Science Quarterly* 54, 1: 66–84.

Black, Earl and Merle Black. 2002. *The Rise of Southern Republicans*. Cambridge, MA: Belknap Press.

Blackstock, Nelson. 1988. *COINTELPRO: The FBI's Secret War on Political Freedom*. New York: Pathfinder.

Blalock, Hubert M. 1967. *Toward a Theory of Minority-Group Relations*. New York: Wiley.

Blee, Kathleen M. 2003. *Inside Organized Racism: Women in the Hate Movement*. Berkeley: University of California Press.

Blumer, Herbert. 1958. "Race Prejudice as a Sense of Group Position." *Pacific Sociological Review* 1: 3–7.

Bobo, Lawrence and Vincent L. Hutchings. 1996. "Perceptions of Racial Group Competition: Extending Blumer's Theory of Group Position to a Multiracial Social Context." *American Sociological Review* 61: 951–72.

Branch, Taylor. 1999. *Pillar of Fire: American in the King Years, 1963–1965*. New York: Simon and Schuster.

Branch, Taylor. 1989. *Parting the Waters: America in the King Years, 1954–1963*. New York: Simon and Schuster.

Brooks, Early L. 1958. *Crucifixion of the South*. Whiteville, NC: self-published.

Brookshire, Stan R. 1963. "It's Time to Solve the Race Problem." *New York Herald Tribune* (16 June): 5.

Brown, Cliff and Terry Boswell. 1997. "Ethnic Conflict and Political Violence: A Cross-National Analysis." *Journal of Political and Military Sociology* 25, 1: 111–30.

Brown, Hugh Victor. 1961. *A History of the Education of Negroes in North Carolina*. Raleigh, NC: Irving Swain Press.

Bullard, Jack L. and Robert J. Stith. 1974. "Community Conditions in Charlotte, 1970: A Study of Ten Cities Using Urban Indicators with a Supplement on Racial Disparity." Charlotte, NC: Charlotte-Mecklenburg Community Relations Committee.

Cagin, Seth and Philip Dray. 1988. *We Are Not Afraid: The Story of Goodman, Schwerner, and Chaney and the Civil Rights Campaign for Mississippi*. New York: Scribner.

Carter, Dan T. 2000. *The Politics of Rage: George Wallace, the Origins of the New Conservatism, and the Transformation of American Politics*. Baton Rouge: Louisiana State University Press.

Carter, W. Horace. 1991. *Virus of Fear*. Tabor City, NC: Atlantic.

Cecelski, David. 1997. "Ordinary Sin." *Independent Weekly* (19–25 March): 11–15.

Cecelski, David S. 1994. *Along Freedom Road: Hyde County, North Carolina, and the Fate of Black Schools in the South*. Chapel Hill: University of North Carolina Press.

Chafe, William H. 1980. *Civilities and Civil Rights: Greensboro, North Carolina, and the Black Struggle for Freedom*. New York: Oxford University Press.

Chalmers, David. 2003. *Backlash: How the Ku Klux Klan Helped the Civil Rights Movement*. Lanham, MD: Rowman and Littlefield.

Chalmers, David M. 1981. *Hooded Americanism: The History of the Ku Klux Klan*. New York: New Viewpoints.

Chapman, G. C. 1965a. "Education Board Retains Lawyers for Court Action." *Greenville Daily Reflector* (8 January).

Chapman, G. C. 1965b. "School Petition's Support Sagging." *Greenville Daily Reflector* (4 January).

Chappell, David L. 2003. *A Stone of Hope: Prophetic Religion and the Death of Jim Crow*. Chapel Hill, NC: University of North Carolina Press.

Chappell, David. 1994. *Inside Agitators: White Southerners in the Civil Rights Movement*. Baltimore, MD: Johns Hopkins University Press.

Churchill, Ward and Jim VanderWall. 1990. *The COINTELPRO Papers: Documents from the FBI's Secret War against Dissent in the United States*. Boston: South End Press.

Churchill, Ward and Jim VanderWall. 1988. *Agents of Repression: The FBI's Secret Wars against the Black Panther Party and the American Indian Movement*. Boston: South End Press.

Clay, Russell. 1966a. "Seawell Blasts Klan." *Raleigh News and Observer* (22 January).

Clay, Russell. 1966b. "Klan Prober Quits, Cites Secrecy in SBI." *Raleigh News and Observer* (26 July).

Clay, Russell. 1965a. "Crisis Nearing Negroes Say." *Raleigh News and Observer* (31 August): 1.

Clay, Russell. 1965b. "Tar Heels Reject State's Label of No. 1 for Klan." *Raleigh News and Observer* (24 October).

Clay, Russell. 1964. "Terry Hurls a Warning at the Klan." *Raleigh News and Observer* (23 June).

Coates, Albert. 1983. *A History of the North Carolina State Highway Patrol*. Chapel Hill, NC: Professor Emeritus Fund.

Cobb, James C. 2004. *Industrialization and Southern Society, 1877–1984*. Lexington: University Press of Kentucky.

Cobb, James C. 1993. *The Selling of the South: The Southern Crusade for Industrial Development, 1936–1990*, 2nd ed. Urbana: University of Illinois Press.

Coenders, Marcel and Peer Scheepers. 2008. "Changes in Resistance to the Social Integration of Foreigners in Germany 1980–2000: Individual and Contextual Determinants." *Journal of Ethnic and Migration Studies* 34, 1: 1–26.

Cole, J. Timothy. 2003. *The Forest City Lynching of 1900: Populism, Racism, and White Supremacy in Rutherford County, North Carolina*. Jefferson, NC: McFarland.

Cole, Willard G. 1952. "Hamilton Gets Four Years in Ku Klux Klan Conspiracy." *Raleigh News and Observer* (31 July).

Connelly, Bill. 1964. "Cox Is Weary of Bickering, but Must Go On." *Winston-Salem Journal* (January).

Cooper, David. 1966. "The State Moves against the Klan's Rally in Robeson." *Winston-Salem Journal* (18 March).

Copeland, Lewis C. 1965. *Tourists and North Carolina's Travel Business in 1964: An Economic Analysis*. Raleigh: Travel Council of North Carolina.

Covington, Howard. 1969. "N.C. Klans Break Ties with Parent." *Charlotte Observer* (9 September).

Covington, Howard. 1968. "Changes in the Activists: How An Informer Faced Klan's Power." *Charlotte Observer* (23 July).

Covington, Howard E. Jr. and Marion A. Ellis. 1999. *Terry Sanford: Politics, Progress, and Outrageous Ambitions*. Durham, NC: Duke University Press.

Cramer, M. Richard. 1963. "School Desegregation and New Industry: The Southern Community Leaders' Viewpoint." *Social Forces* 41: 384–89.

Craven, Charles. 1958. "Cole Is Sentenced to 18–24 Months." *Raleigh News and Observer* (15 March): 1.

Creed, Dick. 1966. "Moderation Is Noted at Rally of Klan." *Winston-Salem Journal* (16 August).

Crespino, Joseph. 2007. *In Search of Another Country: Mississippi and the Conservative Counterrevolution*. Princeton, NJ: Princeton University Press.

Crosby, Emilye. 2011. "'It Wasn't the Wild West': Keeping Local Studies in Self-Defense Historiography." In *Civil Rights History from the Ground Up: Local Struggles, A National Movement*, edited by Emilye Crosby (194–255). Athens: University of Georgia Press.

Crosby, Emilye. 2005. *A Little Taste of Freedom: The Black Freedom Struggle in Claiborne County, Mississippi*. Chapel Hill: University of North Carolina Press.

Cunningham, David. Forthcoming. "Shades of Anti-Civil Rights Violence: Reconsidering the Ku Klux Klan in Mississippi." In *The Civil Rights Movement in Mississippi*, edited by Ted Ownby. Oxford: University Press of Mississippi.

Cunningham, David. 2012. "Mobilizing Ethnic Competition." *Theory and Society*. Published online 21 July.

Cunningham, David. 2009. "Ambivalence and Control: State Action against the Civil Rights-era Ku Klux Klan." *Qualitative Sociology* 32, 4: 355–77.

Cunningham, David. 2008. "Truth, Reconciliation, and the Ku Klux Klan." *Southern Cultures* 14, 3: 68–87.

Cunningham, David. 2007. "Paths to Participation: A Profile of the Civil Rights-Era Ku Klux Klan." *Research in Social Movements, Conflicts and Change* 27: 283–309.

Cunningham, David. 2004. *There's Something Happening Here: The New Left, the Klan, and FBI Counterintelligence*. Berkeley: University of California Press.

Cunningham, David, Colleen Nugent, and Caitlin Slodden. 2010. "The Durability of Collective Memory: Reconciling the 'Greensboro Massacre.'" *Social Forces* 88, 4: 1517–42.

Cunningham, David and Benjamin T. Phillips. 2007. "Contexts for Mobilization: Spatial Settings and Klan Presence in North Carolina, 1964–1966." *American Journal of Sociology* 113, 3: 781–814.

Cunningham, David and Barb Browning. 2004. "The Emergence of Worthy Targets: Official Frames and Deviance Narratives within the FBI." *Sociological Forum* 19, 3: 347–69.

Curtis, Russell L. and Louis A. Zurcher Jr. 1973. "Stable Resources of Protest Movements: The Multi-Organizational Field." *Social Forces* 52, 1: 53–61.

Davenport, Christian, Hank Johnston, and Carol Mueller, eds. 2005. *Repression and Mobilization*. Minneapolis: University of Minnesota Press.

Davis, Jack E. 2004. *Race against Time: Culture and Separation in Natchez since 1930*. Baton Rouge: Louisiana State University Press.

Dees, Morris, with Steve Fiffer. 1992. *A Season for Justice: The Life and Times of Civil Rights Lawyer Morris Dees*. New York: Touchstone Books.

della Porta, Donatella and Herbert Reiter. 1998. "The Policing of Protest in Western Democracies." In *Policing Protest: The Control of Mass Demonstrations in Western Democracies*, edited by Donatella della Porta and Herbert Reiter (1–32). Minneapolis: University of Minnesota Press.

della Porta, Donatella and Dieter Rucht. 1995. "Left-Libertarian Movements in Context: A Comparison of Italy and West Germany, 1965–1990." In *The Politics of Social Protest: Comparative Perspectives on States and Social Movements,* edited by Bert Klandermans and J. Craig Jenkins (229–72). Minneapolis: University of Minnesota Press.

Diani, Mario and Doug McAdam. 2003. *Social Movements and Networks: Relational Approaches to Collective Action*. New York: Oxford University Press.

Dirks, Annelieke. 2006. "Between Threat and Reality: The National Association for the Advancement of Colored People and the Emergence of Armed Self-Defense in Clarksdale and Natchez, Mississippi, 1960–1965." *Journal for the Study of Radicalism* 1, 1: 71–98.

Dittmer, John. 1995. *Local People: The Struggle for Civil Rights in Mississippi*. Urbana: University of Illinois Press.

Dobratz, Betty A. and Stephanie L. Shanks-Meile. 2000. *"White Power, White Pride!" The White Separatist Movement in the United States*. Baltimore, MD: Johns Hopkins University Press.

Donner, Frank J. 1980. *The Age of Surveillance: The Aims and Methods of America's Political Intelligence System*. New York: Alfred A. Knopf.

Douglas, Davison M. 1995. *Reading, Writing, and Race: The Desegregation of the Charlotte Schools*. Chapel Hill: University of North Carolina Press.

Douthat, Strat. 1987. "Suits Knock Wind Out of Klan Sheets." *Washington Post* (26 November).

Drabble, John. 2003. "The FBI, COINTELPRO-WHITE HATE and the Decline of the Ku Klux Klan in North Carolina." Paper presented at Duke University, John Hope Franklin Center Public Lecture Series (24 September).

Dubner, Stephen J. and Steven D. Levitt. 2006. "Hoodwinked?" *New York Times Magazine* (8 January).

Dunn, Mamie. 1974. "'Fighting for White Rights.'" *Durham Morning Herald* (29 December).

Earl, Jennifer. 2005. "'You Can Beat the Rap but You Can't Beat the Ride': Bringing Arrests Back into Research on Repression." *Research on Social Movements, Conflicts and Change* 26: 101–39.

Earl, Jennifer. 2003. "Tanks, Tear Gas, and Taxes: Toward a Theory of Movement Repression." *Sociological Theory* 21, 1: 44–68.

Edwards, Bob and John D. McCarthy. 2004. "Resources and Social Movement Mobilization." In *The Blackwell Companion to Social Movements*, edited by David A. Snow, Sarah A. Soule, and Hanspeter Kriesi (116–52). Malden, MA: Blackwell.

Edwards, Laura F. 1998. "Captives of Wilmington: The Riot and Historical Memories of Political Conflict, 1865–1898." In *Democracy Betrayed: The Wilmington Race Riot of 1898 and Its Legacy*, edited by David S. Cecelski and Timothy B. Tyson (113–41). Chapel Hill: University of North Carolina Press.

Emerson, Robert D. 1998. *Dancing with Devils*. New York: Vantage Press.

Employment Security Commission of North Carolina. 1968. *North Carolina Insured Employment and Wage Payments 1967*. Raleigh, NC: Bureau of Employment Security Research.

Erickson, Gwen Gosney. 2007. "Guilford College." In *Founded by Friends: The Quaker Heritage of Fifteen American Colleges and Universities*, edited by John W. Oliver Jr., Charles L. Cherry, and Caroline L. Cherry (21–42). Lanham, MD: Scarecrow Press.

Erwin, K. (1965). "Tar Heel Baptist Resolution Blasts Klan." *Raleigh News and Observer* (17 November).

Evans, Linda. 1965a. "New Chief Aimed High, but Never Visualized His Position." *Greenville Daily Reflector* (13 March).

Evans, Linda. 1965b. "'Freedom of Choice' Plan Given Final Approval of School Board." *Greenville Daily Reflector* (7 May).

Federal Bureau of Investigation. 1964–1971. Memoranda (various). Washington, DC: FBI National Headquarters Reading Room.

Flowers, Linda. 1990. *Throwed Away: Failures of Progress in Eastern North Carolina*. Knoxville: University of Tennessee Press.

Foner, Eric. 1988. *Reconstruction: American's Unfinished Revolution, 1863–1877*. New York: Harper and Row.

Fossett, Mark A. and K. Jill Kiecolt. 1989. "The Relative Size of Minority Populations and White Racial Attitudes." *Social Science Quarterly* 70: 820–35.

Frankel, Linda. 1991. "'Jesus Leads Us, Cooper Needs Us, the Union Feeds Us': The 1958 Harriet Henderson Textile Strike." In *Hanging by a Thread: Social Change in Southern Textiles*, edited by Jeffrey Leiter, Michael D. Schulman, and Rhonda Zingraff (101–20). Ithaca, NY: ILR Press.

Fry, Gladys-Marie. 1975. *Night Riders in Black Folk History*. Knoxville: University of Tennessee Press.

Fulmer, William E. 1973. *The Negro in the Furniture Industry*. Philadelphia, PA: Wharton School of Finance and Commerce Independent Research Unit.

Gamson, William E., Bruce Fireman, and Steven Rytina. 1982. *Encounters with Unjust Authority*. Homewood, IL: Dorsey.

Garrow, David J., ed. 1989. *St. Augustine, Florida, 1963–1964*. New York: Carlson.

Garrow, David J. 1981. *The FBI and Martin Luther King, Jr.: From "Solo" to Memphis*. New York: W.W. Norton.

Gavins, Raymond. 1998. "Fear, Hope, and Struggle: Recasting Black North Carolina in the Age of Jim Crow." In *Democracy Betrayed: The Wilmington Race Riot of 1898 and Its Legacy*, edited by David S. Cecelski and Timothy B. Tyson (185–206). Chapel Hill: University of North Carolina Press.

Gavins, Raymond. 1991. "The NAACP in North Carolina in the Age of Segregation." In *New Directions in Civil Rights Studies*, edited by Armstead L. Robinson and Patricia Sullivan (105–250). Charlottesville: University Press of Virginia.

Gelber, Steven M. 1974. *Black Men and Businessmen: The Growing Awareness of a Social Responsibility*. Port Washington, NY: Kennikat Press.

Gerhards, Juergen and Dieter Rucht. 1992. "Mesomobilization: Organizing and Framing in Two Protest Campaigns in West Germany." *American Journal of Sociology* 98: 555–95.

Gillette, Paul J. and Eugene Tillinger. 1965. *Inside the Ku Klux Klan*. New York: Pyramid Books.

Gilmore, Glenda Elizabeth. 1996. *Gender and Jim Crow: Women and the Politics of White Supremacy in North Carolina, 1896–1920*. Chapel Hill: University of North Carolina Press.

Goodman, Walter. 1968. *The Committee: The Extraordinary Career of the House Committee on Un-American Activities*. New York: Farrar, Straus and Giroux.

Goodwyn, Larry. 1965. "Anarchy in St. Augustine." *Harper's Magazine* (January): 74–81.

Graham, Fred P. 1965. "President Is Cool to Klan Inquiry by Alabama's Attorney General." *New York Times* (4 July).

Granovetter, Mark. 1978. "Threshold Models of Collective Behavior." *American Journal of Sociology* 83, 6: 1420–43.

Greenhaw, Wayne. 2011. *Fighting the Devil in Dixie: How Civil Rights Activists Took on the Ku Klux Klan in Alabama*. Chicago, IL: Lawrence Hill Books.

Haas, Ben. 1963. *KKK*. New York: Tower Publications.

Haley, John. 1998. "Race, Rhetoric, and Revolution." In *Democracy Betrayed: The Wilmington Race Riot of 1898 and Its Legacy*, edited by David S. Cecelski and Timothy B. Tyson (206–24). Chapel Hill: University of North Carolina Press.

Hall, Jacquelyn Dowd. 1993. *Revolt against Chivalry: Jessie Daniel Ames and the Women's Campaign against Lynching*. New York: Columbia University Press.

Hall, Jacquelyn Dowd, James Leloudis, Robert Korstad, Mary Murphy, LuAnn Jones, and Christopher B. Daly. 1987. *Like a Family: The Making of a Southern Cotton Mill World*. New York: W.W. Norton.

Hamilton, J. G. de Roulhac. 1919. *History of North Carolina* (3 vols.). Chicago: Lewis.

Hanchett, Thomas. 1998. *Sorting Out the New South City: Race, Class, and Urban Development in Charlotte*. Chapel Hill: University of North Carolina Press.

Hannan, Michael T. 1979. "The Dynamics of Ethnic Boundaries in Modern States." In *National Development and the World System: Educational, Economic, and Political Change, 1950–1970*, edited by John W. Meyer and Michael T. Hannan (253–75). Chicago: University of Chicago Press.

Hardee, Roy. 1966a. "Rural, Urban Feud Causes Pitt Klan Rift." *Raleigh News and Observer* (27 January).

Hardee, Roy. 1966b. "Klan Dragon Instructed Klansmen on Voting in First District Race." *Raleigh News and Observer* (8 February).

Hardee, Roy. 1966c. "Ex-Klansman Tells of Plot to Harm Vanceboro Mayor." *Raleigh News and Observer* (25 January).

Hardee, Roy. 1966d. "Klan's Move in Plymouth Is Described." *Raleigh News and Observer* (26 January).

Hardee, Roy. 1966e. "Pitt Ex-Klansman Testifies Today." *Raleigh News and Observer* (28 January).

Hart, Randle J. 2010. "There Comes a Time: Biography and the Founding of a Movement Organization." *Qualitative Sociology* 33, 1: 55–77.

Hart, Reese. 1966. "Klan Jeers Negroes Attending KKK Rally." *Charlotte Observer* (15 August).

Hart, Reese. 1965. "Police Hold 4 in Plymouth after Last Night's Clash; Rights Marches Are Barred." *Raleigh Times* (1 September).

Hartley, Robert W. 1989. "A Long Hot Summer: The St. Augustine Racial Disorders of 1964." In *St. Augustine, Florida, 1963–1964*, edited by David J. Garrow (3–92). New York: Carlson.

Hatch, Richard W. 1966. "Negroes Integrate Rally to Dismay of Klansmen." *Greensboro Daily News* (15 August).

Hayner, Priscilla B. 2001. *Unspeakable Truths: Confronting State Terror and Atrocity*. London: Routledge.

Hechter, Michael. 1975. *Internal Colonialism: The Celtic Fringe in British National Development, 1536–1966*. London: Routledge.

Henderson, Tom. 1939. "Mrs. Graves Sewed White Hoods." *Greensboro Daily News* (17 December).

Herbers, John. 1965. "Klan Head Balks at 73 Questions as Inquiry Opens." *New York Times* (20 October).

Herbers, John. 1964. "Whites Repulsed in St. Augustine." *New York Times* (20 June): 12.

Hinton, Harold B. 1946a. "Klan Head Denies National Status." *New York Times* (19 June): 19.

Hinton, Harold B. 1946b. "Klan in South Keeps under Cover." *New York Times* (1 September): 65.

Hodges, Luther H. 1962. *Businessman in the Statehouse: Six Years as Governor of North Carolina*. Chapel Hill: University of North Carolina Press.

Hofstadter, Richard. 1966. "The Pseudo-Conservative Revolt—1954." In *The Paranoid Style in American Politics and Other Essays*, by Richard Hofstadter (41–65). New York: Alfred A. Knopf.

Hofstadter, Richard. 1964. "The Paranoid Style in American Politics." *Harper's Magazine* (November): 77–86.

Holland, Laurel L. and Sherry Cable. 2002. "Reconceptualizing Social Movement Abeyance: The Role of Internal Processes and Culture in Cycles of Movement Abeyance and Resurgence." *Sociological Focus* 35, 3: 297–314.

Horn, Stanley F. 1939. *The Invisible Empire: The Story of the Ku Klux Klan, 1866–1871*. Boston: Riverside Press.

Horowitz, David A., ed. 1999. *Inside the Klavern: The Secret History of a Ku Klux Klan of the 1920s*. Carbondale: Southern Illinois University Press.

Howard, Henry. 1963. "Pitt's Industrial Growth of 1962 Encourages; Big Hopes in New Year." *Greenville Daily Reflector* (2 January): 5.

Huie, William Bradford. 1965. *Three Lives for Mississippi*. New York: WCC Books.

Hunziker, Karl. 1966. "Klan Cyclops Sees War with Wilson." *Cocoa Tribune* (24 January).

Hwang, Sean-Shong, Kevin Fitzpatrick, and David Helms. 1998. "Class Differences in Rural Attitudes: A Divided Black America?" *Sociological Perspectives* 41, 2: 367–80.

Ifill, Sherrilyn A. 2007. *On the Courthouse Lawn: Confronting the Legacy of Lynching in the Twenty-First Century*. Boston: Beacon Press.

Inman, Tom. 1964. "Preyer Denounces Klan, Warns It's Worming Deep into Politics." *Raleigh News and Observer* (24 June).

Irons, Janet. 2000. *Testing the New Deal: The General Textile Strike of 1934 in the American South*. Urbana: University of Illinois Press.

Irons, Jenny. 2010. *Reconstituting Whiteness: The Mississippi State Sovereignty Commission*. Nashville, TN: Vanderbilt University Press.

Irons, Jenny. 2006. "Who Rules the Social Control of Protest? Variability in the State-Countermovement Relationship." *Mobilization* 11, 2: 165–80.

Jackson, Kenneth T. 1967. *The Ku Klux Klan in the City, 1915–1930*. New York: Oxford University Press.

Jacoway, Elizabeth and David R. Colburn, eds. 1982. *Southern Businessmen and Desegregation*. Baton Rouge: Louisiana State University Press.

James, David. 1988. "The Transformation of the Southern Racial State: Class and Race Determinants of Local-State Structures." *American Sociological Review* 53, 2: 191–208.

Jefferys, Grady. 1966. "Crackdown Ordered on Acts of Violence." *Raleigh News and Observer* (3 January).

Jefferys, Grady. 1965. "Klan Stages Capital City Street Walk." *Raleigh News and Observer* (27 June).

Jeffries, Hasan Kwame. 2009. *Blood Lowndes: Civil Rights and Black Power in Alabama's Black Belt.* New York: New York University Press.

Jenkins, Jay. 1952a. "Klan-Spawned Violence Grips County." *Raleigh News and Observer* (16 January).

Jenkins, Jay. 1952b. "Thomas L. Hamilton Posts $10,000 Bond, Waives Extradition." *Raleigh News and Observer* (25 May).

Jenness, Valerie and Ryken Grattat. 2002. *Making Hate a Crime: From Social Movement to Law Enforcement.* New York: Russell Sage.

Johnsey, Arthur. 1965. "Rivalry Cited as Cause of Shakeup." *Greensboro Daily News* (19 December).

Joseph, Peniel E. 2007. *Waiting 'til the Midnight Hour: A Narrative History of Black Power in America.* New York: Holt.

Justice, John. 1965. "Kluxers Gather to Burn Cross." *Greenville Daily Reflector* (18 October).

Kallal, Edward W. Jr. 1989. "St. Augustine and the Ku Klux Klan." In *St. Augustine, Florida, 1963–1964,* edited by David Garrow (93–176). Brooklyn, NY: Carlson.

Katagiri, Yasuhiro. 2001. *The Mississippi State Sovereignty Commission: Civil Rights and States Rights.* Jackson: University Press of Mississippi.

Kennedy, Stetson. 1990. *The Klan Unmasked.* Gainsville: University Press of Florida.

Kern, Dick. 1966. "Twelve Arrested Following Tension-Packed Klan Rally Here." *Roanoke Rapids Daily Herald* (7 November).

Key, V. O. Jr. 1984 [1949]. *Southern Politics in State and Nation.* Knoxville: University of Tennessee Press.

Kim, Hyojoung and Peter S. Bearman. 1997. "The Structure and Dynamics of Movement Participation." *American Sociological Review* 62, 1: 70–93.

King, Adrian. 1964. "FBI Nabs Them All in Craven." *Raleigh News and Observer* (30 January).

Klatch, Rebecca. 2002. "The Development of Individual Identity and Consciousness among Movements of the Left and Right." In *Social Movements: Identity, Culture, and the State,* edited by David S. Meyer, Nancy Whittier, and Belinda Robnett (185–201). New York: Oxford University Press.

Knox, Joseph. 1965. "Eastern Part of State Most Fertile for KKK." *Greensboro Daily News* (12 September).

Korstad, Robert Rodgers. 2003. *Civil Rights Unionism: Tobacco Workers and the Struggle for Democracy in the Mid-Twentieth-Century South.* Chapel Hill: University of North Carolina Press.

Kotz, Nick. 2006. *Judgment Days: Lyndon Baines Johnson, Martin Luther King, Jr., and the Laws That Changed America.* New York: Houghton Mifflin Harcourt.

Kryder, Daniel. 2009. "Police Chief Ben C. Collins and Law Enforcement in Clarksdale, Mississippi, 1961–1966." Paper presented at the annual meeting of the Southern Political Science Association (New Orleans, LA, 8 January).

Ladd, Everett Carll Jr. 1966. *Negro Political Leadership in the South*. Ithaca, NY: Cornell University Press.

Lahne, Herbert J. 1944. *The Cotton Mill Worker*. New York: Farrar and Reinhart.

Langguth, Jack. 1963. "Protests Puzzle North Carolina." *New York Times* (25 May): 8.

Lassiter, Matthew D. 2006. *The Silent Majority: Suburban Politics in the Sunbelt South*. Princeton, NJ: Princeton University Press.

Laue, James H. 1989. *Direct Action and Desegregation, 1960–1962: Toward a Theory of the Rationalization of Protest*. Brooklyn, NY: Carlson.

Lay, Shawn, ed. 1992. *The Invisible Empire in the West: Toward a New Historical Appraisal of the Ku Klux Klan of the 1920s*. Urbana: University of Illinois Press.

Leach, Damaria Etta Brown. 1976. "Progress under Pressure: Changes in Charlotte Race Relations, 1955–1965." M.A. Thesis, Department of History, University of North Carolina at Chapel Hill.

Leifer, Eric M. 1981. "Competing Models of Political Mobilization: The Role of Ethnic Ties." *American Journal of Sociology* 87: 23–47.

Leloudis, James L. 1999. *Schooling the New South: Pedagogy, Self, and Society in North Carolina, 1880–1920*. Chapel Hill: University of North Carolina Press.

Lewis, George. 2004. "'Scientific Certainty': Wesley Critz George, Racial Science and Organised White Resistance in North Carolina, 1954–1962." *Journal of American Studies* 38, 2: 227–47.

Lewis, Susan. 1965a. "Violence Breaks Out on Plymouth Streets." *Raleigh News and Observer* (1 September): 1.

Lewis, Susan. 1965b. "Plymouth Vigilant as Parley Begins." *Raleigh News and Observer* (3 September): 1.

Lewis, Susan. 1965c. "Plymouth Negroes Announce Recess." *Raleigh News and Observer* (4 September): 1.

Lewis, Susan. 1965d. "Rival Groups Hold Rallies as Plymouth Police Watch." *Raleigh News and Observer* (14 September): 1.

Link, William A. 2008. *Righteous Warrior: Jesse Helms and the Rise of Modern Conservatism*. New York: St. Martin's Press.

Lipset, Seymour Martin and Earl Raab. 1978. *The Politics of Unreason: Right-Wing Extremism in America, 1790–1977*, 2nd ed. Chicago: University of Chicago Press.

Long, Margaret. 1965. "The Imperial Wizard Explains the Klan." *New York Times Magazine* (20 April).

Lubell, Samuel. 1956. *The Future of American Politics*. New York: Harper and Brothers.

Luders, Joseph E. 2010. *The Civil Rights Movement and the Logic of Social Change*. New York: Cambridge University Press.

Luders, Joseph. 2006. "The Economics of Movement Success: Business Responses to Civil Rights Mobilization." *American Journal of Sociology* 111, 4: 963–98.

Luebke, Paul. 1990. *Tar Heel Politics: Myths and Realities*. Chapel Hill: University of North Carolina Press.

Lynch, B. 1968. "Knightdale Popular Klan Meeting Place." *Raleigh News and Observer* (15 February).

MacLean, Nancy. 1995. *Behind the Mask of Chivalry: The Making of the Second Ku Klux Klan*. New York: Oxford University Press.

Markovitz, Jonathan. 2004. *Legacies of Lynching: Racial Violence and Memory*. Minneapolis: University of Minnesota Press.

Marx, Gary T. 1974. "Thoughts on a Neglected Category of Social Movement Participant: The *Agent Provocateur* and the Informant." *American Journal of Sociology* 80, 2: 402–42.

May, Gary. 2005. *The Informant: The FBI, the Ku Klux Klan, and the Murder of Viola Liuzzo*. New Haven, CT: Yale University Press.

McAdam, Doug. 2003. "Beyond Structural Analysis: Toward a More Dynamic Understanding of Social Movements." In *Social Movements and Networks*, edited by Mario Diani and Doug McAdam (281–98). New York: Oxford University Press.

McAdam, Doug. 1999. *Political Process and the Development of Black Insurgency, 1930–1970,* 2nd ed. Chicago: University of Chicago Press.

McAdam, Doug. 1986. "Recruitment to High-Risk Activism: The Case of Freedom Summer." *American Journal of Sociology* 92: 64–90.

McAdam, Doug. 1983. "Tactical Innovation and the Pace of Insurgency." *American Sociological Review* 48: 735–54.

McAdam, Doug, John D. McCarthy, and Mayer N. Zald, eds. 1996. *Comparative Perspectives on Social Movements: Political Opportunity, Mobilizing Structures and Cultural Framings*. New York: Cambridge University Press.

McAdam, Doug and Ronelle Paulsen. 1993. "Specifying the Relationship between Social Ties and Activism." *American Journal of Sociology* 99, 3: 640–67.

McMillen, Neil R. 1994. *The Citizens' Council: Organized Resistance to the Second Reconstruction, 1954–64*. Urbana: University of Illinois Press.

McVeigh, Rory. 2011. "Klan Activism in the 1960s and the Republican Southern Strategy." Paper presented at the Annual Meeting of the Southern Sociological Society (Jacksonville, FL, 8 April).

McVeigh, Rory. 2009. *The Rise of the Ku Klux Klan: Right-Wing Movements and National Politics*. Minneapolis: University of Minnesota Press.

McVeigh, Rory. 1999. "Structural Incentives for Conservative Mobilization: Power Devaluation and the Rise of the Ku Klux Klan, 1915–1925." *Social Forces* 77, 4: 1461–96.

McVeigh, Rory and David Cunningham. 2012. "Enduring Consequences of Right-Wing Extremism: Klan Mobilization and Homicides in Southern Counties." *Social Forces* 90, 3: 843-862.

McVeigh, Rory, Michael R. Welch, and Thoroddur Bjarnason. 2003. "Hate Crime Reporting as a Successful Social Movement Outcome." *American Sociological Review* 68, 6: 843–67.

McWhorter, Diane. 2001. *Carry Me Home: Birmingham, Alabama: The Climactic Battle of the Civil Rights Revolution*. New York: Simon and Schuster.

Medrano, Juan Diaz. 1994. "The Effects of Ethnic Segregation and Ethnic Competition on Political Mobilization in the Basque Country, 1988." *American Sociological Review* 59: 873–89.

Merton, Robert K., with Elinor Barber. 1976 [1963]. "Sociological Ambivalence." In *Sociological Ambivalence and Other Essays*, edited by Robert K. Merton (3–31). New York: Free Press.

Messner, Steven, Robert Baller, and Matthew Zevenbergen. 2005. "The Legacy of Lynching and Southern Homicides." *American Sociological Review* 70, 4: 633–55.

Meyer, David S. and Debra C. Minkoff. 2004. "Conceptualizing Political Opportunity." *Social Forces* 82:1457–92.

Michelson, Melissa R. 2003. "The Corrosive Effect of Acculturation: How Mexican Americans Lose Political Trust." *Social Science Quarterly* 84, 4: 918–33.

Mikell, Robert M. 1966. *They Say—Blood on My Hands: The Story of Robert M. Shelton, Imperial Wizard of the United Klans of America.* Atlanta: Publishers Enterprise.

Miller, Charles W. 1964. *Miller's Greenville, N.C. City Directory*, Vol. 16. Asheville, NC: Southern Directory Co.

Minow, Martha. 1998. *Between Vengeance and Forgiveness*. Boston: Beacon Press.

Mitchell, Memory F., ed. 1970. *Messages, Addresses, and Public Papers of Daniel Killian Moore, Governor of North Carolina, 1965–1969*. Raleigh, NC: State Department of Archives and History, Council of State.

Mitchell, Memory F., ed. 1966. *Messages, Addresses, and Public Papers of Terry Sanford, Governor of North Carolina, 1961–1965*. Raleigh, NC: State Department of Archives and History, Council of State.

Mitroff, Ian I. 1974. "Norms and Counter-Norms in a Select Group of the Apollo Moon Scientists: A Case Study of the Ambivalence of Scientists." *American Sociological Review* 39: 579–95.

Moore, Patricia. 1963. "Hundreds Are Attending the Evening Classes." *Greenville Daily Reflector* (9 February).

Moore, Trudy S. 1987. "Black Lawyer Forces KKK to Pay $7 Million for Lynching Black, 19." *Jet* 71, 24 (9 March).

Moreland, John Kenneth. 1958. *Millways of Kent*. Chapel Hill: University of North Carolina Press.

Morris, Aldon. 1993. "Birmingham Confrontation Reconsidered: An Analysis of the Dynamics and Tactics of Mobilization." *American Sociological Review* 58: 621–36.

Morris, Aldon D. 1992. "Political Consciousness and Collective Action." In *Frontiers in Social Movement Theory*, edited by Aldon D. Morris and Carol McClurg Mueller (351–73). New Haven, CT: Yale University Press.

Morris, Aldon. 1984. *Origins of the Civil Rights Movement: Black Communities Organizing for Change*. New York: Free Press.

Mousseau, Demet Yalcin. 2001. "Democratizing with Ethnic Divisions: A Source of Conflict?" *Journal of Peace Research* 38, 5: 547–67.

Moye, J. Todd. 2004. *Let the People Decide: Black Freedom and White Resistance Movements in Sunflower County, Mississippi, 1945–1986*. Chapel Hill: University of North Carolina Press.

Myers, Daniel J. 1997. "Racial Rioting in the 1960s: An Event History Analysis of Local Conditions." *American Sociological Review* 62, 1: 94–112.

Myrdal, Gunnar. 1944. *An American Dilemma: The Negro Problem and Modern Democracy*. New York: Harper and Brothers.

Nelson, Jack. 1993. *Terror in the Night: The Klan's Campaign against the Jews*. New York: Simon and Schuster.

Nolan, James J. and Yoshio Akiyama. 1999. "An Analysis of Factors that Affect Law Enforcement Participation in Hate Crime Reporting." *Journal of Contemporary Criminal Justice* 15, 1: 111–27.

North Carolina Advisory Committee to the US Commission on Civil Rights. 1962. *Equal Protection of the Laws in North Carolina*. Washington, DC: US Government Printing Office.

North Carolina Board of Higher Education. 1969. *Statistical Abstract of Higher Education in North Carolina, 1968–69* (Research Report 4–69). Raleigh: North Carolina Board of Higher Education.

North Carolina Department of Labor, Division of Statistics. 1964. *North Carolina Directory of Manufacturing Firms*. Raleigh: North Carolina Department of Labor.

North Carolina State Advisory Committee to the United States Commission on Civil Rights. 1962. *Equal Protection of the Laws in North Carolina*. Washington, DC: US Government Printing Office.

Northrup, Herbert R. 1970. "The Negro in the Tobacco Industry." In *Negro Employment in Southern Industry: A Study of Racial Politics in Five Industries,* Volume IV: *Studies of Negro Employment*, edited by Herbert R. Northrup and Richard L. Rowan. Philadelphia, PA: Wharton School of Finance and Commerce Independent Research Unit.

Oakley, Christopher Arris. 2008. "'When Carolina Indians Went on the Warpath': The Media, the Klan, and the Lumbees of North Carolina." *Southern Cultures* 14, 4: 55–84.

Oberschall, Anthony. 1973. *Social Conflicts and Social Movements*. Englewood Cliffs, NJ: Prentice Hall.

Olsen, Otto H. 1962. "The Ku Klux Klan: A Study in Reconstruction Politics and Propaganda." *North Carolina Historical Review* 39: 340–62.

Olson, Mancur. 1965. *The Logic of Collective Action*. Cambridge, MA: Harvard University Press.

Olzak, Susan. 1992. *The Dynamics of Ethnic Competition and Conflict*. Palo Alto, CA: Stanford University Press.

Olzak, Susan. 1990. "The Political Context of Competition: Lynching and Urban Racial Violence, 1882–1914." *Social Forces* 69, 2: 395–421.

Olzak, Susan. 1989. "Labor Unrest, Immigration, and Ethnic Conflict in Urban America, 1880–1914." *American Journal of Sociology* 94, 6: 1303–33.

Ono, Hiromi. 2002. "Assimilation, Ethnic Competition, and Ethnic Identities of U.S.-Born Persons of Mexican Origin." *International Migration Review* 36, 3: 726–45.

Oppenheimer, Martin. 1964. "The Southern Student Movement: Year 1." *Journal of Negro Education* 33, 4: 396–403.

O'Reilly, Kenneth. 1991. *"Racial Matters": The FBI's Secret File on Black America, 1960–1972.* New York: Simon and Schuster.

Parker, Roy Jr. 1966. "Rise in Klan Fever Awaited." *Greensboro Daily News* (13 March).

Parker, Roy Jr. 1965. "Klansman of Wayne Resigns." *Raleigh News and Observer* (22 October).

Patrick, Clarence H. 1964. "Desegregation in a Southern City: A Descriptive Report." *Phylon* 25, 3: 263–69.

Patton, Charlie. 2006. "KKK Book Stands Up to Claim of Falsehood." *Jacksonville Times-Union* (29 January).

Payne, Charles M. 1995. *I've Got the Light of Freedom: The Organizing Tradition and the Mississippi Freedom Struggle*. Berkeley: University of California Press.

Payne, Susan M. 2001. *Adult Education at Guilford College: Past and Present.* Greensboro, NC: Greensboro Public Library.

Perlo, Victor. 1953. *The Negro in Southern Agriculture*. New York: International.

Pfaff, Steven. 1996. "Collective Identity and Informal Groups in Revolutionary Mobilization: East Germany in 1989." *Social Forces* 75: 91–118.

Phillips, Kevin P. 1969. *The Emerging Republican Majority*. New Rochelle, NY: Arlington House.

Platt, Gerald M. and Rhys H. Williams. 2002. "Ideological Language and Social Movement Mobilization: A Sociolinguistic Analysis of Segregationists' Ideologies." *Sociological Theory* 20, 3: 328–59.

Pleasants, Julian M. and Augustus M. Burns III. 1990. *Frank Porter Graham and the 1950 Senate Race in North Carolina*. Chapel Hill: University of North Carolina Press.

Polletta, Francesca. 2006. *"It Was Like a Fever": Storytelling in Protest and Politics.* Chicago: University of Chicago Press.

Polletta, Francesca. 1999. "'Free Spaces' in Collective Action." *Theory and Society* 28: 1–38.

Polletta, Francesca and James M. Jasper. 2001. "Collective Identity and Social Movements." *Annual Review of Sociology* 27: 283–305.

Powell, William S. 1970. *Higher Education in North Carolina*. Raleigh, NC: State Department of Archives and History.

Powell, William S. 1963. *Annals of Progress: The Story of Lenoir County and Kinston, North Carolina*. Raleigh, NC: State Department of Archives and History.

Powers, Richard Gid. 1988. *Secrecy and Power: The Life of J. Edgar Hoover*. New York: Free Press.

Prather, H. Leon Sr. 1984. *"We Have Taken a City": The Wilmington Racial Massacre and Coup of 1898.* Cranbury, NY: Associated University Presses.

Quillian, Lincoln. 1996. "Group Threat and Regional Change in Attitudes toward African-Americans." *American Journal of Sociology* 102: 816–60.

Quillian, Lincoln. 1995. "Prejudice as a Response to Perceived Group Threat: Population Composition and Anti-Immigrant and Racial Prejudice in Europe." *American Sociological Review* 60: 586–611.

Rabby, Glenda Alice. 1999. *The Pain and the Promise: The Struggle for Civil Rights in Tallahassee, Florida*. Athens: University of Georgia Press.

Rabon, Roy. 1965a. "NC Klan Leader: The News Is Faulty." *Raleigh News and Observer* (23 May).

Rabon, Roy. 1965b. "Wake Klan Group Believed One of Strongest." *Raleigh News and Observer* (23 May).

Randel, William Peirce. 1965. *The Ku Klux Klan: A Century of Infamy*. Radnor, PA: Chilton.

Rapoport, David C. 2004. "The Four Waves of Modern Terrorism." In *Attacking Terrorism: Elements of a Grand Strategy*, edited by Audry Kurth Cronin and James M. Ludes (46–73). Washington, DC: Georgetown University Press.

Raynor, George. 1963. "'Revival' of Klan." *Raleigh News and Observer* (3 November).

Reynolds, William J. 1990. *Songs of Glory: Stories of 300 Great Hymns and Gospel Songs*. Grand Rapids, MI: Zondervan.

Rhomberg, Chris. 2005. "Class, Race, and Urban Politics: The 1920s Ku Klux Klan Movement in the United States." *Political Power and Social Theory* 17: 3–34.

Rich, Evelyn. 1988. *Ku Klux Klan Ideology, 1954–1988*. Ph.D. Dissertation, Boston University.

Rollins, Ray. 1966. "He Dislikes Klan, Backs Its Rights." *Winston-Salem Journal* (27 March).

Romano, Renee C. 2006. "Narratives of Redemption: The Birmingham Church Bombing Trials and the Construction of Civil Rights Memory." In *The Civil Rights Movement in American Memory*, edited by Renee C. Romano and Leigh Raiford. Athens: University of Georgia Press.

Roscigno, Vincent J. and William F. Danaher. 2004. *Voice of Southern Labor: Radio, Music, and Textile Strikes, 1929–1934*. Minneapolis: University of Minnesota Press.

Rosenfeld, Richard, Steven Messner, and Eric Baumer. 2001. "Social Capital and Homicide." *Social Forces* 80, 1: 283–310.

Ross, James. 1966. "Did Klan Win in Rowan?" *Greensboro Daily News* (16 November).

Rowan, Richard L. 1970. "The Negro in the Textile Industry." In *Negro Employment in Southern Industry: A Study of Racial Politics in Five Industries*, Volume IV: *Studies of Negro Employment*, by Herbert R. Northrup and Richard L. Rowan. Philadelphia, PA: Wharton School of Finance and Commerce Independent Research Unit.

Rucht, Dieter. 2007. "Movement Allies, Adversaries, and Third Parties." In *The Blackwell Companion to Social Movements*, edited by David A. Snow, Sarah A. Soule, and Hanspeter Kriesi (197–216). Malden, MA: Blackwell.

Salter, John. 1979. *Jackson, Mississippi: An American Chronicle of Struggle and Schism*. Pompano Beach, FL: Exposition Press of Florida.

Sampson, Robert J. 1997. "The Embeddedness of Child and Adolescent Development: A Community-Level Perspective on Urban Violence." In *Violence and Childhood in the Inner City*, edited by J. McCord (31–77). New York: Cambridge University Press.

Sampson, Robert J. and Dawn Jeglum Bartusch. 1998. "Legal Cynicism and (Subcultural?) Toleration of Deviance: The Neighborhood Context of Racial Differences." *Law and Society Review* 32, 4: 777–804.

Sampson, Robert J. and W. Byron Groves. 1989. "Community Structure and Crime: Testing Social Disorganization Theory." *American Journal of Sociology* 94, 4: 774–802.

Savage, Stuart. 1969. "Past Activities of City Police Being Probed." *Greenville Daily Reflector* (14 May).

Savage, Stuart. 1966. "UnAmerican Activities Body Told of Local Klan Functions." *Greenville Daily Reflector* (29 January).

Savage, Stuart. 1965. "H. F. Lawson Sworn in as New Chief of Police." *Greenville Daily Reflector* (4 March).

Scherr, Sonia. 2009. "Crushing the Klan." *SPLC Intelligence Report* 133. www.splcenter.org/get-informed/intelligence-report/browse-all-issues/2009/spring/crushing-the-klan (accessed January 12, 2012).

Schlosser, Jim. 2007. "The Klansman and the Lawman." *Greensboro News and Record* (10 June).

Schussman, Alan and Sarah A. Soule. 2005. "Process and Protest: Accounting for Individual Protest Participation." *Social Forces* 84, 2: 1083–108.

Sexton, William. 1949. "Gastonia Editor Fights KKK Plan to Stage North Carolina Comeback." *Asheville Citizen* (29 April).

Shanahan, Suzanne and Susan Olzak. 1999. "The Effect of Immigrant Diversity and Ethnic Competition on Collective Conflict in Urban America: An Assessment of Two Moments of Mass Migration, 1869–1924 and 1965–1993. *Journal of American Ethnic History* (Spring): 40–64.

Shaw, Clifford and Henry McKay. 1942. *Juvenile Delinquency and Urban Areas*. Chicago: University of Chicago Press.

Shumaker, James. 1952. "The Rise and Fall of the Ku Klux Klan." *Durham Morning Herald* (5 October).

Simi, Pete and Robert Futrell. 2010. *American Swastika: Inside the White Power Movement's Hidden Spaces of Hate*. Lanham, MD: Rowman and Littlefield.

Sims, Patsy. 1978. *The Klan*. New York: Stein and Day.

Small, Mario Luis. 2002. "Culture, Cohorts, and Social Organization Theory: Understanding Local Participation in a Latino Housing Project." *American Journal of Sociology* 108(1):1–54.

Smith, Stephen Samuel. 2004. *Boom for Whom?: Education, Desegregation, and Development in Charlotte*. Albany: State University of New York Press.

Snook, Harry. 1963. "Charlotte C of C Asks Firms to Serve All." *Charlotte Observer* (5 May).

Snow, David A. and Robert D. Benford. 2000. "Framing Processes and Social Movements: An Overview and Assessment." *Annual Review of Sociology* 26: 611–39.

Snow, David A. and Doug McAdam. 2000. "Identity Work Processes in the Context of Social Movements: Clarifying the Identity/Movement Nexus." In *Self, Identity, and Social Movements*, edited by Sheldon Stryker, Timothy Joseph Owens, and Robert W. White (41–67). Minneapolis: University of Minnesota Press.

Snow, David A., E. Burke Rochford, Steven K. Worden, and Robert D. Benford. 1986. "Frame Alignment Processes, Micro-mobilization, and Movement Participation." *American Sociological Review* 51: 464–81.

Sokol, Jason. 2006. *There Goes My Everything: White Southerners in the Age of Civil Rights, 1945–1975*. New York: Alfred A. Knopf.

Spence, James R. 1968. *The Making of a Governor: The Moore-Preyer-Lake Primaries of 1964*. Winston-Salem, NC: John F. Blair.

Stovel, Katherine. 2001. "Local Sequential Patterns: The Structure of Lynching in the Deep South, 1882–1930." *Social Forces* 79, 3: 843–80.

Stryker, Sheldon. 1968. "Identity Salience and Role Performance: The Relevance of Symbolic Interaction Theory for Family Research." *Journal of Marriage and the Family* 30: 558–64.

Stryker, Sheldon and Peter J. Burke. 2000. "The Past, Present, and Future of an Identity Theory." *Social Psychology Quarterly* 63, 4: 284–97.

Tarrow, Sidney. 1998. *Power in Movement: Social Movements and Contentious Politics*. New York: Cambridge University Press.

Taylor, Verta. 1989. "Social Movement Continuity: The Women's Movement in Abeyance." *American Sociological Review* 54: 761–75.

Taylor, Verta and Nancy Whittier. 1992. "Collective Identity in Social Movement Communities: Lesbian Feminist Mobilization." In *Frontiers in Social Movement Theory*, edited by Aldon D. Morris and Carol McClurg Mueller (104–32). New Haven, CT: Yale University Press.

Thomas, Heath. 1957. "Kluxers Hear Wizard Lash Court Race Edict." *Salisbury (NC) Post* (21 July).

Thompson, Holland. 1921. *The New South*. New Haven, CT: Yale University Press.

Thornton, J. Mills III. 1991. "Municipal Politics and the Course of the Movement." In *New Directions in Civil Rights Studies*, edited by Armstead L. Robinson and Patricia Sullivan (38–64). Charlottesville: University Press of Virginia.

Tolnay, Stewart E., Glenn Deane, and E. M. Beck. 1996. "Vicarious Violence: Spatial Effects on Southern Lynchings, 1890–1919." *American Journal of Sociology* 102, 3: 788–815.

Tolnay, Stewart E. and E. M. Beck. 1995. *A Festival of Violence: An Analysis of Southern Lynchings, 1882–1930.* Urbana-Champaign: University of Illinois Press.

Tolnay, Stewart E., E. M. Beck, and James L. Massey. 1989. "Black Lynchings: The Power-Threat Hypothesis Revisited." *Social Forces* 67: 605–23.

Tolsma, Jochem, Marcel Lubbers, and Marcel Coenders. 2008. "Ethnic Competition and Opposition to Ethnic Intermarriage in the Netherlands: A Multi-Level Approach." *European Sociological Review* 24, 2: 215–30.

Trelease, Allen W. 1971. *White Terror: The Ku Klux Klan Conspiracy and Southern Reconstruction.* Baton Rouge: Louisiana State University Press.

Trethewey, Natasha. 2006. *Native Guard.* New York: Houghton Mifflin Harcourt.

Tumin, Melvin M. 1958. *Desegregation: Resistance and Readiness.* Princeton, NJ: Princeton University Press.

Tyson, Timothy B. 2004. *Blood Done Sign My Name: A True Story.* New York: Crown.

Tyson, Timothy B. 2001. *Radio Free Dixie: Robert F. Williams and the Roots of Black Power.* Chapel Hill: University of North Carolina Press.

Tyson, Timothy B. and David S. Cecelski. 1998. "Introduction." In *Democracy Betrayed: The Wilmington Race Riot of 1898 and Its Legacy*, edited by David S. Cecelski and Timothy B. Tyson (3–13). Chapel Hill: University of North Carolina Press.

Ulsperger, Jason S. 2002. "Geezers, Greed, Grief, and Grammar: Frame Transformation in the Nursing Home Reform Movement." *Sociological Spectrum* 22: 385–406.

US Bureau of the Census. 1972a. *Census of Population and Housing: 1970 Census Tracts; Final Report PHC(1)-41 Charlotte, N.C. SMSA.* Washington, DC: US Government Printing Office.

US Bureau of the Census. 1972b. *Census of Population and Housing: 1970 Census Tracts; Final Report PHC(1)-83 Greensboro–Winston-Salem–High Point, N.C. SMSA.* Washington, DC: US Government Printing Office.

US Bureau of the Census. 1963. *U.S. Census of Population: 1960. Selected Area Reports. State Economic Areas.* [Final Report PC (3)-1A]. Washington, DC: US Government Printing Office.

US Bureau of the Census. 1960. *U.S. Census of Population; Vol. I, Characteristics of the Population; Part 35, North Carolina.* Washington, DC: US Government Printing Office.

US Commission on Civil Rights. 1975. "The Voting Rights Act: Ten Years After." Washington, DC: US Government Printing Office.

US Commission on Civil Rights. 1961. "The 50 States Report." Washington, DC: US Government Printing Office.

US Congress. 1872. *Report of the Joint Select Committee to Inquire into the Condition of Affairs in the Late Insurrectionary States* (13 vols.). Washington, DC: Government Printing Office.

US Department of Commerce, Bureau of the Census. 1964. *United States Census of Agriculture; Vol. 1, Part 26, North Carolina.* Washington, DC: US Government Printing Office.

US Department of Labor. 1969. *Labor in the Textile and Apparel Industries (Bulletin No. 1635).* Washington, DC: US Government Printing Office.

US House of Representatives, Select Committee on Intelligence. 1975. *Hearings on Domestic Intelligence Programs*. 94th Congress, First Session. Washington, DC: US Government Printing Office.

US House of Representatives, Committee on Un-American Activities. 1967. *The Present Day Ku Klux Klan Movement*. 90th Congress, First Session. Washington, DC: US Government Printing Office.

US House of Representatives, Committee on Un-American Activities. 1966. *Activities of Ku Klux Klan Organizations in the United States, Parts I-V*. 89th Congress, First Session. Washington, DC: US Government Printing Office.

Vander Zanden, James W. 1965. *Race Relations in Transition: The Segregation Crisis in the South*. New York: Random House.

Vander Zanden, James W. 1960. "The Klan Revival." *American Journal of Sociology* 65, 5: 456–62.

Van Dyke, Jeffrey Alan. 1986. "Bedsheets and Broadsheets: Covering the Ku Klux Klan in North Carolina." MA Thesis: UNC-Chapel Hill.

Van Dyke, Nella and Sarah Soule. 2002. "Structural Social Change and the Mobilizing Effect of Threat: Explaining Levels of Patriot and Militia Organizing in the United States." *Social Problems* 49, 4: 497–520.

Van Valey, Thomas L., Wade Clark Roof, and Jerome E. Wilcox. 1977. "Trends in Residential Segregation, 1960–1970." *American Journal of Sociology* 82, 4: 826–44.

Wade, Wyn Craig. 1987. *The Fiery Cross: The Ku Klux Klan in America*. New York: Simon and Schuster.

Wagy, Tom. 1985. *Governor LeRoy Collins of Florida*. Tuscaloosa: University of Alabama Press.

Walker, Anders. 2009. *The Ghost of Jim Crow: How Southern Moderates Used* Brown v. Board of Education *to Stall Civil Rights*. New York: Oxford University Press.

Wallace, Mike. 2006. *Between You and Me*. New York: Random House.

Walls, Dwayne. 1966. "Is GOP Winner 'Klansville' Sheriff?" *Charlotte Observer* (15 November).

Watters, Pat. 1964. *Charlotte*. Atlanta: Southern Regional Council.

Waynick, Capus M., John C. Brooks, and Elsie W. Pitts, eds. 1964. *North Carolina and the Negro*. Raleigh, NC: North Carolina Mayors' Co-operating Committee.

Webb, Clive. 2010. *Rabble Rousers: The American Far Right in the Civil Rights Era*. Athens: University of Georgia Press.

West, Bernard. 1965. "U.S. Registrars May Skip N.C." *Raleigh News and Observer* (14 September): 1.

West, Bernard. 1964. "Church Is Painted Despite Fire Threat, Klan Warning." *Raleigh News and Observer* (15 July).

Wheaton, Elizabeth. 1987. *Codename Greenkil: The 1979 Greensboro Killings*. Athens: University of Georgia Press.

Whitehead, Don. 1970. *Attack on Terror: The FBI against the Ku Klux Klan in Mississippi*. New York: Funk and Wagnalls.

Whites, LeeAnn. 1998. "Love, Hate, Rape, Lynching: Rebecca Latimer Felton and the Gender Politics of Racial Violence." In *Democracy Betrayed: The Wilmington Race Riot of 1898 and Its Legacy*, edited by Cecelski, David S. and Timothy B. Tyson (143–62). Chapel Hill: University of North Carolina Press.

Wilkes, Rima and Dina G. Okamoto. 2002. "Ethnic Competition and Mobilization by Minorities at Risk." *Nationalism and Ethnic Politics* 8, 3: 1–23.

Williams, Oliver. 1964a. "Klan Runs Students from State." *Raleigh News and Observer* (20 June).

Williams, Oliver. 1964b. "Cleaned-Up Klan Claims Comeback with Old Power." *Raleigh News and Observer* (21 June).

Williams, Oliver. 1964c. "Rebirth of Klan Counters Moderate Action in State." *Raleigh News and Observer* (23 August).

Williams, Oliver. 1964d. "Leaders Promote Klan Extremism." *Raleigh News and Observer* (24 August).

Wiltfang, Gregory L. and Doug McAdam. 1991. "The Costs and Risks of Social Activism: A Study of Sanctuary Movement Activism." *Social Forces* 69, 4: 987–1010.

Wolff, Miles. 1970. *Lunch at the Five and Ten: The Greensboro Sit-Ins, a Contemporary History*. New York: Stein and Day.

Womble, Bill. 1965. "Wilmington Paper Asks Sheriff's Ouster." *Raleigh News and Observer* (12 November).

Wood, James R. 1972. "Personal Commitment and Organizational Constraint: Church Officials and Racial Integration." *Sociological Analysis* 33, 3: 142–51.

Wood, Phillip J. 1986. *Southern Capitalism: The Political Economy of North Carolina, 1880–1980.* Durham, NC: Duke University Press.

Wood, Rob. 1965a. "The Klan Surges Back into Open; Wedding Tonight." *Raleigh News and Observer* (22 May).

Wood, Rob. 1965b. "Klan Has Busy Weekend in East N.C." *Raleigh News and Observer* (7 June).

Woods, Jeff. 2004. *Black Struggle, Red Scare: Segregation and Anti-Communism in the South, 1948–1968.* Baton Rouge: Louisiana State University Press.

Woods, Randall B. 2007. *LBJ: Architect of American Ambition*. Cambridge, MA: Harvard University Press.

Wright, L.M. Jr. 1963. "Charlotte Has Built Its Integration Road: A Special Report." *Charlotte Observer* (19 July).

Wright, L.M. Jr. 1958. "With No Fuss, We Desegregate." *Charlotte Observer* (3 September).

Yancey, Noel. 1965. "Moore Indicates Klan in N.C. Is Small Minority." *Raleigh News and Observer* (28 October).

Young, Pete. 1969. "A Few Soft Words for the Ku Klux Klan." *Esquire* (July): 104–5, 134–37.

PERIODICALS CONSULTED

Asheville Citizen
Carolina Israelite (Charlotte, NC)
Carolina Times (Durham, NC)
Charlotte Daily Observer
Charlotte Magazine
Charlotte News
Charlotte Observer
The Cocoa (FL) *Tribune*
Concord Tribune
Daily Oklahoman (OK)
The Daily Record (Dunn, NC)
Durham Herald Sun
Durham Morning Herald
Fiery Cross (Tuscaloosa, AL)
Fort Lauderdale (FL) *News*
Greensboro Daily News
Greensboro News and Record
Greensboro Record
Greenville Daily Reflector
Harper's Magazine
High Point Enterprise
Huntsville (AL) *Times*
Independent Weekly (Durham, NC)
Jacksonville (FL) *Times-Union*
Kinston Daily Free Press
Life Magazine
New Bern Sun-Journal
The New Citizen
New York Herald Tribune
New York Times
New York World
Raleigh Daily Standard
Raleigh News and Observer
Raleigh Times
The Roanoke Beacon
Roanoke Rapids Daily Herald
The Robesonian
Salisbury Post
Saturday Evening Post
Smithfield Herald

The Southern Patriot
Tampa (FL) *Tribune*
Tucson (AZ) *Citizen*
Washington (DC) *Post*
Wilmington Journal
Winston-Salem Journal and Sentinel
Winston-Salem Journal

ARCHIVES REFERENCED

AFSC (American Friends Service Committee Archives, Philadelphia, PA)
CORE (Congress of Racial Equality Papers, Microfilm, Boston Public Library)
DU (Duke University Archives, Durham, NC)
ECU (East Carolina University Special Collections, Greenville, NC)
FBI (COINTELPRO-White Hate Memos, Microfilm, Scholarly Resources Inc.)
HU (Ralph J. Bunche Collection, Moorland-Spingarn Reseach Center, Howard University, Washington, DC)
HUAC (House Un-American Activities Committee Ku Klux Klan Investigation Files, National Archives, Washington, DC)
Note: Box "X" indicates that document was part of a box compiled by NARA staff of folders from various containers in the collection.
LBJ (Lyndon Baines Johnson Archives, Austin, TX)
MARBL (Manuscript, Archives and Rare Book Library, Emory University, Atlanta, GA)
NCSA (North Carolina State Archives, Raleigh, NC)
SHC (Southern Historical Collection, Wilson Library, University of North Carolina at Chapel Hill)
SNCC (Student Non-Violent Coordinating Committee Papers, Microfilm, Boston Public Library)
UNC (North Carolina Collection, Wilson Library, University of North Carolina at Chapel Hill)
UNCC (J. Murrey Atkins Library Special Collections, University of North Carolina at Charlotte)
UNCG (Civil Rights Greensboro Collection, University Archives and Manuscripts, University of North Carolina at Greensboro)
USM (McCain Library, University of Southern Mississippi, Hattiesburg, MI)

INDEX